Wrapped & Stuffed Foods
Proceedings of the Oxford Symposium on Food and Cookery 2012

Wrapped & Stuffed Foods

Proceedings of the Oxford Symposium on Food and Cookery 2012

Edited by Mark McWilliams

Prospect Books
2013

First published in Great Britain in 2013 by Prospect Books, Allaleigh House, Blackawton, Totnes, Devon, TQ9 7DL.

© 2013 as a collection Prospect Books.
© 2013 in individual articles rests with the authors.

The authors assert their moral right to be identified as authors in accordance with the Copyright, Designs & Patents Act 1988. No part of this publication may be reproduced, stored in a retrieval system or transmitted in any form or by any means, electronic, mechanical, photocopying, recording or otherwise, without the prior permission of the copyright holders.

ISBN 978-1-903018-99-6

The illustrations on the front cover are courtesy of Peter Hertzmann (© 2013 Peter Hertzmann, Inc.).
The illustration on the back cover is of a stuffed baby melon, courtesy of Nilhan Aras.

Design and typesetting in Gill Sans and Adobe Garamond by Tom Jaine and Lemuel Dix.

Printed and bound in Great Britain by Jellyfish Solutions.

Contents

Foreword ... 7
Mark McWilliams

PLENARY PAPERS

Wrapping, Cooking, Civilizing ... 000
Barbara Santich

The Magician's Kitchen: Stuffing and Wrapping at the Pillsbury Bake-Off ... 000
Laura Shapiro

Turning a New Leaf in London? *Paan* Culture in the Metropole ... 000
Jaclyn Rohel

PLENARY PANEL
PROVOCATIVE MISINTERPRETATIONS ON A THEME

The Audacity of Unwrapping and Rewrapping, Unstuffing and Restuffing, Virtually Everything (Including, Especially, Cheese) ... 000
Harry G. West

Care, Control and Commensality: The Game of Stuffed and Stuffing Bodies ... 000
Emma-Jayne Abbots

Chicken Kiev: Material, Social and Discursive Wrappings ... 000
Benjamin F. Coles

Wrapping and Stuffing Food Relationally: Pleasure, Place, Production and Power ... 000
Michael Goodman

SYMPOSIUM PAPERS

Sarma and *Dolma*: The Rolled and Stuffed in the Anatolian Kitchen ... 000
Nilhan Aras

Pasteis de Tentúgal: Serendipity or Cultural Syncretism? ... 000
Paula Arvela

The Haggis ... 000
Adam Balic

Lasagna: A Layered History ... 000
Anthony F. Buccini

Samuel Pepys's Venison Pasties ... 000
Taissa Csáky

Art and Alchemy: The Authentic Air-cured Sausages of Europe ... 000
Jan Davison

MANTI AND MANTOU

Barbarian Heads and Turkish Dumplings: The Chinese Word *Mantou* ... 000
Fuchsia Dunlop

Manti and *Mantou*: Dumplings across the Silk Road from Central Asia to Turkey ... 000
Aylin Öney Tan

Wrapped & Stuffed Foods

A Knish is just a Knish – or is it? The Evolution of a Lowly Street Food to *Haute* Nosh — ooo
Elizabeth Field

All Wrapped Up – A History of Mummy Eating — ooo
Len Fisher and Janet Clarkson

Rich Man's Fowl, Poor Man's Fowl: What's under the Wrapper? — ooo
Alexandra Grigorieva

The Magic of Dumplings: Bringing *Pierogi* into the (New) World — ooo
Naomi Guttman and Frank Sciacca

Modernist Stuffing and Wrapping Techniques and Applications — ooo
Peter Hertzmann

Siberian Stuffed: A Profusion of *Pel'meni* — ooo
Sharon Hudgins

Yufka: Food for the Cook's Imagination — ooo
Priscilla Mary Işın

From Lettuce to Fish Skin: Koreans' Appetite for Wrapped and Stuffed Foods — ooo
Jin Kyung Kim

The Most Frugal of the Phyllo-wrapped Pies (or How to Feed a Crowd with a Handful of Meat) — ooo
Aglaia Kremezi

Kebabs, Bread, and 'Bread': Perugian History Wrapped up in *Torta al Testo* — ooo
Zachary Nowak

Before *Dolma*: A Taxonomy of Medieval Arab Stuffery — ooo
Charles Perry

Bog Butter: A Gastronomic Perspective — ooo
Benedict Reade

The Case for Casings — ooo
Allyson E. Sgro

A Case for Culinary Mongrelism — ooo
May Rosenthal Sloan

'Four and Twenty Blackbirds Baked in a Pie': A History of Surprise Stuffings — ooo
David C. Sutton

Food for Feasting or Food for Fasting? Rabbinical *Krepelach* — ooo
Susan Weingarten

Foreword

In July 2012, the Oxford Symposium on Food and Cookery convened for the thirty-first time. Symposiasts – including academics of all sorts, committed amateur historians and professional chefs – from around the world gathered at St Catherine's College to consider Stuffed and Wrapped Foods.

This year's Symposium opened with David Thompson's Jane Grigson Memorial Lecture on 'Thai Food, Stuffed, Wrapped and Beyond', followed by a surprising tasting of Thai wines. Dinner, a splendid affair prepared by Rowley Leigh of Le Café Anglais, assisted by St Catherine's own chef Tim Kelsey and his team, featured Scottish langoustines and haddock wrapped in filo pastry and a magnificent saddle of lamb Wellington.

Saturday morning's proceedings began with the presentation of the prestigious Sophie Coe Prize to Di Murrell for her entertaining and scholarly essay 'Food on the Move', a study of canal food, and a showing of Anissa Helou and Jane Levi's video introduction to a whole world of wrapping and stuffing techniques. This film set the scene for Laura Shapiro's wonderful talk on the phenomenon of the Pillsbury Bake-Off. Harry West then presided over our first Plenary Discussion Session featuring panellists Emma-Jayne Abbotts, Ben Coles and Michael Goodman.

Lunch, arranged by Ursula Heinzelmann, was a celebration of German sausage-making accompanied by specially baked German breads and appropriate accompaniments, including an unusually good sauerkraut.

After lunch, talks ranged from Len Fisher and Janet Clarkson discussing the surprising history of mummy-eating and Ben Reade describing the preparation and appreciation of bog butter, to Nilhan Aras's paper on the therapeutic properties of *sarma* and *dolma* for the women of Anatolia and Jin Kyung Kim's on Koreans' appetite for an amazing range of wrappings and stuffings. After tea and coffee, parallel sessions resumed with explorations by Fuchsia Dunlop and Aylin Öney Tan of the origins and etymology of *manti* and *mantou*, by Sharon Hudgins on the extraordinary profusion of *pel'meni* throughout Siberia and beyond, by Frank Sciacca and Naomi Guttman on *pierogi* in the New World and by David Sutton on surprise pie-stuffings. One of the late sessions featured Taissa Csáky's recreation of Samuel Pepys's venison pasties, Elizabeth Field's exploration of *haute* knishes and May Rosenthal Sloan's case for 'Culinary Mongrelism'.

And so to dinner, a lovely Turkish supper from Gaziantep, organized by Anissa Helou and Aylin Tan, featuring folded börek, mini spiced walnut-spread rolls and fried cheese rolls, along with Turkish wines and, of course, coffee.

On Sunday morning, Chair Paul Levy opened the proceedings by presenting the Young Chef Scholarship to Lucas Weir, who had already assisted Rowley Leigh and Tim Kelsey with the preparation of the Friday dinner. Following this, Cathy Kaufmann introduced the winner of the Cherwell Prize, Jaclyn Rohel, who treated us to a presentation on *paan* culture in London. In the morning's plenary talk, Barbara Santich discussed Aboriginal paperbark cooking, a technique unappreciated by early Australian settlers all too willing to find the natives uncivilized.

After coffee, symposiasts were treated to a demonstration of the esoteric skill of carving a whole *jamón iberico* courtesy of Joselito, one of the most famous names in Spanish hams. The ham was destined for consumption with our sandwich lunch – a splendid affair in its own right – organized by Susan Haddleston and delivered by Tim Kelsey and his staff, which followed a discussion led by Theodore Zeldin, co-founder of the Symposium, on the importance of table talk.

After lunch, parallel sessions resumed with Adam Balic unwrapping the origins and naming of haggis. Other matters discussed in the concluding parallel sessions ranged from Jan Davison's survey of the artisanal air-cured sausages of Europe and Allyson Sgro making the case for the use of casings, to Susan Weingarten exploring rabbinical *kreplach* and Anthony Buccini tracing the origins of lasagna, all with the Symposium's characteristic mix of expertise, scholarship and wit.

This volume of the Proceedings features many of the papers from these three days in Oxford. The resulting combination is global in scope yet specific in focus. Read alone, each paper illuminates a particular technique, dish or cuisine; read together, this volume testifies to the astounding variety and long history of stuffed and wrapped foods. Many people helped with the preparation of the Proceedings, but I would especially like to thank Elisabeth Luard, Ursula Heinzelmann, Helen Saberi, Peter Hertzmann, Roger Hale and Tom Jaine for their kind assistance.

Mark McWilliams
Editor, Oxford Symposium on Food & Cookery

Wrapping, Cooking, Civilizing

Barbara Santich

When I was young we spent every summer at our holiday house on the central coast of New South Wales. My father went fishing almost every day, and we lived on fish. We had a hierarchy of fish, with first choice snapper (the younger ones we called squire), a daurade-like fish, and another we called rainbow. Nannygai and flathead were slightly inferior. Occasionally we had to make do with kingfish, a slightly dry fish that we often cooked by wrapping in banana leaves from the clump at the bottom of the hill, near the spring where the red-bellied black snakes lurked. This seemed to keep it moist.

Had we gone up the hill instead, we would have come face to face with the grove of paperbark trees, *Melaleuca*, at the bottom of the sandhills. And had there been any indigenous inhabitants there, they might have advised us to wrap the fish in paperbark, as they had done for centuries. We knew that Aboriginal people had lived along the coast. When we played in the sandhills – keeping an eye out for death adders that pretended to be dead sticks – we would come across their middens, huge piles of purple-hued pipi shells, and occasionally find crude tools. But we thought nothing of it.

Nearly two centuries before this, the early Europeans were similarly dismissive. They were happy to accept the foods that had sustained the indigenous people over millennia – or rather, some foods, by some people. But they did not adopt their culinary practices. Their way of accommodating unfamiliar foods was to clothe them in familiar garb – to dress flying fox in curry, kangaroo in the manner of jugged hare, snapper boiled with oyster sauce.

Indeed, with few exceptions, the colonists did not even consider the culinary techniques of the Aborigines as 'cooking'. They viewed them as primitive and savage – not necessarily using these terms as pejoratives, but as what seemed to them plain fact. Aborigines were seen as uncivilized because they lacked the necessary trappings of culture and civilization: they had no permanent shelters, no clothing, no cooking utensils. Sketches and paintings by early explorers and artists, such as Joseph Lycett, depict the Aborigines, often naked, spearing fish in a rocky cove and cooking the catch over open fires.[1] This judgment, which appears to have been generally shared, evoked a range of different responses.

Under the first Governor, the benevolent Arthur Phillip, attempts were made to establish harmonious relations between newcomers and locals. Aborigines were encouraged to supply the colony with fish and to act as guides; sometimes they served as bedmates. Letters, journals and reports written by the accompanying officers (who were generally the only ones to document reactions to a new and distant country) show that some attempted to learn the Aboriginal language. Their observations display a genuine curiosity, a desire to understand, without disparagement, although they still described the indigenous people as primitive, uncivilized. For example, Watkin Tench, a Marine officer in the First Fleet, wrote in 1788 how shocked he was by their nakedness, their lean-tos, and the crudeness of their few tools.[2]

In these circumstances, Governor Phillip seemed to consider it his duty to improve the Aboriginal way of life, writing, 'It is undeniably certain that to teach the shivering savage how to clothe his body, and how to shelter himself completely from the cold and wet, and to put into the hands of men … the means of procuring constant and abundant provision, must confer upon them benefits of the highest value and importance'.[3] Nevertheless, others were more inclined not to intervene. First Fleet surgeon George Worgan, while still viewing the Aborigines as savages, also saw positive aspects in their way of life: 'They appear to be an *Active, Volatile, Unoffending, Happy, Merry, Funny, Laughing, Good-natured, Nasty, Dirty* race of human Creatures as ever lived in a state of Savageness'.[4]

Some years on, as the native populations began to diminish from both disease and warfare, public opinion was divided. Some colonists philosophically concluded that this was no bad result, that the immigrants and settlers could make much better use of the land than had the indigenous people. Yet others believed that, as British subjects, the Aborigines deserved protection; they should enjoy the same rights as the immigrants. Many favoured their assimilation; they believed they should – and could – be civilized, in the English fashion. Indeed, these citizens seemed to believe it was their duty, as superior beings, to civilize inferior beings, as the following letter illustrates:

To the PRINTER of the SYDNEY GAZETTE.

SIR,
The great Creator having made of One Blood all Nations of the Earth, and taking for granted that the Natives of New South Wales are capable of instruction and civilization, I should be extremely obliged by the favor of an Answer to the following Query, either publicly through your Paper, or privately to be left at the Gazette Office.

    Query. – What plan can be adopted, what means used, or what steps taken, whereby we may most speedily and effectualy civilize and evangelize the Natives of New South Wales, local circumstances considered?

I am Sir, your obedient servant,
"PHILANTHROPUS."[5]

By 1816 the Governor of New South Wales had established the Native Institution, 'for the Purposes of civilizing and educating the Black Natives or Aborigines of New South Wales'.[6] The following year, the Lieutenant Governor of Van Diemen's Land issued a proclamation repeating the official command that Aborigines should be considered as under the British Government and its protection, expressly forbidding any ill-treatment of the native inhabitants and instead encouraging 'all Measures which may Tend to conciliate and civilize them'.[7] And in 1826, reclaiming and reforming the indigenous inhabitants had become a gesture of philanthropy. According to the *Sydney Gazette*, 'An enterprise more truly disinterested and philanthropic, than that of instructing and civilizing the very degraded and wretched aborigines of this country, could not be proposed. Such an undertaking cannot fail, we presume, to receive the sincere approbation and earnest support of every humane heart.'[8]

Not all colonists favoured assimilation in these terms. Some, perhaps wiser or more pragmatic, adopted a 'noble savage' perspective. They saw the same lack of clothing, of housing and of cooking implements, but, rather than condemning Aborigines as uncivilized and therefore in need of civilizing, they recognized in Aboriginal practices evidence of a far greater sophistication, at least in the Australian environment, than the ways of the 'civilized' British. For example, Dr James Ross described an Aboriginal hunting party in Tasmania in 1823:

> As we were walking towards one of the little parties, a tall fellow overtook us with a bunch of seven fat, but strong smelling opossums slung on his back and round his neck. We followed him to the fire, and he very deliberately chucked them all upon it, one after the other, just as he had caught them. The company seemed to have little to say, for but few words passed between them, and what was rather mortifying to gentlemen in our rank of life, they scarcely deigned to look upon us. On our parts, however, we could not help admiring their upright and even elegant gait, which would be a pattern to any Bond-street lounger. It was quite indicative of persons who had little to do, with pleasure only to seek. Their air of independence was quite charming, and upon reflection, I know no race of people who have greater claims to that property.
>
> ... As soon as the opossums were singed and well heated on one side, our cook turned them on the other, and then dragging them by the leg from the fire, he scraped off the fur, and with sharp flint cut out the inside, and again threw it on the fire, from which it was soon after taken and eaten, without the trouble of knife or fork, in a half raw state. Occasionally they would take a short walk to the lagoon, and laying themselves on their breast, and dipping their mouth into the water, drank without cups or chalice the pure element of nature. They then returned to their rural hearth, and sitting or reclining on the ground they dozed as deliciously as if they had reposed on a velvet couch.[9]

In similar vein was an article entitled 'The Aborigines of Australia' from *The Spectator* in 1831, republished in *The Australian*:

> The black fellow, as we call him, and as he has learnt to call himself, is a savage – chiefly because he eats half-cooked kangaroo, lizards, rats, and grubs, and

considers the entrails of all animals the choicest of morsels when well grilled on a wood fire. We, however, civilized as we are, eat oysters and muscles raw, to say nothing of periwinkles; we enjoy the trail of woodcock.... They are savage, because they only build temporary habitations when they are always moving about; only frail ones, when it is easier to construct a new abode than to keep an old one. They do not wear clothing, because the climate is beautifully fine....

When the savage has plenty of food, he eats to gluttony – he has the excuse of knowing that days may elapse before another opportunity may occur. When he is hungered he never complains – he appeases nature by means of a tight belt tied round his waist. ... His senses are carried to that degree of perfection, that he hears and sees distinctly where the dull European does not even suspect the existence of either sound or object. When wandering in the depths of the trackless forest, he requires neither mark nor compass to guide; he retraces his path with the utmost security, where the civilized man would lose his way, grow frantic, and eventually lay himself down and die....

This is savagery; nevertheless it has such charms, that no man has as yet voluntarily left it altogether, or when taken young and instructed early in the rules of modern civilization, has not seized a speedy occasion of giving a practical proof of the kind of life he preferred.[10]

Although these two groups of commentators offered diametrically opposed opinions, they nevertheless shared the same concept of 'civilized', and both agreed that the Australian Aborigines, lacking their belief in the necessity of clothing, housing and cooking utensils, were primitive, uncivilized savages. Those who admired the Aboriginal way of life probably saw no need to change it, but the former group, who deplored it, considered it their mission to convert the 'savages'.

Their method of civilizing was a classic example of what Norbert Elias called 'The Civilizing Process', which entailed greater control of impulses and emotions and increased self-restraint, with the individual subsumed into the social world.[11] The vocabulary in this letter to the editor of the *Sydney Gazette* in 1831 – words such as rules, regularity, governed, order, decorum – is eloquently revelatory:[12]

CIVILIZATION OF THE BLACKS;

To the Editor of the Sydney Gazette
... in commencing the task of cultivating uncivilised man. He must be first taught to appreciate the decent customs of society; he must be induced to obey the rules of social life, and be governed by the regularity of domestic habits – clothes must be supplied him ... A regularity in their meals and cooking, I think, should also be attended to, and they should be compelled to sit to their victuals with as much order and decorum as possible....

Such examples emphasize the relevance of cooking (and eating) practices to the concept of 'civilized' – and also to 'culture'. To the early arrivals in Australia, throwing meat, often undressed carcasses, on to fire, without the cultural mediation of a cooking utensil, was a mark of an uncivilized society. Though our nineteenth-century British were unaware, they were anticipating by nearly two centuries the distinctions between nature and culture, roasted and boiled, elaborated by Claude Lévi-Strauss in his classic paper, 'The Culinary Triangle'.[13]

Lévi-Strauss postulated that raw foods can be transformed in one of two ways: by nature, in which case they become rotted; or by culture, to become cooked. Cooking requires human agency; the transformation occurs through the actions of people and is therefore a cultural transformation. This is what distinguishes it from the transformation effected by nature (although human intervention could also produce food that was rotted). In the second phase or elaboration of the culinary triangle, Lévi-Strauss assumed that all forms of cooking, the production of 'cooked' food, require heat, and that the heat can be associated with either air or with water. As an unmediated operation – without receptacle and without water – roasted is placed in the vicinity of raw while boiled is placed near rotted. At the third point of the triangle is smoked, unmediated in the same way as roasted but, like boiled, the result of slow and uniform cooking. Smoking is differentiated from roasting – a kind of sleight-of-hand trick – by the layer of air between the ingredient and the fire; in roasting this layer of air is reduced to a minimum. Boiling represents elaboration, while the roast is unelaborated.

Lévi-Strauss situated the operation of boiling firmly 'on the side of culture: literally, because boiling requires the use of a receptacle, *a cultural object*; symbolically, in as much as culture is a mediation of the relations between man and the world, and boiling demands a mediation (by water) of the relation between food and fire which is absent in roasting'.[14] Boiling requires a cultural means, the cooking pot, a durable utensil.

The reckless and damning judgment of early Europeans was based, in part, on their limited understanding of 'cooking' and their automatic assumption that proper cooking was done with pots and pans and other cultural artefacts. They could not conceive that 'cooking' could be done without man-made culinary utensils and equipment. Therefore they concluded that the Australian Aborigines were uncivilized: they had no durable utensils. We now recognize that this reflected insufficient appreciation of Aboriginal customs, including their modes of cooking. Later explorers, pioneer settlers, botanists, anthropologists and others who took time to observe, communicate and participate in Aboriginal life gave more detailed, and possibly more objective, accounts. Among the practices that they reported was the use of paperbark in cooking, specifically the wrapping of raw ingredients in paperbark before cooking them in the coals or ashes of their fire.

Paperbark comes from one of the many species of *Melaleuca* which can be found throughout much of Australia, from temperate Tasmania to the tropics of north Queensland and the Northern Territory, particularly in coastal zones; they are found in open forest, scrubland and woodland, and near water, along swamps and riverbanks –

which explains why many reports describe cooking fish in paperbark. They do not grow in the desert interior.

These later accounts of Aboriginal cooking practices not only describe the technique of wrapping in paperbark but also show an appreciation of the technique and the result. For example, R. Brough Smyth, in his 1876 book *The Aborigines of Victoria*, reported their way of cooking fish:

> If the fish are not cooked by merely being thrown on the fire and broiled, they dress them in a manner worthy of being adopted by the most civilized nations; this is called *yudarn dookoon*, or 'tying-up cooking'. A piece of thick and tender paper-bark is selected, and torn into an oblong form; the fish is laid in this, and the bark wrapt around it, as paper is folded round a cutlet; strings formed of grass are then wound tightly about the bark and fish, which is then slowly baked in heated sand, covered with hot ashes; when it is completed, the bark is opened, and serves as a dish; it is, of course, full of juice and gravy, not a drop of which has escaped. Several of the smaller sorts of fresh-water fish, in size and taste resembling whitebait, are really delicious when cooked in this manner; they occasionally also dress pieces of kangaroo and other meats in the same way.[15]

Another account of cooking in paperbark was given by naturalist Richard Helms in his paper read before the Royal Society of South Australia in 1893. Referring to the Aborigines of the north-west coast, Helms reported, 'The favourite way of cooking fish is to roll it in paper-bark just as it comes from the river or sea, and bury it in the hot ashes. The skin, bones, and insides come away quite clean when cooked, and the flesh is as white as snow'.[16] Dr W.L. Warner, of the Rockefeller Foundation, reported similar appreciation of this method of cooking in Arnhem Land, twenty-five miles south of the Arafura Sea, in 1927: 'Smaller fish and vegetable foods are put within a piece of paperbark, another piece laid on top, and the whole put in the ashes, and covered with coals, to cook. This is really an excellent cooking device. Food prepared in this fashion, as I can personally testify, is delicious.'[17]

Paperbark could also serve as a makeshift oven, as Roland E. Robinson reported in 1946:

> Back at the camp, the wallaby was thrown down and prepared and cooked in the following manner: First a hollow deep enough to accommodate the animal was scooped in the sand, and this hollow lined with river stones. A reasonably small fire was then made in the stone-lined hollow and allowed to burn down to coals and ash.
>
> By this time, the internal organs of the wallaby had been removed, its hind and forelegs bent and bound to its body, and, unskinned, the wallaby was ready for cooking. Some of the hot stones were then taken from the fire and put inside

the carcase, together with some eucalyptus leaves for flavouring. With this the wallaby was placed in the ground oven and sprinkled over with water.

More hot stones were placed over him and then the oven and its contents were completely covered with a sheet of paper-bark, which in its turn, was mounded over with sand.

This kind of ground-oven produces a great heat, as can be found by placing one's hand on the mound, or by being present at the conclusion of the cooking, when the covering of sand and paper-bark is carefully removed and the steaming, well-cooked, and flavoured wallaby is revealed.[18]

The bark of the tea tree could also be used for wrapping around raw ingredients – for example, Aborigines used paperbark and tea-tree bark to wrap and cook oysters on the Mornington Peninsula in Victoria. In places where neither paperbark nor tea tree grew, the alternative to paperbark might be a wrapping of clay, giving similarly excellent results. The clay-baking technique was applied to both fish and game, large and small, as evidenced by the following reports:

COOKING IN THE DESERT
The half-caste had shot a wild turkey, and found a billyful of Mallee yams no bigger than beans, and some leaves, which appeared to me to be a species of sage in its aboriginal state. He plucked and cooked the bird in the usual manner, and, having stuffed it with the yams, sage, and salt, enclosed it in a lump of well-kneaded clay and then threw the clay into a clear fire. When the clay was baked he placed it on a log, and having separated it into two halves the turkey appeared cooked to a nicety, and as clean as a whistle, and with savoury rapture would have filled dean or chapter, or well filled the crop up of Alderman Topup. Some times the turkey is placed in the clay ungutted, with its feathers on, and nevertheless is taken out equally clean....[19]

The blackfellow, having speared a codfish weighing perhaps five pounds, wraps the fish in a coat of thick mud, and places it in the ashes of a fire which has been made in a hole in the earth. It is covered up and left until it is cooked. Then the hard, caked mud is broken off – it usually came off in a couple of pieces – taking the scales and skin with it, and leaving the beautiful, juicy white flesh quite uncontaminated by either mud or fire.[20]

According to 'J.McG.', writing about the Aboriginals of the western plains of New South Wales between the River Darling and the Paroo:

...the abos. of that locality do their cooking, and wherever possible they encase whatever they wish to cook in moist clay or earth an inch thick, worked up by hand to the consistency of dough.... The object to be cooked, be it kangaroo, goanna, or bird, was so encased just as it was captured and killed and placed in a good fire. When done, the baked mud was removed and the hair, feathers, or skin, as the case, might be, came away with it and left what I have no doubt was a very palatable article of diet.... The abo. of that region was undoubtedly a much more intelligent subject than he is given credit for.[21]

A similar account came from 'Mulga Mick', writing from Tasmania in 1944:

> During my long years of prospecting throughout Australia and Tasmania I have at times been compelled to eat all sorts of food, including snakes, lizards, porcupines, bandicoots, wombats, wallaby, kangaroo, kangaroo rats, opossums, emus, eagles, hawks, crows, etc., and numerous insects. It is all a matter of cooking. The native hen can be made as delicious as any other fowl … roll the bird in damp clay, feathers and all, bury it in hot ashes for about one and a half hours. When taken out the skin and feathers will easily leave the flesh, which, with the retention of its natural juices, will melt in the mouth. This was the method of cooking practised by the natives and runaway convicts, bushrangers, explorers, and prospectors.
>
> MULGA MICK.
Glenorchy.[22]

Sometimes the wrapping could be dispensed with altogether. It is significant that adventurers Mossman and Banister considered the Aboriginal method of cooking superior to 'civilised cookery':

> We confess ourselves a little bit of an epicure in the mode of cooking fish; and their simple method seems to us the best we have ever seen for preserving the natural juices of a delicate fish. They first collect the hot ashes from a large fire made of the mangrove-tree, which are white and free from burning embers; then the fish is taken 'all alive,' without being gutted or scaled, and buried in these hot ashes for a quarter of an hour or twenty minutes. When it is sufficiently baked the gut comes out in one mass, and the skin peels off whole, leaving the flakes of meat firm, white, and savoury, with the natural fat and gravy of the fish, which in civilised cookery are lost; the former being thrown away with the gut, and the latter escaping through the scraped skin.[23]

From these diverse accounts it is clear that paperbark and clay, in Aboriginal culture, performed the same function as a cooking pot, allowing the food to be fully cooked. It was effectively steamed rather than boiled, which would probably place it closer to grilled/roasted in the culinary triangle. Paperbark wrappings were therefore equivalent to a cooking pot. But unlike a pot, which qualifies as a 'cultural object', bark and clay are products of nature rather than of culture; they are ephemeral, transitory, rather than permanent, durable.

Wrapping Cooking, Civilizing

So how would this be accommodated in the culinary triangle? The cooking process could not be called roasting, in which the food is exposed directly to the flames in an 'unmediated conjunction' with the fire. In effect, the paperbark wrapping served as a mediation between the food and fire, and in this respect might be seen as somewhat analogous to the *buccan*, a wooden frame used by American Indians for smoking game (and, incidentally, Lévi-Strauss's argument in relation to smoking was based on this single example). The *buccan* was a cultural object, because it was constructed and necessitated human agency. Nevertheless, it was not a durable cultural object in the same way as is a cooking pot because the *buccan* was perishable, destroyed after use. The same logic could be applied to the paperbark container; it involves some degree of construction, albeit minimal, and despite the fact that it is not durable it could be considered a cultural object in the same way as the *buccan*.

Other uses of paperbark confirm that it could serve as the prime material for a cultural object. Helms noted that 'Water vessels are made by tying a piece of bark of the paper-bark tea-tree at both ends with rushes, but as they have to be carried with both hands the water is not conveyed in them any great distance.'[24] Shelters and huts were also constructed from paperbark, as were canoes and burial caskets.

Because the *buccan* was a cultural object, Lévi-Strauss considered smoking to be related to boiling, and 'smoked' to be closest to the abstract category of 'cooked'. In other words, smoking represented a cultural transformation of the raw. By this logic, the wrapping of raw ingredients in paperbark then setting the package on hot coals similarly represents a cultural transformation.

In this light, the initial judgment by the newly arrived Europeans that Australian Aboriginals were uncivilized, on the basis that they lacked culinary equipment and, as a corollary, the cultural skills to transform 'raw' to 'cooked', was singularly mistaken. Applying Lévi-Strauss's analysis and theory of cooking, it is clear that the technique of wrapping foods in paperbark qualifies as cooking. One of the most elementary of culinary techniques – wrapping in a natural material like paperbark – displays not only ecological efficiency but culinary sophistication.

Notes

1. See, for example, these works by Joseph Lycett: 'Aborigines cooking and eating beached whales', Newcastle, New South Wales, *ca.* 1817; and 'Aborigines spearing fish, others diving for crayfish, a party seated beside a fire cooking fish', *ca.* 1817; and 'Drawings of Aborigines and scenery', New South Wales, *ca.* 1820.
2. Inga Clendinnen, *Dancing with Strangers* (Melbourne: Text, 2003), p. 64.
3. Clendinnen, pp. 29–30.
4. Clendinnen, p. 28.
5. *Sydney Gazette and New South Wales Advertiser*, 7 July 1810, p. 2.
6. *Sydney Gazette and New South Wales Advertiser*, 21 Dec 1816, p. 1.
7. *Hobart Town Gazette and Southern Reporter*, 24 May 1817, p. 1.
8. *Sydney Gazette and New South Wales Advertiser*, 11 Feb 1826, p. 2.
9. *The Australian*, 12 March 1830, p. 3.
10. *The Australian*, 22 July 1831, p. 4.
11. Norbert Elias, *The Civilizing Process* (New York: Urizen Books, 1978).
12. *Sydney Gazette and New South Wales Advertiser*, 10 March 1831, p. 3.
13. Claude Lévi-Strauss, 'The Culinary Triangle,' *Partisan Review* 33 (1966), pp. 586–595.
14. Lévi-Strauss, p. 588.
15. R. Brough Smyth, *The Aborigines of Victoria*, first publ. 1876 (South Yarra, Vic: John Currey, O'Neil, 1972): vol. 1, pp. 204–205.
16. 'Royal Society of South Australia,' *South Australian Register*, 8 November 1893, p. 5.
17. *Western Mail*, 22 September 1927, p. 32.
18. *Sydney Morning Herald*, 16 November 1946, p. 7.
19. *Border Watch*, 27 December 1876, p. 4.
20. *Northern Star* (Lismore), 5 December 1903, p. 1S.
21. *The Mail* (Adelaide), 1 August 1925, p. 18.
22. *Mercury*, October 31 1944, p. 3.
23. Samuel Mossman and Thomas Banister, *Australia Visited and Re-Visited: A Narrative of Recent Travels and Old Experiences in Victoria and New South Wales*, first publ. 1853 (Dee Why: Ure Smith, 1974), pp. 294–295.
24. 'Royal Society of South Australia,' *South Australian Register*, 8 November 1893, p. 5.

The Magician's Kitchen: Stuffing and Wrapping at the Pillsbury Bake-Off

Laura Shapiro

Edna Holmgren was fifty-five years old and a deputy village clerk in Eden Prairie, Minnesota, just outside Minneapolis, when she got the idea to wrap pastry dough around a marshmallow and bake it.[1]

This was not something she was planning for a specific meal, or even because she wanted something to eat. In fact, cooking, as we usually think of it, may have been the last thing on her mind. What she was trying to do was invent a recipe for the Pillsbury Bake-Off, the biggest cooking contest in America and probably the most successful promotion in the history of the American food industry.[2] Started in 1949, it's still going strong today. Back in 1967, the year of the first contest that Edna Holmgren entered, the grand prize was $25,000, and there were a number of smaller prizes. Today the top prize is a million dollars.

Thousands of recipes from ambitious home cooks like Edna Holmgren pour into Pillsbury for months before every Bake-Off. Various teams of home economists study the recipes, screen them for originality, test them, and gradually winnow them down to one hundred finalists. Then comes the moment that everyone who sends a recipe to the Bake-Off waits for – the phone call. If it comes, people remember it for the rest of their lives: someone from Pillsbury calls and tells you that you have been chosen as one of the hundred finalists. You're flown to a city like Orlando or Houston or San Diego, put up in a luxury hotel, photographed and interviewed and entertained, and finally comes the day you cook. The contest takes place in the ballroom of the hotel, where General Electric has installed a hundred mini-kitchens. On the morning of the Bake-Off, all the contestants march into the ballroom together, to the tune of 'When the Saints Go Marching In', and then fan out to their stoves to prepare their recipes. The judges, who are usually food editors from around the country, are sequestered; nobody is even supposed to know who they are until the contest is over. They sit all day in a closed-off room and taste the 100 entries – main dishes, snacks, breads, pastries, appetizers and – famously – desserts. Lots of desserts. The next day the awards are announced at an elaborate ceremony, televised live; and there is always a celebrity onstage who personally congratulates the winners. At the first Bake-Off, in 1949, the celebrity was Eleanor Roosevelt; at the second it was the Duchess of Windsor; and at the forty-fifth Bake-Off in March 2012, it was Martha Stewart. You can make of that trajectory what you will.

But Edna Holmgren's recipe did not get her to the Bake-Off in 1967. It didn't make the cut. No phone call. So she went back to the kitchen and tried again. Nowadays

Stuffing and Wrapping at the Pillsbury Bake-Off

the Bake-Off is held every other year, but back then it was annual, so she had a year to work on the recipe.

As you know, historians do not speculate. But food writers speculate all the time, so I am going to tilt that way for the moment and speculate about what Edna Holmgren was thinking when she contemplated the reasons for her failure. She had one important piece of information to study, and that was the 1967 Bake-Off cookbook. Every time there's a Bake-Off, Pillsbury puts out a paperback cookbook with all the recipes from the hundred finalists in it. So there they were, the people who got the call in 1967. They had to be doing something right. And many of them, like Edna Holmgren, were wrapping dough around things, which is a motif in American cooking that goes back ... as far as American food. Certainly as far as American leftovers. In fact, you could have created a kind of diorama of American stuffed-and-wrapped history just from the recipes in the 1967 Bake-Off cookbook. First you'd have Grandmother's Dessert Rolls, a recipe from Mrs G.R. Taylor of Memphis, Tennessee, who rolled out a biscuit dough, cut it into squares, then filled them with cinnamon and sugar and folded them up to make little packets, which she baked.[3] In other words, Grandmother was making good use of some leftover biscuit dough. But American cooking has also been long known for its efficiency. Why round up several complementary ingredients when a single powerful one will shoot right to the point? In that spirit Mrs Lowell Domers, of Burbank, Ohio, made a sweet pastry dough, cut it into long strips, and stacked them in layers with candy bars between them. These stacks were cut into slices and baked, and she called them – again going straight to the point – Candy Bar In-Betweens.[4] And of course, American cooking has always had a way of absorbing cultural insignia and remaking them in its own image, which is perhaps what inspired Mrs E. Miles Brown of Riverton, New Jersey, to roast a frozen turkey breast, spread it with Spam and anchovy paste, then wrap the whole thing in dough and bake it. She named it Turkey Eleganté, accent and all.[5]

But I'm guessing that, as far as Edna Holmgren was concerned, the most interesting of the numerous ventures in stuffing and wrapping was the one attributed to Moreen Ivice of Chicago. In response to all these culinary cues – economy, efficiency, cultural zeal – she took her dough and wrapped it around a meat loaf, covered it with slices of mozzarella cheese, and called it Pizza Wellington.[6] This, of course, was an homage to Beef Wellington, and in doing this she was right on top of the times: the Chicago *Tribune* announced that very year that 'the current rage among hostesses is any recipe that has the name Wellington'.[7] More importantly, she was also ahead of the times, because her dough was not made from scratch. Instead, this recipe called for a package of refrigerated fresh dough – a ready-made dough sold in a special cardboard tube that keeps it from rising as long as it's chilled. You just pull the dough out of the tube, and depending what kind it is, you can stretch it into rectangles, or divide it into triangles or separate it into biscuits. Moreen Ivice specified a package of Pillsbury refrigerated pizza dough, which in those days came with a can of 'pizza sauce', which she mixed into the meat loaf.

Stuffing and Wrapping at the Pillsbury Bake-Off

Obviously, and this is what Edna Holmgren would have noticed right off the bat, Moreen Ivice had not used refrigerated fresh dough in her original recipe – she couldn't have. The one requirement for a Bake-Off recipe was that it had to use at least half a cup of Pillsbury flour. That's why Edna Holmgren and everybody else who wrapped things made their dough from scratch. But Pillsbury, which technically owned all the Bake-Off recipes, plainly stated in the headnote to Pizza Wellington that it had 'adapted' Moreen Ivice's recipe.

A little more reading in the cookbook, especially the section with the entry blank and rules for next year's contest, and it became clear what Pillsbury was up to. For the first time in the history of the Bake-Off, the company was changing the rules. Or, as it said in the huge newspaper ads that began to appear that year, 'Because baking has changed, we've changed the Bake-Off'.[8] Starting with the 1968 Bake-Off, Pillsbury would award prizes in three categories. You could use Pillsbury flour, you could use a Pillsbury mix, or you could use refrigerated fresh dough. What's more, there would be a new approach to judging the recipes. As always, flavour and appearance would count. But another standard would now be applied: the judges would look specifically for recipes that were quick, and that featured the use of packaged foods.

This new approach had been in the works at Pillsbury for some time. In fact the ads got it wrong: it was because baking hadn't changed enough that Pillsbury was changing the Bake-Off. We think of post-war American home cooking as a panorama of the quick 'n easy, with cake mixes and frozen dinners lined up on every kitchen counter, but the truth is, even as late as the 1960s, packaged foods were still making rather slow progress; they had not yet transformed people's cooking habits. The food industry was really puzzled by this. Why wouldn't homemakers leap at the chance to jettison their familiar recipes and everything they knew and felt about cooking? There were surveys and focus groups, and in 1969 a Pillsbury home economist reported, in a speech to the baking industry, what the company believed was going on. '[C]ommercially processed foods do not represent the "good life" for today's young housewife', she explained. 'In the mass market, there is still a strong anti-progressive, anti-change and anti-modern strain in American culture. In the face of sophisticated advertising and merchandising, the young consumer's sales resistance is phenomenal'.[9]

So Pillsbury had its work cut out. They had to make convenience-oriented cooking both respectable and permanent. That was why they were changing the Bake-Off, and they had actually initiated this change two years earlier when they introduced into their rhetoric about home cooking an entirely new word: 'shortcutted'.

This word was formally presented to the nation's food writers at a brunch sponsored by Pillsbury in 1965. Ruth Ellen Church, who wrote about food for years at the *Chicago Tribune* under the *nom de plume* Mary Meade, was horrified when she heard it. 'I had always thought the past tense of "cut" was "cut"', she wrote. 'I have never "cutted" my cookies; but a Pillsbury public relations man ... says that "shortcut" is a noun, and shortcutted an adjective.'[10] To her dismay, the word had a long life, but happily it seems never to have been deployed outside the confines of Pillsbury.

At any rate, with the new rules, the new judging, and the new word, it could not have been more evident that cooking from scratch was no longer necessary or even desirable in the Bake-Off. And just to make sure nobody missed the point, Pillsbury had temporarily changed the name of the Bake-Off: the company was now calling it 'The Pillsbury Busy Lady Bake-Off.'[11]

Edna Holmgren got the message. She realized that her original recipe had been, as she later put it, 'too long and complicated'.[12] So she did exactly what the company advised, she used a packaged food, or what Pillsbury called a 'convenience product.'[13] She used one of their refrigerated doughs, and she chose the kind that made buttermilk biscuits. This definitely changed her recipe, it certainly wasn't long or complicated anymore – but even so, once again, the phone didn't ring. She was not selected as a finalist. What could be wrong? She decided it had to be the new biscuits. They were, after all, buttermilk-flavoured. Maybe not the best wrapping for a marshmallow. So she tried again, using a different product – Refrigerated Quick Crescent Dinner Rolls. This time, she made history.

Refrigerated Quick Crescent Dinner Rolls had been around since 1961. When you opened the tube of dough, you were supposed to separate the dough into flat triangles, then roll them up, curve them slightly into a crescent shape, and put them in the oven. The idea was that you would end up with the equivalent of a French croissant. People liked this product, and they were buying it, but Pillsbury had bigger plans. They wanted refrigerated dough to be like canned soup – yes, it would make soup, but more to the point it would make sauces and casseroles and would have a whole separate life as an ingredient, not just as an end in itself. If refrigerated dough was going to fulfil its great potential, it too would have to become an ingredient, and crescent rolls in particular seemed versatile enough to have immense possibilities. You didn't have to just use the dough in triangles – you could make rectangles, even big rectangles, and you could fill, and roll, and wrap, and twist, and braid, and slice, just about endlessly.

Nonetheless, the only place crescent rolls appeared, in most households, was the bread basket. Not many people were doing anything else with them. They did start to show up as ingredients in the 1968 Bake-Off, the first one with the new category for refrigerated dough, but far more striking in that Bake-Off was the extent to which breads and pastries made from scratch – America's old way of baking – held their own almost defiantly. There were coconut rolls made with a yeast dough, there was a brioche from scratch, Danish pastries, home-made pretzels, home-made English muffins. Refrigerated dough was out there, but when it came to displaying their skills as bakers, a lot of contestants were still relying on their skills.

So refrigerated dough was not on any obvious path to glory until the day Edna Holmgren opened a tube of crescent rolls, separated out the triangles, and did the following: First, she took a marshmallow and dipped it in melted butter. Then she rolled it in a mixture of sugar and cinnamon and wrapped it in a triangle of refrigerated dough. Then she dipped one end of the little dough package in melted butter, and placed it in one of the cups of a muffin tin. She made 16 wrapped marshmallows this way, baked them for 10 or 15 minutes, and finally drizzled each one with a mixture of powdered sugar, milk and vanilla. She called them Magic Marshmallow Crescent Puffs. And here's the magic. When you bite into one, it's quite gooey and sticky, but there is no marshmallow. You're tasting an empty space. You're tasting pure sweetness, held aloft by the cinnamon.

This time, Pillsbury called. Edna Holmgren became a finalist, she went to the 1969 Bake-Off in Atlanta, Georgia, and she won the Grand Prize – $25,000. Magic Marshmallow Crescent Puffs became a landmark recipe in the history of the Bake-Off. People made them, and made them, and made them. Thirty years later the recipe was inducted into the Bake-Off Hall of Fame, one of the ten most popular recipes ever to emerge from the contest. People still make them, and in recent years they have become especially popular for breakfast on Easter Sunday. Families that make them at Easter call them Resurrection Rolls, because the empty space that once held the marshmallow is a reminder of the empty tomb.[14]

Resurrection Rolls – you can't get more immortal than that. But what happened to refrigerated crescent-roll dough went far, far beyond Magic Marshmallow Crescent Puffs. After Edna Holmgren's victory, the Bake-Off was inundated with crescent-roll recipes. People who were trying to come up with dessert recipes wrapped crescent dough around mincemeat, canned apple pie filling, miniature marshmallows, peanuts, coconut, peanut brittle, Rice Krispies. Or if they were making snacks and entrees, they made Crescent Ravioli, Crescent Taco Pie, Pork 'N Crescent Polish Pasties, Crescent Easy Egg Rolls and Crescent Samosa Sandwiches. (That was not a sandwich with a samosa in it as the filling. It was a samosa, redefined as a sandwich.) They made Flaky Crescent Chicken Wellington, and Chicken Wellington A la Crescent. They made Crescent Hamwich, Crescent Pizza-Wiches, Easy Crescent Pizza-Wiches, Crescent Beef and Baconwiches, and Crescent Corned-Beef-wich. And countless more. As one of the judges remarked, after the 1984 Bake-Off, 'The human mind will stop at nothing when it comes to stuffing a crescent roll'.[15]

It's safe to say that refrigerated dough, and the crescent roll in particular, transformed the Bake-Off, turning it into a showcase for some of the most startling and ingenious emblems of stuffing and wrapping that American cuisine has ever known. But it wasn't just the product that made this happen. It was the product in combination with a particular kind of culinary imagination, a fiercely activist approach to the kitchen that took off like a rocket when Pillsbury pushed the right buttons.

Pillsbury likes to represent the Bake-Off as a mirror of what's happening every day in the nation's kitchens. According to the company, it's a contest for 'amateur cooks like you, whose recipes reflect and set trends in American cooking'.[16] But the fact is, most Bake-Off recipes over the years have not been particularly representative of American home cooking; they've tended to survive chiefly in the Bake-Off cookbooks.

Stuffing and Wrapping at the Pillsbury Bake-Off

Occasionally a Bake-Off recipe does make a noticeable impact on the outside world, the way Magic Marshmallow Crescent Puffs did, but in general there has been little crossover. The reason, I think, is that Bake-Off recipes are exactly that – Bake-Off recipes. The people sending them in are home cooks, but they're not sending in home cooking. They're sending in contest cooking.

The Bake-Off is the oldest national cooking contest in America, and it's the one with the biggest prizes, but it's far from alone. There are dozens and dozens of cooking contests, large and small, local and national. They're usually sponsored by a specific product – chicken, beef, ice-cream, hot sauce – and the really passionate contest cooks spend all year working on recipes and sending them in to one or another contest. The Bake-Off is the pinnacle of these contests, and attracts so many contest cooks that over the years they've effectively swamped it. You're allowed to send in as many recipes as you want to every Bake-Off, and the really extreme contest cooks come up with ten, twenty, forty at a time. What's more, these expert contest cooks know how to win. They study previous winners; they handicap the chances of chocolate versus caramel, and apples versus blueberries. Even before Pillsbury introduced packaged foods to the Bake-Off, back when many of the recipes were still fairly traditional, there were contest cooks figuring out how to get their recipes to the top. In 1961 a magazine called *Contest* interviewed several Bake-Off winners and asked for the secrets of their success. 'Submit a recipe that is DIFFERENT from any you have ever seen', advised Della Ruth Emerson of Coshocton, Ohio, whose cheesecake with chocolate and coconut was a finalist at the tenth Bake-Off. Leona Schnuelle of Beatrice, Nebraska, whose Dilly Casserole Bread won the Bake-Off in 1954, told would-be contest cooks to have the courage of their convictions. 'When your recipes do not win, then DARE to go beyond the conventional', she urged. 'Dream – experiment – measure'.[17]

This kind of thinking was not in circulation when the Bake-Off began in 1949. The early Bake-Offs were similar to their predecessors, the cooking competitions at 4-H clubs and state fairs, which celebrated American agriculture and farm life. These cooking competitions honoured tradition; they were about excellence within familiar categories. Everybody knew what made a good peach pie, that was what you tried to achieve, and the winner was the best peach pie. Nobody said, 'Invent something.' The most Pillsbury did at the beginning was stretch the boundaries a little. The company encouraged Bake-Off contestants to send in recipes that were family favourites and just give them a touch of the unexpected – what it called a 'bright idea'.[18] The winner of the second Bake-Off, for instance, in 1950, was Orange Kiss-Me Cake, a recipe sent in by Mrs Peter Wuebel of Redwood City, California. 'Here is the cake with the $25,000 flavor', said the headnote to this recipe in the Bake-Off cookbook. 'You start out with a single orange, using the inside and the rind, ground up with raisins and nuts. And no frosting needed – you put the juice of that same orange on top of the warm cake with sugar and chopped nuts. … It stays moist for days and has just about the finest, freshest flavor you ever put into your mouth'.[19]

Stuffing and Wrapping at the Pillsbury Bake-Off

So the $25,000 flavour is, first and foremost, a flavour. Everything about this description praises honest ingredients used for a clear purpose. The goal of this recipe is food, not originality for its own sake. But with the development of convenience foods, originality began edging towards the center stage of American cooking. It was so extremely easy to make an instant pudding come out right – this was the era when recipes began to include instructions like 'Follow directions on package' – that the food industry began to fear that women would start feeling irrelevant in their own kitchens. Originality, creativity – these became the counterweight. Sometimes 'creativity' was about making the food taste better – add a little sherry to the canned soup – but more often it was about making the cook feel better. *Be* creative, urged the ads and magazines; be a 'creative cook'.[20]

Year by year at the Bake-Off, this lunge towards creativity became more and more apparent, in part because contest cooking, with its relentless need to be different, was showing up more and more frequently, and also because culinary creativity was simply in the air. There was a great deal of faux sophistication in the mid-century American food press – there was even some real sophistication – but the food industry preferred the quick 'n easy version, hence the garish combinations of packaged products that dominated food advertising. At the Bake-Off, recipes like Cranberry Whirl Ham Dinner were becoming the new normal. This was a 1955 finalist, which you made by taking a sweet biscuit dough studded with cranberries, spreading it with ham, canned pineapple and sweet potatoes, rolling it up like a jelly roll, then slicing it into chunks and baking them. You could eat this, but it wasn't about eating; it was entirely about an idea. Finally Pillsbury, which had been promoting convenience single-mindedly for years, redid the rules once more. In 1970 the company announced that Bake-Off recipes would continue to be judged on convenience – but that 'convenience' from now on meant 'originality and creativity in the convenient use of ingredients'.[21] As English, this doesn't make much sense. At the Bake-Off, it settled in for a long run.

After forty-five years of the Bake-Off, and hundreds of published recipes, there are maybe a dozen that have moved from the contest to the home kitchen and put down roots there. This isn't surprising. The impulse behind contest cooking has nothing to do with the time-honoured culinary quest of looking for something to eat. Most Bake-Off cooking is about novelty; it has no other culinary rationale. Which is why, when we look at typical Bake-Off recipes against their ritual backdrop of kitchen-table Americana, they seem so frantic and silly. These are wild-eyed accumulations of ingredients, assembled for no purpose other than to clamour for attention.

But suppose we change the backdrop. Forget the kitchen table. Take away the pretence that this is home cooking. Think of these contest cooks as exactly the kind of cooks they are – single-minded, driven, passionately in pursuit of ideas. Food is only their medium. Appetite is beside the point. Here are cooks who know how to invent, manipulate and cajole; these are the skills that sweep them to victory. And when you look at the Bake-Off in that light, perhaps you will be reminded – as I was – of a very different branch of cuisine, far more exalted than the Pillsbury Bake-Off: in fact it's the most rarefied branch of cuisine in our time, the chemistry-lab pursuit known as molecular gastronomy.

Edna Holmgren, whose Magic Marshmallow Crescent Puffs achieved pure sweetness, and Ferran Adrià, whose spherical olives achieved pure 'oliveness' – it seems to me that these two are working under the same star. Maybe you've read about the turnaround moment in the life of Ferran Adrià – an incident that has been told and retold with the reverence usually associated with the lives of the saints. This was the day in 1987 when he heard a French chef say, 'Creativity means not copying.' As one of the disciples reported later, 'This simple sentence was what brought about a change in approach in our cooking.'[22] In other words, from that moment on, Ferran Adrià dedicated his life and work to the same principle that had been operating at the Bake-Off for decades. Creativity – over here it means wrapping refrigerated dough around canned crab, mayonnaise and Worcestershire sauce and calling it sushi; over there it means wrapping a translucent disc made of potato starch and soy lecithin around a mixture of pine nuts and pine-cone oil and calling it ravioli. If the former recipe is most likely to be regarded as inane, and the latter as brilliant, I'm not sure the difference has to do with the food.

Perhaps what's most telling about these two versions of culinary extremism is how very far they have come from the modest origin they share – that sensible practice of wrapping one food around another in order to benefit both foods. The arrival these days of new cookbooks promising to bring the techniques of molecular gastronomy right to your own kitchen will not, I think, have any discernible effect on the way most Americans put food on the table, but it does underscore – once again – the high hopes and long reach of commercialized creativity. Today the disparity between cooking to feed people and cooking to show off has never been greater, maybe because the tradition of ordinary, comfortably unexciting home cooking doesn't seem to get much traction anymore, not in a culinary world made dazzling by restaurants and TV chefs. Let's go back to Edna Holmgren for a minute. All she wanted to do was to win the Bake-Off; she had nothing more portentous in mind. But when I think about that marshmallow disappearing, I can't help seeing the plainspoken traditions of American cooking that disappeared with it, leaving nothing behind but the sweetness.

Notes

1. Pillsbury, *100 Bake-Off Recipes* (1969), p. 5. See also 'Mrs Edna Holmgren is Bake-Off Recipe Winner," *Delta Democrat Times*, 12 February 1969, p 6, and Pillsbury, *Hall of Fame Inductee Biographies* (1999).
2. For the history of the Bake-Off, see Laura Shapiro, *Something from the Oven* (New York: Penguin, 2005), pp. 34–40, pp. 82–83.
3. Pillsbury, *Bake-Off Cook Book* (1967), 73.
4. Ibid., p. 34.
5. Ibid., p. 61.
6. Ibid., p. 57.
7. Mary Meade, 'Veal Wellington Tower Buttressed by Pastry', *Chicago Tribune*, 3 April 1967, p. B12.
8. *Chicago Tribune*, 17 September 1967, p. C8.
9. 'Your Customer and What She's Up To', speech by Barbara Thornton to the American Bakers Association, 28 October 1969, Barbara Thornton Lockwood Papers, Minnesota History Center.
10. Meade, *Chicago Tribune*, 27 September 1965, p. B10.
11. Pillsbury, *Bake-Off Cook Book* (1967), p. 92.
12. Ann Burckhardt, 'Bake-Off', *Minneapolis Star*, 18 March 1981, p. 3T.
13. Pillsbury, *Bake-Off Cook Book* (1967), p. 95.
14. See, for example, raisinglittledisciples.blogspot.com, 30 March 2012.
15. Margaret Sheridan, 'Pillsbury Bake-Off Ends with an Oink," *Chicago Tribune*, 1 March 1984, p. DC2.
16. Pillsbury, 'Sixty Years of the Bake-Off Contest', 1 July 2012: pillsbury.com/BakeOff/About/History.
17. 'Warm-Up for the Bake-Off', *Contest Magazine* (June 1961), p. 33.
18. 'Just a Simple Recipe with a Bright Idea…' in Pillsbury, *Pillsbury's 7th Grand National Cookbook* (1956): n.p.
19. Pillsbury, *100 Prize-Winning Recipes* (1951), p. 2.
20. See, for example, 'The Cake Mix: Gilded Variety', in *Living for Young Homemakers* (April 1958), p. 98, which claims, 'The creative cook can go as far as her imagination will take her'.
21. Advertisement, *Los Angeles Times*, 13 September 1970, p. 53.
22. El Bulli, 'History: 1961–1982': elbulli.com/historia, 1 July 2012.

Turning a New Leaf in London?
Paan Culture in the Metropole

Jaclyn Rohel

In eighteenth- and nineteenth-century Europe, coffeehouses and taverns spatialized the modern Western public sphere as a masculinized, bourgeois relation between private individuals engaged in debate about common issues of concern (Habermas, 1991).[1] The intersection of these public spaces with what Wolfgang Schivelbusch (1993) calls 'articles of pleasure' was not an accident (p. xiii). They were intimately connected with both new forms of sociality and burgeoning industrial and capitalist markets, offering not only venues for doing local business and stimulants for increasing alertness and productivity, but also opportunities for consuming foreign products mined from the colonies (Cho, 2010; Cowan, 2005; Goodman, 2007; Mintz, 1985; Smith, 2007). Yet *paan* – the wrapped package of areca nut, slaked lime and catechu in betel leaf – was absent from these forums.[2] The case of *paan*, rather, upsets the strict delineations between public and private that have developed out of the modern Western experience. For centuries, this wrapped comestible has occupied a privileged place in the homes, temples and streets of the Indian subcontinent, deployed as a sign of hospitality, an aphrodisiac, an Ayurvedic medicine, a Hindu offering and a social lubricant. The *paan* stall – a preeminent gathering place – predated the coffeehouse; it continues to typify Indian streetscapes, and increasingly those of global cities such as London. While scholars have thoroughly examined how stimulants such as sugar, tea, chocolate, coffee and tobacco were embedded in networks of social and state power, the cultural politics of *paan* in the West has received surprisingly little attention (Cowan, 2005; Mintz, 1985; Norton, 2006; Schivelbusch, 1983). This paper examines how *paan* as a wrapped – and unwrapped – comestible has transitioned to London, a global city deeply embedded in transnational and postcolonial networks. I do not aim to offer a complete history of *paan* within the context of London and the British Empire, the scope of which would be far too wide to do justice to here. Rather, I seek to illuminate key moments in the shifting materiality of this wrapped comestible to show how it has taken on different meanings and uses over time, given its location in British imperial and postcolonial global networks. Attention to global hierarchies and power relations reveals that *paan* is a (post)colonial comestible through which values associated with the public sphere, capitalism, leisure and sociality come to be negotiated.

The widespread chewing of *paan* is a product of multiple migrations in recent decades just as in centuries past. Almost one-fifth of the global population chews this comestible (Courtwright, 2001; Gupta and Warnakulasuriya, 2002). Though most popular in the tropics, across South Asia, South East Asia and East Africa, it is increasingly common in Europe and North America by way of Asian diasporic communities. Men and women across India have indulged in betel-chewing since at least the fourth century, when it travelled to the subcontinent from South East Asia (Ahuja and Ahuja, 2011). Over the last several centuries *paan* has become embedded in both everyday life and festive celebrations, as a necessary component of domestic hospitality rituals, as an exchange in gift economies for royal patronage during the Mughal empire, as an offering in Hindu temples, as a vehicle of celebration at weddings, as an aphrodisiac, as a tool of Ayurvedic medicine, as a mild stimulant and as a quotidian digestive aid, palate cleanser and breath freshener (Achaya, 1995; Ahuja and Ahuja, 2011; Gode, 1961; Guha, 2006; Reid, 1985; Sen, 2004; Williams et al., 2002; Strickland, 2002). It continues to be crafted not only in homes but also at roadside stalls and on street corners, where its procurement consolidates the nucleus of local communities, often next to a sign publicizing *pan* or *paan*, or even simply an icon of a single green leaf.

There are hundreds – if not thousands – of recipes for *paan*, most of them not written down but rather embodied in the fingers of street-side *paanwallahs* (*paan*-makers) and domestic women across the subcontinent. The recipes are often classified into three categories: simple *paan*, sweet *paan* and tobacco *paan*. Yet even the simplest form has multiple variants, each subtly changing the taste of this wrapped comestible. Its base consists of the betel leaf, which comes from the climbing *Piper betle* vine, a plant in the pepper family *Piperaceae* (Guha, 2006). There are several different varieties of *Piper betle*, bearing leaves that range from crisp, hot and spicy in taste to tender, delicate and subtly bitter. The betel leaf is then smeared with slaked lime (otherwise known as calcium hydroxide or pickling lime). An additional paste, catechu, may also be added and mixed with the lime and other flavour enhancers. Catechu is a tannic reddish-brown paste that is crafted by reducing the heartwood of a tree, normally the *Acacia catechu* or *Areca catechu*. Many *paan*-makers consider catechu to be the backbone of a good *paan*, and for this reason few are willing to part with their recipes. Finally, areca nuts (also known as *Areca catechu* or betel nuts, though the plant bears no resemblance to the *Piper betle*) complete the simple *paan*. Areca nuts, which contain a stimulating alkaloid, are the fruit of the areca palm. The nut is sun-dried, roasted or fermented, and then either chopped, grated, sliced or shaved. Its slightly astringent and bitter taste is sometimes offset with additives such as saffron. The betel leaf is then folded over the other ingredients and neatly wrapped into a triangle or a cone before it is placed into the mouth whole and chewed for at least several minutes, perhaps even more than an hour.

The sweet version of *paan*, which is both familiar in everyday contexts and a quintessential ingredient of many celebrations, contains a range of additional ingredients, including rose petal syrup, coconut, mint and spices such as fennel, coriander, cloves and cardamom, particular combinations of which produce different tastes and aid in the treatment of different ailments. Some versions even call for the final wrapped betel-quid to be coated in silver leaf, a process that not only alters this comestible aesthetically but promises to improve health by moderating blood pressure and serving as an antibacterial agent. The inclusion of tobacco, a New World colonial crop, to simple *paan* is a relatively recent phenomenon, though the precise moment of its adoption is unclear (see Gode, 1961; Ott, 1995; Reid, 1985). Tobacco, added as a paste or in dried leaf form (sometimes flavoured), provides a very strong stimulant effect to the uninitiated. Recipes for *paan* thus range from the simple and rudimentary to the elaborate, along the same spectrum of habitual consumption and luxury consumption. P.K. Gode (1961), the prolific chronicler of Indian history and culture, claims that *paan* – known in Sanskrit as *tambula* – was one of the three Ts of Indian social life, alongside tobacco and tea. Though this social pillar long preceded the popularity of tea and tobacco, comestibles introduced by the Europeans in the modern period, *paan* was also intimately bound up with British imperial power.

The management of areca nut and betel leaf were important to the success of the British in India. Sidney Mintz's (1985) study of sugar shows how a complex network of production and consumption was central to the realization of modern imperial power. In the seventeenth century, Britain's expanding empire had mobilized the raw supplies, labour and fiscal resources to support a substantial increase in the supply of sugar for the British people, thus creating a preference for sweet tastes. Sugar thereby transitioned from a luxury good to a specialized commodity to a ubiquitous commodity over the course of the modern era, a phenomenon that extended to other colonial products and that ultimately subsidized the Empire's operations (Bickham, 2008; Mintz, 1985). While *paan* and its associated ingredients did not follow the trajectory of sugar, tea, coffee, tobacco and chocolate as pillars of mainstream European forums of consumption, the British Empire benefited no less from its involvement in India's betel nut industry. In the mid- to late eighteenth century, shortly after the institution of the East India Company's power, British officials in Bengal forged a monopoly on local products, forbidding subjects of the Empire from participating in the trade of tobacco, salt and betel nut. These restrictions, combined with the imposition of taxes on these commodities, enabled the East India Company to exploit the well-established and extensive commodity trade networks in the subcontinent and South East Asia, thus accumulating local currency to fund British operations and expansion (St John, 2012). Since the monopoly did not prohibit employees of the East India Company from trading these commodities privately, many used the opportunity to trade betel nut as a supplement to their personal profits (Dirks, 2006; St. John, 2012). Company consultations revealed that the European trade of salt, tobacco and betel nut entailed that 'the poor of this country, which used always to deal in salt, beetle nut [*sic*] and tobacco, are now deprived of their daily bread' (Fort William Select Consultation, 1764). Though the monopoly was short-lived, trade restrictions and enduring taxation policies on the betel nut trade not only served to generate revenue for a burgeoning Empire, but also became a means of managing the consumption of its Indian subjects.

By the early nineteenth century, when areca nut trees were well integrated with the sugar plantations on the south-western coast of the peninsula, British officials widely considered areca nut an apt object of taxation due to its local luxury status and its intoxicating capacities. Some even proposed that the betel leaf, a necessary part of *paan*, also be subject to inter-regional import duties.

These trade networks provided British officials and merchants with the opportunity to chew *paan*, but how widely the habit was taken up in India remains unclear. Some chroniclers of colonial India maintain that Company merchants ate curries, wore local clothing and chewed *paan* to preserve the health of their teeth and stomach, noting that *paan* as a post-meal digestive echoed the voidee, the British custom of distributing palate-cleansing and digestive spices after a banquet (Burton, 1993; Collingham, 2006; Sen, 2004). Gode (1961), however, offers a very different perspective, insisting that 'the Europeans settling in India have not adopted the habit of eating *Tambula* owing to their insular attitude. On the contrary every European who travelled to India and has left a record of his travel, has wondered at this peculiar habit and has made a note of it with sometimes elaborate descriptions' (p. 174). Indeed, there were frequent attempts in the British press to de-mystify the practice for the benefit of those in the metropole. One London newspaper carried a short note, 'Betel: By a Hindoo', which sought to promote the exotic commodity to England's masses:

> The chewing of the betel is a favourite habit with the Indians, Burmans, and other peoples of South-Eastern Asia. It is taken after meals, it is chewed during a visit, it is offered when you meet and when you separate – in short, at all times of the day, and even in the night, you will find the lips of most men and women in those countries slightly tinged with red, and the mouth breathing an aromatic smell, the result of chewing betels. … It would be thought a breach of politeness among the Indians to take leave for any length of time without presenting each other with a purse of betels. … Betels are a constant accompaniment of smoking, and, like a glass of wine or a cigar, contribute largely to the pleasure of conversation, and often soften the asperities of social intercourse.
>
> (D.N.D., 1886)

Alluding to the similarities between betel, wine and cigars, the author attempts to establish *paan* as a highly respectable vehicle of civility that should appeal to the upper echelons of the metropole.

Yet despite the increasing visibility of Raj items, *paan* itself did not occupy a role in the emergence of the modern Western public sphere. Advertisements for London's first Indian restaurant, the Hindostanee Coffee House, boasted Indian curries alongside wine and hookahs with spice-blended tobacco for Anglo-Indians and former colonial officials, merchants and traders (Buettner, 2008; Highmore, 2009; Mahomet 1997). Dean Mahomet, the prominent Indian immigrant who ran the restaurant from 1809–1812, is also widely credited with introducing the practice of 'shampooing' (a form of massage) to London. But, despite his demonstrated appreciation for *paan*-chewing and interests in personal hygiene and health, there is no record that London's first Indian restaurant promoted *paan*-chewing alongside the hookah as a post-meal stimulant to aid digestion. Rather, collective drinking and the smoking of flavoured tobacco cultivated a forum of civility and luxury in this bourgeois meeting space. Some suggest that *paan* failed to appeal to European consumers because of its aesthetic as a chewed comestible, its unfamiliar sensations and its bitter taste (Courtright, 2001; Smith, 2007; Von Bibra, 1995 [1855]). But the taste of *paan* (and particularly of areca nut and catechu), while bitter and astringent, was also largely recognized to offer a sweet and subtle finish. Its flavour components would therefore not have troubled palates already accustomed to the tannic yet sweetened beverages of tea and coffee. Moreover, as historian Marcy Norton's (2006) study of chocolate in Europe demonstrates, the European palate was flexible: chocolate, for example, challenged pre-existing categories and preferences, such that 'Europeans in the New World and then the Old World somatized native aesthetic values' (p. 660). Instead of taste, context proved an obstacle: on the global scale masticatories were seen to compete with, rather than complement, drinking cultures (Clarence-Smith, 2008). Coffee, tea, chocolate and sugar were easily compatible with drinking, an already established forum of popular European consumption (Cowan, 2005). Following this logic, *paan*-chewing would have challenged the very European norms and structures of civility that enabled the successful transition of these other commodities into the European market.

While *paan* as a wrapped comestible did not penetrate modern European domains of popular consumption, its various ingredients were commonly used in British industry. By the mid-nineteenth century, areca nut was regularly imported to England for the hygiene and medical industries. The incorporation of areca nut in nineteenth-century English toothpastes is well documented (Courtright, 2001; Flückiger and Hanbury, 1879; Raghavan and Baruah, 1958; Reid, 1985; Von Bibra, 1995 [1855]; Williams et al., 2002). In a brief research note, medical historian and oral pathologist Peter A. Reichart (1984) describes how burnt areca was used as a tooth powder, a phenomenon accompanied by a material culture of porcelain tooth powder pots that circulated through England's pharmacies. Reichart states, 'The belief that Areca nut protects the teeth from decay and at the same time strengthens the gums was based on empiric observation through the centuries; observations of caries-free dentition in India may have particularly enhanced the use of Areca nut in toothpastes', a fact that is corroborated by many travel accounts of India in nineteenth-century British newspapers (p. 68). Interestingly, Reichart adds that toothpastes were also produced from powdered areca nuts mixed with aromatics such as clove oil, cinnamon oil, glycerine, sugar and rose water. In its early popularity in England then, areca nut was not consumed in the wrapped form that was so common in colonial Asia, nor was it consumed as a comestible or a stimulant, but the similarities between the toothpastes and the sweet *paan* should not be missed. The toothpastes not only promised to improve hygiene and health, but they also mimicked the sweet Indian masticatory in fragrance and flavour. Moreover, newspaper advertisements for the pastes and powders promised improved domestic happiness for England's upper classes. Advertisements for Woods' Areca Nut Tooth Paste in popular newspapers vowed that it would 'sweeten the breath' and facilitate intimacy and domestic bliss: 'The great falling-off of marriages should induce all desirous of matrimony to add to their attractions by using Woods' Areca Nut Tooth Paste'. Such claims gently leveraged the aphrodisiacal qualities of *paan*, locating the significance of areca nut for nineteenth-century England squarely in the realm of the private, domestic sphere.

Catechu followed a similar trajectory, though it was used in a larger range of contexts. Catechu first circulated to Europe, via Japan, in the mid-seventeenth century (Gode, 1961). By the nineteenth century, it was frequently shipped to Britain in small blocks. In the metropole, William Morris (1892), the famous designer and leader of the nineteenth-century Arts and Crafts movement, noted how 'catechu, the insipid juice of a plant or plants which comes to us from India, also gives rich and useful permanent browns of various shades' (p. 218). Catechu was instrumental not only as a dye in orientalist British textiles, but also in the Empire's hide and tanning industries (Von Bibra 1995 [1855]; 'Indigenous Indian Dyes,' 1917). It was also employed as an ingredient in European comestibles by virtue of its colouring properties and its medicinal potential. Catechu was used as a colour additive in adulterating tea to stretch the profit margin of tea produced and shipped through imperial routes. Its medicinal qualities prompted one newspaper reader to write to *The Times* of London regarding 'the welfare of our noble army', promising that betel nut and catechu would cure British troops suffering from dysentery (T. G., 1855). This advice was partially absorbed into Western scientific discourse by the end of the nineteenth century. Medical historian Richard Barnett (2012) notes that travellers to the tropics were encouraged to 'make up a simple bitters a month or so before they planned to leave, comprising of quassia chips, powdered catechu, cardamom, dried orange peel, strong whiskey, and water' (p. 1384), to prevent and treat ailments such as indigestion and fever. Catechu thus became an important ingredient in commercial bitters and tonics, sometimes blended alongside cinnamon, coriander, nutmeg, cardamom, allspice and licorice, thereby mimicking sweet *paan* in craft, flavour and therapeutic usage. The importance of catechu to the British imperial imagination is perhaps best encapsulated on one page of the popular nineteenth-century cocktail guide, *How to Mix Drinks or the Bon Vivant's Companion*; a recipe for 'British Brandy' calls for a half-drachm of finely powdered vanilla, one gallon of good quality Cognac and nine gallons of pure proof spirit, and one ounce of catechu (Thomas, 1862).

The shifting cultural significance of *paan* and its various ingredients in London must therefore be contextualized through its colonial and postcolonial history. Betel, areca nut and catechu were considered exotic substances in the nineteenth-century British popular imagination. Their frequent appearance in newspaper crossword puzzles and as the names of racehorses illustrates the extent to which these foreign comestibles were deeply embedded in the display of imperial knowledge, worldliness and cultural capital. However, *paan* as a wrapped package was not widely circulated in the metropole, in part because of logistical limitations on importing fresh betel leaves. More importantly though, the process of removing key ingredients from the wrapped package so as to refine and transform them (as tooth powders, bitters and dyes), while simultaneously drawing on the knowledge that surrounded their usage in the colonies, highlights an important dimension of imperial power, consumption and the civilizing process in the metropole.

Over the course of the twentieth century, *paan* as a wrapped comestible has remained far removed from mainstream consumption in London. Rather, the chewing of *paan* is largely confined to Asian immigrant communities. In London, areca nuts (more portable and shelf-stable than fresh betel leaves) may have been chewed by the Indian travellers, seamen and students who patronized the early twentieth-century canteens that preceded the Indian restaurant. Some speculate that areca nuts may have been available in early London from Chinese apothecaries (Ott, 1995), a claim that is bolstered by early twentieth-century accounts of the streets of London that describe how the bitter yet sweet aroma of the areca nut perfumed Chinatown. During the last century, increased migration from Asia and East Africa, the establishment of more Indian groceries and shops and improved transportation infrastructures brought increased opportunities to purchase areca nuts and betel leaves (Collingham, 2006; Hamlett et al., 2008). The *paan* shop, though, only established itself as a British-Asian cultural institution in the last few decades, multiplying quickly since the early 1970s (Williams, 1995). These stalls and shops announce their presence throughout London with the image of a betel leaf. While most often located on busy High Streets, they are easy to miss; the icon of the leaf calls out to a British-Asian public that, though comprised of different diasporas, languages and migration trajectories, shares a taste for this little-known wrapped comestible. While *paan*-chewing in London is largely associated with the Bengali diaspora, and most especially with Bangladeshi women (Williams, 1995), the clientele of London's *paan* shops far exceeds this population, encompassing Gujaratis, Punjabis, Sri Lankan Tamils and East-African Asians.

Despite the limited popularity of *paan*-chewing outside of these spheres, there are a number of ways in which *paan* is translated for a broader British public. At the shops, London *paan*-makers and customers often describe *paan* as an after-dinner mint and, more specifically, as an 'After Eight'. On the one hand, likening *paan* to an After Eight chocolate-covered mint-thin is a way of positively translating *paan* in a context in which its status and value are increasingly debated by public health experts and community members. But the allusion to temporality and the clock is particularly important. Unlike an After Eight, *paan* is most often crafted at the moment of ordering, valued for its freshness and for the *paan*-maker's skill at blending the ingredients to the taste of each customer. The process of making and wrapping a *paan* is brief, but it provides an important forum of social exchange and community formation. While the *paan* stall in India can be a primary site for 'doing timepass' (that is, for waiting and passing unproductive time), the metaphor of the After Eight describes the busiest times of the London shops (that is, after 8 p.m.) and locates *paan* in the capitalist model of work and leisure; the practice of crafting and chewing *paan* in the public space of the shop becomes measured by the clock. Using After Eight as a descriptive representation for *paan* therefore not only conveys some shared flavours and uses, but also enhances the potential value of *paan* as a cultural product in multicultural Britain.

In spite of the common proclamation of chicken tikka masala as cosmopolitan Britain's national dish (Buettner, 2008; Highmore, 2009) and the ever-growing curry industry, *paan*-chewing does not occupy the role of post-curry digestive in Britain's popular consciousness. However, bartenders and chefs at upscale Indian restaurants increasingly draw on its flavours to provide innovative cocktails and dishes for their broad clientele. From the *Paan* Fizz Cocktail and the Betel Leaf Baba at the Michelin-starred Benares (2012), to more widely available *paan* liqueurs and ice-creams, *paan* is unwrapped, scaled up and made accessible to a broader public in a global city. While such innovations retain its flavours, they transform its substance such that it is a comestible that is no longer chewed, but rather nibbled or delicately sipped at the end of a leisurely meal. *Paan*, once again, undergoes a process of transformation to reach a broader British market; its substance is reconfigured, but its flavours and common uses (in this case, its deployment as a digestive) are maintained. These changes in *paan* – from wrapped comestible to unwrapped colonial and postcolonial product – are a product of its position in global power networks. *Paan*'s trajectory to London differed from those of other once-exotic commodities, such as coffee, sugar, tea, chocolate and tobacco. Along this specific trajectory, cultural values relating to ideas of modernity, private and public, capitalism and leisure continue to be inscribed upon the shifting materiality of this comestible.

Notes

1. This paper forms part of a continuing project. My dissertation analyses the cultural politics of *paan*, public culture and migration in New York and London. This research has been supported by the Cherwell Food History Studentship from the American Friends of the Oxford Symposium on Food and Cookery, a Doctoral Scholarship from the Social Sciences and Humanities Research Council of Canada, and a Provost's Graduate Fellowship for residence at New York University's Global Research Institute in London.
2. *Paan* is the commonly-used Hindi term for the betel-quid.

References

Achaya, K. T. 1998. *A Historical Dictionary of Indian Food*. New Delhi: Oxford University Press.
Ahuja, S.C. and Uma Ahuja, 2011. 'Betel Leaf and Betel Nut in India: History and Uses.' *Asian Agri-History* 15 (1), pp. 13–35.
Barnett, Richard, 2012. 'Bitter Medicine: Gout and the Birth of the Cocktail.' *The Lancet* 379, pp. 1384–85.
Benares, 2012. *Benares Restaurant: Menu*. March 26. Retrieved from http://www.benaresrestaurant.com/.
Bickham, Troy, 2008. 'Eating the Empire: Intersections of Food, Cookery and Imperialism in 18th Century Britain.' *Past and Present* 198, pp. 71–109.
Buettner, Elizabeth, 2008. '"Going for an Indian": South Asian Restaurants and the Limits of Multiculturalism in Britain.' *The Journal of Modern History*, 80, pp. 865–901.
Burton, David, 1993. *The Raj at Table*. London: Faber and Faber.
Cho, Lily, 2010. *Eating Chinese: Culture on the Menu in Small Town Canada*. Toronto: University of Toronto Press.
Clarence-Smith, William G. 2008. 'The Global Consumption of Hot Beverages, c.1500–c.1900.' In *Food and Globalization: Consumption, Markets and Politics in the Modern World*, edited by Alexander Nützenadel and Frank Trentmann, pp. 37–55. Oxford and New York: Berg.
Collingham, Lizzie, 2006. *Curry: A Tale of Cooks and Conquerors*. New York: Oxford University Press, 2006.
Courtwright, David T. 2001. *Forces of Habit: Drugs and the Making of the Modern World*. Cambridge and London: Harvard University Press.
Cowan, Brian, 2005. *The Social Life of Coffee: The Emergence of the British Coffeehouse*. New Haven: Yale University Press.
D. N. D. 1886, July 17. Letter. 'Betel: By a Hindoo.' *The Graphic* (868).
Dirks, Nicholas B. 2006. *The Scandal of Empire: India and the Creation of Imperial Britain*. Boston: Harvard University Press.
Flückiger, Friedrich A. and Daniel Hanbury, 1879. *Pharmacographia: A History of the Principal Drugs of Vegetable Origin, Met with in Great Britain and British India*. London: Macmillan.
Fort William Select Consultation, No. 32. 1764, October 17. In *Fourth Report on the Nature, the State and the Condition of the East India Company, and of the British Affairs in the East Indies*, House of Commons (1773). London: Great Britain, Parliament.
Gode, P.K. 1961. *Studies in Indian Cultural History*, Vol I. Hoshiarpur: Visveshvaranad Vedic Research Institute.
Goodman, Jordan, 2007. 'Excitantia: Or, How Enlightenment Europe Took to Soft Drugs.' In *Consuming Habits: Global and Historical Perspectives on How Cultures Define Drugs*, edited by Jordan Goodman, Paul E. Lovejoy and Andrew Sherratt, pp. 121–41. London and New York: Routledge.
Guha, P. 2006. 'Betel Leaf: The Neglected Green Gold of India.' *Journal of Human Ecology* 19 (2), pp. 87–93.
Gupta, P. C. and S. Warnakulasuriya, 2002. 'Global Epidemiology of Areca Nut Usage.' *Addiction Biology* 7, pp. 77–83.
Habermas, Jürgen, 1991. *The Structural Transformation of the Public Sphere: An Inquiry into a Category of Bourgeois Society*, translated by Thomas Burger, with Frederick Lawrence. Cambridge, Massachusetts: MIT Press.
Hamlett, Jane, Adrian R. Bailey, Andrew Alexander and Gareth Shaw, 2008. 'Ethnicity and Consumption: South Asian Food Shopping Patterns in Britain, 1947–1975.' *Journal of Consumer Culture* 8, pp. 91–116.
Highmore, Ben, 2009. 'The Taj Mahal and the High Street.' *Food, Culture and Society* 12 (2), pp. 173–90.
'Indigenous Indian Dyes.' 1917. *Journal of the Royal Society of Arts* 65 (3369), pp. 534–36.
Mahomet, Sake Deen, 1997. *The Travels of Dean Mahomet: An Eighteenth-Century Journey in India*, edited by Michael H. Fisher. Berkeley: University of California Press.

Mintz, Sidney, 1985. *Sweetness and Power.* New York: Penguin.

Morris, William, 1892. 'Dyeing as an Art.' *The Decorator and the Furnisher* 19 (6), pp. 217–18.

Norton, Marcy, 2006. 'Tasting Empire: Chocolate and the European Internalization of Mesoamerican Aesthetics.' *American Historical Review* 111 (3), pp. 660–91.

Ott, Jonathan, 1995. 'Technical Notes.' In *Plant Intoxicants: A Classic Text on the Use of Mind-Altering Plants*, translated by Hedwig Schleiffer, pp. 223–61. Vermont: Healing Arts Press.

Reichart, Peter A. 1984. 'Toothpastes Containing Betel Nut (*Areca catechu* L.) from England of the 19th Century.' *Journal of the History of Medicine* 39 pp. 65–68.

Reid, Anthony, 1985. 'From Betel-Chewing to Tobacco-Smoking in Indonesia.' *The Journal of Asian Studies* 44 (3), pp. 529–47.

Raghavan, V. and H. K. Baruah, 1958. 'Arecanut: India's Popular Masticatory: History, Chemistry and Utilization.' *Economic Botany* 12 (4), pp. 315–45.

Schivelbusch, Wolfgang, 1993. *Tastes of Paradise: A Social History of Spices, Stimulants and Intoxicants*, translated by David Jacobson. New York: Vintage Books.

Sen, Colleen Taylor, 2004. *Food Culture in India.* Westport, CT: Greenwood Press.

Smith, Stefan H. 2007. 'De-mystifying a Change in Taste: Spices, Space and Social Hierarchy in Europe, 1380–1750.' *The International History Review* 29, 2, pp. 237–57.

Smith, Woodruff D. 2007. 'From Coffeehouse to Parlour: The Consumption of Coffee, Tea and Sugar in North-Western Europe in the Seventeenth and Eighteenth Centuries.' In *Consuming Habits: Global and Historical Perspectives on How Cultures Define Drugs*, edited by Jordan Goodman, Paul E. Lovejoy and Andrew Sherratt, pp. 142–57. London and New York: Routledge.

St. John, Ian, 2012. *The Making of the Raj: India under the East India Company.* Praeger, ABC-CLIO: Santa Barbara, CA.

Strickland, S. S. 2002. 'Anthropological Perspectives on Use of Areca Nut.' *Addiction Biology* 7, pp. 85–97.

T. G. 1855, May 5. Letter. 'The Betel Nut.' *The Times*: 12.

Thomas, Jerry, 1862. *How to Mix Drinks, or the Bon Vivant's Companion.* New York: Dick & Fitzgerald Publishers.

Von Bibra, Baron Ernst, 1995 [1855]. *Plant Intoxicants: A Classic Text on the Use of Mind-Altering Plants*, translated by Hedwig Schleiffer. Vermont: Healing Arts Press.

Williams, S. A. 1995. 'Betel-Quid Chewing: A Community Perspective.' In *Betl-Quid and Tobacco Chewing among the Bangladeshi Community in the United Kingdom*, edited by R. Bedi and P. Jones, pp. 11–25. London: Centre for Transcultural Oral Health.

Williams, S., A. Malik, S. Chowdhury, and S. Chauhan, 2002. 'Sociocultural Aspects of Areca Nut Use.' *Addiction Biology* 7, pp. 147–54.

Plenary Panel
Provocative Misinterpretations on a Theme

These essays were presented in one of the Plenary Discussion Sessions at this year's Symposium. The format is new to the Symposium, and the task given to plenary contributors was both challenging and irresistible, namely 'to stimulate ideas' (interpreted as a mandate to be playful and provocative), preferably by moving beyond the year's theme. Each of the contributors therefore sought to stretch the theme – to 'misinterpret' it in, hopefully, productive ways – in order to explore what might be stuffed within it, and in what it might be wrapped. In the first paper, Harry G. West looks at how the making and eating of artisan cheese entails not only wrapping but also unwrapping and rewrapping, not only stuffing but also unstuffing and restuffing – in some cases audacious acts that not only reveal or conceal but actually become part of the cheese itself. Following this, Emma-Jayne Abbots looks at how the act of stuffing bodies – even if in the name of generosity or care – is inevitably bound up with hierarchy and the exercise of control, whether over others or over one's self, from doting hosts to corporate food producers, from those watching their waistlines to those seeking glory in eating competitions. Ben Coles then unwraps and unstuffs a box of pre-prepared Chicken Kiev to illustrate how new technologies revolutionizing the wrapping and stuffing of food include not only 'broiler chicken' husbandry and refrigerated supply chains, but also new conceptions of food expressed in its marketing and in consumers' engagement with this 'ready-meal'. Finally, Michael Goodman argues that, through the wrapping and unwrapping, and the stuffing and unstuffing of food, we create and recreate a wide range of relationships whether between ourselves and others, ourselves and our environments, or ourselves and our bodies – relationships that he examines under the headings of pleasure, place, production and power.

The Audacity of Unwrapping and Rewrapping, Unstuffing and Restuffing, Virtually Everything (Including, Especially, Cheese)

Harry G. West

A couple of years ago – while in the midst of a four-year research project on artisan cheese-making and cheese-mongering in Europe and beyond – I spent a brief stint working for a highly reputable French *affineur*. On my very first day in the hallowed inner-sanctum of the aging cave, I was set a shocking task: removing foil wrappers bearing the producer's name from delectable full-fat, blue-veined, sheep's milk cheeses, and rewrapping them so that they bore only the name of the *affineur*. Here, craft has turned cunningly crafty, I thought. What artifice! What guile! What audacity!

I was relieved when presented with the next cheeses I was to work with. They were semi-hard, sheep's-milk cheeses called Lavort. Their shape – like a ring of concrete anchoring a signpost in the ground – was almost completely obscured by the shaggy strands of mould that had enveloped them in recent weeks in the aging cave, giving them the appearance of tiny, woolly mammoths. Here, I thought, was honest, natural wrapping, unsullied by human artifice – wrapping that was part and parcel of the thing itself, revealing rather than concealing an inner essence. And what was I to do with these cheeses, I asked? 'Brush the mould off of them,' I was told. Now, the symbolic violence of unwrapping and rewrapping – of breaking the seal on a primordial truth – became physical violence. The brush I was given to work with seemed to me to mow down lush stalks of *mucor* much as the superheated ash clouds spawned by the region's volcanic eruptions three million years ago had mowed down trees, leaving in its wake an apparently barren landscape.

I reflected then – as I have from time to time since – on the unwrapping and rewrapping, the unstuffing and restuffing, that is inevitably involved in the making of any artisan cheese. After I asked a cheese-maker one day in the Turkish village of Divle if he used lamb's rennet in making his cheeses, my interpreter (who struggled with English) asked me what rennet was. 'Enzymes from the lamb's stomach, which curdle the milk,' I told him, wrapping my hand around some imaginary fluid and holding it close to my own stomach, as if stuffing it gently inside. Understanding well how cheese is made, he was then able to translate my question to the cheese-makers with whom I was speaking, but others less familiar with the process have sometimes asked me, 'How do they get the rennet out of the lamb's stomach?', prompting me to explain this with gestures portraying the unstuffing of the stomach from the lamb, and the unwrapping of the rennet within it (not the most appropriate verbs for what is done, but close

The Audacity of Unwrapping and Rewrapping

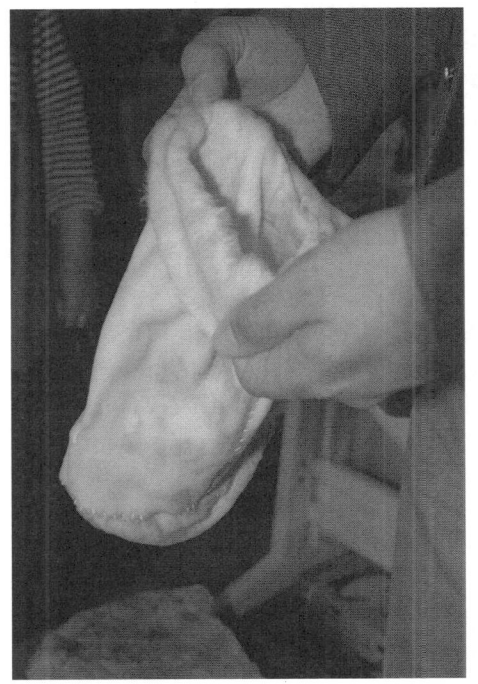

The Audacity of Unwrapping and Rewrapping

enough to convey what it entails for the lamb). The flesh of such lambs might then be minced and stuffed in sausages, or it might be stuffed as lamb chops, depending upon where its meat is sold.

In any case, once cheese-makers in Divle have extracted milk from their ewes and deposited it into a container, they introduce rennet into the milk, causing the clustered molecules of casein proteins in the milk (called micelles) to form a lattice, or curd, that wraps around globules of fat and squeezes out the milk's water content in the form of whey. They then stuff this curd into tidy little sacks that they have made from the skins of the ewes' slaughtered offspring, and stuff these sacks into a cave more than a hundred meters underground, where they are left for months to age. Audacious? It seems to me spectacularly so.

By the time Divle's cheese-makers pull their lambskin sacks from the cave, and unwrap the skin from the cheese, the rennet and a range of other enzymes and microorganisms in the milk have broken down its long-chain casein proteins into peptides, amino acids and amines, and its globules of fat into fatty acids, releasing from this microscopic wrapping a splendid array of flavour notes. Wrapped in warm pockets of bread, the cheese ends up stuffed in mouths and, ultimately, in the stomachs of its makers and others fortunate enough to eat it.

But is it just the making of artisan cheeses that involves such audacious unwrapping and unstuffing, rewrapping and restuffing of . . . well . . . virtually everything? From the simplest cell to the most complex organism, life breaks down in order to build up; unwraps by enveloping or rewrapping; unstuffs only to restuff. Warm enclosures, cosy pockets, moist cavities – these may hold components together in stable configurations, facilitating life and its reproduction. The integrity of such vessels – wrapping around or stuffed with things, be they elements of self or of something else – may be the means of creating or sustaining life, or they may be life's very ends.

When I was done with them, the woolly Lavort cheeses I had been asked to shear of their shaggy wrapping by the French *affineur* were stuffed back in their cave where, in coming weeks, they hosted on the detritus of *mucor* stumps the growth of splendid little bursts of a rusty-golden-coloured mould that their makers poetically call *fleurs*. From death, life. From unwrapping, rewrapping.

And so, our unwrappings and rewrappings may displace the wrappings actualized by other agents in our ecology, may imitate them, may facilitate them, or may do any combination of these things, but they inevitably become a part of the thing they hold within. This is, in the end, true even of the French *affineur*'s audacious unwrapping and rewrapping, for if he does his work as most in France think he should, his inviolable aging cave and his trusted brand hold secure the relationship he mediates between producers and consumers, to the benefit of both. Borne of his artifice is another truth, in another wrapper, with another seal eventually to be broken. I should confess, I like to be there when it is.

Acknowledgement

My thanks to Aylin Öney Tan, who graciously orchestrated my journey through the landscape of Turkish cheese-making in the summer of 2012.

Care, Control and Commensality: The Game of Stuffed and Stuffing Bodies

Emma-Jayne Abbots

Picture a stuffed goose.

Perhaps the image of a glistening roast bird springs to mind: a Dickensian symbol of festivity, abundance and indulgence. Expectant faces look down at the burnished and crispy skin, which hints at the rich and succulent flesh encased within – meat that is flavoured, perhaps, with dried and fresh fruits, chestnuts, even Armagnac. Or maybe another stuffed goose image materializes. One in which a live animal, straddled by a man who, with his hands placed around the creature's neck, is forcing the bird to ingest the grain being pumped into its body through a feeding pipe.

As this second image suggests, the act of stuffing is not benign. It can be a practice of power, a reiteration of hierarchies – in this context one between humans and animals – and an act of violence against the body. Foie gras production and the practice of *gavage* are often held up as an explicit and visceral example of this violence, but it can also take more insidious and less overtly politicized forms. For it is not just the livers of geese that are being stuffed to obscene proportions: changes in diet and the increased availability for many to 'simple' and processed foods, replete with refined carbohydrates, saturated fat and sugars, such as high-fructose corn-syrup, are arguably transforming our own organs into 'fatty livers'. But should it be the multi-nationals, the billion-dollar agri-food corporations, and the supermarket chains that are held to account for creating populations of human foie gras? Are they solely responsible for this stuffing?

In what follows, I would like to argue that the answer to this question is no. For while the structures of contemporary industrial food systems play a significant role in informing our eating practices, our access to certain foods and our dietary preferences – and it is not my intention to dispute this – they are not the only agents in this story. Individuals, family and friends also stuff food into others' mouths. This is often an act of love and affection, or at least is ostensibly expressed as such, but it can also be, I suggest, an exercise of power and domination. Granted, the intentions behind feeding loved ones and producing foie gras for the market differ, but I wish to float the possibility that the 'politics of stuffing' in these seemingly unrelated examples are not, perhaps, so dissimilar.

As children – and, for a number of us, as parents – many of us have experienced the game of 'finishing the plate': a charade that also takes the form of 'eat those vegetables or you won't be allowed to get down from the table' and 'you can have dessert when you've finished your main course'. Even in adulthood, when, in theory, we are able to opt out of this game of coerced eating, it is difficult to say no to stuffing. At a dinner party, for example, adults squeeze in another spoonful of dessert, even when they 'couldn't possibly', or feel obliged to tuck into a dish they dislike, forcing down every mouthful through gritted teeth and quelling waves of nausea while feigning enthusiasm and gusto.

I recall my fieldwork in the Ecuadorean Andes, where I 'enjoyed' this type of 'guerilla hospitality'. In order to be polite and maintain relationships, it was not an uncommon experience to consume three meals in quick succession (with obvious pleasure) as I visited the homes of my research participants, each one of which wanted to feed me. Likewise, I was strongly encouraged to eat more than I wanted during festive occasions, and even when I felt stuffed to the brim, I would respond to my fellow eaters' urging to 'eat, Emita, you haven't had enough, have more' by reaching towards the communal bowl and taking another helping. In the field, I was never socially able to say no for fear of offending my host, whose status, in these contexts, is based on their generosity, hospitality and cooking skills. Following Mauss, saying no – rejecting the hospitality – is tantamount to rejecting the host, and damages the social relationship.[1] Consequently, like my fellow guests, I became adept at avoiding stuffing: I learnt the sleight of hand required to slip pieces of food from the plate to household dogs or into a napkin, as well as how to look like I was draining the glass at every toast while just taking a sip.

Eating thus becomes a game, with hosts trying to (over)stuff their guests' bodies and their guests, in turn, attempting to assert their own agency and set the limits of how much they are willing to be stuffed. And as battles over dinner tables and uneaten plates of vegetables testify, this game can become fraught and tense. Commensality, so often associated with the positive affirmation of relations and social cohesion, can just as easily descend into arguments and rupture relations; a process further exemplified by the unfortunate case of a meal-time row over vegetables resulting in a jail sentence for one of the protagonists.[2]

But just as we are stuffed, we also stuff ourselves.

From the all-you-can-eat buffet to extreme eating competitions, as exemplified by the annual Nathan's Hot Dog Eating Contest in Brooklyn, New York, and the popular television show *Man v. Food*, examples of over self-stuffing can be commonly located. This form of stuffing appears diametrically opposed to self-starvation or the regulated, disciplined intake of food we have come to anticipate and expect in 'civilized' society, and are encouraged to practice by medical and health advisers.[3] Eating bodies in these extreme eating contexts seem to be undisciplined, unruly even, in their efforts to stuff in as much food as possible. Moral judgements are made against the actors involved, in a way that parallels the discourse – albeit, at times, well-meaning – on obesity.[4] People are consuming more than their fair share of finite resources, do not know what they are doing to themselves or, perhaps even worse, the environment, which can no longer sustain this type of excessive practice. Over-stuffing yourself – eating more than your daily recommended intake of calories – becomes irresponsible, wasteful even, and morally reprehensible. People who over-stuff become symbolic of the excesses of a capitalist, consumer-led society. Consumption in this context becomes less of a creative practice and is more akin to its original etymology: to consume is to destroy and waste that which did not need destroying and wasting so thoroughly.[5]

Yet, I would like to suggest that this form of eating also takes discipline. As my experiences in the Ecuadorean Andes and as the reluctant dinner party guest gamefully forcing down another mouthful of an undesirable dish both indicate, significant willpower is required to resist the visceral, bodily urges to reject stuffing. Moreover, as the preparation for the egg-eating challenge in *Cool Hand Luke* and the victors of extreme eating competitions suggest, bodies need to be trained to accept this quantity of food; it takes discipline to stuff.

In these contexts of the all-you-can-eat buffet, Nathan's hot dogs and *Man v. Food*, stuffing becomes a 'spectacle'.[6] It is a visible rather than a hidden process – a voyeuristic show in which all can participate. Viewers may be repulsed, revolted, awed or entranced, but by gazing on the spectacle they all uphold the event and validate the 'stuffers'. An orgy of excess then, in which the quantity and the easy availability of food, and, perhaps more importantly, those who eat it and feed it to others, are on full display. There are echoes here with the excesses of the historical (and contemporary) feasts of the aristocracy, the upper-classes, and the wealthy; forerunners all to the middle-class dinner party. Here the status of the host, like that of my Ecuadorean research participants, is conferred by the spread of foods on display and the hospitality on offer. As such, by participating in these food events, either as viewers or fellow eaters, guests aid and abet in the reinforcement of their hosts' social status and position in the social hierarchy. Dinner becomes a potlatch, a display of excess and wastefulness through which hierarchies are created and maintained, not through the acquisition of wealth but its distribution.[7] Refusing to be stuffed, as with rejecting the gift of hospitality, takes the eater out of the status game. The eater thereby potentially contests the hierarchy through the expression of their own agency and a reassertion of their own bodily boundaries.

Stuffing then – both of other people and of the self – is not a benign act, but rather a battleground in which individual eating bodies are subjected to the will of the stuffer. Whether they take the form of a generous dinner-party host, a farmer force-feeding a goose, a caring parent urging a child to eat their vegetables, or a corporate-sponsored contest urging competitors to eat as many hot dogs as possible, stuffing is an exercise of power in which social hierarchies are created, reinforced and maintained. Yet these hierarchies are also contested. Children refuse to eat their vegetables and parents capitulate, bringing dessert out before the main course is finished; guests politely say no to a second helping; consumers stop purchasing foie gras and seek alternatives; and viewers switch channels away from *Man v. Food* and televised extreme eating competitions. Stuffing thereby presents an opportunity to contest power dynamics just as much as it does to enact them.

Returning to the theme of extreme eating and decadent feasts, it is tempting to consign them to the places and times of 'other' people. They are, by definition, extremes – exceptions rather than quotidian examples. Yet we are surrounded by the spectacle of food, and the orgy of excess encourages us to stuff ourselves and those around us. Upon strolling through supermarket aisles or meandering around a market, we are greeted with laden shelves and tables, groaning under the array of foods on offer. But we are supposed to select from the menu on display, exercise discipline, and make 'good choices'.[8] Our time for stuffing is supposed to be set aside from our everyday life, and contained by the sanctioned moments of dinner parties, ritual occasions and 'celebrations', such as Christmas. Stuffing is allowed, even encouraged it seems, on such occasions; they are the one-off events, the carnivals in which the rules of 'civilized eating' and disciplined bodies are suspended.[9] But, like all rituals and carnivals that subvert the rules, they only provide a temporary outlet – a release of pressure – before the status quo is resumed. To stuff one's body outside of these authorized moments – to steadfastly turn one's liver into human foie gras – is then, potentially, just as much an act of resistance and contestation as the refusal to be stuffed by others during celebrations.

All of which brings me back to the stuffed festive goose, the remnants of which are now sitting on the Christmas dinner table. Diners are loosening their belts and caressing their stomachs. The satisfaction of a good meal and satiated eaters is palpable. Yet on being offered a final mince pie by their 'generous' host, one guest reluctantly takes the plate: 'Thank you, but I shouldn't really; I'm absolutely stuffed'.

Notes

1. Marcel Mauss, *The Gift: The Form and Reason for Exchange in Archaic Societies*, trans W.D. Halls, 1950 (London: Routledge, 1990).
2. Barbara Hijek, 'Table Scrap over Eating Veggies Land Man in Jail', *South Florida Sun Sentinel* 14 May 2011: http://weblogs.sun-sentinel.com/news/specials/weirdflorida/blog/2011/05/table_scrap_over_eating_veggie_1.html (accessed 28th November 2012).
3. Deborah Lupton, *Food, the Body and the Self* (London: Sage, 1996); Stephen Mennell, *All Manners of Food: Eating and Taste in England and France from the Middle Ages to the Present* (New York: Basil Blackwell, 1985).
4. See Lucy Aphramor, Jennifer Brady and Jacqui Gringa, 'Advancing Critical Dietetics: Theorizing Health at Every Size', *Why We Eat, How We Eat: Contemporary Encounters between Foods and Bodies*, ed. Emma-Jayne Abbots and Anna Lavis (Aldershot: Ashgate, 2013).
5. Cf. Jonathan Friedman (ed.), *Consumption and Identity* (Chur, Switzerland: Harwood Academic, 1994); Daniel Miller, *Material Culture and Mass Consumption* (Oxford: Basil Blackwell, 1987); and Miller, *A Theory of Shopping* (Oxford: Polity, 1998); David Graeber, *Possibilities: Essays on Hierarchy, Rebellion and Desire* (Oakland, CA: AK Press, 2007), p. 59.
6. Jean Baudrillard, *Simulations* (Los Angeles: Semiotext(e), 1983) and Guy Debord, *Society of the Spectacle*, trans. D. Nicholson-Smith (New York: Zone, 1995).
7. Cf. Franz Boas, *Kwakiutl Ethnography* (Chicago: University of Chicago Press, 1966).
8. See Sally Brooks, Duika Burges Watson, Alison Draper and Michael Goodman, 'Chewing on Choice', Abbots and Lavis.
9. Mennell.

Chicken Kiev: Material, Social and Discursive Wrappings

Benjamin F. Coles

Take a chicken breast; remove its skin and bones; flatten it *en escalope*; fill it with butter and parsley; wrap it back up; coat in flour, egg-wash and breadcrumbs; and fry it until golden brown, turning once. It takes about 8 minutes. Slice and serve. Or, conversely, wander to the frozen food aisle at Marks and Spencer's (M&S); grab a packet of chicken Kievs from the freezer; unwrap and stuff them into the oven at about 190° for thirty minutes. The fun part is when they're cut open and the *beurre de maitre d'* (that is to say herby butter) oozes onto the plate. It is a dish that comes stuffed with its own sauce. The wrappings and stuffings of chicken Kiev go beyond its ingredients, the ways in which they combine, or indeed what happens to them after assembly and cooking. The chicken Kiev is also the material embodiment of a particular kind of history and historicization as well as a particular kind of material geography. All of which wrap chicken Kiev up with material, social, and discursive relations, and stuff chicken Kiev with moral and ethical entanglements. As we consider eating such a food we should consider the ways in which chicken Kiev, and any food, can be un-stuffed and un-wrapped. And, as we un-wrap and un-stuff we can question the relations that comprise chicken Kiev, and we can challenge the implicit ethics and moralities with which they are entangled.

Chicken Kiev has a long, somewhat contentious history. Historian Patricia Bunning Stevens locates the dish within the culinary traditions of the Ukraine – hence the name, 'chicken Kiev' – but she notes that several 'national' cuisines also have some kind of pounded, stuffed, rolled and wrapped, fried meat – Austrian schnitzels perhaps being the most famous, but similar offerings can be found in France, Switzerland, Hungary and Italy.[1] Even a precursory glance at the ways in which the political geography of that part of Europe has developed over history reminds us that when it comes to food, boundaries, like butter, are leaky. The popular imagination of chicken Kiev associates it with Muscovite nobility. This toponymy further complicates notions of its authenticity. Chicken Kiev's development is said to be linked to expatriate Parisian chefs preparing new dishes for the grand tables of Moscow. The dish, it would seem, is wrapped up within imperial and colonial histories, as well as a culinary history, and this is just some of the stuff wrapped up in chicken Kiev.

Harry Wallop, writing in the *Telegraph*, reminds us that chicken Kiev is stuffed with more than butter.[2] As Britain's 'first ever' ready-meal, appearing on the market in 1979, it is wrapped up in a culinary imagination that transcends meat and two veg to become at once a symbol for the modern diet and a chic retro food wrapped in irony. The oft-slighted ready-meal is of particular interest to me and to the themes of wrapping and stuffing. A ready-meal is food stuffed in a box, wrapped in plastic, stuffed in another box, cooled off in a freezer, only to be un-wrapped, un-stuffed, and then re-stuffed into an oven, before getting stuffed into the body.

These material wrappings and stuffings are bound up with other wrappings and stuffings – some of which are material, and some are discursive. The M&S chicken Kiev was only made possible by the convergence of numerous technological exploits: namely, the cold chain – a complex system of refrigerated production, processing, storage, transportation and retail – and the broiler chicken. Both the cold chain and broiler chicken, and by extension the 'modern' diet, are M&S inventions.

Let's start with the chicken. Broiler chickens – what we mostly eat – started off as a bi-product of the egg industry in the 1930s.[3] Non-egg-laying male chicks were separated from their egg-laying sisters, raised on scraps and sold locally. Some of us might even remember when chickens were very expensive, and for this reason often eaten only during times of celebration. Raising chickens for market, before particular techno-science innovations, was difficult, inefficient, risky and therefore costly. Simply put, chickens couldn't be easily raised indoors, whilst living outdoors subjected them to predation, exposure and disease, and unlike beef and lamb, both of which benefit from a posthumous maturation process, once killed, poultry meat goes off very quickly. This is one reason why some might have images of poultry being sold live at markets in other parts of the world. In absence of adequate technology, the only way to assure fresh poultry is to deliver it live to market and let the end-consumer wring its neck. For chicken production to be profitable and therefore commercially viable, they must be produced in large quantities, protected against the rigours of outdoor life, and transported to market before decay sets in. To meet these demands of production, new vitamin- and antibiotic-fortified feeds were developed, which allowed for vast numbers of chickens to be grown under lights indoors, and food scientists, working for newly emerging supermarkets, established the 'cold chain', a set of procedures and technologies that tackled the transportation 'problem'.

As a socio-techno-science device, the cold chain emerges through two separate but interrelated 'phases'. The first revolves around cutting-edge materials and engineering coupled with micro-biological research. It has long been known that meat's decay can be slowed indefinitely by refrigeration. The technologies required to cool a chicken to temperatures low enough to inhibit bacteria growth and subsequent decay, however, are energy intensive – which, by the way, wraps up chicken Kiev in a separate yet interrelated complex of geopolitics, energy markets, violence and looming environmental catastrophe. Given the distances between producers and final consumers, it is necessary to efficiently keep dead chickens cold for long periods of time. Ultimately this leads to an assemblage of technologies – such as portable refrigeration, insulated transport containers, and, as M&S also discovered and pioneered, supermarket display cabinets, all of which come together to keep the 'chain' intact, and scientific knowledge(s) to govern the system, control and mitigate against bacteria growth and ensure end-products like frozen chicken Kievs arrive to consumers

Chicken Kiev: Material, Social and Discursive Wrappings

before they expire. Chicken Kievs are discursively wrapped up in these assemblages, and materially stuffed into them.

The second phase of this development is infrastructural. Deploying multiple cold chains, linking multiple producers to multiple retail and consumption outlets over long distances, is inefficient. To make it efficient, and indeed plausible, such concepts as centralized processing, warehousing, and distribution emerge to effectively shorten the distances between 'production' and 'consumption'. For those interested in short supply chains, food miles, and related concepts, one only has to look as far as a major supermarket for a lesson in lean and efficient supply chain management – perhaps the critique of such things, popular in both academic and lay discourses, should lie not in the supposed inefficiency that seems to characterize industrialized supermarket food, but focus rather on its being too efficient, cannibalizing itself figuratively, through a shifting politics of production and consumption, and literally, as demonstrated by recent foot-and-mouth disease outbreaks and other such animal-born agricultural diseases, when in a never-ending drive for efficiency the diseased-dead are stuffed into the living.

Therefore, to make the modern chicken work economically, and therefore give us the modern-day chicken Kiev, chicken production had to be both scaled up and centralized – but what of the ethics and moralities wrapped-up in such scaling? I am reminded of a piece of recently completed fieldwork. I was talking with the managing director of a 'global' chicken producer at his head office. We were in a boardroom located on the twenty-seventh floor of an office tower in Sao Paulo: a vista of the Sao Paulo skyline and the new Brazil lay out in front of me through the picture window. The MD was telling me about a new, state-of-the-art factory-slaughterhouse in Matto Grosso that can supposedly process, from live birds wandering a paddock to individually packed and frozen chicken Kievs (and other such products) stuffed in boxes, 500,000 chickens a day – and it is 'more sanitary, safer, and "ethical" when it comes to animal welfare to do it this way' because the human component, the risky variable, is replaced by mechanization that slaughters and packs efficiently before the bird or anything else can grasp what is happening. Ethics may well be dependent on perspective and subject to instrumental aims. Moralities, however, are intrinsic and cannot be so easily hidden away by so-called 'good' ethical practice that displaces the capacity for an ethical human component, efficiently wraps it in bulk processing and stuffs it away into a box. Moralities instead are dependent upon not only how we see the world, but how we construct it through our everyday actions – like when we choose to eat a chicken Kiev or not. Morality dictates that regardless of what we choose to eat, we are complicit, bound, wrapped and stuffed with and in the relations that come with it.

Notes

1. Patricia Bunning Stevens, *Rare Bits: Unusual Origins Of Popular Recipes* (Athens, OH: Ohio University Press, 1998).
2. Harry Wallop, 'Chicken Kiev Back in Fashion', *The Telegraph* 26 March 2011.
3. William Boyd and Michael Watts, 'Agro-Industrial Just-in-Time: The Chicken Industry and Postwar American Capitalism', *Globalising Food: Agrarian Questions and Global Restructuring*, eds. David Goodman and Michael Watts (London: Routledge, 1997), pp. 192–225.

Wrapping and Stuffing Food Relationally: Pleasure, Place, Production and Power

Michael Goodman

Food is not food. Food is literally and figuratively wrapped and unwrapped, stuffed and unstuffed with all manner of relationships. Food is full of relationships: the wheel of cheese, the stuffed goose, the chicken Kiev are all containers of sorts for the relations that go into the making and unmaking of these particular foods. But so too does food work to create sets of relationships, whether these are between and amongst those eating and making the wheel of cheese, stuffed goose or chicken Kiev; the wider ecologies and micro-biologies of growing, transforming and preparing these foods; or the sets of cultures, economies and politics that go into defining these foods as things and these things as food. The eating of food, as we know, is one of the most intimate relationships we, as corporeal beings and bodies, can have with the world, with others, with nature. As Elspeth Probyn puts it in her book *Carnal Appetites*, 'eating [is] a visceral reminder of how we variously inhabit the axes of economics, gender, sexuality, history, ethnicity and class'.[1] Food's relationalities also contain what might be called – after Appadurai – the 'social life' of food and foodways as they simultaneously contain and make the 'material life' of food and foodways.[2] For Emma Roe, getting at these relationalities of food involves a 'tracing' of food's 'liveliness', whereby this 'liveliness … set[s] up two forms of connections with humans. On the one hand, to trace food through a network is in fact to trace energies through a metabolic network, and on the other hand it is to trace meaning-making enacted through how foodstuff is handled'.[3] Through eating and the metabolization of food, then, the outside becomes the inside, the inside (eventually) becomes the outside, all the while the socio-material relationships embedded in and created by food literally and figuratively become who, what and how we are, suspending us, transforming us, making and unmaking us.

But much like the critic and analyst Raj Patel, who writes about our *Stuffed and Starved* world, I feel that some of the relationships that food contains and creates are more prescient than others.[4] In this, there are four relationalities of food that I want to briefly highlight – all of which resonate across the papers by West, Abbotts and Coles – and suggest that they are worthy of much more sustained empirical and theoretical engagement in the making of contemporary foodscapes.

The first set of relationships I want to highlight, then, are those of pleasure. Amongst other things this is about the pleasure of being stuffed and full for the hungry, or the pleasure of being unstuffed for the anorexic or dieter. This is about the pleasure of the conviviality of eating together on a birthday or holiday or the pleasure of eating an instant soup from Aldi on one's own, at one's desk, to be able to finish one's paper for this volume. In general then, what I am talking about are the feelings and affects associated, created and produced by food, from those gut feelings of pleasure we feel way deep-down inside to those feelings of joy laughing over a shared meal. Of course, the flip side of all this involves those feelings of disgust we might feel in our relationship to food or particular foods, or even the people we have to share a meal with. These tensions of pleasure and disgust can even be played out in one single food item like the deep-fried Mars bar which, while truly a health disaster, tastes damn good! This, then, involves drawing on what Elspeth Probyn and Alison and Jessica Hayes-Conroy describe as the *visceral* aspects of food: the ways it feels good/bad to us and those around us, the ways it tastes good/bad to us and those around us and, especially important for these authors, the ways that this viscerality connects us to a multi-scaled politics, from the personal, all the way to the global.[5]

One of the most interesting sets of relationships embedded in pleasurable foods are those of authenticity. Am I eating a 'real' New York steak, English breakfast, German *Schweinhaxen* or American hotdog? Debates over authenticity rage, my favourite at the moment being that over the San Francisco burrito.[6] Does it have rice or not? Does having the rice make a burrito a San Francisco burrito? And, who really cares? I certainly don't, because if I am eating one, full of rice or not, it means I am back in San Francisco, eating something scrumptious and most likely sitting across from my brother-in-law talking about the Giants; thankfully, I can now also get – to my extreme delight – a relatively good simulacrum of a San Francisco burrito in London as they have recently begun to spread across the city's foodscapes. For me, anyway, the viscerialities of taste reign supreme here, rather than any kind of overt authenticity, bringing me both the pleasures of taste as much as the pleasures of the memories of places, people and relationships; in a way, then, pleasure and authenticity easily slip in and out of each other, are in tension or in agreement in fascinating and important ways in the context of food's relational wrappings and stuffings.

The second set of relationships embedded and created by food are those of place. In this, we eat in place, out of place and literally and figuratively eat places in their cultural, economic and material constitution.[7] And food place can travel: we talk more and more about the McDonaldization and Coca-colonization of the world's cuisines, and coffee, cheese and wine varietals move the world over.[8] One of the things we are literally obsessed with now is the making visible of the relationships we have with food, its production and its travel. From organic, fair trade and PDO/*terroir* food labelling, to the ability to use smartphones and QR codes to find out the origins and provenance of your tomato, figuring out your relationship to your food's place involves yet another set of relationships to supply chains, accounting practices, technologies and visual representations.[9] And, for Coles and Crang, in their exploration of the 'place' of Borough Farmers Market in London, it is the 'ethical consumption' of food that is particularly coincident in the constructions and development of food(s') place. As they put it, 'the dynamics of place and place-making play a central role in ... "alternative" forms of consumption' through the ways that (ethical) consumption is a placed activity, the ways it creates 'better' food consumption places *vis a vis* the supermarket, and the ways that it works to connect the places of production and consumption through the commodity form of food.[10]

The third set of relationalities in food are those of production, but here I want to talk about, specifically, the visual, spectacular and image-drenched production of food through the various media and mediums that it is now so thoroughly wrapped in and stuffed with. From celebrity chefs, to cookbooks, to television networks, to advertisements and marketing, to magazines, to radio programmes, to major motion pictures, to online discussion groups, social media and recipe blogs; food has colonized and been colonized by literally every form of media available, making it the serious big business of an everyday, 'spectacularized' engagement.[11] Indeed, along with the tatty old recipe folders and slips from my mother and grandmother, Google is now my recipe book for whenever I cook at home. More than anything, this has led me to ask a series of questions about the relationalities created and embedded in this mediatized food: Is food part of the realm of the 'real' anymore, or is it simply one more spectacular image flashing across our collective eyes and tongues in the pursuit of the next best-selling cookbook, food exposé, or new celebrity chef personality? Where do we find real food, or is this spectacular food the new 'real'? What relationalities do these food spectacles produce, with whom and why? How do new technologies make food even more mobile, social and, perhaps, edible and relatable? And, as food researchers, how might we find all of this out?

The final set of relationalities wrapped and stuffed in and through food are those of power, which, by definition are imbued with inequalities in one form or another.[12] Here the power of supermarkets in the UK – with just four having 75% of the total market for food and two of these having over 50% of the market for organic foods – is about the ability to set up relationships with eaters, buyers, shoppers, suppliers, regulators, politicians, ecologies and the environment and, of course, farmers.[13] This is not without resistance, as the group known as Tescopoly attests.[14] Yet there is also a new set of power players here in the form of the aforementioned celebrity chefs and their abilities to increasingly define for us what 'good food' is and should be.[15] The cultural and economic power of, for example, Hugh Fearnley-Whittingstall to get us to buy sustainable fish, or Jamie Oliver to get us to better supply kid's school meals should not be underestimated.[16] But even in these 'good food' networks, inequalities abound: those strawberries used in the strawberry tart made by the multi-millionaire celebrity chefs of today are grown by particular people, under particular conditions and embedded in particular supply chains that often reek of the inequalities of power. Thus, to ask a strong yet continuingly important question: How and in what ways is that tasty strawberry tart flavoured with the sweat and, dare I say, exploitation that often defines the contemporary food networks created and maintained by celebrity chefs?

Wrapping and Stuffing Food Relationally

I want to end where I started: food is not food, but rather it is wrapped and stuffed and stuffed and wrapped in and by relationships of pleasure, place, production and power; it is these crucial relationalities of food that are not only worthy of a further and much longer chewing over, but it is these relationships that are key in defining our relationships to ourselves, each other and the contemporary (food) worlds that we inhabit.

Notes

1. Elspeth Probyn, *Carnal Appetites: FoodSexIdentities* (London: Routledge 2000), p. 9.
2. A. Appadurai, ed., *The Social Life of Things* (Cambridge: Cambridge University Press, 1986); see also D. Lind and E. Barham, 'The Social Life of the Tortilla: Food, Cultural Politics, and Contested Commodification', *Agriculture and Human Values* 21 (2004), pp. 47–60.
3. Emma Roe, 'Things Becoming Food and the Embodied, Material Practices of an Organic Food Consumer', *Sociologia Ruralis* 46.2 (2006), p. 109.
4. Raj Patel, *Stuffed and Starved: From Farm to Fork, the Hidden Battle for the World Food System* (London: Portobello Books 2007).
5. Probyn; Alison and Jessica Hayes-Conroy, 'Taking Back Taste: Feminism, Food and Visceral Politics', *Gender, Place and Culture* 15.5 (2008), pp. 461–473; and Alison and Jessica Hayes-Conroy, 'Visceral difference: Variations in Feeling (Slow) Food', *Environment and Planning A* 42.12 (2010) pp. 2956–2971. See also M. Goodman, 'Towards Visceral Entanglements: Knowing and Growing the Economic Geographies of Food', *The Sage Handbook of Economic Geography*, eds. R. Lee et al. (London, Sage, 2011), pp. 242–257 and M. Carolan, *Embodied Food Politics* (Aldershot: Ashgate, 2011)
6. 'San Francisco Burrito', *Wikipedia*: http://en.wikipedia.org/wiki/San_Francisco_burrito and 'Once and for All – Rice in a Burrito – Yay or Nay?' and *Chowhound*: http://chowhound.chow.com/topics/357410.
7. L. DeLind, 'Of Bodies, Place and Culture: Re-situating Local Food', *Journal of Agricultural and Environmental Ethics* 19.2 (2006), pp. 121–146; R. Feagan, 'The Place of Food: Mapping Out the 'Local' in Local Food Systems', *Progress in Human Geography* 31.1 (2007), pp. 23–42; M. Goodman, D. Maye, L. Holloway, 'Ethical Foodscapes?: Premises, Promises and Possibilities', *Environment and Planning A* 42.8 (2010), pp. 1782–1796.
8. e.g. G. Ritzer, *The McDondaldization of Society: An Investigation into the Changing Character of Contemporary Social Life* (Los Angeles: Pine Forge Press, 1996).
9. D. Rangneker, J.Wilkinson, '(New) Borders of Consumption', *Environment and Planning A* 43.9 (2011), pp. 2007–2011, and D. Goodman, E.M DuPuis, and M. Goodman, *Alternative Food Networks: Knowledge, Practice and Politics* (London Routledge, 2012); Harvestmark, 2012: http://www.harvestmark.com/
10. B. Coles and P. Crang, 'Placing Alternative Consumption: Commodity Fetishism in Borough Fine Foods Market, London', *Ethical Consumption: A Critical Introduction*, eds. T. Lewis and E. Potter (London: Routledge, 2011), 88–89.
11. D. Bell and J. Hollows, 'From River Cottage to Chicken Run: Hugh Fearnley-Whittingstall and the Class Politics of Ethical Consumption', *Celebrity Studies* 2.2 (2011), pp. 178–91; J. Hollows and S. Jones, 'At Least He's Doing Something': Moral Entrepreneurship and Individual Responsibility in Jamie's Ministry of Food', *European Journal of Cultural Studies* 13.3 (2010), pp. 307–22 and 'Please Don't Try This at Home: Heston Blumenthal, Cookery TV and the Culinary Field', *Food, Culture and Society* 13.4 (2010), 521–37; P. Naccarato and K. LeBesco, *Culinary Capital* (London: Berg, 2012); S. Rousseau, *Food*

and Social Media: You Are What You Tweet (London: Rowman and Littlefield, 2012) and *Food Media: Celebrity Chefs and the Politics of Everday Interference* (London: Berg, 2012).

12. P. McMichael, 'The Power of Food', *Agriculture and Human Values* 17 (2000), pp. 21–33; J. Guthman, 'Bringing Good Food to Others: Investigating the Subjects of Alternative Food Practice', *Cultural Geographies* 15 (2008), pp. 431–47 and '"If They Only Knew"': Color Blindness and Universalism in California Alternative Food Institutions', *Professional Geographer* 60.3 (2008), pp. 387–97.
13. '2012 UK Supermarkets (Marketshare)', *Grocerynews.com*: http://grocerynews.org/2012-06-16-08-27-26/supermarkets-market-share/grocery-stores; Soil Association, *Organic Market Report*, (Bristol: Soil Association, 2012).
14. Tescopoly, 2012: http://www.tescopoly.org.
15. Goodman et al., 2010.
16. Fish Fight, 2012: http://www.fishfight.net/; see R. Slocum et al., '"Properly, with Love, from Scratch": Jamie Oliver's Food Revolution', *Radical History Review* 110 (2011), pp. 178–91; Hollows and Jones, 'At Least He's Doing Something'.

Sarma and *Dolma*:
The Rolled and the Stuffed in the Anatolian Kitchen

Nilhan Aras

While different examples of stuffed vegetables and leaves exist all around the world, they form a distinct main group of dishes in Turkish cuisine. They are important because each of them, in one way or another, has a place in Anatolian social life: their ingredients and the techniques used in their preparation reveal regional, ethnic and religious references; because they unveil many things about human as well as natural history. Rolled and stuffed vegetables and leaves are sometimes served as *meze* or as a first course, but more often they are the main dish themselves. Their importance is captured best by the inhabitants of Denizli, a city in the Aegean Anatolian region of Turkey. Instead of *sarma sarmak*, meaning 'rolling stuffed vegetables', or *dolma doldurmak*, meaning 'stuffing stuffed vegetables', they use the term *aş doldurmak*: the word *aş* has many meanings in Turkish, but its first meaning is *yemek*, 'food'.

To a Turkish man, rolled and stuffed vegetables and leaves mean only food. He has of course heard that they are time-consuming dishes for the cook, but this information does not have any significance for him. It is the taste of the dish that he is mostly interested in. However, to a Turkish woman, rolled and stuffed vegetables mean absolutely something more than food. Although she cannot name it, rolling or stuffing vegetables is a sociological phenomenon in which she has a part. Furthermore this part is not limited to the sociology of cuisine, and sometimes it has its own strict rules.

It is not easy to learn how to roll stuffed leaves. Therefore, in many regions of Anatolia, the task is a test applied by a groom's family to any prospective bride. Her success is proof of her potential as a housewife. Believe it or not, *sarma*, stuffed leaves, are a critical factor in the family's decision. They should be rolled thin, and sometimes they have to be small as well: so thin and small that the cook holds five or six in her palm and places them altogether in the pot, rather than putting them in the pot one by one. The rolls must also be made quickly, which is another measure of skill. Speed matters because making delicious dishes is not the only work of an Anatolian woman; she has to keep her house clean and tidy, take good care of her child, her husband and herself and, moreover, she must work outside the home. In short, it is hard to make stuffed leaves.

Perfect *sarma* are both evidence of a bride's skill and a sign of her beauty. An Anatolian girl has to have strong hands, but her fingers must be thin and fine-looking since long fingers are a sign of beauty and grace. Perfect *sarma* are indicative of this. Perfectly rolled leaves, which neither open during the cooking process nor at the time

The Rolled and the Stuffed in the Anatolian Kitchen

of serving, also indicate the candidate's ability to maintain order in the house. Failure in the test, by contrast, reveals a careless, untidy, insensitive girl.

Sarma and *dolma* have such a dominant image in Turkish cuisine and social life that they are mentioned in many *türkü*s, the traditional Turkish folk music with lyrics revealing true stories, good and bad memories, happiness, sorrow, wishes, the pains of the Anatolian people and even *sarma* and *dolma* determining the fate of a bride. Within this context, two anonymous *türkü*s (one of which comes from Kastamonu, a city situated in the eastern Black Sea region of Anatolia, and another from Kayseri, situated in the central Anatolian region) seem especially worthy of note. In both cities, traditional family structure and social customs survive. Their cuisines are extremely rich. The lyrics of these *türkü*s tell of a bride sent back to her mother's house because she did not make rolled leaves as she should have. What is more, the bride ate some of the cooked dish, and the cat ate some of the rest. The lyrics (my translation is literal) underline how hard it is to roll stuffed leaves, but insist that their taste is great:

> I took and ate one by one thinking that it is endless
> Thought that she won't tell about it to my parents
> Thought that grape vine leaves will not cause a bride to be driven away
> I sit in the morning to roll grape vine leaves
> My mother-in-law went for getting water
> Oh grape vine leaves I won't exchange you with dates[1]

The Rolled and the Stuffed in the Anatolian Kitchen

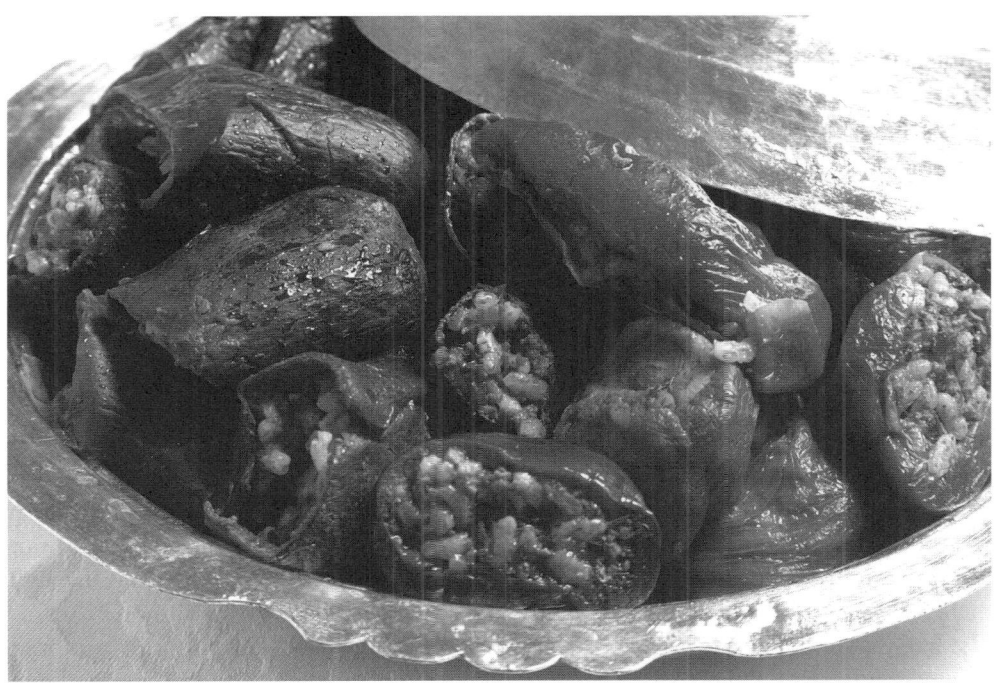

The Rolled and the Stuffed in the Anatolian Kitchen

In some districts – including Yalova and some villages of Çorum – when leaves are stuffed with minced meat they are thought better loosely rolled, not tightly. This is a particularly fine test of the bride's skills. The traditional view is that *sarma dediğin, kendini salmalı*, 'stuffed leaves should spread out themselves'.

The importance of this dish is also plain from a glance at the counters of shops selling small kitchen utensils. Over the last fifteen years in Anatolia, a machine that assists in the rolling of stuffed leaves has become very popular. The tradition of many hands making light work around a single table has perhaps declined in step with the rise in popularity of this useful aid. It is a simple design, perfect for domestic use, and some indication of the enduring love of Anatolians for this dish.

The significance of sarma in Anatolian society is demonstrated by the sequence of rituals that accompanies picking suitable leaves to be stuffed and ends when the dish itself is served. These rituals may encompass the reasons for the dish being made in the first place, as well as how it is consumed.

A team of women, both friends and family, assemble to pick suitable leaves. On some occasions, people from villages close-by will also be invited, and work will not begin before the whole group is gathered. Day by day the group will progress through members' vineyards or gardens picking the leaves while singing *türkü*s and other songs. The harvest complete, the woman with the 'most suitable hand' prepares the brine and pickles the leaves for the entire village, making ready for their consumption through the winter.

Anatolia, a land of rich flora, has many gifts for the woman in the kitchen. Among these are vegetables, edible herbs and the leaves of some trees, which differ from one region to another as they are exposed to dramatic variations in climate. For centuries, Anatolian women used every kind of edible leaf to make *sarma* in response to both the scarcity of ingredients and seasonal necessity. However, this virtue of necessity has now hardened into traditions and the result is our current perception of regional differences. For example, in Malatya, a city bathed in the warmth of south-east Anatolia, the leaves they use range from the vine, to the mulberry, sour cherry and quince. Other places, it stands to reason, cannot boast such variety. Thus there are no stuffed hazelnut leaves in Manisa, on the Aegean; nor are there bulgur-stuffed sour cherry leaves in Trabzon, on the Black Sea.

This a short list of the most popular leaves in Asia Minor for making *sarma*: vine leaves (number one); hazelnut; horse chestnut; cherry; sour cherry; white mulberry; white cabbage; kale; mallow; sheep sorrel; other species of *Rumex*; *melevcen* (*Smilax excelsa* L.); *şalba* (*Salvia forskaohlei* L.); *yılan yastığı* (*Arum dioscoridis* Sm); lettuce; Swiss chard; spinach; leek; onion. It should be stressed however that not every stuffed dish on the Anatolian table has a leaf as its wrapping: many are encased in caul.

Stuffed vine leaves are the perfect example of a dish assembled piece by piece. These individual atoms are never cooked singly, but in large numbers in big pots because, over centuries, it has been a festive dish for weddings and holidays, not only among the people at large but in the homes of the élite. Even today, in some villages, stuffed vine leaves are served for breakfast on religious holidays. On occasions such as this the large number of rolls required demands collaboration among the women of the village. Sociologically speaking this undertaking might be viewed as group therapy. The women sit around a cloth spread on the floor, or sometimes round a table. While their hands are busy making the dish, tongues are too, as they tell their troubles, worries and sorrows; exchange opinions and thus relax; find comfort for their souls; and enjoy singing songs and *türkü*s. Once the pots are full, although arms and backs may tell the tale, hearts and souls are 'as light as a bird'.

Sometimes a bead, or a coin (even a gold coin, depending on the occasion) is inserted in one or more of the rolls. This may be to encourage children to eat or to choose by lot the next host of the party. In some cases, the current host makes a gift to the host in waiting who may also take any requests for dishes on the menu from the guests. In the village of Taşpınar (Tokat province), the token in the roll is seen as a lucky charm. As the meal begins, everyone makes a wish, and whoever finds the charm will be granted his desire. This practice is usually restricted to family meals, and there is a variation which has the mother making wishes for each of her children.

Like the roll or *sarma*, the *dolma* – the stuffed vegetable or stuffed something-else – has similar techniques and rituals. Although *dolma* requires a more robust technique than *sarma*, it is also widely liked. Its popularity can be seen in an idiomatic expression from the Daday district of Kastamonu: when describing a lady of embonpoint, a much-relished feature there, people say, '*dolma gibi kadın*', that is, 'a woman like *dolma*.' There is another turn of phrase, '*dolma parmak*', which translated literally means, 'finger like stuffed vegetable'. In other words, the fingers are fat, not slim.

Dolma are an everyday dish, but are also sometimes an essential part of a special feast-day menu. The preparation is time-consuming as each vegetable has to be dealt with in turn. As the usual way is to prepare a lot at once, some collaboration between friends, family and neighbours does not go amiss (although this is not so marked a feature as it is with *sarma*).

In traditional Turkish cuisine, there are few vegetables or even fruits that may not be stuffed. The centre is hollowed out and then filled with the stuffing mixture. The vegetables and fruits that come to mind for *dolma* include green and red bell peppers, aubergines, courgettes and gourds as the most popular candidates, and then some kinds of fungi, hairy cucumbers (*Cucumis melo*), tomatoes, potatoes, celeriac, onions, cabbage, carrots, fava beans, peas, turnips, cucumbers, melons, watermelons and quinces. Stuffed vegetables figured among the dishes served at banquets in the Topkapı palace. One of these was stuffed okra, which requires meticulous craftsmanship. Fruits such as apricot, fig, apple and pear, were stuffed with different mixtures and served as light desserts.

The material to be stuffed, the outer part, does not always have to be a vegetable or fruit. From antiquity to the present day, poultry like quail and turkey as well as bigger animals like lamb and kid have been stuffed whole. These kinds of stuffed dishes signal

The Rolled and the Stuffed in the Anatolian Kitchen

wealth and higher social status, which makes them suitable for feasts and other special events. Some parts of these animals, such as the flank, ribs, trotters and tripe, may be stuffed separately, although this category of *dolma* is not easy to make. Indeed, the preparation is so long and involved that the assembly is often completed up to 36 hours before the dish is actually served. Fish are also stuffed: sometimes large species such as carp for a group of diners, or mackerel for a single diner.

Over time, a special vocabulary has evolved around stuffed vegetables and stuffed leaves. This vocabulary is not limited to metaphors for beauty, but includes terms used for differentiating the ingredients to be used as the outer part and those for the inner mixture; such terms include *sarmalık yaprak*, grape vine leaves for making stuffed leaves, and *dolmalık biber*, meaning bell pepper. Furthermore, dried vegetables – particularly in south-eastern Anatolia, especially the city of Gaziantep – and zucchini flowers in the Aegean and Mediterranean regions, are used as materials to be stuffed – even though they are not identified by the Turkish adjective *dolmalık*, meaning 'to be stuffed with'. Dried vegetables are so relished that aubergines, a kind of red bell pepper and hairy cucumbers are prepared and carefully dried in summer, ready for winter consumption. The adjective *dolmalık* is used to qualify not only the item to be stuffed, but also the stuffing. Hence pine nuts are called *dolma fıstığı*, short or broken rice is called *dolmalık pirinç* and both grades of bulgur are also qualified with the adjective *dolmalık*. However, the epithet is not applied to the oil, fat, tomatoes and/or other miscellaneous ingredients that make up the stuffing mixture.

The generic names *sarma* and *dolma* derive from the technique used in their preparation. If the filling is wrapped by an outer material which is then shaped into rolls, the technique is called *sarma*, literally 'rolled'; if the filling is placed inside the hollowed outer material, the technique is called *dolma*, meaning stuffed. The name of each individual confection is generally taken from the identity of the wrapping or the fruit, vegetable or other foodstuff that is being stuffed. Less frequently, the name of the dish will relate to the chief ingredient that makes up the stuffing itself; and much less frequently, rarely indeed, the name of the dish will identify both the suffing and the wrapping and/or stuffed. However, in the case of mulberry leaf *sarma* or sour cherry leaf *sarma*, the dish made with the leaves of trees is called nothing more than *sarma* – the species of leaf is only identified when specifically enquired about. Examples of *sarma* and *dolma* getting their names from the outer part of the dish include stuffed grape vine leaf, stuffed cabbage leaf, stuffed *Rumex* leaf, stuffed zucchini flower, stuffed morel, stuffed ribs, stuffed tripe and others.

Dishes named according to the filling designate the subcategory to which the dish belongs. This subcategorization normally reflects the Anatolian division between those dishes made with olive oil and those with meat. Dishes in which olive oil is used are served and consumed cold or at room temperature, whereas dishes made using meat as an ingredient are served and eaten hot. The dishes in these two categories not only differ in their consumption but also by the techniques used in their preparation and cooking.

The Rolled and the Stuffed in the Anatolian Kitchen

For example, there is a technique which dates back to the Ottoman period but which is still found today where the fat that rises to the top of a broth is skimmed off and the remaining broth is used in olive oil-based dishes to add flavour.[2] In cosmopolitan cities like İstanbul and İzmir, some *dolma* tend to a certain sweetness, either from sugar or from other spices. Leaving such categorization aside, some examples of rolled or stuffed dishes named according to their filling are: *zeytinyağlı sarma* (most often vine leaves made using olive oil), *baklalı sarma* (stuffed leaves with broad beans), *zeytinyağlı dolma* (usually applied to stuffed green bell peppers made with olive oil) and *yalancı dolma* (meaning pseudo-*dolma*). Although nowadays in some places *yalancı dolma* is used to designate the dish having bulgur in its filling instead of rice, during the Ottoman period it was used to indicate that stuffed or rolled dishes were made with olive oil instead of meat.[3] Furthermore, as in the case of some districts of Rize, a city situated on the Black Sea coast of Anatolia, *yalancı dolma* signifies stuffed cabbage leaves made without meat.

Among the dishes named according to both the outer material and the filling are *etli kuru dolma*, which is stuffed dried vegetables with meat in the filling, and *zeytinyağlı kuru dolma*, stuffed dried vegetables with olive oil in the filling. Leek and onion *dolma*s are technically and visually rolled vegetables but called *dolma* instead. The leaves of these vegetables are separated from each other and poached in boiling water. In some regions these leaves are spread when they are hard and the filling is put on them for rolling. Although they are rolled in thin and long rolls, the dish is still called *dolma*.

Other kinds of *sarma* and *dolma* are special because of the heat control needed during their cooking. If all the ingredients were layered in a pot, the taste of the cooked dish would be different. But with the rolling or stuffing technique the ingredients are cooked in another way. Thus the names of the dishes in this category give a clue about how they are cooked. There are also dishes which are named *dolma* or *sarma* although they are not. One example is *İskilip dolması*. This is a very special dish, made with caramelized onion, rice and meat put into a cloth bag and cooked in a big copper cauldron. *İskilip dolması* is called a *dolma* because the preparation and the cooking process are similar to other dishes that fall under the generic name *dolma*. Similar examples of cross-categorization can be found where a roll is made with a piece of meat as the wrapping (an 'olive'); they are called *sarma*.

In order to make *sarma* and *dolma*, the first step is to prepare the outer layer. If vine leaves are used, they are cleaned, poached in hot water and put aside for draining. If leaves are not fresh but in brine, first the salt is rubbed off then the leaves are washed and left to drain. If it is *dolma*, the ingredient to be stuffed is generally hollowed out, washed and left to drain; sometimes the top is only opened, not cut off. While the outer layer ingredients are draining, the filling is made.

In fact, ingredients used as outer material and as filling signify more than their own meaning because they both define the exact name of the dish and sometimes refer to ethnic roots and religious codes. Moreover, they often refer to the place or region where

The Rolled and the Stuffed in the Anatolian Kitchen

they are made most frequently. Especially where *sarma* dishes are concerned, there is a great diversification in the ingredients used as outer material. In Istanbul and the Aegean region, vine leaves are the most common outer material of *sarma*. However, in eastern parts of Anatolia, those of various fruit trees are used as well. In Malatya (ancient Melitene, in eastern Anatolia), about seventy different dishes are recorded which employ the technique of rolling or stuffing.

As well as reflecting their geographical points of origin, stuffed and rolled dishes are also mirrors of the social status of their makers – depending on the ingredients used. The staple grain of Anatolia is wheat, and its by-products *yarma* and *bulgur* are the foundation of the cuisine.[4] *Bulgur* is the main ingredient in the filling of the stuffed and rolled dishes in the rural areas. It is easily available, it keeps for a long time, it has high nutritional value and is often consumed before heavy work. However, in the cities rice takes the place of bulgur. Since rice is relatively more expensive than *bulgur*, it serves as a sign of wealth. In the eastern Black Sea region, cracked maize is used in the filling instead of *bulgur* or rice. There appears another sign here, because the kind of maize used gives signs of the socio-economic situation of the family. In this region, sundried maize is used in many dishes whereas the maize dried in the oven, which is not an ordinary ingredient, is preferred for making stuffed dishes. When it comes to stuffed or rolled dishes in which the meat is an ingredient, the minced meat ratio to the overall weight of the dish is another sign of status. The quantity of minced meat is an important and generally accurate indicator of the wealth of the family. Sometimes, however, the amount of meat used in the filling will reflect not so much the wealth of the makers but rather their respect for traditional recipes and customs, as well as a wish to make a better-balanced dish.

The other ingredients which make up the filling are often calling-cards of the makers' ethnic origins. The kinds of spices, and their quantity, the kind of the sauce – such things whisper the name of the ethnic cuisine to which the dish belongs. Furthermore, seeing the same ingredient for the outer part and/or the same filling across the seven geographical regions of Turkey hints at the great cultural mosaic and the migrations that have taken place within Anatolia. For example, stuffed zucchini flower is made in the same way in İzmir, on the Aegean, and in Mersin and Antalya on the Mediterranean, but not in Adana on the furthest eastern reach of the Turkish Mediterranean, nor in Çorum, on the Black Sea, bordering central Anatolia. But in all these places, dishes made by rolling and stuffing are the *sine qua non* of Turkish cuisine.

KUBBEŞEN DOLMASI

Although it is a dish very specific to Ankara and often specially cooked there for guests, *kubbeşen dolması* is not cooked in all parts of the city. Prof. Dr Ayşe Baysal briefly describes this dish, whose shape looks like a dome, 'You can either cut the cabbage so as to make cabbage stew or carve the cabbage and fill it in.'[5] Semiha Bostancı from Kalecik (Ankara), on the other hand, describes it in detail:

> Boil the outer leaves of the white cabbage until they get soft and put them in a basin. You will not need more than 7 leaves. While they rest to one side, prepare the filling. Fry together melted butter, a bowl of rice, 4–5 onions, 1 teaspoon of dried mint, 1 bunch of parsley, 1 bunch of dill, dried red pepper, pepper, red pepper and tomato pastes with 200 grams of dry mince. Spread a cabbage leaf over the bottom of the pot and then lay the rest, from bottom to top, round the sides of the pot. Put the filling inside and spread it and close the leaves over the top. Make a cut across the centre of the top to let water in. Add half a litre of water by pouring it gently down the sides of the dish. Cook it slowly until the rice is cooked. Place it on a round tray upside down. Cut it as triangles as if cutting a cake. It will taste delicious.

ROLLED LEAVES WITH PASTRAMI AND BULGHUR[6]

For 5
500g vine leaves • 1 *parçalanmış* rib[6] bone

For the filling:
150 g pastrami • 2 cups thick bulghur
1 cup green lentils • 4 onions • 4 tbsp butter
2 tsp of tomato paste • 1 bunch dill • salt, pepper

If the vine leaves are in brine, soak them in cold water overnight; if fresh, boil them a little. Boil the lentils until tender and strain the water. Dice the onions, fry in butter until they turn pink and add the paste. Add the chopped pastrami. Cook the bulghur stirring in butter together with the lentils in hot water. Add all the ingredients together and leave to cool. Finely chopped dill and spices are added. Roll the mixture into the leaves. First place the rib bones and then the rolls in the pot. Cook on a low heat with a little water. Serve hot.

Acknowledgements

Special thanks to Priscilla Mary Işın, Nazlı Pişkin and Aylin Mutlu, who translated my original Turkish texts (both abstract and full text) into English; to Mehmet Ali Sağbili, who prepared the photo film, and to Hasan Uslu, who made the film about *sarma* and *dolma* in Anatolian.

Notes

1. *Türkü* compiled from Kayseri.
2. Personal interview with Vedat Başaran, March 2012.
3. See Mehmet Kâmil (1844), *Melceü't-Tabbâhîn (Aşçıların Sığınağı)-İlk Basılı Türkçe Yemek Kitabı,* Haz. Cüneyt Kut, 1997, Unipro.
4. Boiled and cracked wheat.
5. Ayşe Baysal, s. 226.
6. Meryem Kadife, b. 1971, Çorum. The information given was edited by Huriye Alkan (b. 1930, Çorum) and Kamile Hatun (d. 1960, Çorum), mother-in-law Hasibe Kadife and mother Raife Aydınlı. See Ahmet Örs vd., s.302.

Pastel de Tentúgal: Serendipity or Cultural Syncretism?

Paula Arvela

Introduction
Pastel de Tentúgal, a wrapped sweet pastry and a popular item of the traditional *Doçaria Conventual Portuguesa*, is simultaneously a food and an item of cultural history.[1] As a food, the cigar-shaped pastry constitutes a distinctive item of confectionery. It exhibits most of the culinary attributes that seem mandatory in sweet-making – balanced symmetric shape with perfect texture, colour and flavour. *Pastel de Tentúgal* strikes a flawless balance between visual structure and the gustatory experience, with its multi-layered crispy wrapping enclosing a filling that teases the taste buds and senses. One bite breaks through the crunchy, delicate wrapping to expose the yellow, sweet content. Texture and flavour constitute the hallmark of the *pastel de Tentúgal*.

But the *pastel* is more than food; it is also an artefact of culinary history, a signifier of cultural identity and an exciting storyteller. Its significance derives from its embeddedness in many different narratives, as for example in the story of the *pastel*'s 'original' creation

Pasteis Tentúgal – Pastel de Tentúgal (cigar shape).
(Courtesy of Olga Cavaleiro – Confraria da Doçaria Conventual de Tentúgal)

Pastel de Tentúgal: Serendipity or Cultural Syncretism?

by barefoot Carmelite nuns who, working on floors covered with white clean sheets, meticulously stretched the dough to a paper-thin pastry that wrapped and hid the voluptuous filling. But the *pastel* also lures us into yet untold stories of plausible links with other cultures, culinary practices and alternative techniques that generate look-alike products.

Pastel de Tentúgal's wrapping is puzzling. It looks like filo pastry yet, according to its traditional artisans, it is a unique product that has been integral to Tentúgal's pastry-making repertoire for five centuries.[2] These claims of originality by the *pastel*'s pastry-makers raise some troublesome questions because of similar claims made for other cognate forms of wrapping. For example, filo-like pastry is used in the making of the Turkish *börek* and *baklava*; the Greek *spanakopita* and *baklava*; the Moroccan *bestilla* and the Tunisian *brik*.[3] Likewise, in Central Europe, Vienna is famous for its strudels and Bulgaria for its *banitsa*.[4] These traditional pastry products share a well-documented Arabic culinary heritage. Hitherto, the five-century long Arab-Moorish presence in Portugal and its consequences for Portuguese culture have been acknowledged but under-valued.

This paper explores the impact of Arab-Moorish influence on the Portuguese culinary heritage. It specifically examines the possible links between the *pastel de Tentúgal*'s pastry wrapping and Moorish culinary influence on Portuguese cuisine. Rather than brazenly amend *Tentúgal*'s pastry legacy, my purpose is to explore a number of narratives that feed into an overarching story about paper-thin pastry that tends to generalize and gloss over many local specificities and techniques. My aim is not re-classification but instead to acquire a better understanding of the broader pastry-making tradition with which *pastel de Tentúgal* might be associated. Is serendipity or cultural syncretism at work here?[5] Either way, the Carmelite nuns deserve acknowledgement for their accomplishment in producing an item that, although similar to filo pastry, also bears characteristics of its own.

Stories of Tentúgal
The nuns
Tentúgal is a small coastal village in central Portugal. According to the *pastel de Tentúgal*'s professional pastry-makers and cultural gatekeepers, the product was first devised in the sixteenth century by the nuns of the convent *Nossa Senhora da Natividade*, and it remained an integral part of its kitchens' culinary repertoire for three consecutive centuries until the closure of the convent in 1898 upon the death of the last Carmelite nun.[6]

Exploring the *pastel de Tentúgal* takes us inside the walls of a sixteenth-century convent, where women were forced into celibacy for reasons other than individual choice. The institutionalization of the system of *morgadio* had a detrimental impact on the lives of young women. *Morgadio* enforced male primogeniture so that the elder son was the only lawful inheritor of the family patrimony. Initially a customary practice, *morgadio* was sanctioned in 1603 during the Iberian unification.[7] This inequitable system of inheritance particularly hurt females, who fell victim to substantially decreased monetary allowances made to their marriage dowries and were subsequently forced into a life of celibacy. Voiceless and cast out, they faced uncertain futures. Forced to choose between a life of tightened circumstances and voluntary entry into monastery life, the latter was the solution most had to accept.

Tentúgal's convent was founded in 1565, well before the institutionalization of *morgadio*. However, by the time the convent was established, this customary practice was already observed, and women were already entering monastic life to comply with social expectations rather than in accord with their religious beliefs. As a result, the establishment of a convent in Tentúgal was regarded as a positive measure because it fulfilled the need to 'shelter many orphans and the daughters of many honourable nobleman who could not afford to pay for their marriages'.[8] The great majority of these women were literate and well educated. Secular habits were not necessarily shed at the convent's door. Despite their lives of privilege being abruptly denied from the moment they entered the convent, these nuns-to-be brought with them the eating habits of their family homes. From a life of comfort, abundance and perhaps even exposure to exotic foods, they were thrown into a lifestyle of unexpected limitations. Their engagement in crafts and sweet-making offered them respite from the boredom of monastery life.[9] This is how the tradition of confectionery in Portuguese convents emerged. It is usually referred to as *doçaria conventual*, and this story and practice are recognized as part of the national culinary heritage.

Cooking in the family home was not an activity in which these women would have been expected to engage. However, once in the convent, cooking turned out to be a soothing and gratifying activity that kept them occupied and gave them a sense of self-worth. As Goes asserts, 'These nuns were women from wealthy families, some of them connected either to the royal family or aristocracy, it is therefore possible that they would have taken into the convent their family recipes and since they did not have any other way to keep themselves motivated, they engaged in sweet-making'.[10] Thus, convents offered the perfect conditions to become busy hubs of culinary practice.

Pastel and secrecy

Some of the major convents were very wealthy. Their active role in the kingdom's territorial organization and development had always been recognized, approved and promoted by the king and the royal house. In return, convents were granted valuables and land, which they leased out in return for cash payment or equivalent value in goods.[11] According to Saramago, convents ranked second only to the royal house in land and wealth.

The institutionalization of *morgadio* and the consequent increased demand for female convents made admission highly competitive and costly.[12] This is not to say that every woman entering a convent would have had to pay for her right to admittance.

Pastel de Tentúgal: Serendipity or Cultural Syncretism?

However, women from wealthy families opting out of secular life for non-religious motives were expected to pay a dowry. This sum, although less than what would have been expected as a wedding dowry, might still be substantial.[13]

In addition, women were also expected to be accompanied by a 'wedding chest' when entering a convent. It might contain fine linen, kitchen equipment and expensive ingredients such as spices.[14] Consequently, convents' kitchens became well-equipped places with a resourceful female workforce, willing to occupy their free time with cooking.

Convents had easy access to the ingredients required for sweet-making – flour from the local mill; eggs, milk, honey and fruits from the convent's farmyard. Sugar, which at the time was an expensive commodity in Europe, was easily accessible in Portugal due to its production in the Madeira Islands and later in Brazil and Africa.[15] In the sixteenth century, sugar was considered to have medicinal effects and was used in confectionery for its alleged therapeutic qualities.[15] Thus, the sweets made by the nuns were either used as a remedy for sick children and adults or as gifts to the convent's benefactors, and the leftovers were utilized for the convent's own consumption. The shape and filling of the *pastel* indicated its recipient. The traditional cigar-shape made with a filling of *ovos moles* was distributed to the sick and poor. In turn, the half-moon shaped *pastel*, with almond meal incorporated in its filling, was used as a gift for the convent's sponsors.[17]

Primary evidence of the *pastel*'s history is sparse, thus making its validation difficult. For example, there are no recipes or written descriptions of the *pastel*-making process. The only written records that have survived four centuries of the likely routines are the convent ledgers and other financial records, which ought to be acknowledged as a tribute to the literacy levels and organizational skills of the nuns. These records have been essential for our current knowledge of the *pastel de Tentúgal*. For instance, according to Carvalho, as early as 1611 there are entries in the Convent's ledger for products named as '*pastel*', which she argues are reference to the *pastel de Tentúgal*. Likewise, Carvalho argues that the Convent's *livro de receitas* (receipt book) and *despesas do convento* (expenditure book) illustrate that the purchase of large amounts of flour, sugar and honey match the increased kitchen pastry production.[18] These records, which form the only written documentation witnessing the production of the *pastel*, have been essential in piecing together its story.

Artefacts and the convent's architectural drawings constitute valuable secondary evidence in Carvalho's argument. Reference to thirty *cazas de cozinha* (kitchens) and separate *casas de amassar* (dough-making rooms), illustrate the high level of kitchen productivity and the need for specialization of space and tasks. Likewise, textual descriptions of 'two flour chests, bowls, trays and flour sieves' give an accurate idea of the equipment and practices carried out in those spaces.[18] According to the *Associação do Pastel de Tentúgal*, this equipment has remained unchanged with exception of adopting electric dough-mixers.

The convent's inventory includes a puzzling piece of equipment. It refers to *bacias de*

Pastel de Tentúgal: Serendipity or Cultural Syncretism?

lavar os pés (foot washing basins). According to Carvalho, this equipment is uncommon and not generally required in kitchens unless, she argues, the basins were meant to be used by the nuns to sanitize their feet before entering the rooms where the dough was stretched. The presence of the foot-washing basins together with the evidence provided in earlier paragraphs has been used by the *Associação* and the *Confraria de Tentúgal* to substantiate their claim of a dynamic and unique practice of pastry-making which gives the *pastel de Tentúgal* its legitimate claim to regional authenticity.

Pastel's claim to authenticity

In 2011, the *Associação dos Pasteleiros de Tentúgal* (APT) and *Confraria do Pastel de Tentúgal* submitted an application to the Portuguese government requesting a Protected Geographic Indication nomination.[20] When approved, this nomination will officially recognize and legitimate the *pastel* as a unique item of the Tentúgal area. Their case was based on the alleged specificity of the *pastel*, its unique relationship with the locale's cultural history and its geographic distinctiveness. The forty-two-page document is thorough, referenced and clearly defines and codifies the specificities of the *pastel*: 'Classified as *doçaria conventual*, the dough is a mix of flour and water, and the filling made by mixing eggs with sugar-syrup cooked to soft-ball stage (105 °C). The *pastel* has two presentations – the *palito* (cigar-shape) and the m*eia-lua* (half-moon or crescent).'[21] The document is a detailed and precise description of a process that complies with rigorous standards of production. The dough is stretched over floorboards covered with white sheets to a thickness ranging between 0.06mm–0.15mm. The ingredients' quality is clearly specified and so is the technique required for the shaping of the *pastel* (*armar o pastel*).[22] According to the professionals involved in this process, the application of butter between the layers of pastry can only successfully be achieved with the traditional use of a chicken's feather. In their experience, only this technique can guarantee the delivery of the precise amount of butter required for a crunchy pastry. Finally, the *pastel*'s shape is of paramount importance. It is prescribed in accordance with tradition: *palito* (cigar) or *meia-lua* (half-moon). The former has a filling of *ovos moles*, the latter with added ground almonds.

The strict guidelines established for the confection of the *pastel* safeguards its PGI nomination which depends as much on the methodology of production as it does on the specificity of its geographic location in Tentúgal. According to the document, the *pastel*'s uniqueness results from its location in Tentúgal. The local optimum temperature-humidity ratio makes 'the natural conditions that are specific to Tentúgal … paramount for a successful end product.'[23] Only they can guarantee a pastry with the required degree of crunchiness. This constitutes the product hallmark and underpins its claim to authenticity.

The association between the *pastel* and Tentúgal is framed by the discourse of authenticity. It implicitly and explicitly reflects a natural, rooted and inherent relationship between locale and product. The *pastel*'s location makes it legitimate,

*Figure 1. Initial stages of stretching the dough.
(Courtesy of Olga Cavaleiro – Confraria da Doçaria Conventual de Tentúgal)*

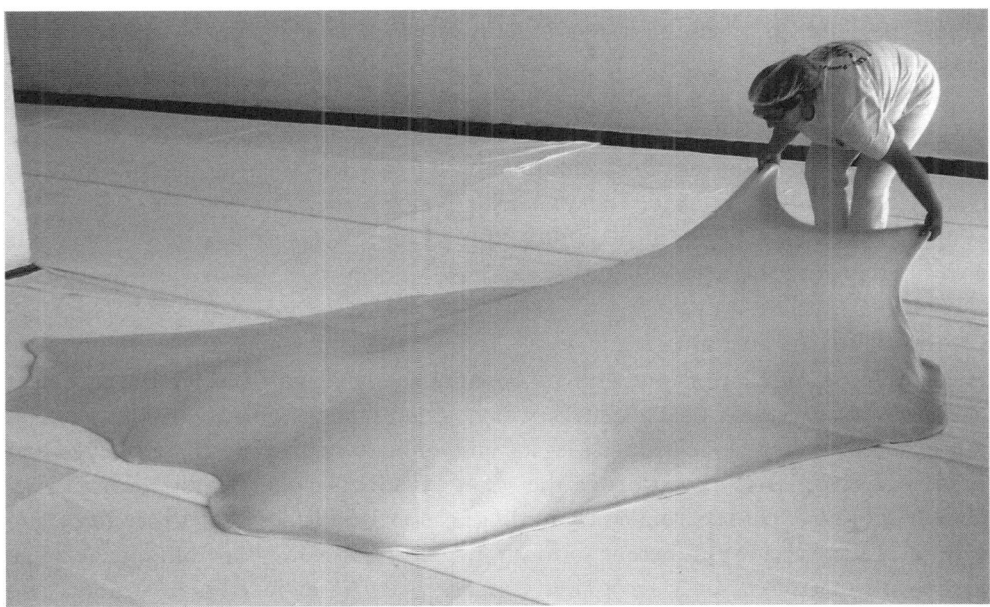

Figure 2. Stretching the dough. The air caught underneath the dough assists the process.

authentic and unique. However, the document also pays tribute to the essential human factor by acknowledging the 'original' producers – the Carmelite nuns who kept an oral tradition alive and developed a 'very specific know-how that created the *pastel*.'[24] According to the same document, the last nun, D. Maxima de Loreto, later passed down this oral tradition to the laywomen of Tentúgal who perpetuated and promoted it.

No recipes or written descriptions of the practice survived the ravages of time, especially given the effects of the nineteenth-century French Napoleonic invasion and the religious persecution that accompanied Liberalism. Instead, oral tradition has ensured the rigorous preservation of a practice that would have otherwise been lost.

It is generally accepted that the convent's special recipes were kept secret to zealously preserve their 'uniqueness' and to enable differentiation from the products of competing convents. The mother superior was the only person with access to any of the existing written records, thus assuring confidentiality. Amongst the nuns, oral tradition was the mainstay of cooking practices. To guarantee recipes would not go beyond the convent walls, any nun exiting or being transferred to another convent was required to pledge her silence about the convent's culinary practices. Within the convent, oral tradition efficiently preserved the passage of knowledge and skills over generations of nuns. However, it also safeguarded them against the devastating effect of looting and the destruction of written records during the nineteenth century. The institutionalization of liberalism, secularization and the progressive closure of convents and monasteries would have been the fatal blow to the nuns' sweet-making practice had it not been preserved orally.

For three centuries oral tradition protected the nun's secret recipes and later became the vehicle that divulged it to the outside world. Oral tradition gave the women of Tentúgal the chance to learn the technique through the teachings of the last Carmelite nun before her death in 1898. Today's female pastry-makers preserve the 'know-how' that makes them the twenty-first-century cultural gatekeepers who diligently assert the *pastel*'s originality and authenticity.

Other claims to authenticity

Pastel de Tentúgal's claim to authenticity needs further analysis. Thus far, the argument has been based on secondary sources which ground the originality of the *pastel* as much in its location as in its social legacy and culinary specificity. The challenge that needs to be met is to acknowledge the *pastel*'s distinctive traits whilst exploring its place in a broader context where new findings can expand its already rich culinary and cultural narrative. My aim here is to locate the *pastel de Tentúgal* within a conceptual framework that discursively recognizes culinary practices as markers of regional and national identities but also takes into account the dynamic characteristics of cultural syncretism.

Thus, this paper uses the *pastel de Tentúgal* as a launching pad to articulate and

Pastel de Tentúgal: Serendipity or Cultural Syncretism?

*Figure 3. Final stages of stretching the dough.
(Courtesy of Olga Cavaleiro – Confraria da Doçaria Conventual de Tentúgal)*

*Figure 4. Outcome: paper-thin pastry.
(Courtesy of Olga Cavaleiro – Confraria da Doçaria Conventual de Tentúgal)*

Pastel de Tentúgal: Serendipity or Cultural Syncretism?

encompass different narratives. On the one hand, it acknowledges the claims made by the *pastel*'s gatekeepers who name it as an icon of national cuisine and declare it to be in a class of its own. On the other hand, it recognizes the need to explore the apparent resemblances between the *pastel*'s paper-thin wrappings and similar products that equally assert themselves as integral to traditional local culinary practices.

It is important to consider the diverse geographic locations that incorporate paper-thin pastry in their traditional culinary repertoire. Such a consideration alerts us to the potential common cultural legacy, but at the same time as it highlights the pastry's versatility and wide range of utilization. However, it also underscores contested claims to authenticity. Analyzing some of the most popular items that use the paper-thin pastry takes us to many places and introduces us to a wide range of foods. It is not my intention to analyse in detail the differences amongst these wrappings. However, I can briefly note that, for instance, in the Mediterranean basin we find the Moroccan *bestilla* made with paper-thin *warqa*, the Tunisian *brik* made with paper-thin *malsouqua*, the Turkish *börek* and *baklava*, the Egyptian *göllash* and the Greek *baklava* and *spanakopita*, all made with filo-like pastry.[25]

As Davidson suggests and the thirteenth century *Anonymous Andalusian Cookbook* illustrates, paper-thin dough was documented in recipes for the *khabis* and the *muwarraqa musammana* which technically resemble the making of the Moroccan *warqs*.[26] The commonalities represented by these techniques in traditional dishes of the Mediterranean basin strongly suggest their shared culinary and cultural legacy despite a time gap of seven centuries.

Likewise, in Central Europe the Austrian strudel and the Bulgarian *banitsa* also use paper-thin pastry in their production.[27] Both Austrians and Bulgarians admit their confectionery icons to be a culinary legacy from the Ottoman presence in Central Europe in the sixteenth century.[28] In turn, the dispute over the origins of the celebrated *baklava* is a topic of contention between Greeks and Turks, with claims made by the former being disputed by counterclaims of *baklava*'s Turkish heritage made by Charles Perry and echoed by Alan Davidson.[29]

Perry traced the origins of filo pastry to the Turkic nomads who, due to lack of ovens, devised the technique of making bread by multi-layering sheets of thin dough cooked on a griddle. Later technical developments in the kitchens of the Topkapi Palace led to the 'invention' of the Turkish *baklava* whose distribution in the streets of Constantinople during Ramadan became integral to the Baklava Procession.[30]

As these examples illustrate, there are grounds to support the claim that the paper-thin pastry might indeed have a common cultural and culinary heritage perhaps indebted to the expansion of the Ottoman Empire in these areas. But what is the link with the Portuguese *pastel de Tentúgal*?

Let's for a moment ponder the Moors' legacy in Portugal.[31] Their presence in the Iberian Peninsula dates from 711 CE. They inhabited the southern areas of the Peninsula and named them *Al-Andalus* (Spain) and *Garb-Al-Andalus* (Portugal). The Catholic

Pastel de Tentúgal: Serendipity or Cultural Syncretism?

Figure 5. 'Brushing' the melted butter on the pastry using a chicken's feather. (Courtesy of Olga Cavaleiro – Confraria da Doçaria Conventual de Tentúgal)

repossession of these territories is generally referred to as *Reconquista* (re-conquest). In Portugal it took place in 1249 under the monarch Afonso III and in Spain under the Catholic monarchs Ferdinand of Aragon and Isabella of Castile, who claimed the Moors' last bastion – Granada – in 1498. This five-century presence of the Moors in Portugal is historically documented. Porto, Coimbra and Lisbon were consecutively claimed by the Catholics in 868, 1064 and 1147. Faro, the Moors' last stronghold in *Garb-Al-Andalus*, fell in 1249.[32]

The presence of Mozarabs in Coimbra has been a topic of research.[33] Curiously, one of the relevant figures referred to by Saraiva and Carvalho is Mozarab Sesnando, born in Tentúgal.[34] He studied in Seville, was elected Seville's Vizier and became an eminent Moorish figure. Later, in 1064, Sesnando returned to Coimbra where he held important administrative roles in the Moorish political system.[35] The evidence of Sesnando's political role in Coimbra and his birth filiations to Tentúgal illustrate the ethnic and religious inclusiveness of the Moorish cultural system. But, more importantly, it also demonstrates that Tentúgal is no stranger to the presence and influence of the Moorish culture.

In fact, the Moorish legacy is patently illustrated in many aspects of Portuguese culture. For example, the Portuguese language includes up to a thousand words of Arabic derivation.[36] Most of these words are related to concepts newly introduced by the Arabs' more advanced technology which therefore did not have referents in the local vernacular. Agricultural practices and irrigation techniques were introduced, dramatically changing and improving hitherto archaic methods. Likewise, the Moors are credited with the introduction of many new foods, cooking techniques and eating habits which are still current today.[37] According to Lima-Reis, the wide use of fresh coriander, bread-based soups (*migas* and *açorda*) as well as the renowned Portuguese 'sweet-tooth' bear witness to the Moorish influence in Portuguese cuisine.[38]

The scarcity of primary evidence attesting the Moorish legacy should not be equated with its absence, in particular since the signs that substantiate it are still strongly embedded in language and everyday practices. Unlike Spain, Portugal does not have the equivalent of the *Anonymous Andalusian Cookbook* yet, as illustrated, the evidence of Moorish influence on cooking is still present and cannot be discounted.

José Saraiva and Alfredo Saramago assert that during and since the process of territorial Catholic *Reconquista* there was a conscious effort by Catholic hegemonic élites to erase any previous signs of the Arab presence in Portugal. Saraiva calls it 'cultural genocide' which methodically aimed to erase any cultural or religious evidence of the Muslim and Jewish traditions, a process that dramatically culminated in the Inquisition.[39] Ironically, and demonstrating the power of embedded cultural practices, the attempt to erase the totality of those vestiges failed. Ingrained oral traditions, tastes and preferences that resonate in the everyday practices of eating and cooking have lasted and still prevail in the twenty-first century, thus speaking more meaningfully than any written document or preserved artefact.

Let's return to our rhetorical question – where does the paper-thin wrapping of the *pastel de Tentúgal* sit in this continuum of narratives, evidence and speculation?

Is there any link between the layered bread of the nomadic Turks and the stretchable dough that the barefoot nuns skilfully and patiently pulled and tugged over the clean white sheets spread out on the floor? Are these two separate culinary moments in the culture of two geographically distant places and peoples? Are there any yet undiscovered links? Did the nuns learn about the technique used in the Topkapi Palace from books or travellers to the Middle or Far East? Or alternatively, did they revive a dormant practice from the previous presence of the Moors in Tentúgal? Is the pastry wrapping of the

Pastel de Tentúgal: Serendipity or Cultural Syncretism?

pastel de Tentúgal an act of serendipity or, is its similarity with those other wrappings that I have mentioned the result of cultural syncretism?

At this stage it is difficult to find a convincing answer to these questions. However, the specific techniques used in the making of the *pastel de Tentúgal*, in particular the stretching of the dough, need to be recognized because to my knowledge they are unique to Tentúgal. Nevertheless, as I have demonstrated, the wide geographic distribution of similar pastries needs to be investigated to substantively assert the place of the *pastel*'s wrapping in the narrative of paper-thin pastries.

Figure 6. *Final stages of shaping the pastel* (armar o pastel)
(Courtesy of Olga Cavaleiro – Confraria da Doçaria Conventual de Tentúgal)

Pastel de Tentúgal: Serendipity or Cultural Syncretism?

Notes

1. *Doçaria Conventual Portuguesa* (Portuguese Conventual Confectionery-Making) is a branch of traditional dessert-making, purportedly made only in female convents. It is usually rich in eggs, sugar and almonds.
2. Filo means leaf in Greek usually associated with 'a dough of many paper-thin layers separated by films of butter', *The Oxford Companion to Food*, ed. Alan Davidson (Oxford: Oxford University Press, 2006), p. 300.
3. With 'Borek the wrapper is… characteristically either filo or rough puff paste…the filling is usually savoury of meat or cheese, but sweet versions have been made throughout the pastry's recorded history" (Davidson, p. 91). For a comprehensive reading on *baklava* see Charles Perry, 'The Taste for Layered Bread Among the Nomadic Turks and the Central Asian Origins of Baklava', *A Taste of Thyme: Culinary Cultures of the Middle East*, eds. Sami Zubaida and Richard Tapper (London: Tauris Parke, 2001) and Davidson. According to Davidson, 'Bestilla is a round pie made with numerous layers of paper-thin pastry called *warqa* (leaf), inside which are separate layers of three different fillings, two savoury and one sweet' (p. 518). The most popular form of *briq* is known as *briq à l'oeuf* which is 'an egg cooked (by deep-frying) inside a triangle of paper-thin folded pastry (*warq*) perhaps with a little tuna added' (Davidson, p. 812).
4. Strudel is an Austrian pastry made with paper-thin pastry and filling of apples; *Banitsa* is a Bulgarian creation of 'paper-thin pastry-wrapped around a cheese filling which is often served with coffee', M. and F. Field, *A Quintet of Cuisines* (Time-Life International, 1972), p. 142.
5. P. Brooker, *A Concise Glossary of Cultural Theory* (London: Arnold, 1999), p. 91; J.N. Pieterse, 'Globalization as Hybridization', *Global Modernities*, eds. Mike Featherstone, Scott Lash and Roland Robertson (London: Sage, 1995), p. 55. Pieterse refers to syncretism as the 'methodology of montage and collage' (p. 55), and Brooker defines the term as 'a combination of kinds or styles' (p. 106).
6. Clive Seal defines 'gatekeeper' as the 'sponsors, officials and significant others who have the power to grant or block access to and within a setting' (*Researching Society and Culture* (London: Sage Publications, 1999), p. 221). I name the *Associação dos Pasteleiros de Tentúgal* (APT – Tentúgal's Pastry Makers Association) and the *Confraria dos Pasteis Conventurais de Tentúgal* (CPCT) – *Pastel de Tentúgal*'s gatekeepers. The *Nossa Senhora da Natividade* convent was founded in 1565 in the village of Tentúgal by the Carmelite nuns.
7. M.A. Goes, *Doçaria Tradicional do Alentejo* (Sintra: Colares Editora, 2002); J.H. Saraiva, *História Concisa de Portugal* (Mira-Sintra, publicações Europa-América, 1979). Cardeal D. Henrique died without a direct heir to the throne. In 1580 the Spanish monarch Filipe II was elected king. Portugal and Spain became a political entity until 1640. Unless otherwise noted, all translations are the author's.
8. Coimbra University Archives (AUC), *Livro de Sentenças e Aforamentos*, doc. no. 6, p. 5, 1569–1592: http://apTentúgal.com.sapo.pt/convento.html (accessed 1-05-2012).
9. Goes and A. Saramago, *Cozinha Algarvia. Enquadramento Histórico e Receitas* (Lisboa: Assírio & Alvim, 2003).
10. Goes, pp. 20–21.
11. Goes, p. 14.
12. Saramago.
13. Goes.
14. Saramago.
15. The Arabs had brought sugar cane to the Iberian Peninsula. There were some plantations in the Algarve but the plantations in Madeira were enough to produce enough sugar for local production and export (Goes, p. 12).
16. Goes.
17. *Ovos moles* are a filling made with sugar syrup cooked to reach 108 °C and to which egg yolks are added.

18. S. Carvalho, '*Levantamento Histórico do Pastel de Tentúgal*', *Revista Monte Mai* (Montemor-o-Velho em Colaboração com o Arquivo da Universidade de Coimbra, 2007).
19. Carvalho.
20. Protected Geographic Indication (PGI) is a programme instituted by the European Union to register certain foods and agricultural products.
21. *Pastel de Tentúgal – IGP*: http://www.gpp.pt/Valor/CE_pastel_Tentúgal_Jan12.pdf, p. 5.
22. The document's technical specifications include flour: 'wheat type 55 or 45' (p. 5); egg yolks: 'category A, Class Land'. The yolk's specifications include colour characteristics 'between 12 and 14 in the Roche scale'.
23. *Pastel de Tentúgal – IGP*, p. 11.
24. *Pastel de Tentúgal – IGP*, p. 11.
25. Field and Field, p. 144 and Davidson, p. 838; Field and Field, p. 184 and Davidson, p. 838.
26. The *Anonymous Andalusian Cookbook* was compiled by a scribe in the 1400s borrowing directly from several well-known cookbooks. One is usually referred to as al-Baghdadi (AD 1239) yet some of the recipes are recognized as being authored by gastronome Abu Ishaq Ibrahim ibn al-Mahdi (779–839). This book has been translated into English by Charles Perry and is available at http://italophiles.com/andalusian_cookbook.pdf. See p. 33 and p. 147.
27. Field and Field, p. 142.
28. J. Wechsberg, *The Cooking of the Vienna's Empire*, Time-Life International, 1978, p. 176.
29. Perry and Davidson.
30. Perry, p. 91.
31. Moors refer to Northern African populations and connotes the word's etymological link to Mauritania (Blackmore, p. 29). They were converted to Islam after the Arab territorial invasion of North Africa. In 711 they invaded the Iberian Peninsula.
32. Saraiva, p. 34.
33. Carvalho; Saraiva. *Mozarab* is a Christian living in territories under Moorish jurisdiction. A *Mozareb* has kept his/her religious affiliation but is completely integrated in the Moorish cultural lifestyle (Saraiva, p. 76).
34. Saraiva, p. 43.
35. Saraiva, p. 34. Coimbra is located 20 kilometres from Tentúgal.
36. J.P. Lima Reis, *Algumas Notas Históricas para a História da Alimantação em Portugal* (Porto Lima-Reis: Campo de Letras, 2008), p. 35; Saraiva, p. 34.
37. Moors recognized by introducing sugar cane, rice, buckwheat (*Fagopyrum esculentum*), olive and almond trees as well as new fruits and vegetables such as eggplant, oranges, lemons, almonds, pomegranate and lentils (Lima-Reis, p. 38).
38. Lima-Reis, p. 39. My research includes interviews with Portuguese chefs Unanimously they acknowledged wide use of fresh coriander in southern cuisine as a Moorish legacy. Lima-Reis signals that the Moors made soups with bread and called them *ath-thorde* (*açorda* in Portugues). Davidson also refers to *shorba* as the word for soup in most Islamic countries and *çorba* in Turkey (Davidson, p. 719). *Livro de Cozinha da Infanta D. Maria* (fifteenth century) is recognized as the first Portuguese collection of manuscripts containing recipes. Recipes for *almojavenas* and *alfitetes* (p. 18 and p. 78) share a recognized Arab legacy.
39. Saraiva, pp. 79, 78.

The Haggis

Adam Balic

The haggis addressed

For over two centuries, the poetry and life of the eighteenth-century Scottish poet Robert Burns has been celebrated in Scotland and around the world as a *de facto* Scottish National Day on 25 January. The day concludes with the traditional Burns' Supper, which can be a casual gathering of friends and family or a much more formal occasion. In its most evolved form, a key part of the Burns' Supper involves the ritual procession and presentation of a large haggis to the assembled crowd (Figure 1), followed by a recital of Burns' address *To a Haggis*:

> Fair fa' your honest, sonsie face,
> Great Chieftain o' the Puddin-race!
> Aboon them a' ye tak your place,
> Painch, tripe, or thairm:
> Weel are ye wordy of a *grace*
> As lang's my arm.
>
> The groaning trencher there ye fill,
> Your hudies like a distant hill,
> Your *pin* wad help to mend a mill
> In time o' need,
> While thro' your pores the dews distil
> Like amber bead.
>
> His knife see Rustic-labour dight,
> An' cut ye up wi' ready slight,
> Trenching your gushing entrails bright,
> Like onie ditch;
> And then, O what a glorious sight,
> Warm-reeking, rich!
>
> Then horn for horn, they stretch an' strive:
> Deil tak the hindmost, on they drive,
> Till a' their weel-swall'd kytes belyve
> Are bent like drums;
> Then auld Guidman, maist like to rive,
> *Bethankit!* hums.

The Haggis

Is there that owre his French *ragout*,
Or *olio* that wad staw a sow,
Or *fricassee* wad mak her spew
Wi perfect sconner,
Looks down wi' sneering, scornfu' view
On sic a dinner?

Poor devil! see him owre his trash,
As feckless as a wither'd rash,
His spindle shank a guid whip-lash,
His nieve a nit;
Tho' bluidy flood or field to dash,
O how unfit.

But mark the Rustic, *haggis-fed*,
The trembling earth resounds his tread,
Clap in his walie nieve a blade,
He'll make it whistle;
An' legs, an' arms, an' heads will sned
Like taps o' thrissle.

Ye pow'rs, wha mak mankind your care,
And dish them out their bill o' fare,
Auld Scotland wants nae skinking ware,
That jaups in luggies;
But if ye wish her gratfu' prayer,
Gie her a Haggis![1]

After the poem's recital, the haggis is formally toasted, and then, finally, the haggis is eaten. The haggis is typically accompanied by whisky, mashed potatoes and 'neeps' (*Brassica napus* var. *napobrassica*, Swedish turnip or rutabaga). The Burns' Supper can be formal and serious, mock-heroic or simply a fun night for all involved. Whatever the case, Burns' Night is an important part of Scottish culture, both within Scotland and in the larger Scottish diaspora, with the haggis featuring as both an object of adoration and ribaldry.

So what exactly is this haggis so central to this celebration of Scottish identity? The standard definition is that it is a savoury pudding made of a sheep's stomach stuffed with the minced heart, liver, lungs, onions, oatmeal, suet and spices. Hence, for many, the haggis perfectly encapsulates the idea of egalitarianism and unapologetic dietary economy; in short, a food of thrift and virtue. A near-perfect cultural icon, some would say. However, as an example of national identity the haggis can be more difficult to swallow. Oliver Thring has argued that, while haggis is enjoyable enough, it is 'a mean old tribute to such a rich array' of Scottish food, and that '[t]he Scots have rejected haggis in their millions'.[2] Furthermore, Nigel Slater states that he has 'met many a Scot who wouldn't touch what has become their national dish, insisting that it is actually just a joke on tourists'.[3] While some Scots might support this view that the haggis is not the sum of modern Scottish identity, in my own experience there seems no evidence of it being either rejected or treated as a joke. Far from it: haggis is made in vast quantities from the artisanal to the industrial scale; it is served at school dinners, work canteens, fast food shops and restaurants. It is a topping for pizza, artfully crafted into towering ziggurats in restaurants, stuffed into wontons and pakora, used as a flavouring for potato chips and, most recently, encased in Polish breads. How did the haggis become a regional food item in Scotland, and why does it elicit such a wide range of opinions regarding its worthiness both as a food item and as a cultural icon? This paper will attempt to answer this question by tracing the developmental history and social context of the haggis from the medieval period to the present.

What is a haggis?

The *Oxford English Dictionary* (*OED*) defines haggis as 'A dish consisting of the heart, lungs, and liver of a sheep, calf, etc. (or sometimes of the tripe and chitterlings), minced with suet and oatmeal, seasoned with salt, pepper, onions, etc., and boiled like a large sausage in the maw of the animal.' Although the *OED*'s definition of haggis is generally correct, it does not address the changes that have occurred in this dish within the last fifty years, nor does it give an indication of the regional variation that is present in the extant range of haggis produced throughout Scotland. One of the major changes that have occurred within the last fifty years is that haggis is now rarely, if ever, made in a sheep's stomach. The haggis stuffing is encased in either a synthetic casing or an ox bung (a prepared bovine caecum, generally used for large diameter sausages). Interestingly, when interviewed for this paper, most of the Scottish people I spoke to seemed to be largely unaware that the haggis was now made without a sheep stomach casing, an indication of how central this idea is to the concept of the haggis. There is also little appreciation of how much regional variation there is in Scottish haggis production. Having sampled haggis from the Islands, Highlands, Lowlands and cities of Scotland, it is clear that there is a wide range in the composition, appearance and taste of Scottish haggis. So how did this ball of offal and oats become Scotland's national dish?

The early history of the haggis

Popular histories of the haggis often mention other similar, ancient and outlandish sausages, such as the Roman stuffed sow womb or the ancient Greek roasted, stuffed sheep stomach.[4] There may even be descriptions of other quasi-haggis dishes such as Catalan/Aragonese *chireta*; Cajun *chaudin*; Swedish *pölsa*; German *Knipp, Stippgrütze* and *Saumagen*; Cincinnati *goetta*; Lebanese *ghammeh*; Persian *gippa*; Icelandic *slátur*; Norwegian *lungemos*; Faroese *garnatálg*; and Lithuanian *kepenin*. In fact this is only a tiny selection from a huge number of haggis-like dishes. However, this similarity does not mean that these other dishes are related developmentally to the haggis. While it is true that food items which are prepared using the same ingredients and/or culinary technique often have a shared history of development, this is not necessarily the case, and there is no evidence that the Scottish haggis is directly related to any of these dishes. The Romans did not invent the haggis, and there is no evidence that the Norse introduced the haggis to Scotland and England.

Based on available evidence, the earliest clear references to haggis come from thirteenth-century English sources. These occur as a limited number of Anglo-Norman glosses in Latin texts and in one instance within the main text of an Anglo-Norman manuscript.

Glosses to *The Satires of Persius*:
tucetaque: hacys[5]
tuceta: pudding, hagiz[6]

Glosses to *De Nominibus Utensilium* of Alexander Neckam:
tuscetis: agys[7]
tu(n)cetis: bodeyns[8]

Figure 1. Piping in the haggis. Burns' Night celebrations in Scotland during the 1930's.

*tu(n)cetis: puddingis*⁹
*tu(n)cetis:de puudincques*¹⁰

Walter de Bibbesworth *Le Tretiz*,
'*estrere le hagis del postnez*' ('take the haggis out of the pot').¹¹

While the appearance of haggis in these Anglo-Norman glosses and *Le Tretiz* suggests that the term would be familiar to a French speaker, it does not necessarily mean that the word origin (or dish origin for that matter) is French. It could also represent an Anglo-Saxon language influence on the insular French spoken by the elite classes in thirteenth-century England. There are several Anglo-Saxon glosses of Latin texts in the tenth century that potentially refer to a haggis-type pudding:

Farcimen: Gehæcca oððe mearhæccel
Isica: mærhgehæc, mearhhæccel
Lucanica: mærh ¹²

In this case the glosses are variations on the combination of the Anglo-Saxon terms '*mearh*' (sausage/pudding) and '*haccian*' (to hack). The *OED* refutes the French origin of the term 'haggis', suggesting that its etymology is 'unknown' and that*:*

> The analogy of most terms of cookery suggests a French source; but no corresp. French word or form has been found. The conjecture that it represents French *hachis* 'hash', with assimilation to *hag*, *hack*, to chop, has apparently no basis of fact; French *hachis* is not known so early, and the earlier forms of the English word are more remote from it. Whether the word is connected with *hag* vb., evidence does not show.

However, this entry is now rather out of date. In an early French medieval cookery text dated to *c.*1300, the instructions for the chopping of ingredients for a stuffing is followed by '*Puis hagiez tout*' ('Then hack/chop it all').¹³ The verb *Hacher* in fact dates to around 1225.¹⁴ So there is some evidence to suggest a continental French origin for the term haggis independent of Anglo-Saxon influences.

In summary, the first definite references to a class of sausage/pudding as 'haggis' appear in thirteenth-century Anglo-Norman texts, with a possible derivation from continental French terms that describe the preparation of the ingredients as a hash. There are earlier Anglo-Saxon terms that also perhaps describe a similar sausage/pudding of hacked ingredients, and these terms potentially influenced the formation of the thirteenth-century Anglo-Norman terms. As there is no continuity between the Anglo-Saxon hacked sausage references and the first Anglo-Norman reference to haggis, it is not yet clear if this is the case.

Even less clear is what these early haggis were actually like. These early references do give us some information on the nature of these early haggis. There are thirteenth-century Anglo-Norman glosses for the Latin terms for sausage/pudding (*hirna* and *hilia* for example) that consist of variations on the words 'sausage', 'pudding' or *andouille*, but never 'haggis'. This indicates that 'haggis' was not a general term for pudding/sausage in the thirteenth century and that it represented either a distinct type of sausage/pudding or a regional term for a sausage/pudding. The earliest detailed descriptions of haggis preparation and ingredients come from the manuscript recipe collections of the fifteenth century.

Early haggis recipe descriptions

> For hagese
> *The hert of schepe, the nere thou take,*
> *The bowel not thou shalle forsake,*
> *On the turbilen made, and boyled wele,*
> *Hacke alle togeder with good persole;*
> *Isop, saveray, thou shall take then,*
> *And suet of schepe take in, I ken,*
> *With powder of peper and eggs gode wonne,*
> *And seethe hit wele and serve hit thenne;*
> *Loke hit be saltyd for gode menne.*
> *In wyntur tyme when erbs ben gode,*
> *Take powder of hom I wot in dede,*
> *As saveray, mynt anf tyme, fulle gode,*
> *Isop and sauge I owt by the rode.*[15]
>
> Hagws of a schepe
> *Take þe Roppis with þe talour, & parboyle hem; þan hakke hem smal; grynd pepir, & Safroun, & brede, & ʒolkys of Eyrour, & Raw kreme or swete Mylke: do al to-gederys, & do in þe grete wombe of þe Schepe, þat is, the mawe; & þan seþe hym an serue forth ynne.*[16]

There are some clear differences between these two recipes. In the first recipe, it seems unclear whether the haggis is intended as a stuffing or simply a hash, and there is also no mention of a grain or bread component. This latter ingredient does appear in the second recipe, as it does in the majority of recipes published from the sixteenth century to the present. However, comparing these early descriptions of haggis reveals some key similarities. In both cases, there are instructions to hack up sheep offal as a main ingredient, season the mixture with spices and bind it with eggs. Further evidence that they represent a distinct class of sausage/pudding is indicated by the fact that, during the fourteenth and fifteenth centuries, a number of similar stuffed stomach sausage/pudding recipes appeared that were not referred to as 'haggis' even when they appeared in recipe collections with haggis recipes. The 'haggis' is clearly identified as a specific class of sausage/pudding in these early English recipe collections rather than a generic term for 'something stuffed into a stomach'.

The Haggis

By the sixteenth century, haggis recipes were relatively common in English cookery books, with published recipes persisting into the late seventeenth century. Recipes for haggis were also represented in English manuscript recipe collections of the seventeenth and eighteenth centuries. Regional variations on the haggis were found in England (especially the north) until the nineteenth century. Again these haggis recipes contain minced offal. However, close examination of these English recipes indicates that the definition of 'haggis' is not necessarily consistent:

For to make the Hagges.
Take the mawe and wasshe hit clene and let him soke in water also, & the guttes of the same dere and slytte them faire and scrape them clene & washe them clene and let them lie in water all a night, or els as longe as ye maye, and then caste them into a faire potte with brothe freshe, and cast ther to a quatite of Noumbleis, some of the herte, and some of the kidnes & a great quantite of suette for to make them fate Inough, & when that it is bolied al together Inough, then ley them vpon a fayre borde, & cast ther|to fayre gratid brede and perseley feayre picked and a litel saueren and time & faire yelkes of Egges aboute, vi. or vii. in on, and the powther of Peper and safron but not to moche, lete them haue sum what a browne cullor, and then take. ii. knifis and hewe them small, and then take the Hagges gut that I spake of before and putte the same stuffe therin, but fyll him not to full for he wyl swel, pricke him, close him and caste in a potte and gefe him a boyle, and let him soke a while, & take him vp & ley him in a disshe and cute of the grette ende that is pricked, & loke that he be fatte Inough with in him selfe, & cast brothe aboute him and serue him forth for a good Hagges.[17]

To make a Haggesse Pudding
Take a fat Haggesse; perboil it wel, take out the Kernels, shred it smal, and temper it with a handful or two of grated Manchet, then take three or four Eggs wel beaten, Rosewater and Sugar, Cloves, Nutmegs, Cinnamon, Mace, very finely beaten, Currans and Marrow good store, temper them all together, with a fit quantity of Cream, being first moderately seasoned with Salt.[18]

To make Haggus-puddings
Take a Calves Chaldron, being well scoured and parboiled, and when it is cold mince it very small; then take four or five Eggs, and leave out halfe the whites, and take thick Creame, grated Bread, Sugar, Nutmeg, Salt Currans and Rosewater, and (if you will) Sweet-majerome, Thyme and Parsley; mix it well together: then having a Sheeps Maw ready dressed, put it in, and boyle it a little: remember Suet or Marrow.[19]

To make a Haggis Pudding
Take your Haggis or Calves ginne clean scowred and watered, and parboyl it well; then take out the Kernels, and chop it fine; season it with salt, Sugar and

beaten spice; then put to it a little Cream, and ten or twelve yolks of Eggs, as much grated bread, a few minced Dates and plumped Currans, and so fill your skins, and boyl them carefully.[20]

In the fifteenth century, there were also haggis recipes without any offal at all. This may indicate a figurative use of 'haggis', either because these meatless haggis consisted of hacked ingredients or because the finished dish resembled a haggis in appearance. Either case indicates that the haggis was a recognizable enough class of food to be imitated. What is interesting about these English haggis pudding recipes is that while the stuffing ingredients are all very similar, the way in which the 'haggis' is used differs between recipes. In fact there are two broad classes of haggis recipes. In the first category, the haggis pudding consists of the haggis (defined as the maw, most likely the rumen stomach) stuffed with other offal, especially the intestines. However, in the second class of recipes the haggis is not used as the casing, but is finely minced and used as a stuffing ingredient itself. So a 'haggis' pudding is really a description of a pudding that includes a haggis (stomach) either as a casing or as a stuffing ingredient, not a description of a stuffed stomach dish *per se*.

Scotland and the haggis

The earliest Scottish references to haggis date from the beginning of the sixteenth century, which postdates English references by several hundred years.[21] One consequence of this late appearance is the surprising claim that 'the jury is still out on whether this dish is authentically, verifiably Scottish'.[22] This has resulted in some negative responses in Scotland, as might be expected.[23] Given the facts that vast quantities of haggis are consumed in Scotland, that it is perceived as a national dish both within and outside Scotland and that these haggis-related activities are largely restricted to Scotland, one could be forgiven for thinking that it is an authentic Scottish dish.

Unfortunately, there is a tendency to equate primacy of historical records of a particular dish with 'authenticity'. 'Authenticity' is a dangerously nebulous concept beyond the scope of this paper; however it should be noted that while early records of a particular dish establish *termini post quem*, they do not tell us anything about the history of a particular dish before this date.[24] Between 1500 and 1790 at least 188 new and 426 reprinted cookery books were published in England; during the same period in Scotland less then twenty cookery books were produced.[25] We simply cannot tell if haggis was made and eaten in Scotland for as long as it was in England because of this unequal weight in the two countries' historical documents.

With this disparity in mind, what do we know about the earliest history of haggis in Scotland, what was it like and who ate it? Historically, the haggis has been assumed to be a food of the poor. A haggis is a way of using offal, after all, and offal is a dish of the poor. The problem with this assumption is that to make a haggis you need a sheep. Sheep, in general, are not owned by the poor, and even their offal was sold, not given away. Another issue is the size of the haggis: an adult sheep rumen can hold up to seven litres, which would make an enormous pudding.[26] I have made several haggis in the much smaller rumen stomach obtained from a six-month-old lamb; these produce a haggis of approximately 1.5 kg, enough for a family. I have great doubts that the haggis was ever a regular feature of diet for the poor. It seems more likely that it was eaten in wealthier households, which either owned sheep or could afford to buy them, and had large households to feed. There are historical documents to support this idea. The daily menu from Dunrobin Castle between 22 August and 9 November 1703 lists haggis on the menu twenty-eight times, only once mentioned as being 'for servants'.[27] In contrast, the records of Ochtertyre House between 22 January 1737 and 16 February 1738 list haggis thirty-five times with every instance specified as being 'for servants'.[28] It seems that haggis is a far more egalitarian dish than commonly realized, with its status on the table differing from estate to estate.

In terms of what these early Scottish haggis were like, recipes in early eighteenth-century Scottish manuscript recipe collections are very similar or identical to those published in England during the seventeenth and eighteenth centuries. The first Scottish recipe for haggis, Susanna MacIver's, was not published until 1773, and it is for

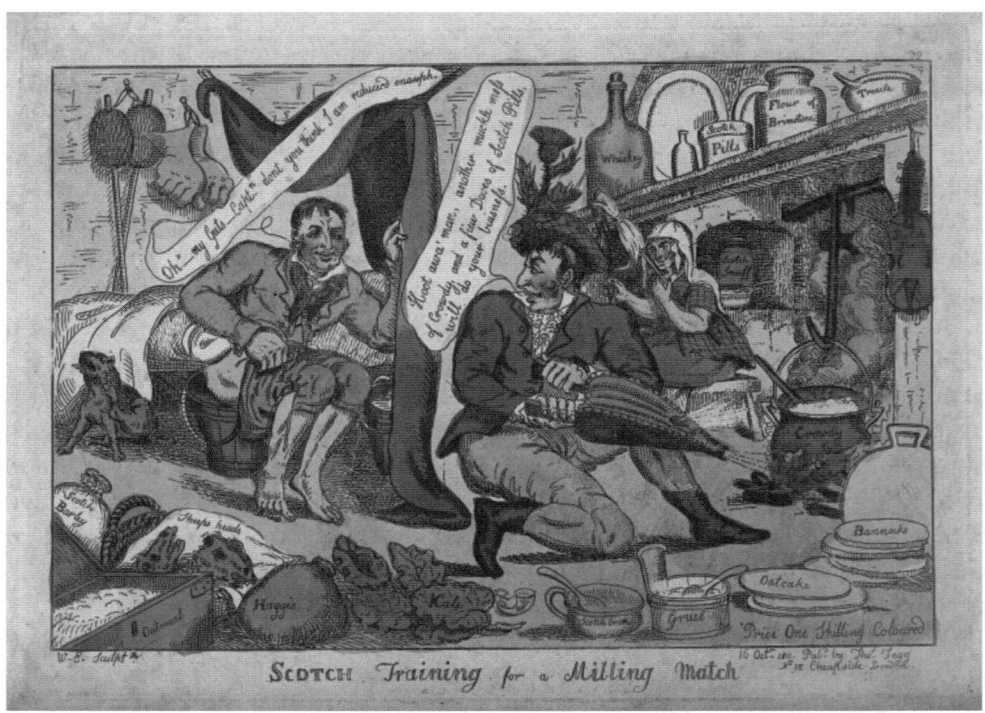

Figure 2. Some early nineteenth-century views on the Scottish and their foods. (Wellcome Library no. 12206i.)

a significantly different style of haggis. Gone are the breadcrumbs, eggs, cream, herbs and dried fruit of the earlier recipes:

> *A Good Scotch Haggies*
> Make the haggis-bag perfectly clean, parboil the draught; boil the liver very well, so as it will grate; dry the meal before the fire; mince the draught and a pretty large piece of beef very small; grate about half of the liver; mince plenty of the suet and some onions small; mix all these materials very well together, with a handful or two of the dried meal; spread them on the table, and season them properly with salt and mixed spices; take any of the scraps of beef that are left from mincing, and some of the water that boiled the draught, and make about a choppin of good stock of it ; then put all the haggis meat into the bag, and that broth in it; then sew up the bag: but be sure to put out all the wind before you sew it quite close. If you think the bag is thin, you may put it in a cloth. If it is a large haggis, it will take at least two hours' boiling.[29]

Over two hundred years later this remains the archetypical Scottish haggis recipe. While some variation exists in extant haggis recipes, most recipes show little change from the basic elements here.

Interestingly this is not the only recipe for a 'Scottish haggis' to appear at this time: several 'Scottish Haggis' recipes were also published in English cookery books. Within a century haggis had gone from a dish eaten throughout the British Isles to a Scottish regional dish. If the haggis was known in England since at least the thirteenth century, why is the dish suddenly identified with Scotland? There is often an assumption made that regional foods develop in situ; however in many cases food regionality results from restricting the range of a product that had been more widely made. In this respect, regional food could be interpreted as an example of cultural inertia, and potentially this is the case for haggis.

Regardless of this, by the end of the eighteenth century the haggis was firmly established as a symbol of Scottish vulgarity and barbarism (Figure 2), and in turn reclaimed by the Scottish as an icon of Scottish egalitarianism, economy and rustic virtue.

In 1773 the Edinburgh poet Robert Fergusson criticized the principles of St. Andrews University for their lavish treatment of the outspoken critic of all things Scottish, Samuel Johnson, by suggesting they should have presented Johnson with a real Scottish meal, and in this case a real Scottish meal means haggis for first course:

> Imprimis, then, a haggis fat,
> Weel tottl'd in a seything pat,
> Wi' spice an ingans weel ca'd thro',
> Had help'd to guft the stirrah's mow,
> An' plac'd itsell in truncher clean
> Before the gilpy's glowrin een.[32]

The Haggis

Fergusson's use of the haggis to portray the Scots joined its characterization in the poems of Allan Ramsay, who shows the haggis as an example of honest, rugged Scottishness, to influence Robert Burns in his production of the most famous haggis poem of all time, his address 'To a Haggis'. Burns' poem has a simple message: Don't like us? Don't like our haggis? Well too bad for you.

After this watershed, there was no going back: there was so much momentum generated around the haggis as an icon of Scottish identity that all opposition was swept aside. From the early nineteenth century, hearing the word 'haggis' triggered thoughts of Scotland. As the 'vulgar barbarism' of the Scottish became romanticized and idealized, all things Scottish, including the haggis, became popular. Finally, after centuries of being the prime example of the untrustworthy neighbour, the Scots were in vogue with the English. This popularity continued throughout the nineteenth century, when all things Scottish – or at least a pastiche of traditional Highland culture and romantic medievalism – became fashionable. What more fitting dish than the haggis for a Highland Tour?

MacIver's 1773 haggis recipe was copied in cookbook after cookbook throughout the nineteenth and into the twentieth centuries. During this period not only was the totality of the English history of the haggis largely forgotten, but so too was general use of haggis on Scottish estates to feed servant and master alike. Its iconic status as a virtuous food of the common Scotsman overshadowed its known history. At the present time, although a whiff of the cultural icon still surrounds the haggis, by and large it is eaten and enjoyed on a daily basis by thousands of Scots who do not give a second thought to its role as a national dish or its seven-hundred-year history in the British Isles. It is a delicious food item in its own right, and its continuing popularity does not have to be justified or explained by its role as cultural icon. Perhaps this is the best position to be in for the continued survival of any regional food item.

Notes

1. Robert Burns, *Poems, Chiefly in the Scottish Dialect* (Edinburgh: William Creech, 1793), p. 61.
2. Oliver Thring, 'Consider Haggis', *The Guardian* 25 January 2011: http://www.guardian.co.uk/lifeand-style/wordofmouth/2011/jan/25/consider-haggis.
3. Nigel Slater, *Eating for England: The Delights and Eccentricities of the British at Table* (London: HarperCollins, 2007), p. 203.
4. 'Haggis', *Wikipedia*: http://en.wikipedia.org/wiki/Haggis (accessed May 29, 2012).
5. MS British Library, Harley 4967; f.140v., qtd. Tony Hunt, *Teaching & Learning Latin in 13th-Century England* (Cambridge, D.S. Brewer 1991), pp. Vi–iii.
6. MS Cambridge, Trinity College R.3.18, ff. 45–54v., qtd. Hunt.
7. MS Worcester Cathedral Chapter Library q.50 ff.28ra., qtd. Hunt.
8. Cambridge, Gonville and Caius College 136 pp. 3–20., qtd. Hunt.
9. Dublin, Trinity College 270 ff.157r–169v., qtd. Hunt.
10. Lincoln Cathedral Chapter Library 132 ff.36vb–51ra., qtd. Hunt.
11. Walter de Bibbesworth, *Le Tretiz*, ed. William Rothwell (London: Anglo-Norman Text Society, 1990), p. 27.
12. MS. British Library, Cotton, Cleopatra A iii.
13. *Enseingnemenz qui enseignent a apareillier toutes manieres de viandes*, ed. G. Lozinski, *La bataille de caresme et de charnage*, édition critique avec introduction et glossaire (Lutetiae 1933), pp. 181–87.
14. William Sayer, 'The Genealogy of Haggis', *Miscelénea* 39 (2009), pp. 103–110.
15. Richard Morris, *Liber cure cocorum: Copied and edited from the Sloane MS. 1986* (Berlin: A. Asher & Co., 1862), pp. 52–53.
16. *Two fifteenth-century cookery-books: Harleian MS. 279 (ab 1430), & Harl. MS. 4016 (ab. 1450), with extracts from Ashmole MS. 1439, Laud MS. 553, & Douce MS. 55*, ed. Thomas Austin (London: Early English Text Society, 1888), p. 39.
17. John Lacy, *wyl bucke his testament* (London: Wyllam Copland, 1560), pp. 4–5.
18. *The Ladies Cabinet Enlarged and Opened* (London, printed by T.M. for M.G. Bedell and T. Collins, 1654), p. 206.
19. Joseph Cooper, *The Art of Cookery Refined and Augmented* (London: R. Lowndes, 1654), p. 139.
20. Hannah Woolley, *The Cook's Guide: or, Rare Receipts for Cookery* (London, peter Dring, 1664), p. 42.
21. *The Makars*, ed. J.A. Tasioulas (Edinburgh: Cannogate Books, 1999), p. 344.
22. Thring.
23. 'Haggis Is English, Historian Says', BBC: http://news.bbc.co.uk/1/hi/8180791.stm (accessed May 29, 2012).
24. Walter de Bibbesworth.
25. Gilly Lehmann, *The British Housewife* (Totnes, Prospect Books, 2003), p. 383.
26. D.B. Purser and R.J. Moir 'Rumen Volume as a Factor Involved in Individual Sheep Differences', *Journal of Animal Science* 25 (1956), pp. 509–15.
27. National Library of Scotland, Manuscript Dep. 313/555
28. National Library of Scotland, Manuscript MS.21106
29. Susanna MacIver, *Cookery and Pastry* (Edinburgh: [n. pub.], 1773), p. 63.
30. Robert Fergusson, *Selected Poems*, ed. James Robertson (Edinburgh, polygon, 2007), p. 165.

Lasagna: A Layered History

Anthony F. Buccini

A Pasquëta, 'na bonn-a lasagnata a l'é consueta.

Genoese Proverb

Introduction[1]

In 2003, there appeared a news story in Britain which reported the alleged discovery of the true English origins of lasagna, citing the recipe for *los(e)yns* from *The Forme of Cury* as indisputable proof.[2] Though one suspects (and hopes) that the claim that lasagna is English in origin was made with tongue in cheek, given the ample, earlier attestations of the word 'lasagna' and evidence for the dish in Italian sources, there is a body of scholarly work about the history of pasta in general and of lasagna in particular that argues they are to be attributed in the first place not to the Italians but to the Arabs. In the general case of pasta, the arguments that have been adduced are complex and involve various kinds of evidence, from the palaeoethnobotanical to textual to linguistic, but for many food scholars, the claim of Arab origins has been limited to the invention of dry pasta made from durum wheat, while the origins of fresh pasta have generally been felt to be murkier and likely more diffuse; nonetheless, some food historians, such as Clifford Wright (e.g. 1996–1997), are clearly inclined to attribute all early forms of pasta, including lasagna, to the Arabs.

Evidence for the putative Arab origins of lasagna is largely limited to an etymological assertion, namely, that 'lasagna' comes from the name of an almond paste confection known in Arabic as *lawzīnağ*. Beyond that, the claim rests for the most part on the merits of the broader theory that pasta is of Arab origin.

In this paper, I examine the etymologies of the word 'lasagna' that have thus far been proposed and demonstrate that they are all unsatisfactory: the etymologies offered and championed by food historians have paid little or no heed to the historical linguistic issues involved in producing a plausible etymology. The linguistic evidence and the earliest textual and culinary evidence, taken together and viewed against the backdrop of the political and socioeconomic history of the western Mediterranean in the late Middle Ages, provide us with the clues needed to reconstruct an interesting and complex path of the dish's development. This path starts in southern Italy but crucially involves a journey across the Tyrrhenian Sea to Genoa and the regions of Liguria and Provence, a return voyage back to southern Italy, as well as a spread throughout central and northern Italy and ultimately back to Provence, northern France and beyond. It is, moreover, a path that involves travel across social space, starting with humble origins but then moving to the very highest layer of society, only gradually to find its place with all levels of society in Italy. What is conspicuously absent throughout the early history of lasagna is any evidence of Arab involvement.

Preliminaries

In recent decades, lasagna has become enormously popular outside of Italy, particularly in the United States and Britain, but in the process the dish has been changed in a number of ways, rendering the versions known in the Anglophone world fundamentally different from those of Italy. The following points need therefore to be made before we proceed.

First, we note that, in referring to baked versions of the dish, regional usage in Italy favours the plural form *lasagne* in the north and the singular form *lasagna* in the south; from the former usage stems the British use of 'lasagne' and from the latter the American 'lasagna'. Neither usage can be considered 'more correct', though, depending on one's cultural prejudices, one may think one or the other superior for entirely irrational reasons.

Also to be noted is the fact that, whereas outside of Italy lasagna-type noodles appear almost exclusively in stuffed and baked form, within Italy there are regionally non-baked applications of such noodles, served with a simple condiment as a *pasta asciutta* dish or appearing in a soupy (*minestra*) form. In addition, Italian usage of the word operates at two levels, one with a more specific sense akin to that known outside of Italy and another, more general sense, referring to noodles that are flat, broad and thin but not necessarily to a specific shape, i.e., square, rectangular, etc. In this sense of the word, it is perfectly reasonable to speak of 'round lasagne', as when Ratto & Ratto (2003 [1863]: 80) describe the Genoese pasta *corzetti stampati* as a 'specie di lasagne tonde'. In effect then, the word can overlap with the term *sfoglia*, a sheet of rolled-out dough, from which various pasta shapes can be cut, as well as for a range of cuts made from such a pasta sheet, but then also serves as an overarching term for shapes that are felt to be related – *lasagnone, lasagnette,* the *sagne* of Adriatic regions, and the *lagane* of the continental south.

Regarding the method of producing these noodles, considerable regional variation obtains, though in general these are traditionally fresh products which tend to be made more often in the north with soft wheat flour and eggs and more often in the south with durum wheat flour and water. Commercially manufactured dry noodles are, of course, used nowadays but in Italy are still not the norm, as they are in other countries where lasagna is popular. And in this regard we come to an important point about the status of the dish, especially in its stuffed and baked forms: whereas in the United States and Britain, it is a dish consumed relatively frequently by many people, it is in Italy a dish that remains special, closely linked to specific holiday meals, and otherwise it is seldom or not at all consumed. In other words, for the broader population of Italy the dish has deep contextual meaning in the overall culinary repertoire and in the culinary calendar.

Earliest Attestations

In seeking the origins of lasagna it makes sense *prima facie* to look to Italy not only because it is that country whence in modern times the dish has clearly diffused into other countries but also because all of the earliest attestations of the word 'lasagna' are found in texts written in Italy. Indeed, a century and more before the recipe which was recently claimed to prove the dish's English origin was composed, probably around 1390 (Hiett & Butler 1985: 24), there had already appeared in Italy numerous references to the dish in various kinds of texts, including a cookbook. 'Lasagna' or 'lasagne' are mentioned in poems by the Umbrian Jacopone Da Todi (1230–1306) and the Senese Cecco Angiolieri (1257–1312), in a chronicle by the Parmesan Salimbene di Adam (1221–c.1290) and also once in poetic marginal notes on legal records of the city of Bologna, the *Memoriali bolognesi*, for the year 1282.

Besides these references to the dish, which are all occasionally cited in recent commentaries on the history of pasta, we find two other, neglected references. First, in one of the works by the 'Anonymous Genovese' poet, also known as Luchetto, there appears a clear mention of 'lasa[g]na' – rhyming with 'castagna' – as a food (Cocito ed. 1970: 304); this poem dates to around the end of the thirteenth century or just thereafter. Second, what is to my knowledge the earliest attestation of lasagna occurs in an etymological work on Latin, the *Derivationes*, written by Uguccione da Pisa and dating to the last quarter of the twelfth century, perhaps around 1180 (Cecchini ed. 2004: v. II 642). In the entry on the word 'lagos' (rabbit), Uguccione goes on also to discuss the seemingly related Latin 'laganum' (from Greek *laganon*) and in that context then mentions 'lasania'.

This word 'laganum(/laganon)' is well attested in classical sources, where it clearly indicates a dough product that is flat, broad and thin but it was either baked or, as several Greek and Latin texts indicate, often fried in oil, rather than boiled in the fashion of pasta as we know it. This matter of the method of cooking has led some scholars, most notably Grocock and Grainger (2006: 349–50) to reject the idea that the laganum of classical times was already a sort of lasagna-noodle to be boiled and dressed or cooked in a *minestra*. But it must also be said that there is no doubt whatsoever that at some time in southern Italy, lagana did become exactly that, broad noodles, and though we cannot say precisely when the treatment of lagana as 'pasta' began, there are good indications that it was long ago and, *pace* the cautionary observations of Perry (1981: 43) and Grocock and Grainger, quite possibly already in classical times. Certainly, the broad distribution of the term across the dialects of the continental Mezzogiorno, together with the fact that the dialectal reflexes of the word show a considerable amount of variation with regard to sound-shape in accordance with local phonological developments, bespeaks continuous active use of the term from classical times to today.[3]

Direct evidence for the manner of cooking employed in the preparation of southern Italian *lagane* is lacking before recent times, but looking at the evidence starting in the nineteenth century, when scholarly interest first turned to the underclasses of southern

Italy and popular descriptions of regional foodways also find their way into print, the term 'lagane' appears as the regional name for fresh broad noodles which are used in both sauced and soupy preparations, most famously in combination with chick peas – *lagane e ceci* – in a preparation which in many localities enjoys the status of a sacral dish, served at the feast or vigil of the feast of Saint Joseph, a particularly important figure in the region's religious life.

There are two very striking aspects to this dish which have relevance to the history of pasta. First, the dish appears in the Salentine peninsula (the heel of the Italian boot), an area that was historically Greek-speaking and still maintains, to a now very restricted degree, the use of the inherited Greek dialect, with the same form of pasta but under the name of 'tria', from the Greek *itria*; already in late antiquity (and in my opinion earlier than that), there are strong indications that 'itria' indicated at least on occasion a form of pasta and, as some scholars have remarked (e.g. Grocock and Grainger 2006: 349; Weingarten 2004), there was considerable overlap between *itria* and *lagana* and a third product, *tracta*, the name of which does not seem to have survived anywhere. Given this analogous appearance of lagane and tria in essentially identical special dishes, it is very tempting to conclude that, in a sense, 'lagane' was the Romance-speakers' name for what their southern Italian Hellenophone neighbours called 'tria'. And in this regard it is also noteworthy that there is a tradition in the Salentine peninsula of finishing the *tria e ceci* with some of the noodles fried in oil, a usage that recalls the treatment in classical times not only of *itria* but also of *lagana*.

Second, there is a famous passage in one of Horace's satires in which he argues that he is not a social-climber but rather a person content with a simple life; to illustrate his claim, he relates how, after a night-time stroll through Rome, he betakes himself home to enjoy a simple meal of leeks, chick-peas and lagana: 'inde domum ad porri et ciceris refero laganique catinum.' Though how this meal was prepared is not explicitly stated, the phrasing strongly points to the three items forming a single dish. My own interpretation of the text is that they most likely formed a unity, and so too thought Ullman (1912: 443), who wrote a century ago that 'Certainly Horace's language is entirely in favor of the view that the three articles were cooked together: "I come back home to my *pot* of leek, peas, and *laganum*."' In other words, there is a strong possibility that Horace, speaking of the food of the humble poor, is talking about a boiled *piatto unico*, the forerunner of the *lagane e ceci* still eaten many centuries later. That the dish maintains in many places a status as the required meal for an important festive fast-day reinforces the likelihood of the connection, given the tendency for special meals of that sort to resist change. It should also be noted that Horace was himself of humble origins and a native of the town of Venosa (today in Basilicata, near the border with Puglia), a place that stands fully in the zone where the dish of *lagane e ceci* is to this day part of the regional culinary tradition.

Returning now to Uguccione's comments about the word 'laganum', we note that he explicitly links the 'lagana' of classical times and two foods he knows from his own times: lagana that are fried in oil and dressed with honey and those that are first boiled and then fried in oil correspond to what are called commonly ('illa vulgo dicuntur...') 'crustella' and 'lasania' respectively (Cecchini 2004: II.642). Whatever the accuracy of these comments might be, offered not by a cook but by a scholar and future bishop, Uguccione's description of 'lasania' rings true at a basic level – lasania are boiled and then cooked again. But what exactly does he mean by 'fried in oil (in oleo friguntur)', necessarily deep-fried or simply finished in a pan with an oil-based condiment? And does he know lagana only as a term from classical Latin texts or is he familiar also with the still-living tradition of *lagane* in the Mezzogiorno?

That lagana and lasania coexisted to some degree during this period (mid twelfth to mid-fourteenth centuries) in Italian culinary practice is proven by their co-occurrence in the earliest extant medieval cookbook from Italy, the *Liber de coquina*. This Latin text dates to around 1300 and is generally regarded as having been composed in association with the court in Naples of the Angevin king of southern Italy, Charles II (Maier 2005: 13; Martellotti 2005: 14). It is here that we find the first known recipe for lasagne which calls for one to make a sheet of (leavened) dough and roll it out as thin as possible, then to cut the dough into small squares which one then boils in salted water and serves up laid out on a platter with grated cheese; a further variant is indicated in which one composes the dish with alternating layers of the noodles and layers of grated cheese and powdered spices (Maier 2005: 114–5). Conforming more to the modern notion of lasagna as a baked dish is the recipe for the *torta de lassanis*, that is, a lasagne pie (Maier 2005: 131) which involves layers of lasagne stuffed with cooked eggs, ravioli, cheese, bacon, etc., somehow surrounded by a stuffed intestine; the assembled 'torta' is then baked in the oven.

Also in the *Liber de coquina* we find a recipe for 'Monk's Head' (*de capite monachi*), a particularly elaborate and rich preparation that includes no animal products and thus is suitable for consumption during fast-days (Maier 2005: 127–8). Noteworthy is the fact that this dish calls for a large quantity of dough, out of which are made lagana: of these, one third are coloured with saffron and fried, another third boiled, and the last third used to make nut-filled ravioli; these items, together with fruits, nuts, spices, honey and oil, are all composed into a layered dish which is then baked under live coals.

From these early attestations of the word 'lasagna/lasagne', we can draw the following conclusions:
1) Already in the twelfth century lasagne existed in Italy as a flat and very thin form of pasta, and by end of the thirteenth century lasagne were widely known across Italy, at least among the upper classes.
2) This form of pasta was served in the style of *pasta asciutta* – boiled, drained and simply dressed – but also used to form layers in stuffed preparations that were then baked.
3) Uguccione clearly identifies the Latin word *lagana* with a colloquial word of his time, *lasania*, i.e. lasagne.

4) From the *Liber de coquina*, a cookbook originating in Naples, it is apparent that at least in a southern Italian context, the local food item *lagane* partially overlapped with the item *lasagne* and that both terms could indicate thin, broad cuttings of dough that were boiled.

Problematic etymologies

The close relationship between classical *lagana*, southern Italian *lagane* and *lasagne* has long been recognized and, given the fact that in certain contexts these terms have essentially the same meaning, many food scholars have assumed that the word *lasagna* is itself derived from the word *lagana*; e.g. Serventi & Sabban (2000: 33): 'Se torniamo al fatto che il termine lasagna deriva dal latino *laganum*, il significato di «sottile foglio» trova una spiegazione.' But this derivation is hardly a fact; indeed, it is an assumption without any justification from linguistic analysis. Put simply, in no Romance dialect does the historical development allow for the change of 'lagana' to 'lasagna' by regular sound-law. Of course, the superficial resemblance of the two words is eye-catching, but in reality they differ crucially in the location of the syllabic prominence (accent) – *lágana* vs. *laságna* – and the very neutral vocalic environment for the medial consonants is hardly propitious for the required changes of [-g-] to [-z-] and of [-n-] to [-ñ-]. However clear the semantic connection between the two is, the two words are themselves quite unambiguously unrelated from an etymological standpoint.

Recognizing the mismatch, some philologists have suggested an alternate derivation of the word *lasagna*. A commonly cited version links *lasagna* directly to a Latin (from Greek) term *lásana*, attested in Latin as a word meaning 'chamber pot' but in Greek also as a sort of cooking pot. From a phonological standpoint, this etymology is only slightly better than the one just discussed as it too fails to account for the same mismatch of place of accent and also leaves unexplained the development of the sequence [-ana-] to [-aña-]. A further suggestion by Ullman (1912: 448) builds off this etymology and resolves the phonological problems: '*Lasagna* must be derived from **lasania*, the neuter plural of the Greek diminutive form.' An early form **lasánia* would indeed yield *lasagna* in most, if not all, Italian dialects; however, the semantic motivation of this etymology is strained and, more damningly, unsupported by any clear attestation of *lasanum/lasana* as a cooking pot in Latin; I know, moreover, of no reflexes of the term in any Italian dialects. Finally, it seems odd that it is precisely in southern Italy, where Greek influence was strong and a putative *lasana* cooking-pot would most likely have existed, that the old word *lagana* survives robustly and the word *lasagna* seems to be an intrusive late-comer (more on this anon).

One last proposed etymology for *lasagna* needs mention here, namely, that of Vollenweider (1963: 440–443) and Rodinson (1986: 19), which – with the ever-growing inclination of food scholars to see the Arabs as central players in the invention and diffusion of pasta in the West – is encountered with considerable frequency nowadays (e.g. Wright 1996–7: 156–7 and Martellotti 2001: 88). Both Vollenweider and Rodinson argue that the term *lasagna* is best seen in relationship to the French heraldic (and later culinary) term *losange*. Vollenweider in particular draws a connection between the two via the attested forms of the Provençal analogue of lasagna, namely *lausan, lozan*, etc., and the English forms derived ultimately from Provençal, *lozeyn, lozen, losan*. Both scholars are of the opinion that the etymology of the heraldic term *losange* is not to be derived, as a number of linguists have suggested, from an old word, *lausa/losa* 'stone slab, tile', found throughout the Romance dialects of Iberia, southern France and parts of northern Italy, but rather from the name of the Arab confection *lawzīnağ*. This confection was made from a fine paste of almonds and, according to these scholars, cut in rhomboid form and it is from this characteristic shape that the term came to be applied in the one direction to the rhomboids used in heraldry, and in the other to the square or otherwise angular cuts of fresh pasta that are the Provençal *lausans* and the Italian *lasagne*.

There are three objections to be levelled against the Arabic etymology. First, according to Perry (2006: 223) *lawzīnağ* was often cylindrical in form and by no means necessarily rhomboidal: 'This deals a blow to Maxime Rodinson's theory that the word "lozenge" derives from *lawzīnaj*.'

Beyond this observation, I have two broader objections to this etymology. First, at no point does Rodinson or Vollenweider (or others) make any attempt to account for the phonological relationship between the putative Arabic source word *lawzīnağ* and the attested forms of both 'lozenge' and 'lasagna/lausans'; particularly striking is the disparity between the accented vowel of the Arabic, a long high front vowel, and the low vowel of almost all of the attested Romance forms – why do we not get something like the actual borrowing or at least rendering of *lawzīnağ* that we find in Giambonino da Cremona's translation of an Arabic text (*c*.1400), namely, *lawzīniz* (Martellotti 2001: 288)? Under all normal circumstances we would expect a borrowing of *lawzīnağ* to have as its accented vowel -*i*- and if we do not find that in *lasagna* etc. – and we do not – one must offer an explanation as to why.

A final and very grave objection to the Rodinson/Vollenweider etymology is that it focuses primarily on the later attested forms, from the fourteenth century on, and then especially on ones from French and Provençal, but it does not address the earliest attestations from Italy discussed above, where we find no trace whatsoever of influence on the culinary term in question from either a heraldic term or an Arab confection. That such influences come in later, secondarily and marginally, seems clear, but they certainly do not constitute an explanation of the rise of the word 'lasagna' and ultimately are without relevance to the history of pasta.

A new, layered view
If we consider the general time-frame from which come the earliest attestations of the word 'lasagna', we note that the first one, by Uguccione da Pisa, is dated to just a few decades after one of the most famous early references to pasta in Italy, namely, the

mention of the production and export of *itria* from the town of Trabia, near Palermo, Sicily, by the Arab geographer, Al-Idrisi (Jaubert 1836: v.II, 78). Al-Idrisi's text is dated to 1154 and was written while the author was serving King Roger II of Sicily, a clear indication of a significant level of continuing Arab cultural influence on the island even well after its conquest by the Normans. The fact that this early mention of pasta from Italy occurs in an Arabic text is, of course, important and possibly suggestive of an Arab role in the history of pasta during this period, but it is also the case that Al-Idrisi's observation has been regarded in a strangely myopic way, that is, only as evidence regarding pasta and the Arabs. But the reality is that we are told nothing about who it was that was producing the *itria* of Trabia, under whose impetus this industry had begun, and who it was that was carrying out the commerce that involved exportation of the product from Sicily to 'Calabria and to Muslim and Christian countries'. Indeed, the text was written more than eighty years after the Norman conquest of Palermo, and it is precisely in this period, after the reduction of Muslim dominance in the western Mediterranean, that trade in the area is increasingly dominated by the Italian maritime powers, most notably Pisa and especially Genoa. Of particular relevance here is the fact that throughout the twelfth century, Genoa and Pisa took the pre-eminent role in the commercial exploitation of the agricultural wealth of Sicily and southern Italy, with considerable amounts of durum wheat and presumably also some quantities of prepared pasta products being bought up by the northerners, both to supplement the dietary requirements of those cities' growing populations and to sell in other markets as well, such as, in the case of Genoa, Provence. In other words, the trade in pasta that Al-Idrisi observed was almost certainly being carried out by Genoese and/or Pisan merchants and the primary markets were in northern Italy and Provence.[4]

Though we do not know to what degree there was already a tradition of making pasta in northern Italy before this period, indications are strong that a pasta culture existed both in Sicily and in the south of the mainland, and the likelihood is that the importation of grain and especially durum wheat, as well as some pasta products, into northern Italy and Provence may well have been the stimulus for the development of a pasta culture in those areas. If we regard the appearance of 'lasagna' in northern texts in the late twelfth and thirteenth century and remember the semantic connection, expressly articulated by Uguccione, between 'lasania' and 'lagana', it is reasonable to consider the possibility that the word itself, *lasagne*, was a new and specifically northern name for a form of pasta the Genoese and Pisans had encountered in southern Italy, namely, *lagane*.

The word *lausa/losa* (stone slab, tile) is the key to accounting for the variety of forms that we find indicating flat, thin noodles in northern Italy and Provence, as already proposed by Nigra in 1898 (286–87). Alongside the unitary form we encounter in Italy, *lasagna*, we find a range of forms attested for Provençal, in part involving the use of different suffixes but, more significantly, also with two distinct root forms – *lausan*, *lauvan* (Mistral, vol. 2, 193) – which correspond to variants of the word for 'stone slab/

tile', *lausa/lauva*. In Piemontese dialects in Italy we also find this word in the form *losa* (corresponding to the Provençal *lausa*) but in some places there and further east in the sub-Alpine regions of northern Italy, we also find a variant *lasa* with the same meaning. These stone slabs are throughout these regions cut into square or rectangular forms and used in various functions, most notably as roof tiles. The semantic sense fits perfectly the form of pasta under discussion and the occurrence of all three root variants of the tile-word makes the direct connection to the pasta words all but assured: *lausa – lausan, lauva – lauvan, lasa – lasagna*.

It remains to account for the suffixes of these forms and the apparent difference between the Provençal and Italian forms. It seems easiest to account for the Provençal forms as secondary to the Italian one: the Italian form shows the use of a well-known nominal derivational suffix, *-agna* < *-anea*, found in a number of word pairs, such as *monte – montagna, campo – campagna*, where the suffix sometimes, but not always, has a collective sense, which would hardly be incompatible with the application to the particular form of pasta under discussion.

In Provençal, as in other Romance languages, there is a nominal/adjectival suffix *–an*, and it is possible that it is this suffix that appears in the forms *lausan/lauvan*. A more likely explanation, however, is that, building these forms on the model of the Italian *lasagna*, the Provençal speakers adapted the root form to their local words for 'tile' and that they additionally preferred to assign the pasta words masculine gender, thus **lausanh, *lauvanh*; between Old Provençal and modern Provençal, most dialects reduce final *-nh* ([-ñ]) to *-n* ([-n, -ŋ]) by regular sound change. This explanation accounts well for the Middle English form attested as *loseyn*, where the sound [-ñ] in loan words is normally resolved as the sequence [-yn] and where [ai] and [ei] fall together as *-ey*. With regard to the plausibility of the change of gender in Provençal from the putative original Italian feminine to masculine, we can only note other early Provençal names for pasta also appear as masculine nouns, namely, *croset* and *menudet*.

Finally, with regard to the localisation of the source of *lasagna* in Italy, it seems that the possibility exists that the word was formed in any of a number of places in northern Italy, but historical and linguistic contexts point to the most likely place of the word's origin being Genoa. First, there is the particularly central role played by Genoa in trade with southern Italy, as discussed above, and then also the close relationship of Genoa and Liguria to their immediate neighbour to the west, Provence. Second, the linguistic evidence that groups the forms just discussed together also points toward Genoa as source, as does the very much parallel occurrence of another early pasta name in Liguria and Provence, namely, *croset*; Buccini 2012a demonstrates that Genoa is also the source and point of diffusion for the term *fidê/fideus*.[5]

The appearance of *lasagna* in the *Liber de coquina* also finds ready explanation in the scenario proposed here for the etymology of the word. The Angevin royal court in the Kingdom of Sicily after Charles I's conquest in 1266 was the meeting place of French-speakers (the king's own family and closest men), Provençal speakers – for Charles of

Anjou was also the Count of Provence – and, of course, southern Italians. It is then no surprise really that a cookbook compiled in a courtly context in Naples around 1300 would include recipes for *lagane, crosets* and *lasagne*. And finally, it seems likely that the culinary culture of the Angevins played a role in the further spread of pasta culture across northern Italy.

Notes

1. A mæ moggê, Amy Dahlstrom, graçie pe-o se-i aggiutto.
2. See the article by Sue Leeman, available online: http://www.smh.com.au/articles/2003/07/16/1058035074218.html. For the original recipe, see Hieatt & Butler 1985: 128–9.
3. See, for example, the several forms included on the AIS map 992, vol V. (Jaberg & Jud 1928–40); other forms showing various local phonological developments can be found in dialect dictionaries from Campania, Basilicata, etc.
4. For an overview of the relationship between the northern Italian cities and the Norman Kingdom of Sicily, see Abulafia 1977. Focusing on Genoa's relationship with the south in the period, see Epstein 1996, esp. chaps. 1–2.
5. Buccini 2012b presents a broader refutation of the theory that the Arabs played a central role in the diffusion of pasta in Italy; this research will constitute a chapter in my forthcoming monograph (Buccini in preparation).

References

Abulafia, David, 1977. *The Two Italies.* Cambridge: Cambridge University Press.
Buccini, Anthony F. 2012a. 'The Etymology of *fide/fideus* and its Historical Context: New Evidence for the Rôles of Southern Italy and Genoa in the Early History of Pasta.' (Presented at the Global Gateways and Local Connections Conference, NYU/New School, New York, June, 2012.)
———, 2012b. 'The Early History of Pasta: Post-Modern Myth and Medieval Reality.' (Presented at the Chicago Foodways Roundtable, Kendall College, August, 2012.)
———, In preparation. *From Green to Gold: On the History of Mediterranean Foodways with Particular Reference to the History of Olive Oil.* Columbia University Press.
Cecchini, Enzo (ed.), 2004. Uguccione da Pisa: *Derivationes.* Firenze: Sismel/Edizione del Galluzzo.
Cocito, Luciana (ed.), 1970. Anonimo Genovese (Luchetto): *Poesie.* Roma: Edizione dell'Ateneo.
Epstein, Steven, 1996. *Genoa and the Genoese, 958–1528.* Chapel Hill: University of North Carolina Press.
Grocock, Christopher, & Sally Grainger (eds.), 2006. *Apicius.* Totnes: Prospect.
Hieatt, C.B. & Sharon Butler, 1985. *Curye on Inglysch,* Oxford: Oxford Univeristy Press (EETS).
Jaberg, K., & J. Jud, 1928–40. *Sprach- und Sacnatlas Italiens und der Südschweiz* (8 vols.). Zolfingen: Ringier.
Jaubert, P. Amédée (ed., trans.), 1836. *Géographie d'Édrisi.* (Two volumes.) Paris: Imprimerie Royale.
Maier, Robert (ed.), 2005. *Liber de Coquina. Das Buch der guten Küche.* Frankfurt am Main: Friedrich.
Martellotti, Anna, 2001. *Il Liber de ferculis di Giambonino da Cremona.* Fasano: Schena.
———, 2005. *I ricettari di Federico II. Dal 'Meridionale' al 'Liber de coquina'.* Leo Olschki.
Mistral, Frédéric. n.d. *Lou tresor dóu Felibrige, ou Dictionnaire Provençal-Français.* (2 vols.) Aix: Veuve Remondet-Aubin.
Nigra, C. 1898. 'Note etimologiche e lessicali.' *Archivio Glottologico Italiano* 14: 353–384.
Perry, Charles, 1981. 'The Oldest Mediterranean Noodle: A Cautionary Tale.' *Petits Propos Culinaires* 9: 42–45.
———, 2006. 'What to Order in Ninth-Century Baghdad.' In: *Medieval Arab Cookery,* pp. 217–23. Totnes: Prospect.
Ratto, G.B, & Giovanni Ratto, 2003 [1863]. *La cuciniera genovese.* Genova: Fratelli Frilli.

Rodinson, Maxime, 1986 [orig. 1956]. 'On the Etymology of 'Losange'.' (Charles Perry trans.) *Petits Propos Culinaires* 23: 15–23.

Serventi, Silvano, & Françoise Sabban, 2000. *La pasta. Storia e cultura di un cibo universale.* Roma/Bari: Laterza.

Ullman, B.M. 1912. 'Horace Serm. 1.6.115 and the History of the Word Laganum.' *Classical Philology* 7: 442–449.

Vollenweider, Alice, 1963. 'Der Einfluß der Italienischen auf die französische Kochkunst im Spiegel der Sprache (Zweiter Teil: Wortmonographien).' *Vox Romanica* 22: 398–443.

Weingarten, Susan, 2004. 'The debate about ancient tracta: evidence from the Talmud.' *Food & History* 2: 21–39.

Wright, Clifford A. 1996–1997. 'Cucina Arabo-Sicula and Maccharruni.' *Al-Masaq* 9: 151–177.

Samuel Pepys's Venison Pasties

Taissa Csáky

Samuel Pepys (1633–1703), England's most famous diarist, kept his diary from 1 January 1660, the year of the Restoration, to 31 May 1669. In the diary, Pepys often records meals he has enjoyed at home or in company. He does not always remark on what he ate, but one dish that is specifically named, many times, is the venison pasty. On 1 September 1660, he writes, 'Mr. Moore and I and several others being invited to-day by Mr. Goodman, a friend of his, we dined at the Bullhead upon the best venison pasty that ever I eat of in my life, and with one dish more, it was the best dinner I ever was at'.[1] Then again, on 5 July 1661, he notes, 'At home, and in the afternoon to the office, and that being done all went to Sir W. Batten's and there had a venison pasty, and were very merry. At night home and to bed'. This paper seeks to answer two questions: why was venison pasty worth mentioning, and what was it like?

Pepys was born in London, the son of a City tailor, and grew up during the Civil War and Protectorate. Thanks to education, hard work and family connections Pepys worked his way from relative poverty in his parental home to a comfortable life as an adult.

For a brief period as a teenager Pepys attended grammar school in Huntingdon. He lodged with his uncle Robert, who was bailiff on the Hinchingbrooke estate a couple of miles outside town. Here he got to know his uncle's employers, Edward and Jemima Montague, who were also distant relatives. Pepys developed a warm but respectful relationship with the couple and after more schooling at St Paul's in London and a degree at Cambridge he went to work for Montague at his London home in Westminster.

Edward Montague had fought for Parliament during the Civil War but was skilled enough as a politician to survive the regime change during the Restoration. He secured a seat on Charles II's Council of State and was even ennobled as Earl of Sandwich. In his new role Montague helped Pepys secure a job as Clerk to the Navy Board in 1660, the first year of the diary. Pepys remained at the Navy Board, steadily advancing in seniority and influence, until 1688.[2]

Pepys's job came with a house attached to the Navy offices at Seething Lane in the City. Claire Tomalin describes the houses provided for officials as 'substantial, with up to ten rooms apiece and two or three storeys high, with cellars'.[3] With space to entertain, Pepys and his wife gave numerous dinners for six guests or more.

The house is no longer standing, but some general assumptions can be made about the cooking facilities based on the available technology of the time. In the mid-seventeenth century most cooking was done over an open fire, possibly contained within a fire basket, with hooks and grates to support cooking pots and spits for roasting meat. An oven (essential for baking pastry) was built into a brick wall alongside or within the fireplace.

It was not heated directly but filled with fuel which was ignited and left to burn. When the oven was hot the ashes and embers were swept out so baking could begin. This method would give a hot oven that gradually cooled as cooking time elapsed.[4]

Not every house had an oven – many city-dwellers sent baked dishes out to a commercial bake-house – but it seems safe to assume that a house the size of Pepys's did. Like other men of his time and class, Pepys took no part in food preparation. His wife Elizabeth did some cooking, for example making fashionable quince jelly on 4 November 1663 and helping prepare for more elaborate entertainments, but most cooking was done by the household servants.

During the diary years Pepys was well-off. Taking stock of his position on the last day of 1666, he writes, 'One thing I reckon remarkable in my own condition is, that I am come to abound in good plate so as at all entertainments to be served wholly with silver plates, having two dozen and a half'. We can assume that his food habits were driven by choice rather than necessity. But however much he wanted to eat venison pasty he could not have it at will. Venison had an exclusive social status. Only the aristocracy could afford the deer parks where venison destined for the table was kept in a condition between farming and wilderness, enclosed by a fence but killed in a hunt.

A rich array of traditions surrounded the deer hunt that stretched back to the Norman era, when deer parks first became widespread in England. A Norman deer hunt ended with a ritual called the 'unmaking'. First the deer was laid on its back and the king or senior noble present cut its throat. Then the dogs were called in to eat their share of the entrails. When they had been called off (an exercise in restraint for the hounds), the tongue, testicles and intestines were strung on a stick and reserved for the landowner. Finally the pelvis bone was thrown into the air for the crows. Only then was the meat butchered for eating. The haunches went to the landowner and the shoulder and sides to hunt servants.[5] Memories of the unmaking ritual gave venison a touch of courtly glamour.

While the full unmaking was no longer practised in Stuart England, the tradition of reserving the haunch for the lord and allotting the shoulders and other lesser parts to hunt servants persisted. On 13 September 1665, Sir William Hickes, the Keeper of Waltham Forest, served Pepys and friends a dinner of venison shoulder and umbles (deer offal) alongside some beef and pigeons. Pepys complained that the dinner was of the 'meanest'.

The desirability of and demand for venison was further enhanced by restricted supply. Hunting had been tightly controlled in England since the arrival of the Normans, and possibly earlier. Venison could not be bought (at least not legally), and punishments for men and dogs found poaching could involve mutilation or even death. Legal access to venison was restricted to those who owned land on which they could hunt, who had a Warrant (permission from the King to hunt in a royal Forest) or those who received it as a gift. In practice some people might also acquire venison illegally from a poacher – a Tudor proverb warned 'Never enquire whence venison comes'.[6]

Samuel Pepys's Venison Pasties

Pepys was concerned for his social status and lived in the capital where access to poached venison would have been more difficult than in the country. His aristocratic patron, Edward Montague, had a deer park at Hinchingbrooke and occasionally gave Pepys venison. Pepys also had friends who regularly invited him to eat venison. So while he may have bought poached venison, it seems more likely that he received it through the proper channels.

Receiving venison as a gift must have given Pepys a rosy glow of contentment at his secure social status. Being given venison meant you were friends with the sort of people who could advance your career and located on a spectrum of social respectability that stretched all the way to the King. As Pepys writes on 18 July 1660, 'to my Lord about business, and being in talk in comes one with half a buck from Hinchinbroke, and it smelling a little strong my Lord did give it me (though it was as good as any could be). I did carry it to my mother … and so I did leave the venison with her to dispose of as she pleased'. It is interesting that Pepys immediately re-gifts the gift. He may have been avoiding imposing the task of preparing the venison on his own household or, perhaps more likely, taking pleasure in extending the generosity and patronage. Two days later Pepys and his wife were invited round to eat the venison in pasty form. The diary implies there were ten or more guests, perhaps asked to witness how well Pepys was doing and how strong was his relation with Montague. In September 1663, another piece of venison was gifted and re-gifted, and when Pepys cannot help consume it on 13 September he plans to send his wife as a proxy: 'by and by comes my uncle Wight to bid us to dinner to-morrow to a haunch of venison I sent them yesterday, given me by Mr. Povy, but I cannot go, but my wife will'.

At such meals, venison was prepared in several different ways. In *The Queen-Like Closet* (1670), Hannah Woolley gives recipes for potted venison; venison baked in blood; roast haunch with a sweet, spicy, red wine sauce; venison boiled with cauliflower and cow's udder and seasoned with lemon, parsley and barberries; and many more venison recipes of which venison pasty is but one. John Evelyn, a contemporary of Pepys, wrote about dinners including venison a dozen times but never mentioned a pasty.[7] In Pepys's diary venison is also served boiled, potted, roasted and 'baked in pans', but on more than half the occasions venison is mentioned, it is eaten in pasty form.

One reason why Pepys's circle most often ate venison in a pasty might be that pastry made a desirable commodity go further so more people could be invited to enjoy it. Another might be that, while Woolley perhaps wrote with the country home in mind (the urbanized population of London was less than 10 per cent of the total in England), Pepys spent most of his time in London, further from the sources of game. The pastry kept venison – which had already travelled some distance from the countryside – fresh for longer. While some venison was salted before it travelled long distances (or for local storage), other venison, like the half-buck Montague gave Pepys, seems to have travelled fresh. The Hinchingbrooke estate is about sixty miles from London. On 7 August 1661 Pepys, returning from his parents' house near Hinchingbrooke, broke his journey at an inn and notes, 'as I was eating my breakfast I saw a man riding by that rode a little way upon the road with me last night; and he being going with venison in his pan-yards to London, I called him in and did give him his breakfast with me, and so we went together all the way'. Pepys and the venison carrier complete the Huntingdonshire–London journey in two days. *The Oxford Companion to Food* suggests venison can be hung for 12–22 days.[8] Provided the weather was not too warm and the venison was packed in such a way that it was moderately cool yet had a good air-flow around it, travelling time could be counted as hanging time and was not a great risk to the quality of the meat. But once the meat reached its final destination it needed to be dealt with quickly to keep it at its best. A carefully made pasty would exclude air and add another few days, or even weeks, to the life of the valuable venison within.

Once made, a pasty was a very substantial food item: a fallow deer haunch weighs at least 3kg and a red deer haunch can weigh up to 8kg. Venison pasty was therefore of a suitable size and status to be served at dinner parties.

Pepys socialized with his own family, who were generally middle-class, and neighbours who were prosperous tradesmen. He also mixed with City officials, like mayors and aldermen, and with members of the nobility, either as a guest at a private home or an inn (usually the Mitre or the Bullhead, where Pepys claimed to have eaten the best pasty he ever had in his life). Whether eating in public or private, there were usually six to eight people sitting down to meals including venison pasty. On 14 August 1666, for example, Pepys writes, 'We had invited to a venison pasty Mr. Batelier and his sister Mary, Mrs. Mercer, her daughter Anne, Mr. Le Brun, and W. Hewer; and so we supped, and very merry'. On 21 August 1662, Pepys went to the Mitre on Fenchurch Street where 'my uncle Wight and my aunt, and some neighbour couples were at a very good venison pasty'. Visiting friends in Bristol on 13 June 1668 at least five people, including Pepys, enjoyed a 'good entertainment of strawberries, a whole venison-pasty, cold, and plenty of brave wine, and above all Bristoll milk'.

In the 1660s, in wealthier homes, it was the fashion to serve several dishes at once, including meat and vegetables, hot dishes and cold, savoury and sweet. There was no expectation that everything on the table would be finished, and a large pie or piece of roast meat might be brought back to the table several times over a few days until it was gone. Each person helped themselves, or was helped to some of each of the dishes they liked. The more dishes served per course, the grander the occasion. In *The Queen-like Closet*, Hannah Woolley's menu for a summer 'Feast' has three courses, of fourteen, twelve and eight dishes each. The scathingly titled 'Bill of Fare for Gentlemens Houses of Lesser Quality, by which you may also know how to order any Family beneath another, which is very requisite' suggests two courses of seven dishes, followed by cheese and fruit. Venison pasty is considered grand enough for the Feast but is also included on a menu for 'Houses of Lesser Quality'.[9] The meals at which Pepys was eating venison pasty ranged from 'Familiar' (at home) to 'Feast' (with his patron Edward Montague).

So what was Pepys's venison pasty? How was it prepared? What did it taste like?

Samuel Pepys's Venison Pasties

Although Pepys recorded fascinating detail about the events at which pasties were eaten he never described a venison pasty. Fortunately contemporary cookbooks offer numerous recipes for venison pasty. These volumes include Joseph Cooper's *The art of cookery refin'd and augmented: containing an abstract of some rare and rich unpublished receipts of cookery* (1654), Kenelm Digby's *The Closet of Sir Kenelm Digby Knight Opened* (1669), Gervase Markham's *The English Housewife* (1664), William Rabisha's *The Whole Body of Cookery Dissected* (1673), Robert May's *The Accomplish't Cook, or, The Art and Mystery of Cookery: Wherein the Whole Art is Revealed* (1678) and Hannah Woolley's *The Queen-like Closet* (1670). These books reveal a pasty a world away from the contemporary Cornish pasty, with its single meal-sized portion of cubed beef, swede, potato and onion encased in flaky pastry. Instead, these authors describe venison pasties encasing a whole, boned joint, enriched with additional fat and seasoned with spices or sauces, cooked long and slow with the aim of cooking the meat gently without either burning or completely drying the pastry.

Despite these common features, there is also surprising variation. Red deer haunch was baked in a strong rye crust. A smaller, more tender fallow deer haunch could be baked in a light wheat flour crust. Some pasties were encased in short-crust pastry made with cold fat rubbed into the flour. Others (for example, Sir Kenelm Digby's) seem more like contemporary pork pies, made of a hot-water pastry with a raised crust. Sometimes, but not always, the venison was larded (with pieces of lard 'as big as your finger') or spread with a thick layer of butter. Sometimes pepper was specified as a seasoning; other recipes recommended ginger. Some pasties were moistened with red wine, others with a broth made with marrow from the deer's broken bones. One recipe from *The Accomplish't Cook* suggests filling the pasty, when partly cooled, with 'gallendine', 'made with strained bread, vinegar, claret wine, cinnamon, ginger, and sugar; strain it, and being finely beaten with the spices boil it up with a few whole cloves and a sprig of rosemary'.[10]

Woolley's menus suggest pasties could be served hot or cold. In summer, when Pepys ate most of his pasties, cold pasty offered many advantages. It could be prepared in advance leaving more capacity in the kitchen for other dishes. It could tolerate late guests. For the parsimonious household it would provide an excellent dish to return to at subsequent meals *en famille*. Pepys's Royal Society associates were happy to return to a cold pasty. On 1 September 1660, when Pepys dined with them at the Bullhead:

> Here rose in discourse at table a dispute between Mr. Moore and Dr. Clerke, the former affirming that it was essential to a tragedy to have the argument of it true, which the Doctor denied, and left it to me to be judge, and the cause to be determined next Tuesday morning at the same place, upon the eating of the remains of the pasty, and the loser to spend 10s.

Occasions on which Pepys was disappointed in his pasty are also revealing. On 6 January 1660, after a morning at the office paying soldiers' wages, Pepys 'went home and took my wife and went to my cosen, Thomas Pepys, and found them just sat down to dinner, which was very good; only the venison pasty was palpable beef, which was not handsome'.

A beef pasty would not be intrinsically awful so it must have been the deceit that offended Pepys. Faked venison was not uncommon. Gervase Markham gives this recipe in *The English Housewife*:

> *To bake beef or mutton for Venison*
> And if to your meat sauce you add a little Turnsole, and therein steep Beef, and Ramm mutton; You may also in the same manner take the first for Red-Deer Venison, and the latter for Fallow, and a very good judgement shall not be able to say otherwise, than that it is of it self perfect Venison, both in taste, Colour, and the manner of cutting.[11]

Turnsole is a herb used to make blue paint and dye cloth.[12] Mixed with sauce it must have given beef or mutton a darker, more gamey hue. Markham also gives a method for making mock-venison with pounded hare, and Robert May suggests soaking beef or mutton with beer, vinegar and turnsole. Such recipes for mock-venison indicate how desirable genuine venison was to ambitious hosts.

One feature of the pasty which Pepys never mentions, but which must have enhanced its contribution to the table, is the pastry decoration. The potential has been beautifully illustrated by Ivan Day.[13] The designs he illustrates, from Edward Kidder and Robert May, are applied to lamb pasty but would be most fitting for venison pasty: a crow recalls the ritual of tossing the pelvis bone at the unmaking, arrows recall the hunt, a stag surrounded by leafy branches reminds diners that this is a beast of the forest.

The venison pasty was desirable for pragmatic and aesthetic reasons. Venison pasty suited Pepys's seventeenth-century world of city dining because it was a sensible way of dealing with meat that had travelled and could be used as an attractive centrepiece for a large gathering. It was also, thanks to the company in which it was eaten and its flavour and appearance, enjoyable. In the twenty-first century the restrictions of game laws, transport and storage no longer apply. Venison pasty deserves a revival. To this end, and to illustrate the diversity between recipes, three contemporary interpretations of historic pasty recipes are given here.

Samuel Pepys's Venison Pasties

A COLD PASTY: RED DEER WITH RED WINE VINEGAR IN A RYE CRUST

On 7 July 1663 Pepys was 'Up by 4 o'clock and to my office, and there continued all the morning upon my Navy book to my great content. At noon down by barge with Sir J. Minnes (who is going to Chatham) to Woolwich, in our way eating of some venison pasty in the barge'. This recipe is based on a method for preparing cold venison pasty given in Gervase Markham's *English Housewife*.[14] The zingy sourness of the rye pastry and vinegar are a wonderful foil to the darkness of the meat.

> 2kg joint of red deer haunch (or shoulder) • 12 finger-sized pieces of pork fat
> 500ml ale (avoid hoppy beer) • 250ml red wine vinegar • 2 tbsp salt
> 750g rye flour • 350g wheat flour • 250g butter • 500ml water
> egg yolk • 4 tbsp red wine vinegar • 8 tbsp red wine

Cover the meat with water and parboil for about 10 minutes or until the outside is brown but the middle remains raw.

Drain and leave to cool a little before threading the pork fat through the meat at regular intervals. This would be best done with a larding needle but can also be achieved with a sharp knife.

Wrap the larded meat in greaseproof paper, put it in a high-sided dish and leave it in the fridge for about two hours with a heavy weight on top.

Combine the ale, red wine vinegar and salt. Unwrap the meat, pour this mixture over, cover again and leave overnight.

Preheat the oven to 200°C.

To make the pastry, cut the butter into cubes and stir it with the water over medium heat until the butter is completely melted. Stir this mixture into the flour. If the mixture is too sticky add more flour.

Take about three quarters of the pastry and make a 'coffin' (raised pie crust). You can either do this by rolling it out then placing a baking dish or other suitably sized container on top of the pastry and turning the pastry up to create a free-standing crust. Or roll your pastry out and use it to line a spring-form cake tin.

Spread soft butter in the bottom of the pastry case. Remove the venison from the vinegar bath and dry it with kitchen paper. Lay it carefully into the pastry.

Roll out the remaining pastry to make a lid, reserving some for decoration. Leave a hole in the lid. When your pasty is ready to bake, brush it with egg yolk.

To simulate the cooling of a bread oven, bake for 45 minutes at 200°C, 30 minutes at 180°C, then 30 minutes at 160°C.

Remove the pasty from the oven and allow it to cool. Combine 4 tbsp red wine vinegar with 8 tbsp red wine. Pour this mixture into the hole in the pasty lid and leave to cool. Ideally keep the pasty loosely covered at room temperature for 3–4 days – the crust will soften slightly and all the wine and vinegar will soak into the pastry.

Samuel Pepys's Venison Pasties

A cold pasty: red deer with red wine vinegar in a rye crust

A FAMILIAR PASTY: VENISON WITH CLARET IN WHEAT FLOUR CRUST

On Tuesday 14 August 1666, the anniversary of a naval victory over the Dutch, after a trying day at the office Pepys took his wife to a bull-baiting show, then:

> In the evening our company come to supper. We had invited to a venison pasty Mr. Batelier and his sister Mary, Mrs. Mercer, her daughter Anne, Mr. Le Brun, and W. Hewer; and so we supped, and very merry. And then about nine o'clock to Mrs. Mercer's gate, where the fire and boys expected us, and her son had provided abundance of serpents and rockets.

To feed this number a whole haunch or shoulder would be required, but for contemporary purposes this recipe uses the smaller, more delicate saddle and will feed three to four. It is based on Recipe 276 of Hannah Woolley's *Queen-Like Closet*.[15] The pastry uses cream rather than water as the moistening agent. The result is a melt-in-the-mouth pastry. The seasoning (salt, pepper and wine) is simple but effective as the wine reduces and combines with the meat juices to make a sweet, tart gravy.

Samuel Pepys's Venison Pasties

750g white wheat flour • 150g butter • 400ml whipping cream
about 50g butter for spreading • 500g saddle of venison
roughly ground black pepper • salt • 250ml claret (Bordeaux) • egg, beaten

Rub the butter into the flour. Add cream little by little until you have a very smooth pastry.

Roll the pastry out into a square (save the trimmings to decorate the pasty). It should be large enough for the saddle to sit in one half of the square with a 5cm margin all around.

Spread butter over the pastry. Lay the meat on the square and season it generously. Brush the edges of the pastry with beaten egg then fold it over to cover the meat. Pinch the pastry all around to give a sealed, wavy edge. Cut a round hole in the top, apply decorations with more beaten egg and brush again.

Finally pour the wine carefully through the hole and bake at 200°C for 30 minutes, then 180°C for 20 minutes.

Rest for 10 minutes before serving.

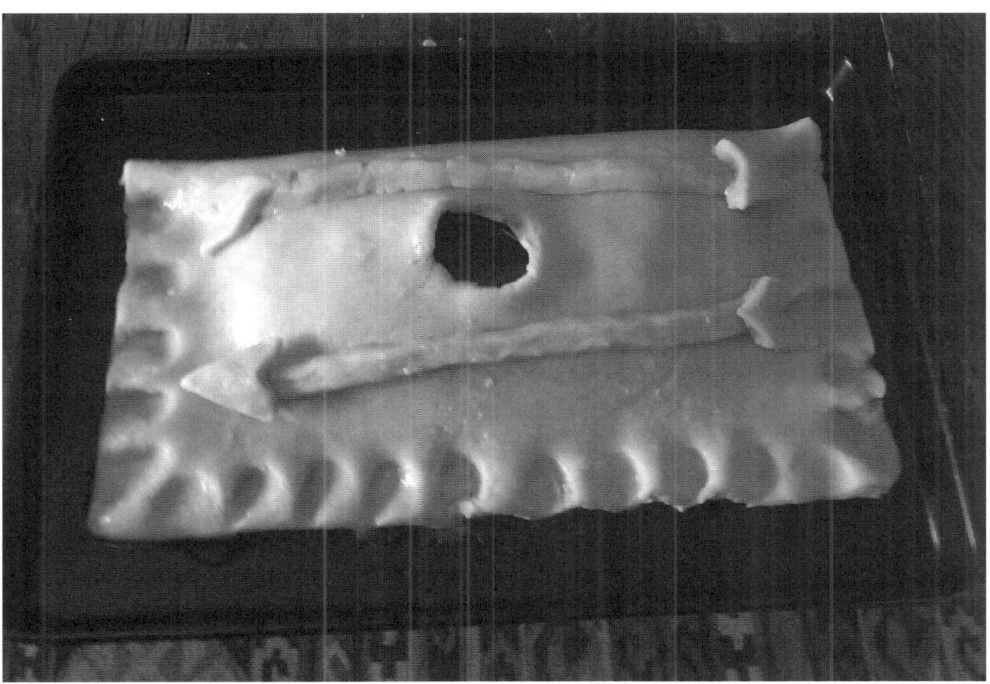

A familiar pasty: venison with claret in wheat flour crust

Samuel Pepys's Venison Pasties

Lady Newport's pasty: red deer in marrow broth

LADY NEWPORT'S PASTY: RED DEER IN MARROW BROTH

In 1660–61 Edward Montague was Keeper of the Wardrobe, looking after the financial affairs of the royal household. Samuel and Elizabeth Pepys went to dinner at the Wardrobe with Montague and his wife ('my Lady') on 25 October 1661:

> To Whitehall, and so to dinner at the Wardrobe, where my wife met me, and there we met with a venison pasty, and my Lady very merry and very handsome, methought. After dinner my wife and I to the Opera, and there saw again *Love and Honour*, a play so good that it has been acted but three times and I have seen them all [...].

This more elaborate hot pasty draws together three sections of *The Closet of Sir Kenelm Digby Knight Opened*: a method for making the broth; another for pastry; and a third the method of assembly, as practised by Lady Newport.[16]

The distinctive feature of this pasty is the difference between the pastry below and above the meat. The lower part is soaked in broth and remains soft (Digby calls this 'pudding') while the upper part bakes tough and hard. If removed with care it can be used as a lid, preserving the attractiveness of the dish even when the meat is half eaten.

Samuel Pepys's Venison Pasties

2–3 leg bones • venison trimmings (or chicken thighs)
1l meat or vegetable stock • 1.5kg white flour • 250g butter • 1.5l water
2kg red deer or fallow deer, boned haunch or shoulder • egg, beaten

First prepare the broth. With a hammer, crack the bones so the marrow can easily escape. Place them in a large pan with the extra meat and stock. If necessary add more water to cover the bones. Simmer gently for about an hour. Allow to cool slightly then remove the large pieces of bone and strain through a colander to remove small pieces.

To make the pastry, heat the water, add the butter and simmer gently until it is melted. Allow to cool slightly, then use a large spoon to skim off the butter bit by bit and stir it into the flour. When all the butter is combined, add water from the pan until you have a smooth, elastic pastry.

Roll out two thirds of the pastry and use it to line a high-sided dish large enough to take the meat without it touching the sides. Put the meat into the dish and roll out a lid. Reserve some pastry for decoration.

Brush the edges of the pastry with egg and add the lid, sealing the edges well. Cut a hole in the top of the lid and add decoration. Brush the whole lid with egg. Finally pour the broth very carefully into the hole. It should ideally cover the meat without touching the lid.

Bake at 180°C for about one and a half hours. If the pastry looks brown enough before the cooking time is over cover it with foil. Allow the pasty to rest for at least 15 minutes before serving.

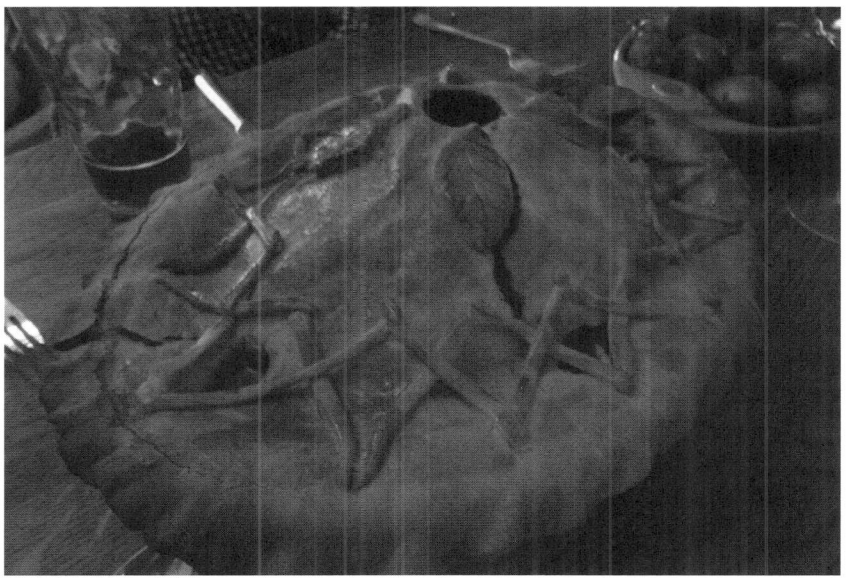

Notes

1. Phil Gyford, ed., *The Diary of Samuel Pepys: Daily Entries from the 17th-Century London Diary*, 1 September 1660: http://www.pepysdiary.com/archive/1660/09/01/. All subsequent citations from Pepys's diary refer to this source and are cited by date in the text.
2. Claire Tomalin, *Samuel Pepys – The Unequalled Self* (London, penguin, 2002), pp. 3–48.
3. Tomalin, p. 408.
4. Molly Harrison, *The Kitchen in History* (Reading: Osprey, 1972), p. 64.
5. Barry Lewis, *Hunting in Britain* (Stroud: History Press, 2009), p. 131.
6. Lewis, p. 125
7. William Bray (ed.), *The Diary of John Evelyn* (New York: M. Walter Dunne, 1901) passim.
8. Alan Davidson, *The Oxford Companion to Food* (Oxford: Oxford University Press, 1999), p. 825.
9. Hannah Wolley, *The Queen-like Closet or Rich Cabinet*, 1670 (accessed via www.gutenberg.org).
10. Robert May, *The Accomplish't Cook, or, The Art and Mystery of Cookery: Wherein the Whole Art is Revealed* (London: [n. pub.], 1678).
11. Gervase Markham, *The English Housewife*, 1664.
12. 'Turnsole,' www.wikipedia.org/wiki/Turnsole.
13. See www.historicfood.com.
14. Markham, pp. 73–75.
15. Available online at http://www.gutenberg.org/ebooks/14377
16. Kenelm Digby, *The Closet of Sir Kenelm Digby Knight Opened* (1669), pp. 203, 215, 169. Available online at http://www.gutenberg.org/ebooks/16441

Art and Alchemy:
The Authentic Air-cured Sausages of Europe

Jan Davison

Take meat, add salt, stuff it into a gut; provide fresh air and time. Together, in an act little short of alchemy, these simple elements combine to turn raw flesh into cured meat, to render what would otherwise spoil into a form that will keep. That the resulting sausage is not only durable, but also exceptionally good to eat, is down to the skill of its maker. It is a craft that has been practised and honed across much of Italy and the uplands of southern Europe through the centuries.[1] Associations with heritage and tradition do much to foster perceptions of a product carefully handed down one generation to the next, made in the same way as always, from time immemorial; yet for the most part this is no longer the case.

As with most foods, technology has revolutionized the production of air-cured meats and sausages. The greatest innovation has been the development of climate-controlled curing units. At a flick of a switch the perfect conditions for curing meat can be created, quite literally, anywhere. Large-scale industrialization has inevitably followed. Today, it is factories – with an emphasis on standardization and speed – that produce most of the salami and other cured sausages eaten in Europe. The authentic, slow-cured sausage – true to local tradition and place – is a rarity few of us have the opportunity to savour.

This paper reviews the principal factors involved in making traditional air-cured pork sausages and examines the skills, techniques and application of the artisan maker working solely with nature. It highlights three critical factors that cannot be replicated at a flick of a switch: tradition, *terroir* and time. The paper also reveals the historical and culinary significance embodied in the simple act of stuffing salted meat into a casing and hanging it to cure. The findings presented here are the distillation of eighteen months field research across Europe researching the making, use and cultural importance of the sausage in all its diversity.[2]

Air-cured sausages – traditional centres of production
The fundamental process underlying all curing is the removal of water from the meat. This is achieved through the action of salt drawing moisture out of the meat tissue and its gradual evaporation into the surrounding air. It is for this reason the terms 'air-dried', 'air-cured' and 'cured' are interchangeable. To facilitate this loss of moisture naturally requires the right combination of environmental conditions. These are determined by climate and topography. To minimize risk of the sausages spoiling in the initial drying phase, which traditionally takes place between November and early March, the winters

must be dry and cold, hovering at freezing or below (0°C to 2°C).³ Altitude also plays an important role: 500–800 metres above sea level is the ideal. At this height there is circulating air to remove moisture from the surface of the casings as the sausages continue to dry. Critically, there must also be a constant relative humidity of between 70–80%. This is vital for successful curing: too damp and the meat becomes mouldy, too dry and the casing develops a crust preventing the essential loss of moisture.

This set of conditions occurs most readily across southern Europe in clearly defined areas. Starting on the Iberian Peninsula and travelling east, Portugal has just one location, the town of Barrancos on the high Serra Morena, in the south-east of the country. Spain, a major producer of air-dried hams and sausages, has three principal centres: Guijuelo, near Salamanca; Jabugo in the Sierra de Huelva, western Andalusia; and the high Plana de Vic, just north of Barcelona. In neighbouring France there are also three areas particularly suited to air-curing: the Plateau of Lacaune in the Midi-Pyrenees; the Auvergne; and the city of Lyon and its environs. However, it is in Italy where the right combination of altitude and climate occurs most often, afforded by the foothills of the Alps in the north and the Apennines running down the length of the country. Traditional areas of air-dried salami production include Calabria in the south, Tuscany and Umbria in central Italy, and Lombardy, Piedmont and Emilia Romagna in the north.⁴

Continuing eastwards across Europe, Slovenia also benefits from the presence of the Alps. The Karst region, Sebrelje Plateau and Upper Savinja Valley all have microclimates suited to curing meat. Despite the mountainous nature of the Balkan Peninsula, only Bulgaria has a significant tradition of air-cured sausages.⁵ They are made in numerous locations along the Balkan range stretching across the centre of the country and between the Rila and Pirin mountains in the south-west. Greece is able to air-dry meats; surprisingly it is not on the mainland, but on the islands, notably the Ionian Islands of Corfu and Lefkáda and the Cyclades: Paros, Tinos, Syros, Sérifos and Mykonos. There is also one lone 'outpost' to the southern band of natural curing centres: Germany has a suitable pocket in the middle of the country comprising northern Hesse, Eichsfeld in neighbouring Thuringia and the southern reaches of Lower Saxony.

The specific microclimate of each locality, the seasonal and diurnal changes in temperature and humidity, influence the rate at which the sausages cure. Producers in Italy also attach great import to the local winds, which they claim impart a special flavour to their particular salami. Romance apart, the unique climate and daily weather conditions of each area are important contributory factors to a traditionally cured sausage's individual character – its *terroir*.

At this point it is important to make a distinction between natural weather-dependent maturation, which concerns us here, and that which takes place in temperature and humidity controlled curing units with pumped, circulating air. The high demand for cured products year-round means that, even in the regions cited above, recourse to such technology is now the norm. While sausages cured under these optimum conditions can, if this is the only form of intervention, be very good, they mature faster than those dependent on external weather conditions.[6] The result is a consistent product of a fine quality, but without the extra dimensions in flavour and character that can be attained in the best sausages cured more slowly.

Making traditional air-cured sausages

Traditionally produced, slow-cured sausages are essentially all made in the same way. The distinctiveness of each – the variations in texture and flavour – are brought about by the complex inter-relationship of many factors. These include the selection of the raw material, the age and in some instances the breed of pig, the cuts of meat and type of fat used, and how they are both prepared. In addition there is the salt, spices and aromatics, all of which, in varying degrees, affect flavour. The choice of gut into which the seasoned meat is stuffed also plays a critical role, as does the unique effect of the local microflora.

Selection of the pig

The age of the pig is an important contributory factor to the ultimate quality and flavour of the sausage. The best cured sausages are made from slow-growing mature pigs, typically nine months to a year old and weighing between 140–170 kilos.[7] In Germany, artisan butchers have a saying that a pig must hear the Christmas carols twice before slaughter. Older pigs have three distinct advantages over their quick-growing, younger counterparts: their meat has significantly more flavour; they have more fat, which enables the meat to lose moisture without becoming overly dry; and finally, the meat tissues contain less water, so there is less to lose during curing.

For the most part, the breed or sex of pig (boars are always castrated) has little bearing on the character of the cured sausage. Indigenous and old breeds, which may (or may not) have had distinctive eating qualities, have largely been replaced across Europe by standard commercial Celtic breeds such as the Large White, Landrace and Pietran. The dominance of these breeds makes it difficult for makers today to truly replicate the sausages of their forbears. However, there are a few exceptions; of particular note is the indigenous black *Ibérico* pig of the Iberian Peninsula. Free grazing, fattened on acorns, and slaughtered at around eighteen months, the *Ibérico* produces cured sausages with unique melt-in-the-mouth qualities and a pronounced, richly nuanced flavour.[8]

The selection of meat and fat

The balance between the various cuts of pork used and the type of fat selected influences the final texture of the cured sausage. The emphasis among traditional producers is on using prime, lean pieces of meat, commonly from the shoulder.[9] This produces a firm sausage – a characteristic of most salami. For softer-style cured sausages a proportion of meat from the belly, with more integral fat, or from the leg, which contains more water than the shoulder, may also be included. Similar principles apply to the choice of fat:

hard fat from the back produces a dry, firm, cured sausage whereas fat taken from the belly or throat, which is itself soft, produces a softer style. Typically, sausages that are to be cured are made of 75–80% lean meat and 20–25% fat.[10]

The firmness or softness of the sausage is also determined in part by how the meat and fat are prepared. As a general rule, both are coarsely minced (8–12mm). If they are minced together, as in *salame finocchiona* and *sbricolona* from Tuscany, a soft texture will result, even after long curing; minced separately and then combined the sausage will be supple but firm; if the back fat is cut into distinct cubes, rather than minced, the lean meat, which has little integral fat to lubricate and keep it moist, cures to a marked chewy firmness; *salame di Napoli* is a good example of this style of cured sausage.

Salt, seasoning and aromatics

The best makers attach great importance to the source and quality of seasonings. They use freshly ground whole spices, the finest sea salt, fresh aromatics and pungent, locally grown herbs.

Across Europe producers show remarkable consistency in the amount of salt they use in the making of cured sausages: 25–26g per kilo is the norm. The use of other seasonings and aromatics is dictated by tradition. For many makers, the primary role of seasoning is to enhance the flavour of the meat. Often only salt and black pepper are used, such as in the *salchichón de Vic* produced in northern Spain and *salame Brianza* from Lombardy, Italy. Where spices and aromatics are added, the general intention is to give nuance rather than a distinctive flavour. This subtle seasoning is typical of Germany's traditional *Alte Wurst* made in northern Hesse and of the salami produced in northern Italy: *salame Brianza, salame di Felino, salame piacentino, salame Piemonte* and *salame di Varzi*.[11] Similarly, in Spain, the finest examples of the large cured sausages *chorizo cular* and *lomo* are seasoned, almost imperceptibly, with the fiery red spice, *pimentón*. However, there are exceptions to this general rule, including the smaller cured *chorizo* of Spain and the equally spicy *soppressata* of Calabria, Italy where significant quantities of *pimentón* and *pepperoncino* are used respectively to flavour the meat. Greece also produces a highly aromatic cured sausage, *lefkados*, redolent with coriander, allspice and whole peppercorns. The use of herb seeds can also be used to create a distinctive flavour such as in *finocchiona Toscana*, fennel *salame*, from Tuscany, Italy.

Wine is used in minute quantities, just 1–5ml per kilo of meat, yet makers insist it helps with both preservation and flavour. Given curing is about removing water from the meat it is important not to add liquid unnecessarily.

Art and Alchemy: The Authentic Air-cured Sausages of Europe

Typical seasonings for air-cured sausages

Seasoning	*Per kilo of meat*	*Observations*
Salt	25–26g	Usually sea salt. A minority of makers use as little as 20g and some up to 28g/kilo. Along with the salt producers are required to add preservative: either potassium nitrite, sodium nitrite or sodium nitrate.[12] Most makers use a proprietary curing salt which includes nitrite at the approved levels. The salt also contains the antioxidant ascorbic acid.[13]
Black pepper	2–5g	Used as whole peppercorns, or coarsely or finely milled, often in combination. White pepper is occasionally added along with black.
Ground spices	0.5g in total	Occasionally up to 2g/kilo.[14] Common spices, often used together, include: cinnamon, nutmeg, cloves and coriander.
Dried herbs	0.5–1g	Rarely used, exceptions include: marjoram in *chorizo cular*, Spain; oregano and savoury in air-dried *loukanika*, Mykonos, Greece.
Herb seeds	2–5g	Typically fennel or aniseed in Italy and Greece, coriander in Bulgaria and caraway in Germany. Quantity depends on pungency of the seed and desired effect.
Fresh garlic	0.5–1g	Minced or chopped and added to the meat or infused in wine and then discarded.
Wine	1–5ml	Dry red or white from the locality.

Stuffing – the importance of the gut

It is the casing into which the meat is stuffed that ultimately, and perhaps surprisingly, determines much of a cured sausage's character. Despite it being the most unlikely of contenders, the pig's gut used to encase the meat, with its variations in calibre and wall thickness, influences the curing time and in so doing, the final flavour of the sausage.[15] The fundamental premise is this: as the sausage hangs and dries so it acquires flavour. The longer it takes to dry, the greater the depth and complexity of flavour that results.

The desire to extend the curing time was also once shared by much earlier generations. Indeed the diversity of air-cured sausages made today is a legacy of the European peasant's judicious planning. The peasant, however, was not striving for gastronomic excellence, but simply seeking to eke out the meat from the slaughtered pig, prolonging the time over which it would remain fit to eat. The slabs of back fat were salted, while the flesh and remaining fat were cut small, salted well, and stuffed into the pig's cleaned intestines, bladder and stomach. The sausages were made in various sizes and thicknesses: small, thin sausages that dried quickly; thicker ones to keep a month or two and others that would cure slowly over several months. Often a special sausage would be made from the best meat with its maturation timed for Easter. *Louza,* prepared from the pig's loins on the Cycladic Islands and Corfu (where it is called *noumboula)* is such an example. Fortunately the pig obliged the peasant's quest for sequential curing and eating. Along the length of its intestine are sections of gut that are narrow in diameter and others that are larger; there are thin walled parts and thick walled parts – each section influencing how long the sausage will take to cure and ultimately last.

Today, as in the past, slow curing through the selection of gut is achieved in three main ways. First, a sausage stuffed into a section of gut with a large calibre will, simply by virtue of its size, lose moisture more slowly and so mature over a longer period. Second, the thickness of the wall of the intestine acts in a similar way: a thick-walled gut allows the moisture to escape more slowly than a thin-walled part. Third, some sections of gut contain a fatty lining that also slows down moisture-loss, again facilitating slower curing. In addition, human ingenuity can also play a part: a speciality of the region of Extremadura, Spain is *lomo blanco*, made from a whole pig's loin which is dipped into melted fat before being stuffed into the intestine. The moisture-retaining fat slows the meat's curing from three to five months or more.

The small intestine, with its relatively thin walls and small diameter, is used for small sausages destined to cure within a month or so. Meanwhile, the large intestine affords the opportunity for a variety of slow cured sausages, giving each their characteristic size, shape, flavour, and in some instances their name. The pouch-like *caecum* creates distinctively large, lumpy sausages: *Jesus de Lyon* from France and *morcon* made in Spain are two examples. A particularly thick-walled section, close to the rectum, is favoured for large, straight sausages. In Spain, for example, this section of gut is known as '*cular*' and gives its name to the popular *chorizo cular,* which is as thick and straight as a large church candle. Similarly, in France, the large dried sausage *rosette* is named after the rose-like shape formed by the scrunched anus at one end. In Italy, producers refer to a specific section with thick walls and an integral fatty layer as *gentile*. Despite its relatively small diameter, the *gentile* affords slow curing and is used for a number of high-quality salami including authentic *salame di Felino*, giving the *salame* its characteristically slightly irregular, slender shape and delicate aroma and flavour.[16]

Fermentation and curing

The transformation of a raw sausage into one that is preserved relies on two parallel processes: fermentation and curing. Fermentation adds flavour to the meat through the action of bacteria, particularly those producing lactic acid and organic flavour compounds such as nutty aldehydes and fruity esters. Curing renders the meat stable, primarily through the action of salt drawing moisture out of the tissues but also through the effect of nitrites which produce a rosy coloration.[17] Both fermentation and curing contribute to its textural qualities.[18]

For producers seeking to manage these processes in tune with the seasons and wholly dependent on the vagaries of the weather, there is a significant risk involved.[19] The greatest threats are damp and sluggish air, both of which hinder drying and prevent the product from curing sufficiently – the meat becomes mouldy and spoils. In summer, if temperatures are unusually hot, there is a danger of fat melting and dripping from the maturing sausage. There are two distinct stages in the fermentation and curing of sausages, preliminary drying and maturation.

Typically, producers manage preliminary drying in one of two ways. Artisan makers preparing sausages during the winter months, and sticking to time-honoured practices, hang them in the ambient temperature of their drying room, typically around 3–6°C. The sausages hang at this temperature for two to three months, as the room gradually warms up through the spring.[20] If it is particularly cold or if the air is damp, a small fire may be lit in the first few days after making to raise the temperature slightly and dry the air, thus helping to dry the casings, but being careful not to smoke the sausages. This traditional method of curing requires significant skill: both fermentation and drying are temperature dependent and at low temperatures there is greater risk of spoilage. However, where it is managed successfully, slow fermentation produces sausages with a superior depth of flavour.

A more common approach today, even among artisan producers, is to get drying and fermentation underway as quickly as possible. To this end, the freshly made sausages are hung in a warm environment, with the temperature between 15–25°C and a relative humidity of 70–85%, for several days and up to a week. Those advocating this approach argue that the introduction of warmth is little different to the custom of lighting a fire to raise the temperature. During this period the temperature is progressively reduced and the sausages continue their natural curing at the ambient temperature.

As the sausage matures, a stage also known as seasoning, ripening or aging, the continued drying of the sausage is of primary concern.[21] For this to happen effectively requires first humidity, to prevent the casing from developing a crust that seals in the moisture, and second circulating air, to swiftly remove any dampness. The walls of traditional drying rooms also help in this regard; being of brick, clay or occasionally wood, they absorb moisture, while moderating the temperature.

The ideal conditions during maturation are an ambient temperature of 12–15°C with a relative humidity of 70–80%. If the humidity is higher, drying will be slower. To ensure a good through-flow of air, drying rooms are usually well above the ground, first storey upwards. In some parts of Italy a *cantina* (cellar) is used. However, these vaulted rooms are only semi-underground and small, high windows provide ventilation.

Producers that rely solely on natural conditions to dry their sausages manage the ambient air temperature, humidity and flow of air in the drying room through opening and shutting vents or windows. In the winter, when the weather is dry, the windows are opened through the day. At night and when it is too humid, damp or cold, they are closed. In the summer the vents are closed during the day and open at night. If more humidity is required, the floor is dampened with water.

The value of yeasts and moulds

The microflora – yeasts and moulds present in the air – is different in every area, and slight variations in local conditions can also be unique to a particular producer. Readily air-borne, the microflora settles on the casings of the sausages as they hang; the principle benefit is extending the curing time with the resultant effect on depth of flavour. Initially the yeasts flourish but are soon overtaken by the growth of moulds comprising various species of *Penicillinum* and *Aspergillus* which form a visible protective 'bloom' on the sausage, slowing down moisture loss.

The amount of mould is monitored carefully. Too much can seal moisture in and prevent drying so excess is brushed off. The mould's colour is an indicator of the level of moisture in the meat. Green mould is found on sausages at an early stage of their maturation, with a high moisture content, a greyish-white mould on ones that are part or fully cured. The moulds appear damp, but a gentle tap and they drift in the air like icing sugar.

Producers regard the contribution moulds make to their cured sausages as invaluable, believing they also contribute a distinctive flavour to the meat itself. One top Italian producer of *salame di Felino*, on commissioning a new drying shed ran it in parallel with the original building. Gradually the curing salami were moved from the old premises to the new, with the hope that the microflora that had helped give the salami their unique character would move too. In this respect natural curing is not simply a repeatable science; to make products that have individuality and convey a sense of place, *terroir,* they must be made in collaboration with capricious nature. The producer of this traditional *salame di Felino* advises its customers to slice it with the skin on so that the mould 'perfumes' the meat as it is cut.

The waiting game

For makers wholly dependent on the rhythm of the seasons and fluctuations in local weather conditions, time has to run its course. Sausages maturing in a traditional drying room at ambient temperature and humidity will take up to twice as long as the same product hung in a climate-controlled unit, where perfect curing conditions are replicated every day. For some large, naturally air-cured sausages this means anything from six months up to a year. It takes a trained hand to tell with a gentle squeeze if the sausages are fully cured and ready to eat.

Conclusion

In the hands of a master craftsman, continuing time-honoured practices, relayed through generations, the natural, slow, weather-dependent aging adds much to a sausage's individuality and flavour. Only a tiny minority of producers are prepared to take the risk of natural air-curing in pursuit of the elusive extra 'something' that makes their products unique and a true expression of place. In the hands and hearts of these artisans a sense of art and alchemy remains amid the science of curing. Every year their sausages vary a little, just as wines change with each vintage. For many artisans and their customers it is this aspect of the cured sausage's making, the successful collaboration between man and nature, which continues to be celebrated today. As one Italian artisan producer, whose *salama da sugo* is in such demand it is sold '*en-primeur*', a year before it is ready to eat, explained: 'My customers take the risk with me. They understand that it could be a good year, in which case their *salama* will be superb, or a bad year, in which case we will weep together.'

Five artisan air-cured sausages

Alte Wurst – Landfleischerei Thomas Koch, Hesse, Germany
As a country butcher Thomas Koch slaughters his own animals. He needs to, for contrary to all usual sausage-making conventions, the best *Alte Wurst* is made from a freshly killed pig with the meat still warm. Warm meat, says Thomas, is better able to absorb the spices, giving the sausage a superior aroma and flavour. Made only in the winter months, the *Alte Wurst* cures for up to a year, well deserving of the name 'old sausage'.

Babichka – Deshka Kashta, Rila Mountains, Bulgaria
A large air-cured sausage made by the family for their own use. Loin of pork is cut small and seasoned with salt and pungent herbs. It is stuffed into the pig's caecum, which is then flattened between boards. Once cured, the *babichka* is plunged into wood-ash keeping it in perfect condition for two years or more.

Corallina di Norcia – Fratelli Ansuini, Umbria, Italy
The Umbrian town of Norcia gave its name to Italy's specialist pork butchers, and today the Ansuini family, third and fourth generation *norcini*, still produce hams and salami in the town. In a small vaulted cellar row upon row of salami hang on sweet chestnut branches. Each *salame* matures here for six to twelve months. Sparing use of aromatics and unhurried curing give Ansuini's *corallina di Norcia* its outstanding depth of flavour – one of the finest salami in Italy.

Mortadella di Camaiore – Salumi Gombitelli, Tuscany, Italy[22]
Alderigo Triglio's family have been making sausages in the tiny hilltop village of Gombitelli since 1797. Alderigo insists on mature pigs fattened on whey as only they provide meat of the required flavour and texture. He collects herbs from the

Art and Alchemy: The Authentic Air-cured Sausages of Europe

hillside to flavour the meat, and the walnuts he harvests in June find their way into the sausages he makes in November.

Salchichón de Vic – Casa Reiera Ordeix, Catalonia, Spain
An area described as cool and misty for almost two thirds of the year would not appear an auspicious location for curing meat, but on the Plana de Vic, 40 kilometres north of Barcelona, Spain's most distinctive sausage is still made traditionally. It owes its subtle and intense flavour to the unique microclimate and hence microflora of the area that enables it to undergo an exceptionally long maturation.

Notes

1. Examples include: Italy, *salami*; France, *saucissons secs;* Spain, *chorizo* and *salchichón;* Germany, *Rohwürste;* Bulgaria, *sudjuk;* Slovenia, *želodec.*
2. Austria, Bulgaria, Czech Republic, France, Germany, Greece, Hungary, Italy, Latvia, Lithuania, Poland, Portugal, Romania, Slovakia and Spain.
3. Historically, pigs were slaughtered in the late autumn and winter.
4. In Calabria, the limestone Apennines end. Much of the peninsula is dominated by the granite mountain range known as the Sila.
5. In Romania a very small proportion of sausages (*salam*) are air-cured. From empirical evidence it would appear that suitable conditions are not found elsewhere in the Balkans: sausages for keeping are traditionally smoked.
6. It is common industry practice to add starter cultures and sugar to speed up fermentation (with extra salt to compensate). In many products milk protein, soya or cereals are also added to bulk out the meat and absorb excess moisture, so reducing curing time as well as adding weight. A standardized culture of microflora may also be applied to the sausage's external casing to ensure a consistent flavour.
7. In Spain and Italy these heavy pigs are raised for ham production; air-cured sausages are the by-product. These characteristics are in marked contrast to the industry standard of three to six months with a weight of 60–90 kilos.
8. Known as Porco Alentejana in Portugal.
9. The meat is prepared by hand to remove any fat, tendons or nerves. In ham-producing areas trimmings from the leg are also used.
10. During drying, the lean meat loses moisture, but the fat does not, and so the proportion of fat ostensibly increases – fully cured sausages typically have a fat content of 30–35%.
11. These salami are of an excellent quality and have either DOP or IGP protection, they are made in accordance with traditional practices – no starter cultures or other additives can be used, although most are cured in climate-controlled units.
12. Nitrite suppresses microbial activity (in particular *Clostridium botulinum* is the cause of sometimes fatal food poisoning, botulism); it also has a secondary role, giving cured meat its characteristic pink coloration (see n. 19). The amount of potassium nitrite or sodium nitrite added to the meat is set by EU regulations at 150mg/kilo (European and Council Directive, 95/2/EC). In some cases sodium nitrate (300mg/kilo) is used in place of sodium nitrite. The nitrate is slower acting, in that it first has to be transformed by salt-tolerant bacteria into the active form, sodium nitrite. The slower, on-going bacterial production of nitrite from nitrate is beneficial in sausages that are curing over a long period. For more on nitrites in cured meat, see Harold McGee, *On Food and Cooking, The Science and Lore of the Kitchen* (New York: Scribner, 2004).

13. Ascorbic acid (vitamin C) slows down oxidation of the meat when the cured sausage is sliced and the meat exposed to the air, so preserving its red coloration for longer. Producers typically add between 0.5–1.0g/kilo of fresh meat.
14. There are exceptions: for small cured *chorizo* (Spain) between 7 to 35g of the spice *pimentón* is used per kilo of meat. Greek *lefkados* is seasoned with around 8g each of ground coriander, ground allspice and whole black peppercorns per kilo of meat.
15. In the home the pig's bladder or stomach may also be used. In commercial production, some large calibre sausages are now made in cow gut.
16. This style of salame is widely copied; the traditionally made product has IGP (protected designation of origin) status.
17. The nitrite reacts with the protein myoglobin in the muscle fibres to form a pink compound, nitrosomyoglobin.
18. For more information on fermentation and curing see McGee and Len Fisher, 'Fermented, Cured and Smoked: The Science and Savour of Dry-Fermented Sausages', *Cured, Fermented and Smoked Foods: Proceedings of the 2010 Oxford Symposium on Food and Cookery*, ed. Helen Saberi (Totnes: Prospect Books, 2011), pp. 102–105.
19. It is why the majority of producers following traditional procedures in every other respect have installed computer-controlled plants with regulated temperature, humidity and airflow. Some use these only when the weather is poor, but most large producers use it as a matter of course to optimize curing conditions and enable year round production.
20. Many traditional producers now undertake year round production – to this end, they seek to mimic the cold winter period by keeping the sausages in chilled conditions for up to a month, before continuing curing traditionally, at the ambient temperature.
21. Through the process of curing and dehydration a sausage loses from 25–40% of its original weight.
22. This is an air-cured sausage. It should not be confused with the large cooked sausage, Mortadella Bologna.

Mantı and *Mantou*

Along the Silk Road, dumplings hint at a shared common past. In these two papers, we explore these parallels, historical and contemporary, using our complementary linguistic skills and respective areas of expertise. Since the same forms of dumpling are reproduced and reinvented across the Eurasian landmass, we hope to shed new light on the connections between different forms of stuffed flour foods across this vast region.

Aylin Öney Tan investigates the Turkish end of the Silk Road, while Fuchsia Dunlop focuses on its Chinese termination. Fuchsia also draws on her knowledge of Uyghur foodways, gathered during two field trips to Xinjiang, to examine the ways in which this vast region, which is still little known outside China, can be seen as an important bridge between Chinese and Central Asian food cultures. Aylin explores the Anatolian and Central Asian Turkic variations of mantı, *listing stuffing and folding techniques, fillings, and cooking methods, to try to trace the Asiatic roots through Fuchsia's findings.*

Barbarian Heads and Turkish Dumplings: The Chinese Word *Mantou*

Fuchsia Dunlop

Chinese legend has it that the *mantou* (馒头), a plain steamed bun that is one of the staple foods in the north of the country, was originally a 'barbarian head' (*mantou* 蛮头).[1] The great statesman and strategist Zhuge Liang – so the story goes – was on a military campaign in the south in the third century AD when he encountered some difficulties, and was told to propitiate local spirits with offerings of human heads. Unwilling to make such a sacrifice, he fooled the gods with dough balls stuffed with meat. These 'barbarian heads' entered Chinese culinary tradition, though their name eventually lost its original, gory meaning, with the replacement of the original character *man* 蛮, referring to the southern barbarian tribes, by the innocuous 馒, which sounds the same, but has no particular meaning.

In modern Chinese, the term *mantou* (馒头) has evolved to cover a range of foods that include, in different regions, plain steamed buns and stuffed dumplings. And, while the Chinese may lay claim through the tale of Zhuge Liang to be the originators of the word, strikingly similar terms are used to describe a whole range of flour-based

Barbarian Heads and Turkish Dumplings:

foods from Xinjiang in the far north-west of China (where, for the Turkic Uyghurs, *manti* are large steamed dumplings stuffed with mutton and onion) to Turkey (where tiny *manti* dumplings are stuffed with minced lamb and served with yoghurt, butter and chilli). In this paper, I review the history and usage of the Chinese word *mantou* and offer some observations that might support the argument that the term is of Turkic or Central Asian origin.

The earliest extant Chinese written reference to *mantou* is in the *Rhapsody on Bing* (饼赋) written by the scholar Shu Xi (束皙) during the Western Jin Dynasty (AD 265–316), which survives only in fragments quoted by later works.[2] This prose-poem, a lively account of the pasta-type foods known as *bing* in ancient China, suggests that *mantou* should be served at feasts and banquets in early spring, when the harsh cold of winter has eased and the weather is warm but not yet sweltering. In Shu Xi's time, *mantou* is thought to have referred to fairly large pastries filled with meat, or perhaps with sweet stuffings – which may explain why they were linked to the idea of 'barbarian heads'.[3]

A version of the Zhuge Liang story first appears centuries later, during the Song Dynasty (AD 960–1279), when Gao Cheng's 'Recording the Origins of Things' tells how, during a campaign against the rebel Chinese soldier Meng Huo and his army of Man barbarians, Zhuge Liang was advised that the people of the south used sorcery in battle, and that it was necessary to pray to the gods to send out a spirit army to assist him. According to Man custom, a man should be killed and his head offered up in sacrifice before the gods would send out their forces, but Zhuge Liang instead used mutton and pork wrapped in dough to resemble a human head, and the gods, satisfied by this trickery, sent out their ghostly soldiers to help him.[4]

Another version of this legend appears in the Ming Dynasty (AD 1368–1644) novel, the *san guo yan yi* (三国演义), which describes how Zhuge Liang's soldiers were unable to cross a river in the south because of wild waves, and discovered that according to local custom the savage river spirits had to be appeased by the sacrifice of forty-nine human heads, along with oxen and goats or sheep. Zhuge Liang was unwilling to embark on such 'senseless slaughter', so he ordered his cook to make models of human heads from flour dough stuffed with beef or mutton, which were to be called *mantou* (馒头), a homonym, as already explained, for 'barbarian head'. They made their offerings on the banks of the river, the waves calmed and they were able to cross.[5] Another source suggests that the name *mantou* is a play on the word *man*, meaning 'to deceive' (瞒), so the stuffed pastry is a 'false head'.[6]

Early Chinese sources consistently refer to the ritual use of wheaten foods called *mantou*: for example, Shu Xi's *Rhapsody on Bing* describes their use to mark a particular season, when the *yin* energy of the winter months merges into the *yang* of early summer, while one Ming Dynasty literary work mentions them as a food used in temple rituals.[7] *Mantou* still have some ritual uses in China: for example, in one village I've visited in northern Gansu province, each household sends nine very large, round, steamed *mantou* buns to a neighbour who has suffered a death in the family (white, in China,

129

is the colour of mourning and of funeral vestments).⁸ Furthermore, the habit of using human heads in sacrifice was known in ancient China, as Qiu Pangtong remarks in his history of flour-foods, so it is possible that there is some truth in the Zhuge Liang legend.⁹ However, it is conspicuous that there are no references to the story in sources earlier than the Song. And, as Qiu also notes, *mantou* would anyway have been a natural development of the 'steamed *bing*' of the Han Dynasty (206 BC–AD 220) rounded flour-foods that, by the time of Shu Xi, are known to have had stuffings.¹⁰ There is no need to suppose that they were suddenly invented, independently, as a substitute for human heads – although of course it is possible that the word *mantou* was applied to a pre-existing flour-food as a result of Zhuge Liang's adventures.

In modern China, the most common Chinese *mantou* is a substantial, unfilled steamed bun made from leavened wheatflour dough, which is very different from the stuffed dumplings that go by similar names in Central Asia. For example, in Xinjiang, the *manti* is a generously-sized steamed dumpling with a thin, unleavened wheaten wrapper stuffed with seasoned lamb/mutton and onions; in Turkey, the *mantı* may be a tiny dumpling made from a square of unleavened wheaten pastry, stuffed with lamb, boiled and then served with yoghurt, melted butter and chilli; or a 'Tatar' boiled dumpling made from a larger, circular wrapper of unleavened wheaten pastry, folded into a semicircle around a stuffing of seasoned lamb and onion, and served with yoghurt and melted butter, with further seasonings – ground chillies, mint, thyme, sumac – added at the table. (For further examples, see Aylin Öney Tan's companion paper.)

Although the forms of these Central Asian dumplings vary, they clearly have some characteristics in common: namely, a thin, unleavened wheaten wrapper and a stuffing made from seasoned, finely chopped ingredients. In modern China, dumplings with these characteristics are not generally known as *mantou*, but, variously, as *jiao, jiaozi, baozi, bao* or *huntun*. Moreover, large stuffed dumplings made with leavened dough which, one might suppose, most closely resemble the 'false heads' of the Zhuge Liang legend are not known as *mantou* at all, but almost invariably as *baozi* (包子 – 'wrapped things'). The gulf between the modern Chinese *mantou* and this family of stuffed dumplings with *mantou*-like names, encourages some scholars to conclude that they have separate origins and etymologies.¹¹

I'd like, however, to look at evidence that the Chinese word *mantou* and the Turkic *manti* may, in fact, be historically linked, and that while the physical Chinese *mantou* as a leavened, steamed bun is distinct from the unleavened dumplings found across Asia, the Chinese word itself is of Turkic or Central Asian origin.

The history of usage of the word *mantou* in China

There is no doubt that the Chinese word *mantou* has been, and still is, used to refer to a variety of different wheaten foods. Zhu Wei, in his *Philological Researches into Eating*, provides an overview of the Chinese sources, which I will now summarize: After the Jin Dynasty, the period in which *mantou* appear in Shu Xi's *Rhapsody*, the generic pasta-word *bing* continued to be used to describe any kind of food that consisted of a flour-and-water dough encasing a stuffing, including those he referred to as *mantou*. During the Tang Dynasty (AD 618–907), so-called *mantou* were typically small and dainty, and were considered as a type of *dian xin* (little pastries offered as refreshments rather than staple foods). Different sources of this period use divergent Chinese characters to refer to them: variously *mantou* (曼头 – the first character here is yet another *man*, meaning 'large, extended, long') and *man dou* (饅飣 the *dou* here meant 'to set out food').[12]

By the Song Dynasty, *mantou* (with the modern name 馒头) are described as a common snack for university students in the southern capital, the city now known as Hangzhou.[13] At this time – a *mantou* might be stuffed with pork, lamb, beef, chicken, duck, fish, goose or any kind of vegetable. According to Zhu Wei, it was around this time, when *mantou* had shrunk in size and no longer resembled the human heads of the old legend – that an alternative name for them emerged: *baozi* ('wrapped thing').[14] *Mantou* from the Tang and Song periods onwards were made with leavened dough, so they were distinct from the Central Asian *manti*, with their unleavened pastry. It was around this time that the term started to be applied also to steamed buns without stuffing, which presumably were like the common *mantou* of modern China. Both types, stuffed and unstuffed, were still used as ritual foods.[15]

The Mongol invasion of China and the Mongols' establishment of the Yuan Dynasty in 1271 brought with it a wave of influences from Central Asia. The treatise on diet and cookery written in 1330 for the Mongol Qan by his Muslim court doctor, *yin shan zheng yao* (饮膳正要)[16] includes recipes for four types of *mantou* (馒头) that clearly incorporate elements of both Chinese and Central Asian cooking traditions. Two of them, for example, have stuffings in which the lamb, lamb fat and onions typical of Central Asian cooking (and used in the modern Uyghur *manti*) are mixed with Chinese seasonings that include ginger and dried mandarin orange peel.[17] The text also includes two recipes for *baozi*, which are essentially the same as the *mantou* recipes, except that one gives crab ovaries, normally a south-eastern Chinese ingredient, as a possible addition to a stuffing of lamb, sheep's fat and tail, onions, dried mandarin peel, ginger and mushrooms.

Paul Buell and Eugene Anderson suggest that the *mantou* described in this text have nothing to do with the unfilled Chinese steamed bun known as *mantou*, but are Turkic in style – which is presumably why they translate the Chinese characters of the original script (馒头) into English as **Manta*, in accordance with the Turkic pronunciation, rather than *mantou*. It is true that the fillings for these *mantou* appear Turkic/Central Asian in style, with their mutton and mutton fat seasoned with, among other things, some kind of onion (see note 17 below). However, I'd like to make a couple of observations which suggest that the Turkic origins of these *mantou* may be less clear-cut. One is that a recipe for *manti* stuffed with 'deer milk fat' (the fatty part of a deer's udder) includes the observation that 'one can [also] perhaps make "Quick **Manta*", or perhaps "Thin-skin **Manta*"'.[18] Could the reference to 'thin-skin **Manta*'

Barbarian Heads and Turkish Dumplings:

as an alternative to the main recipe imply that the main recipe is in fact for a dumpling with a thicker, leavened dough, like the early Chinese stuffed *mantou*? Certainly, in modern China, the Chinese name for the Uyghur *mantı*, a recognizably Turkic/Central Asian steamed dumpling with a thin, unleavened skin and a mutton/onion stuffing, is 'thin-skin *baozi*', and given that from the Song Dynasty onwards *baozi* emerged as a name for the stuffed buns originally known as *mantou*, it is inviting to suppose that these dumplings may once have been known as 'thin-skin *mantou*'.

The other observation concerns a recipe in the *yin shan zheng yao* ('A Soup for the Qan') for 'Cut-Flowers *Manta*' (剪花馒头 *jianhua mantou*). The words *jianhua* literally mean 'scissor-cut flowers', and the recipe is translated by Buell and Anderson as follows:

CUT FLOWERS *MANTA*

Mutton, sheep's fat, sheep's tail, onions, prepared mandarin orange peel. (Cut up each finely.)

[To] ingredients add, according to recipes, spices, salt and sauce. Make the stuffing. Form the *Manta*. Use scissors to cut out into various flower shapes. Steam. Use safflower to dye the flowers.[19]

If the *mantou* of this recipe are of the thin-skinned, Turkic/Central Asian variety, it is hard to see how they could be cut into flower shapes with scissors without being ruptured. Even if the dumplings were made with unusually large skins, allowing a

flap of pastry to hang loose over them, cutting this would surely give floppy rags of dumpling skin, not flower shapes. However, one pastry-making practice in modern Chinese cookery is to use scissors to snip patterns into the leavened skins of stuffed buns; as these rise, the patterns become more prominent. One example of this is a hedgehog bun made by the Chengdu chef Yu Bo, which is stuffed with sweet bean paste and snipped into quills:

A less delicate scissor-cutting technique may be used to cut an 'X' into the tops of Cantonese barbecued pork buns, which are again made from a leavened dough. Although I have not been able to establish when this technique emerged in Chinese bun-making, from a practical point of view, it might make sense to suppose that the reference in this recipe to scissor-cutting implies that the wrapper is made from a leavened dough.[20] Also, the recipe calls for the use of rouge (胭脂 *yanzhi*) to colour the cut 'flowers' – Buell and Anderson translate this as 'safflower', but I wonder if it might not actually be the natural dye made from red yeasted rice (红曲米 *hong qu mi*) that is commonly used to add an auspicious pink-red decoration to steamed Chinese buns, and has been cultivated in China since the Song Dynasty.[21] Steaming is also a quintessentially Chinese method for cooking dumplings. If these observations make sense, could it be that the *mantou* of the *yin shan zheng yao* are not, in fact, unleavened Turkic/Central Asian dumplings with a Chinese twist, but leavened Chinese *mantou* with hybrid Turkic/Chinese stuffings – and therefore a missing link between the Turkic *manti* and Chinese *mantou* traditions?

Moving swiftly onward through Chinese history, again with Zhu Wei as a guide: by the Qing Dynasty (1644–1911), the modern division emerged between the word *mantou*, which became tied to unstuffed steamed buns, and *baozi*, which came to identify steamed buns with stuffings (there are some geographical exceptions to this distinction, as I'll explain later). Zhu quotes a Qing source as saying that *mantou* are round, steamed buns made from leavened dough, and that because they have no stuffing, they must be served alongside other dishes.[22]

Modern Chinese usage of the word *mantou*

In modern China, as mentioned above, the most common use of the word *mantou* is to describe unstuffed steamed buns made from a leavened dough. These may be shaped with the hands into balls,[23] but are usually made by cutting thick slices from a long sausage of dough, so the steamed buns are slightly squared-off at both ends. In the north, these *mantou* are regarded as a staple food, to be served with prepared dishes as an alternative to noodles or rice; they may also be known as *mo mo* (馍馍), *juanzi* (卷子 'rolls') or even, confusingly, *baozi*.[24] In southern, rice-eating areas such as Guangdong and Sichuan, where they are often made smaller and daintier than in the north, these plain *mantou* buns are normally treated as a supplementary staple, perhaps to be eaten with one's breakfast rice gruel. (In most parts of China, stuffed, leavened steamed buns, reminiscent in form if not size of the Zhuge Liang legend, are now known as *baozi* –

which is presumably why the Chinese in Xinjiang call the unleavened Uyghur *mantı*, with its lamb-and-onion stuffing, a 'thin-skin *baozi*' 薄皮包子.)

In certain parts of south-eastern China however, *mantou* is still used to describe small, dainty steamed buns with fillings. Generally made with an unleavened dough, they are distinct from the more common unstuffed, leavened *mantou*.²⁵ The famous Shanghai 'soup dumplings' for example, although nowadays widely called *xiao long bao* (小笼包 'small steamer *bao*', using the 'wrap' character found in the word *baozi*), are traditionally known in their place of origin (the township of Nanxiang on the outskirts of Shanghai) as *xiao long mantou* ('small steamer *mantou*'). These *mantou* are made with an unleavened dough and stuffed with a mixture of seasoned minced pork and jellied pork stock; they have relatively thin skins, and are usually served twenty at a time, in one layer of a bamboo steamer. They are made by using a spatula to press stuffing onto a disc of dough held gently in one hand, and then turning the dough with this hand as the fingers of the other draw up the edge into tiny pleats, so the final dumpling is a little bun with a neat, twirly top.²⁶

Similarly-shaped *mantou*, steamed with their pleats facing upwards or downwards, and occasionally fried before serving, are found in the broader south-eastern region surrounding Shanghai, including Jiangsu and Zhejiang provinces. I've only been able to find mention of two northern *mantou* with stuffings: one pork bun from Beijing and one ball-shaped bun from Kaifeng, Henan Province, which has a sweet stuffing of candied fruits and walnuts.²⁷ In the south-eastern region, unstuffed steamed buns tend to be known as 'big *baozi*' (大包子).²⁸

Clearly, the picture is very confusing. In Chinese, the *mantou* has been, in various times and in various places, a large stuffed bun, a small stuffed bun, and an unstuffed bun; a ritual food used in seasonal feasts and sacrificial offerings; a snack for university students; a staple food and a dainty pastry. Moreover, all of the various types of *mantou* have been, or are, simultaneously known by one or more alternative names.

Turkic origins?
The translators of *A Soup for the Qan*, Paul Buell and Eugene Anderson, see the various *mantou* described in the text as being primarily Central Asian in character, and unrelated in any way – except for sharing a name – to the unfilled Chinese steamed bun that 'has considerable antiquity, going back at least to Han times if not before.' They argue that the Central Asian terms, including the Uyghur *mantı* and the Kazakh *manty*, are probably derived from the *mamata* of Mahmud al-Kashgari's eleventh-century dictionary of the Turkic languages,²⁹ which is defined as 'dough smeared on fat chicken or meat so that the fat will not run out when the meat is roasted'. This dough-wrapped piece of meat may have developed into the steamed *mantı* bun with dough skin and meat filling that is still found in Uyghur cooking. The echoes in this of the old (stuffed) Chinese *mantou*, and the similarity of sounds, may explain why, as Buell and Anderson suggest, the author of the Mongol dietary treatise and his contemporaries chose to

transcribe the name of this new Central Asian food with the same characters as those used for the Chinese *mantou* bun.[30]

Perhaps, though, *mantou* always was a Chinese transliteration of a foreign word. The origins of the *manti*-type terms in Turkic languages are mysterious, and early written documentation is scarce. Shu Xi, however, in his *Rhapsody on Bing*, does imply that the names of some of the pastry foods he describes are foreign in origin: 'Some of the names originate in the wards and lanes; Some of the methods come from alien lands'.[31]

The Chinese word *mantou*, meaningless in its individual Chinese characters, sounds so like the Turkic *manti* that it's tempting to suppose that this word was in very early use among the nomadic tribes bordering the Chinese empire to the West, and that *mantou* was an attempt to reproduce the sounds in Chinese.

As Endymion Wilkinson explains in his *Chinese History: A Manual*, the northern Chinese language has been influenced at various times by the languages of its Turkic and Altaic conquerors,[32] and loan words from foreign tongues were an important source of new polysyllabic words in classical Chinese.[33] For example, in the first great wave of loan words during the former Han Dynasty, new goods from the Xiongnu tribes in the north and from Western Asia were typically given names that were disyllabic transcriptions of their names in foreign languages: one example Wilkinson gives is the word *luotuo* for camel. Some of these loan words were later sinicized by adding significs that brought them into line with existing Chinese word categories: so, for example, eventually both the characters used for the camel (*luo* and *tuo*) came to include the 'horse' radical used in the names of other transport animals. Another type of loan word was created by attaching the current word for barbarian to an existing Chinese word, as in *hujiao* for black/white pepper (胡*hu* barbarian + 椒*jiao* pepper; *jiao* was originally used for the spice now known as Sichuan pepper).[34]

If the word *manti* or something similar was in use by the nomadic tribes of Central Asia as early as the Han, or at least as early as the Jin Dynasty when it first appears in Chinese, it would very likely have been transliterated into Chinese with the sounds *man* and *tou*, the closest Chinese match for the original sounds. Furthermore, the *man* character that is now used as standard in the word *mantou* includes the radical meaning 'eat', in common with many other Chinese words for types of flour-food now and in the distant past, including another of those described by Shu Xi in his rhapsody, the *putou*, which, as Knechtges notes, has an 'un-Chinese sounding name'.[35] Again, this fits a pattern of the adoption of a foreign concept or thing by the Chinese through the choice of Chinese characters that have similar sounds but no relevant meaning, and then adding the relevant signific that makes the new word conform to Chinese practice, so it sits happily among Chinese words for related things, in this case, breads and pastries, like *bing* (饼*bing*, with the 'eat' signific or radical 饣 on the left, as in the 馒*man* of *mantou*).

Of course, according to the Zhuge Liang legend, the original word for *mantou* used the 蛮*man* character that means 'barbarian', which invites comparison with the practice, mentioned above, of adding a prefix meaning 'barbarian' to an existing Chinese word for something similar. However, there is no real parallel here, because 'head' (头 *tou*) is not a preexisting word for any kind of food, but a meaningless suffix sometimes added to foreign loan words, perhaps to create a more balanced rhythm.³⁶ Moreover, I am not aware of any other cases of the *man* character for southern barbarians being used in this way in food words, unlike the character 胡 *hu*, referring to the north-western 'barbarians', which appears in many food compounds dating back to the Han,³⁷ and the character 番 *fan*, used during the Ming for overseas barbarians, which is also commonly used in food compounds.³⁸

Intriguingly, Zhu Wei cites one Ming Dynasty dictionary as stating that *mantou* were originally known as *tuo tuo qi*. This compound translates as something like 'camel's navels' or 'hunchback's navels', but sounds, to my ears, strikingly like the modern Chinese for Turkey (*tu er qi*). Could this be a reference to an ancient Chinese awareness that the word *mantou* was associated with a food of Turkic of Central Asian origins? According to C.E. Bosworth, there are references to Turks in Chinese as early as in the dynastic annals of the sixth century AD.³⁹

Clearly, the most common type of modern Chinese *mantou* is totally distinct from the Central Asian and Turkish dumplings described briefly here. However, if we take into account the smaller, stuffed south-eastern Chinese *mantou*, the differences are less striking. These small Chinese *mantou* have meat fillings and pleated wrappers like the Uyghur and Central Asian dumplings – although the meat is usually pork and the pleating takes a different form – and they recall the early *mantou* mentioned in Tang Dynasty sources. Also, it's interesting that one Song Dynasty source mentions mutton/goat *mantou* (羊肉馒头 *yangrou mantou*) as a food eaten in the city now known as Hangzhou. Could this use of mutton, with its nomadic associations, be an indicator of a northern influence with possibly Central Asian origins? (The migration of the Song court south to Hangzhou following the fall of the northern capital Kaifeng brought a wave of northern influences. It was said that at this time most of the restaurants in Hangzhou were kept by people from Kaifeng.⁴⁰)

We know that foreign food customs and the words associated with them flowed into China from Central Asia, particularly during the Han and Tang Dynasties and the period of Mongol rule, the Yuan Dynasty. It is also clear that the Central Asian-type *manti* dumpling entered Korea via China during the thirteenth-century Mongol invasion of the Korean Peninsula: this was the ancestor of the modern Korean *mandu* dumpling, a stuffed dumpling made with unleavened pastry that may be boiled, steamed or fried.⁴¹ It seems likely that the northern Chinese would have come into contact both with Central Asian pastry-foods and their associated words at various stages of their history. Given this long history of culinary and cultural contacts, isn't it unlikely that the Chinese word *mantou* would have a completely separate etymology, and that its similarity to *manti* should be purely coincidental?

Barbarian Heads and Turkish Dumplings:

Conclusions

The precise origins of the terms *mantou*, *mantı* and their relatives are mysterious, and there's no solid evidence that the Chinese word has foreign origins. However, what is clear is that the Chinese word *mantou* has been used, over the centuries and in different parts of the country, to refer to a variety of different flour foods, stuffed and unstuffed. Although the most common modern *mantou*, the plain steamed bun, appears to have little in common with the Central Asian and Korean dumplings bearing similar names, the difference is less marked between them and the stuffed *mantou* still eaten today in some parts of the country.

Many of the Chinese words for flour-foods have been fluid in their applications, with meanings that have changed over time and across the regions. The words *baozi* and *mantou*, though now broadly distinct, were used interchangeably during the Song Dynasty, and perhaps also during the Yuan Dynasty as the recipes in *A Soup for the Qan* suggest. They still have varied applications in some places, not only in the case of the modern, south-eastern Chinese *mantou*, but also in the case of the Uyghur *mantı*, a steamed dumpling with a thin, unleavened skin that is known in Chinese as a 'thin-skin *baozi*' – the same term used for the sinicized *mantı*-type dumplings in *A Soup for the Qan*.[42]

Perhaps *mantou* is simply one of the many loan words from foreign languages that entered China through Silk Road contacts with Central Asian tribes, and was borrowed at times of heightened foreign influence as a name for local flour-foods that may have evolved independently, but had some characteristics in common with the flour-foods of Central Asia. The word was transcribed in a few different ways, but eventually standardized as a pair of characters that incorporated the 'eat' radical to bring them in line with Chinese linguistic tradition. And perhaps although the word *mantou* was used interchangeably with *baozi* for much of its history in China, by the Qing Dynasty it had become so strongly associated with an unstuffed bun in the north that it was no longer appropriate to use it for the stuffed dumplings it had once described – this might explain why the Chinese call the modern Uyghur *mantı* '*baozi*'.

The Zhuge Liang legend first appears in a text produced during the Song Dynasty, a period when foreign regimes had conquered parts of China and the court was under constant threat of invasion by northern nomads. Could it have been intended to make a foreign word seem more Chinese? Or was it simply an example of the wit and playfulness of Chinese culinary culture, in which storytelling is one of the ways of heightening gastronomic pleasure?[43]

Whatever its exact origins, it seems hard to believe that the striking similarity between the word *mantou*, in many ways a linguistic misfit in Chinese, and the Turkic *mantı*, is purely coincidental.

Barbarian Heads and Turkish Dumplings:

Name	Country/Region	Shape/Folding	Cooking	Dough/Filling	Serving
Manti (Uyghur language) In Chinese: *bo pi bao zi* 薄皮包子 ('thin-skinned *baozi*')	Xinjiang (Uyghur ethnic group)	Large, floppy steamed dumplings, pleated and pinched along top like cockscomb	Steamed	Unleavened flour/water, dough, rolled discs Lamb or mutton/onion, salt, pepper	May be served on a nan bread 'plate', or on a plateful of *polo* (the local version of a rice pilaf)
Stone-baked *manti* (Kyrgyz language name unknown); Chinese name: 石烤馒头	Xinjiang (Kyrgyz ethnic group)		Baked on a hot stone		
Mantou (generic) 馒头	China, especially north	Usually cut from a thick sausage of dough	Steamed	Fermented flour/water dough No filling	Eaten as a staple food with dishes of meat, vegetables etc. Eaten as a supplementary staple with rice gruel in the south. In at least some parts of north China (eg rural Gansu), used as a ritual food at funerals
Diced pork *mantou* 肉丁馒头	China (north), Beijing	Fluffy buns with stuffing	Steamed	Fermented flour/water dough with sodium carbonate Small cubes of pork, spring onion, ginger, rice wine, sesame oil,	

Barbarian Heads and Turkish Dumplings:

Eight-treasure *mantou* 八宝馒头	China (north), Henan Province, Kaifeng	Ball-shaped	Steamed	Flour, sourdough starter, salt, sodium carbonate; finely-chopped walnuts, dried grapes, candied green plum, candied winter melon, candied tangerine peel, dried jujube, candied water chestnuts, sugar	
Nanxiang small steamer *mantou* 南翔小笼馒头	China (southeast), Nanxiang, Shanghai. (Wuxi in Jiangsu Province has a similar *mantou*)	Dumplings with twirly, pleated tops	Steamed	Unleavened flour/water dough; minced pork, salt, sugar, soy sauce, sesame oil, water, jellied pork stock	Served in the steamer with a dip of rice vinegar and shredded ginger
Pot-sticker *mantou* 生煎馒头	China (southeast), Shanghai	Dumplings with twirly, pleated tops	Steam/fried	Semi-fermented flour/water dough; jellied pork stock, water, ginger and spring onion juices, salt, sugar, soy sauce, sesame oil	Served with rice vinegar dip
Hou kou mantou 喉口馒头 a.k.a. *hou kou man shou* 喉口馒首	China (southeast), Shaoxing, Zhejiang Province	Spheres with twirly, pleated tops and slightly-open mouths so you can just see the filling	Steamed	Fermented flour/water dough with soda; minced pork with some fat, soy sauce, spring onion	Served in the steamer, with a dip of rice vinegar and a soup seasoned with lard, spring onion and egg-skin

139

Barbarian Heads and Turkish Dumplings:

Water-ferment mantou 水酵馒头	China (south-east), Nantong, Jiangsu Province	Buns, stuffed or unstuffed	Steamed	Flour dough leavened with a starter made by fermenting glutinous rice and wheat; may be unfilled, or stuffed with reconstituted dried vegetables, spring onions, nuts, radish, salted-vegetables or sweet bean paste (sweet or savoury)
Five-kernel mantou 五仁馒头	China (south-east), Nanjing, Jiangsu Province	Round buns with stuffing (pleats on underside), decorated with a dot of red food colouring	Steamed	Fermented flour/water dough; deep-fried walnuts, peanuts, sweet apricot seeds, pine nuts, melon seeds, leaf lard, sugar, salt
Fresh yeast mantou 鲜酵母馒头	China (South-east), Changzhou, Jiangsu Province	Unstuffed buns	Steamed	Fermented flour/water dough leavened with fresh yeast; salt and sugar added
Flourishing mantou 兴隆馒头	China (south-east), Jiangsu Province	Stuffed buns, pleats on the underside, slightly flattened	Steamed and then deep-fried	Fermented flour/water dough, salt; minced belly pork, jellied pork stock, toasted sesame seeds, soy sauce, sugar, ginger

Barbarian Heads and Turkish Dumplings:

Oil-scalded *mantou* 油氽馒头	China (south-east), Shanghai	Dumplings with twirly, pleated tops	Steamed and then deep-fried	Flour, warm water, salt; minced pork, jellied pork stock, water, salt, sugar, ginger and spring onion juice.	
Cloud-layer mantou 云层馒头	China (south), Hunan Province	Sections cut from dough that has been rolled out, brushed with lard and then rolled up	Steamed	Fermented flour/water dough	Served with dishes
Milkwhite *mantou* 奶白馒头	China (south), Guangdong Province	Sections cut from a thick sausage of dough	Steamed	Fermented flour/water dough with a little added sugar	
Zhongshan fresh *mantou* 中山鲜馒头	China (south), Guangdong Province	Sections cut from a thick sausage of dough	Steamed	Fermented flour/water dough, sugar, milk, soda	
Mandu	Korean	Seem to be various different shapes…	Steamed, boiled, pan-fried	Flour/water Beef, pork, kimchi or beansprouts… or a whole variety of fillings	May be served with a dip, or in soup

Barbarian Heads and Turkish Dumplings:

Notes

1. I would like to thank Paul D. Buell and Eugene N. Anderson, the joint authors of *A Soup for the Qan: Chinese Dietary Medicine of the Mongol Era as Seen in Hu Sihui's Yinshan Zhengyao*, Sir Henry Wellcome Asian Series (London: Kegan Paul International, 2000), for their invaluable advice and for their readings of a draft of this paper, and Aylin Tan, for sharing with me her discoveries regarding the dumplings of Turkey and Central Asia. David Knechtges was also kind enough to help me clear up my confusion over one of the sources.
2. All the surviving pieces appear in Yan Kejun 严可均, *quanjinwen* 全晋文, *quan shanggu sandai qin han sanguo liuchao wen* 全上古三代秦汉三国六朝文 (1815, republished Beijing 1959).
3. Zhu Wei 朱伟, *Philological Researches into Eating* 考吃 (Beijing: Zhongguo Shudian, 1997): p. 61; David R. Knechtges, 'A Literary Feast: Food in Early Chinese Literature', *Journal of the American Oriental Society* 106.1, p. 60.
4. Knechtges, p. 60; Qiu Pangtong 邱庞同, *zhongguo miandian shi* 中国面点史 (Qingdao: Qingdao Chubanshe, 1995), p. 17; Zhu Wei, p. 61.
5. Zhu Wei, p. 61; Knechtges, p. 60.
6. Zeng Sanyi and Yin Hua Lu (曾三异，因话录), qtd. Knechtges, p. 60.
7. Zhu Wei, p. 63.
8. Personal observation, Gansu Province 1995.
9. Qiu, p. 17
10. Qiu, p. 17.
11. In a footnote to the introduction to their translation of the Yuan Dynasty text *yin shan zheng yao* 饮善正要 ('A Soup for the Qan'), Paul Buell and Eugene N. Anderson say: "In our view, the *man-t'ou* [described in this text and other contemporary sources] has nothing to do whatever, other than sharing a name, with the unfilled steamed bun called *man-t'ou* still eaten, particularly in south China, where it has considerable antiquity, going back at least to Han times, if not before' (n. 75, p. 110).
12. Zhu Wei, p. 62. Zhu suggests that during the Tang Dynasty, *mantou* were used as a kind of display food at banquets.
13. *Wu lin jiu shi* 武林旧事, qtd. Zhu Wei.
14. In modern Chinese, *baozi* generally refers to leavened steamed buns with a stuffing.
15. Zhu Wei, p. 63.
16. Translated as 'A Soup for the Qan' by Buell and Anderson.
17. Buell and Anderson, pp. 238, 302–03. The presence of ginger alongside onions (葱 *cong*) in one of the recipes may suggest that the onions are the long, green-tipped kind known in English as spring onions, because ginger and spring onions are a classic Chinese combination. However, most modern Turkish/Central Asian *mantı* dumplings use the larger, round onions known in modern Chinese as 'foreign/ocean onions' (洋葱 *yangcong*). I'm guessing there may be some ambiguity about which kind of onions is intended for use in these recipes. If the recipes were Turkic/Central Asian in origin, perhaps they originally incorporated 'foreign onions', but were adapted when made at the Yuan Dynasty court in China to use Chinese green onions.
18. A footnote to one Chinese-language edition of this text suggests that 'Quick *Manta' (*cang mantou*) should actually be translated as 'Storehouse' *mantou* rather than 'quick' *mantou*, because the finished dumplings resemble granary storehouses 仓囤 *cangdun*. Li Chunfang 李春方 (ed.), *yinshan zhengyao* 饮膳正要, (Beijing: Zhongguo Shangye Chubanshe 1988), p. 92; Buell and Anderson, pp. 238, 302.
19. Buell and Anderson, p. 303.
20. I should add that the notes in one Chinese edition of the *yin shan zheng yao* (Li Chunfang, p. 94) are not consistent with this analysis: Li suggests that the recipe means that rolled-out, unleavened dough should be cut into flower shapes that are then stuck onto the *mantou* before they are steamed.
21. Xiao Fan 萧帆 (ed.), *zhongguo pengren cidian* 中国烹饪辞典 (Beijing: Zhongguo Shangye Chubanshe, 1992), p. 206.
22. Zhu Wei, p. 64, citing Xue Ke's (徐珂) *qing bai lei chao* 清稗类钞.

23. There seems to be some association of the word *mantou* with the domed shape of a rounded bun: dictionaries cite 'earth mantou' (土馒头 *tu mantou*) as a word for burial mounds. See, for example, Ci Yuan 辞源 (Beijing: Shangwu Yinshuguan, 1998): p. 317.
24. Zhu Wei, p. 64.
25. A minority of recipes suggest a lightly leavened dough should be used.
26. Personal observation, Nanxiang, 2012.
27. See Li Zhengquan 李正权 (ed.), *zhongguo mimian shipin* 中国米面食品, (Qingdao: Qingdao Chubanshe, 1997).
28. Zhu Wei, p. 64
29. *Dīwānu l-Luġat al-Turk*, the first comprehensive dictionary of Turkic languages.
30. Buell and Anderson, n. 75, pp 110–11.
31. Knechtges, p. 60.
32. Endymion Wilkinson, *Chinese History: A Manual* (Cambridge, MA: Harvard-Yenching Institute, 1998), p. 25.
33. Wilkinson, p. 38.
34. Wilkinson, p. 40.
35. 饅餃 Knechtges, p. 60.
36. Wilkinson, p. 38.
37. For example, 胡瓜 *hu gua* 'barbarian squash', for cucumber; 胡萝卜 *hu luo bo*, 'barbarian radish', for carrot; and 胡豆 *hu dou*, 'barbarian bean', for broad or fava beans.
38. For example, 番茄 *fan qie*, 'barbarian aubergine', for tomato, 番椒 *fan jiao*, 'barbarian pepper' for chilli.
39. As C.E. Bosworth notes, 'The Turks themselves appear, as what is in modern Chinese transcription T'u-chüe, in dynastic annals of the sixth century AD, where various branches of them are noted and fanciful tales about their origins retailed', 'Introduction', *The Turks in the Early Islamic World*, ed. C. E. Bosworth (Aldershot: Ashgate, 2007), xii–xiv. Thanks to Will Stockland for sending me this quotation.
40. Jacques Gernet, *Daily Life in China on the Eve of the Mongol Invasion 1250–1276* (London: George Allen and Unwin, 1962), p. 134.
41. Michael J. Pettid, *Korean Cuisine* (London: Reaktion, 2008), p. 15. A popular Korean song of the 13th century, *Ssanghwa-jom*, 'mandu shop', tells the story of a *mandu* shop run by a foreigner, 'probably a man of central Asian origins' (Pettid, p. 58).
42. The Uyghur *manti* appears to be a Chinese-Central Asian hybrid, conforming to the Central Asian pattern in its thin, unleavened skin and lamb stuffing, but using the Chinese cooking method of steaming.
43. There are colourful and clearly fabricated legends explaining the origins of many common foods and famous dishes in China.

Mantı and *Mantou*: Dumplings across the Silk Road from Central Asia to Turkey

Aylin Öney Tan

There are many intriguing parallels among the food cultures from northern and western China and Central Asia all the way west to Turkey. In all these countries, one of the most significant dishes must be the dumplings. Along the Silk Road, dumplings demonstrate intriguing similarities that tell of a shared common past. Some of these similarities are linguistic, such as the use of variants of the word '*mantou*', while others are technical, such as the forms into which dumplings are pleated or folded.

From the Turkish perspective, the origins of *mantı* are long forgotten, and the dish is regarded as quintessentially Turkish. However, the word does not have a specific meaning in Turkish and almost all etymological references state that the origin of the word comes from the Chinese *man tou*. Etymological dictionaries of both Nişanyan and Eren stress the Mongol connection.[1]

Mantı, or similar dumplings under different names, continue to be the signature dishes of a geographical region ranging through today's Mongolia, Kyrgyzstan, Tajikistan, Afghanistan, Uzbekistan, Turkmenistan, Kazakhstan, Azerbaijan, Armenia, Georgia, Russia and Crimea. Though there are several varieties, the ultimate stuffed dumpling in Turkey is the *mantı*. In Turkey, where the nomadic Turkic tribes from Central Asia eventually came to settle, it remains the classic reminder of the Central Asian heritage in present-day food culture. Its basic form is a rolled noodle paste, cut into squares, folded around a meat filling, boiled and served with a garlic yoghurt sauce with a drizzling of paprika butter. However, in Turkey, *mantı* is more or less the generic word for any stuffed dumpling. There are also some stuffed dumplings that are almost identical to *mantı* in shape and cooking technique, but named differently: other common names include *Tatar böreği*, *kulak aşı* (ear dish), *kulak* (ear), *piruhi*, *hingel*, etc.

Documentary evidence for *mantı*

The ancestry of Turkish *mantı* can easily be tracked back to similar dishes that exist in the vast expanses of Turkic Central Asia and the Caucasus. This extensive range indicates shared culinary heritage. However, despite the obvious connection of *mantı* to Central Asian dumplings, documentary evidence is rare, which makes it quite difficult to sketch in an evidence-based account of the history of *mantı*. Instead, one must interrogate the culinary evidence from local and regional cuisines in order to establish a genealogy of influences, which may be connected to mentions of Turkish *mantı* in documentary sources.

Dîwân Lughât al-Turk

In Turkish sources, the first mention of a noodle dish similar to *mantı* is *tutmaç*, found in a Turkish-Arabic dictionary written in Baghdad in 1072–74. Written by the Turkic Scholar Mahmud al-Kāshgari, *Dîwân Lughât al-Turk* (Compendium of the Turkic Dialects) is the first known dictionary of the Turkish language and remains one of the most comprehensive sources for west Asian Turkish dialects. The description for *tutmaç* here has no stuffing.

Tutmaç is also mentioned, as Charles Perry notes, in the name of a certain utensil, *minzâm tutmâj*, described as 'a tool for arranging *tutmaç*'. It is also referred to as the *şiş* (shish), a skewer, which seems to be the first mention of shish in a written document. Perry points out that this has been previously interpreted as a stick for eating noodles, like the Chinese chopsticks, but it might well be a stick for drying the noodles instead.[2] However, the *tutmaç* noodles are not long but rather short-cut matchstick pieces, small squares or triangles and cannot be draped over something, but must be laid on straw mats or fabric to dry.

Soup for the Qan

As Fuchsia Dunlop discusses in her companion paper, one of the earliest mentions of a dumpling similar to Turkish *mantı* is in the treatise written in 1330 by Hu Szu-hui, the Uyghur imperial doctor serving the Chinese Emperor. The treatise, known as *Yin-shan Cheng-yao* (Proper and Essential Things for the Emperor's Food and Drink) combines a recipe book with a manual for health care. Translated into English with the name *Soup for the Qan*, the treatise includes recipes that are clearly related to Turkish *mantı*.[3]

At the time the treatise was written, Mongol rule had spread to China, Turkestan, Siberia, Manchuria, Russia, Iran, Afghanistan, Anatolia, Tibet and part of Vietnam. Early in the thirteenth century, the Mongol leader Temujin (later known as Genghis Khan) defeated his rivals to start the Mongolian Empire, and his successors turned almost the entire continent of Asia into a borderless single united entity, stretching from eastern Europe to the Sea of Japan. This borderless *Pax Mongolica* territory was an encouragement to travellers, with trade flourishing between Europe and Asia. Together with trade and travel, the Mongol ruling system created a mix of ethnicities, religions and cultures that encouraged exchanges between many parts of Asia, in particular with the Central Asian Turkic tribes and the Chinese. By 1276, Kublai Khan, the last of the Mongol rulers to be born in the steppes, had conquered all China and established the Yuan dynasty. He was greatly influenced by Chinese culture but also maintained his Mongolian roots. This was the cultural climate that gave rise to Hu Szu-hui's treatise, for he had been in the service of several of Kublai Khan's successors. The treatise demonstrates the cultural 'globalism' of the period, incorporating gastronomic influences from Middle Eastern, Persian and Turkic cultures.

There are three recipes that are worth mentioning with respect to the origins of *mantı*.

Dumplings across the Silk Road

TUTMAÇ

Tutum Ash (This is a kind of kneaded noodle)
They supplement the centre and increase *ch'i*.
White flour (six *chin*. Make into *tutum ash*), mutton (leg. Roast the meat. [Make into] *quruk qima* [and stuff *tutum ash*]).
Use A Good Meat Soup for ingredients. Add the noodles and roast [cook dry]. Adjust flavours evenly with onions. Add garlic, cream [or yoghurt], finely ground basil.[4]

The recipe for *tutum ash*, which still exists as *tutmaç* in Anatolia, also describes the contemporary Turkish *mantı*. *Tutmaç*, considered one of the earliest pre-Ottoman Turkic and Seljuk dishes, is a noodle dish with yoghurt. Many contemporary variations of *tutmaç* have minced meat or little meatballs cooked together with the pasta but not stuffed in the dough. However, in this very early recipe of *tutmaç*, the meat, *quruk qima* (*kuru kıyma* in Turkish), is stuffed into dough. *Kuru kıyma*, meaning dried minced meat, remains a very popular winter provision in Anatolia. It is actually fried minced meat in its own fat, salted, potted and preserved for winter consumption. The garlic yoghurt sauce is also a feature of typical Turkish *mantı*. This recipe of *tutum ash* (*tutmaç*) is a fantastic example of how a dish can survive for almost seven hundred years, travelling thousands of miles.

CUT FLOWERS 'MANTA'

Mutton, sheep's fat, sheep's tail, onions, prepared mandarin orange peel. (Cut up each finely.)
[To] ingredients add, according to recipe, spices, salt and sauce. Make the stuffing. Form the *Manta. Use scissors to cut out into various flower shapes. Steam. Use safflower to dye the flowers.[5]

The recipe for 'Flower' *mantı*, incorporates a very Chinese ingredient, mandarin peel, but otherwise this recipe is almost identical to some examples of contemporary Turkish *mantı*. The flower-shaped folding is still used in some local recipes in Anatolia; however instead of steaming, the preferred method is baking and steeping in broth, most probably a cooking technique developed long after the nomadic lifestyle had been abandoned. Wood-fired communal ovens are a common feature of Anatolian villages. A similar local speciality from the town of Çorum in central Anatolia, the elaborate flower-shaped oven-baked *mantı*, is a treat for guests, and is rightly served on special occasions. The use of safflowers is also very common in Anatolian cookery.

EGGPLANT MANTA

Eggplant Manta / Mutton, sheep's fat, sheep's tail, onions, prepared mandarin orange peel (cut up each finally), 'tender' eggplant (remove the pith). Combine ingredients with meats into a stuffing. But [instead of making a dough covering] put it inside the eggplant and steam. Add garlic, cream [or yoghurt etc.] finally ground basil. Eat.[6]

This recipe is thought-provoking as it does not have a pastry casing but stuffs a vegetable instead. It must be noted that the word *manta* can be used for 'stuffed' in Uzbekistan but not in Turkey. This kind of stuffed eggplant can be likened to *karnıyarık*, a popular Turkish eggplant dish, meaning 'split belly', though the eggplant is fried first, then stewed with stuffing but never steamed. Although the word *manta* or *mantı* is never used for stuffed dishes in Turkey, it might be used for a dish with a garlic yoghurt sauce, especially if boiled or baked pastry with fried minced meat is involved.

Early Ottoman references

The earliest recorded serving of *mantı* in Ottoman court was to Fatih the Conqueror, who made Istanbul/Constantinople the new capital of Ottoman Empire. Fatih's daily routine consisted of two meals a day; the one in the morning before midday almost always included a *mantı* course. Court documents dated June 1469 record *mantı* as one of the dishes presented to the Sultan Fatih.[7] It was steamed like Chinese *mantou*. Probably the dish was also popular with Fatih's predecessors, but there is no record of the culinary practices of earlier Sultans. However, it is known that *tutmaç* was a favourite dish throughout Anatolia in the pre-Ottoman Seljuk Empire and Principalities period.[8] We do not know if *tutmaç* of medieval Anatolia was stuffed, like the one mentioned in *Soup for the Qan,* or unstuffed, like the one mentioned by Mahmud al-Kāshgari.

Turkish cookbooks

The earliest written Ottoman *mantı* recipe appears in the fifteenth-century Ottoman cookbook written by Muhammed bin Mahmud Shirvani. Shirvani's book, *Kitâbü-t Tabih,* is a revised version of the thirteenth-century Arabic text by Baghdadi; it features a *mantı* recipe as if to register a new entrant to the food vocabulary of the region. Shirvani added 82 recipes to Baghdadi's 174, and also offered advice on food–health connections. This 'new' entrant to the book is a steamed dumpling with a minced lamb and chickpea filling flavoured with cinnamon and vinegar, and served with garlic yoghurt and sumac.[9]

There are no other written records of *mantı* between the fifteenth and nineteenth centuries; the lack of cookbooks leaves us without exact recipes. Early Turkish cookery manuscripts do not mention *mantı*. The first printed recipe book, *Melceü't Tabbâhîn,* published in 1844, gives a recipe for *Tatar böreği,* similar to *mantı,* but without the garlic yoghurt. The first Ottoman cookbook in English, the *Turkish Cookery Book* compiled by

Turabi Efendi in 1862, has the same recipe with the name *Tatar bureghi*. The cookbook *Ev Kadını* (The Housewife), printed in 1880, includes exactly the same recipe with the same name. It is interesting that none are called *mantı*, and that there is no mention of garlic yoghurt sauce in any of them; instead, all are tossed in butter before being served. *Ev Kadını* also mentions *piruhi*, the cheese-filled version of the same dish, and another dish with the name *mantı*, not stuffed but layered dough with mince meat like a *börek*, served with garlic yoghurt.

Contemporary Anatolian varieties of *mantı* and similar dumplings
In Turkey today, *mantı* refers to an array of stuffed and boiled wheaten products, in most cases served with a garlic yoghurt sauce and a drizzle of melted paprika butter. Dishes served in the same manner, in particular baked savoury pastries, may also be called *mantı*.

The dough and stuffing
The dough used for dumplings is unleavened, usually a simple dough of just flour, water and salt, sometimes with eggs. The filling is almost always minced lamb and onion flavoured simply with salt and pepper. There are cases where the filling is sautéed first, but generally the meat filling is stuffed raw into the dumpling. Some versions add herbs and spices, but the classic taste is of meat and onion. Sometimes the meat is extended with cooked chickpeas, lentils or mashed potatoes. Vegetables or greens are not traditionally used. Pork is never used, even among non-Muslim Christian communities like the Greeks or Armenians, who make exactly the same dumplings as their Muslim neighbours. In the past few decades, along with lamb and mutton, minced beef has also become common. On rare occasions finely chopped, cured, spicy beef *pastırma* is added to the filling. Chicken and game is never used as a filling, but the dish can be covered with cooked pieces of chicken for a more elaborate and festive serving. Fish and seafood are never used. There are cases where fresh curd cheese might be used as a filling, but then the name would usually be changed into *piroh, piron, piruhi*, etc., and the finished folded form is usually a triangular pocket. There is also a meat-filled equivalent of *piruhi*, triangular parcels filled with meat and served without the yoghurt sauce; that version is often named *Tatar böreği*, meaning *börek* (savoury turnover) of the Tatars. Both have almost the same dough and filling; the difference between *Tatar böreği* and *mantı* is about the size and folding, with the latter usually tiny and almost always served with a garlic yoghurt sauce.

Cooking technique
Today in Turkey steaming *mantı* is an almost completely forgotten technique. The most common method is boiling. However, some baking might also be involved at a certain stage. Sometimes the prepared *mantı* is dried or slightly roasted in the oven, and then boiled. *Mantı* can also be cooked by baking them in the oven until golden and then

pouring hot water or broth over them before baking the whole tray until all the juices are absorbed by the *mantı*. In this case, the tops are left slightly open, for the steam to escape and the broth to penetrate. This type of dumpling can be shaped like little bundles, folded to rosette or flower shapes, or twisted on the ends to resemble a boat. They can also be dried completely in the oven and kept for later use, to be reconstituted in broth. This method seems quite common in Central Anatolian towns and is shared by both Armenian and Turkish communities. The Armenian cook of the American school in Merzifon, Vağinag Pürad, gives a recipe for such baked *mantı*, folded like 'little confectioner's cones',[10] and Arto der Haroutunian pinches their ends to resemble boats.[11] *Mantı* can also be fried instead of baked.

Size, shape and folding
Turkish or Anatolian *mantı* have moved away from their Asiatic steamed cousins in size and shape. The fist-sized steamed dumplings are long forgotten here. Usually, the smaller the better. In Kayseri, the town often referred as the capital of *mantı*, people take pride in making dumplings so small that at least forty can fit in a tablespoon. In one local example from Kütahya, the dumplings need to be so small that they cannot be rolled and folded; instead, the pastry and the filling is pinched together. In general, the dough is rolled into a large thin sheet, cut into squares and then folded or pinched to close corners. In many cases these squares are really tiny, and the filling just the size of a pea.

Still, there are similarities between the Asian and Anatolian dumplings. The folding technique of certain dumplings can be amazingly similar to their Asian ancestors. The classic, simple folding of a square-cut dough to a bundle by squeezing adjacent sides towards the center is exactly the same as one folding type of Mongolian *buuz*, except in size. This particular type of Mongolian *buuz* is like a magnified version of Anatolian *mantı*.

Triangular folding is common, especially if there is a Caucasian or Crimean connection in the community. In many cases the triangular shape is further folded into a hat shape. Half-moons are rare, but common in communities with Georgian or Caucasian heritage. Rosette, flower, and boat-shaped dumplings are quite common when baking is involved. As meat stock is added after the dumplings are baked, the tops need to be left slightly open for the broth to penetrate.

Serving
As mentioned, today's *mantı* is almost always served with garlic yoghurt. In most cases a drizzling of hot sizzling melted butter flavoured with hot pepper flakes or powdered paprika is also poured over. Sometimes the butter is also mixed with a little tomato paste to add colour and tang. There are always small cups of dried mint, thyme, pepper flakes and sumac on the table, so anyone who wishes may further flavour the dish. One particular herb, *güveyotu* or *mantı otu* with a pretty bluish-lilac colour, is special for *mantı*. This herb is the flower of wild thyme.

There are cases when no yoghurt is involved, and the dumplings are just tossed in butter. These kinds of dumplings are usually of Caucasian, Crimean, Russian or Balkan origin. There can be a sprinkling of dried yoghurt grated like cheese. If broth is involved in cooking then it is likely that some of the broth will be served along with the dish.

Turkish dumplings are never individually eaten in the hand like a snack. *Mantı* in Turkey is always a plated dish served with a spoon, combining all the tastes of the dumpling, yoghurt sauce and butter drizzling in a single gulp. *Mantı* is generally served as a single dish, not preceded or followed by other dishes. It is filling and satisfying, with no need for another accompaniment.

Similarities with Asian dumplings
Apart from size, folding, shape, dough and filling and cooking method, there are amazing links between Asian and Anatolian dumpling culture. In her paper, 'Feasting with the Buriats of Southern Siberia', Sharon Hudgins notes the similarities of Asian and Turkish dumplings:

> These Buriat steamed dumplings are more closely related to the *manti* of Turkey than to some of the Central Asian dumplings made with a raised dough that are also called *manti*, or to the Chinese steamed breads known as *mantou*. Buriat *buuza* (Russian *pozy*) are made from the same dough that is used for making noodles […]. The Buriats also have a larger version of filled, steamed dumplings, made from the same dough and filling as *buuza*, with the dough twisted together to seal the dumpling at the top.[12]

The interesting point here is that the Mongolian *buuz* and the Buriat *buuza* is pronounced as *pozy* in Russian. In Turkish, when making *mantı*, the dough is divided into equal-sized ball-shaped portions called *pazı, pezi, bazı* or *beze*. These little fist-sized portions are then rolled into sheets to be cut and folded. The Turkish etymological sources cannot give an origin to these words for ball-shaped portions of pastry, but it seems likely that their roots may stem from Mongolian connections. Another Turkish word that might be related to Uyghur *çüçürek* is *çörek*, but used in an entirely different meaning, a baked sweet or savoury wheaten product. Nigella seeds are called *çörek otu* (meaning herb for *çörek*) as it is always sprinkled on baked goods and breads.

Various similar dumplings may have different names in the vast Euro-Asian geography, but when cultural interactions are studied these words usually indicate a common shared root. Alan Davidson points out to the etymology of Russian (or Siberian) *pelmeni*, stating that '*pelmeni* are thought to come from *Udmurt-Komi* words for 'bread ear' – *pel* meaning 'ear', *nyan* meaning 'bread', a relative of Indian *naan*, originally being not *pelmeni* but *pelnyani*'.[13] Similarly Iranian *goosh barreh* mean 'lambs' ears'.[14]

The very same forms of dumplings are reproduced and reinvented across the huge Eurasian land mass. Central and Eastern European dumplings like German *Maultaschen*

Dumplings across the Silk Road

and *Kreplach*, Polish *pierogi*, Ukranian *vareniki*, Lithuanian *koldunai*, Belarussian *kalduny* and various others have direct links with Russian/Siberian *pelmeni* and their other relatives in Central Asia and beyond. The accompanying tables attempt to gather various dumplings in geographic zones. It is not easy to draw a general picture, but this study may lead us to map dumplings from eastern Europe to the Sea of Japan, tracing a culinary geography in the region where once trade, travel and cultural interaction flourished in the *Pax Mongolica*.

Appendix

1. Turkish / Anatolian Dumplings

Name	Region	Shape/Folding	Cooking	Dough/Filling	Serving
Mantı	All regions	Rolled pastry cut in squares, folded in bundles or triangles; sizes may vary, though never too big.	Usually boiled	Flour/(egg)/ water/salt	Garlic yoghurt sauce; paprika butter; dried mint or thyme, sumac
				Minced meat/ onion/ salt and pepper	
Fırın mantı (oven mantı)	Not a particular region, practiced in all regions	Rolled pastry cut in squares, folded in bundles boat or flower shape withtops slightly open	Baked and steeped in broth	Flour/(egg)/ water/salt	Garlic yoghurt sauce; paprika butter; dried mint, or thyme, sumac
				Minced meat/onion/ salt and pepper	
Yağ mantısı (Greasy mantı)	Kayseri, Nevşehir	Ball shaped	Fried; or fried and steeped in broth	Flour/yeast/Water/salt	Garlic yoghurt sauce; sizzling paprika butter
				Fried minced meat/ onion/salt and pepper	
Kuru mantı (Dry mantı)	Çorum,	Flower shaped with tops slightly open	Baked, steeped in broth	Flour/water/salt	Garlic yoghurt sauce; sizzling paprika butter
				Minced meat/onion/ salt and pepper	
Boz mantı The name implies origins in Mongol Buuz.	Sivas	Cut in squares, no filling	Boiled	Flour/water/salt	Tossed in melted butter
				If there is a filling it is callad İçli Mantı (meaning stuffed mantı)	

Dumplings across the Silk Road

Name	Region	Preparation	Cooking	Dough	Filling	Serving
Tatar böreği (Tatar börek)	Eskişehir; regions with Tatars or Caucasian settled	Rolled pastry cut in squares, folded into triangles; medium sized	Boiled	Flour/water/salt	Minced meat/onion/salt and pepper	Tossed in melted butter
Sinop mantısı	Sinop	Rolled pastry cut in squares, folded into triangles	Boiled	Flour/water/salt	Minced meat/onion/salt and pepper	Tossed in melted butter
Kayseri mantısı	Kayseri	Rolled pastry cut in tiny squares, folded in bundles or triangular prisms	Boiled	Flour/water/salt	Minced meat/onion/salt and pepper	Garlic yoghurt sauce; paprika butter dried mint, or thyme, sumac
Cimcik (means pinched)	Kütahya	Dough not rolled, very small pieces pinched with minced meat folded into a tiny dumpling	Boiled	Flour/water/salt	Minced meat/onion/salt and pepper	Garlic yoghurt sauce; paprika butter dried mint, or thyme, sumac
Börek Çorbası	Gaziantep	Dough rolled, fried minced meat sprinkled, dough folded, rolled, cut in tiny squares pinched in prisms	Baked, dried, boiled in soup	Flour/water/salt/fried minced meat		Served in yoghurt soup
Kulak means 'ear'	Giresun	Rolled pastry cut in disks, folded in triangles	Boiled	Flour/water/salt	Minced meat/onion/salt and pepper	Tossed in melted butter

Dumplings across the Silk Road

Name	Origin	Shape	Cooking	Dough	Filling	Serving
Kaşık Böreği (means spoon börek)	skişehir (Crimean origin)	Rolled pastry cut in squares, folded in hat shape	Boiled	Flour/water/salt	Minced meat/onion/salt and pepper	Sizzling paprika butter
Haluj, haluşka	People of Caucasian origin	Rolled disks, folded in half moon shape, pleated, pinched	Steamed or boiled	Flour/water/salt	Minced meat/onion/salt and pepper	Tossed in melted butter
Hınkal, hingel	People of Georgian origin	Rolled disks, folded in half moon shape, pleated, pinched	Steamed or boiled	Flour/water/salt	Filling is varied	Plain or tossed in melted butter
Pelmeni	People of Caucasian origin	Rolled pastry cut in squares, folded into triangles; medium sized, never tiny	Boiled	Flour/water/salt	Usually curd cheese	Tossed in butter
Piruhi	Caucasian	Rolled pastry cut in squares, folded into triangles; medium sized, never tiny	Boiled	Flour/water/salt	Fresh curd cheese	Melted butter
Pirob Pirohu	North Cyprus	Filling placed on rolled pastry, a second sheet placed over, cut like ravioli; or cut in squares folded triangles	Boiled	Flour/water/salt	Filled with 'Nor', fresh unsalted curd cheese	Melted butter, dried mint, grated *hellim*
Kaypak (means slippery)	Amasya	Rolled pastry cut in squares, folded in medium size triangles	Boiled	Flour/water/salt	Minced meat/onion/salt and pepper	Melted butter

Dumplings across the Silk Road

Mantikos Sephardic Jewish Çanakkale		Leavened dough hand shaped into balls		Baked	Flour/yeast/water/salt	No sauce
					Fried minced meat/onion/salt and pepper	
Manti Armenian	Central Anatolia	Cut squares, Pinched into open-top boat or slipper shape		Baked in oven, steeped in broth	Flour/water/salt	Garlic yoghurt sauce; paprika butter
					Fried minced meat/onion/parsley/salt and pepper	
Mantabour Armenian	Central & Eastern Anatolia	Cut squares, Little bundles		Boiled in broth	Flour/water/salt	Served in broth, sometimes yoghurt added
					Fried minced meat/onion/salt and pepper	

2. Turkic & Central Asian Dumplings

NAME	REGION	SHAPE/FOLDING	COOKING	DOUGH/FILLING	SERVING
Düşbere	Azerbaijan	Rolled pastry cut in squares folded like tortellini	Boiled in meat stock	Flour/water/salt	Garlic and vinegar
				Mincemeat/onion/garlic/fresh dill/mint/parsley/cinnamon	
Çuçvara	Uzbekistan	Rolled pastry cut in squares folded like tortellini	Boiled	Flour/water/butter	
				Mincemeat/onion	

Dumplings across the Silk Road

Name	Origin	Shape/Folding	Cooking	Ingredients	Sauce/Accompaniment
Kavurma Güçvara	Uzbekistan	Rolled pastry cut in squares, folded like tortellini	Fried	Flour/water/butter; Mincemeat/onion	Plain
Mantı	Uzbekistan	Rolled pastry cut in squares, corners folded in center like a bundle	Steamed	Flour/egg/water; Mincemeat/tail fat/onion/cumin/boiled mashed potato	Yoghurt with mint or *Kaymak* clotted cream
Ashak	Afghanistan	Cut disks, folded in half moons	Boiled	Flour/egg/water	Served with meat sauce yoghurt with mint
Mantou	Afghanistan	Cut squares, folded like tortellini shape	Steamed	Chopped meat/onion/cumin/black pepper	Yoghurt with chopped coriander or with sweet carrot stew
Çöçüre (chuchure)	Uyghur	Rolled pastry cut in squares folded like tortellini	Boiled with onion/garlic/pepper/dill/parsley	Flour/egg/water; Minced meat/onion/cumin/black pepper	Hot and sour sauce
Yumurta Manttsi (chuchure with eggs)	Uyghur	Rolled pastry cut in squares folded into tortellini shape	Boiled	Flour/egg/water; Chopped fried omelette made with soy sauce/garlic vinegar/cumin pepper/onion	Hot and sour sauce

Dumplings across the Silk Road

Name	Group	Shape	Cooking	Dough	Filling	Sauce
Kök çüçüre (Yonca mantısı)	Uyghur	Rolled pastry cut in squares folded into tortellini shape	Boiled	Flour/egg/water	Wild greens (clover?)/spinach fried with onions	Laaze, chilli, garlic, oil, vinegar
Pıtır Mantı	Uyghur	Rolled disks, folded and pinched into bundles	Steamed	Flour/egg/water	Hand chopped meat/onion/black pepper/cumin	Plain
Hoşan yağmantı	Uyghur	Rolled disks, ball-shape twisted top	Fried, shallow steeped	Flour/yeast/water	Hand chopped meat/onion/cumin	Plain
Yutağza	Uyghur	Hand spread very thinly, coated with fat, rolled in ball	Steamed	Flour/yeast/water/salt/fat	No Filling	Plain

Dumplings across the Silk Road

Küçük Yutağza	Uyghur	Hand spread very thinly, coated with fat, rolled into a ball	Steamed	Flour/yeast/egg/water/salt/fat	Plain
Kıymalı Yutağza	Uyghur	Hand spread very thinly, coated with fat, rolled like a sausage	Steamed	Flour/egg/water/salt/sugar/fat	No filling, sprinkled with fresh herbs, dill, parsley or spinach	Hot and sour sauce
					Fried mincemeat/onion/cumin/or Fried onion/carrot	
Kaymaklı Yutağza	Uyghur	Hand spread very thinly, coated with fat, rolled sausage	Steamed	Flour/yeast/egg/water/salt/sugar/fat		Plain
					Clotted cream/sugar/walnuts	
Bolak mantı	Uyghur	Rolled disks, ball-shape twisted on top	Steamed	Flour/yeast/water		Plain
					Hand chopped meat/onion/cumin	

Aş mantı	Uyghur	Rolled disks, pinched half moon	Cooked in rice pilaf	Flour/egg/water/salt	In pilaf

3. Caucasian Dumplings

NAME	REGION	SHAPE/FOLDING	COOKING	DOUGH/FILLING	SERVING
Fıdıgabın (*gabın* with meat)	Ossetia	Cut disks, half moon folded, pleated, pinched	Boiled	Flour/water/salt	Tossed in melted butter
				Minced meat/onion/garlic	
Sıhtıgabın (*gabın* with cheese)	Ossetia	Cut disks, half moon folded, pleated, pinched	Boiled	Flour/water/salt	Tossed in melted butter
				Curd cheese/onion	
Kartogabın (*gabın* with potatoes)	Ossetia	Cut disks, half moon folded, pleated, pinched	Boiled	Flour/water/salt	Tossed in melted butter
				Boiled mashed potato/onion	
Kurzunuş	Chechnya	Cut disks, half moon folded, pleated, pinched	Boiled	Flour/water/salt	Dipped in garlic, broth, butter sauce
				Minced meat/onion or potato/onion	

Name	Region	Shape	Cooking	Ingredients	Sauce
Halttmış	Chechnya	Rolled disks, half moon folded, pleated, pinched	Boiled	Flour/water/salt	Dipped garlic and broth sauce
Etli Hınkal (*Hınkal* with meat)	Daghestan	Cut disks, half moon folded, pleated, pinched	Boiled	Flour/egg/water/salt; Tail fat/corn meal; Minced meat/onion/lemon juice; Curd cheese/egg parsley/dill; Spinach/onion/egg butter	Garlic-vinegar or garlic yoghurt sauce
Pshalive	Hatkoy	Cut squares, triangle folding	Boiled	Flour/water/salt; Potato/onion	Melted butter paprika
Mantaz/Mentaz/Metaz	Hatkoy	Cut disks, half moon folded, pleated, pinched	Boiled	Flour/water/salt; Potato/onion/paprika	Melted butter paprika
Tepsi manttsı	Hatkoy	Cut small squares, Pinched on top like a rosette	Broiled in broth in oven	Flour/egg/water/salt; Minced meat/onion/green pepper/	Plain

Name	Region	Shape	Cooking	Ingredients	Serving
Gedige Halame	Kabardey	Cut disks, Pinched into open-top boat or slipper shape	Boiled	Flour/egg/water; Fried minced meat/egg, black pepper, paprika	Melted butter, paprika
Kruzume	Kabardey	Cut squares, pinched into open-top boat or slipper shape	Boiled	Flour/egg/water; Minced meat, Bulgur	Fried onion, pepper, milk sauce
Pshalıve	Kabardey	Cut squares, triangle folding	Boiled	Flour/egg/water; Potato/fried onion	Melted butter, paprika
Gedige Halame	Kabardey	Rolled disks, half moon folded into bundle, pinched	Boiled	Flour/egg/water; Fried minced meat/onion/egg/parsley/paprika; Whole raw egg	Melted butter, paprika
Metaz	Şapsığ	Hand shaped stuffed balls	Boiled	Corn meal/flour/water/salt; Cheese	Plain
Kaşık Börek	Crimea	Cut squares, folded like hats	Boiled in broth or water	Flour/water/salt; Minced meat/onion/salt and pepper	In broth with adjika, hot pepper condiment

Üyken börek	Crimea	Cut disks, folded in half moons	Boiled	Flour/water/salt	*Adjika*, hot pepper paste to accompany
				Minced meat/onion/salt and pepper	
Tabak Börek	Crimea	Cut disks, folded in half moons	Boiled	Flour/water/salt	Tossed in butter
				Minced meat/onion/salt and pepper	
Pilmän	Volga Tatars	Cut disks, folded in half moons	Boiled in broth	Flour/water/salt	Served in clear soup
				Minced meat/onion/salt and pepper	

4. Bosnian & Balkan Dumplings

Name	Region	Shape/Folding	Cooking	Dough/Filling	Serving
Klepa (mantı)	Bosnia	Rolled pastry cut in squares, folded in triangles	Boiled	Flour, water, salt	Garlic yoghurt, melted butter, paprika
				Minced meat, onion, salt and pepper	
Pečeni klepa (fırında mantı)	Bosnia	Pastry rolled in three oiled layers, cut in squares, folded in triangles	Baked	Flour, olive oil, yoghurt, water, salt	Garlic yoghurt, melted butter, paprika
				Minced meat, onion, salt and pepper	

Börecik	Bosnia	Rolled thin pastry (*yufka*), spread with oil, stuffed sausage roll	Baked	Flour, water, salt	Garlic yoghurt, melted butter, paprika
				Minced meat, onion, salt and pepper, paprika	
Tutmaç çorbası	Bosnia	Small cut squares of pasta, not folded or filled	Boiled in broth	Flour, egg, water, salt	Served like a soup in broth
				Little meatballs	
Gulnar (gülnar)	Bosnia	Rolled pastry cut in disks, filling placed on one covered with second disk, edges sealed	Fried	Flour, egg yolk, yoghurt, olive oil.	Served soaked in syrup
				Egg white beaten stiff with sugar	

Notes

1. Hasan Eren, *Türk Dilinin Etimolojik Sözlüğü* (Ankara: AÜ, 1999), p. 287; Sevan Nişanyan, *Sözlerin Soyağacı-Çağdaş Türkçenin Etimolojik Sözlüğü* (İstanbul: Adam, 2003), p. 279.
2. Charles Perry, 'The Horseback Kitchen of Central Asia', *Food on the Move, Proceedings of the 1996 Oxford Symposium on Food and Cookery*, ed. Harlan Walker (Totnes: Prospect Books, 1997), p. 244.
3. Paul Buell and Eugene N. Andersen, *A Soup for the Qan: Chinese Dietary Medicine of the Mongol Era as seen in Hu Szu-hui's, Yin-shan Cheng-yao*, Henry Wellcome Asian Series (London: Kegan Paul International, 2000), pp. 298–99, 313–14.
4. Buell and Anderson, pp. 298–99.
5. Buell and Anderson, p. 314.
6. Buell and Anderson, p. 313–14.
7. Ömer Lütfi Barkan, *Belgeler IX* (Ankara: TTK, 1979), p. 187.
8. Haşim Şahin, 'Cuisine During the Turkish Seljuk and Principalities Eras', *Turkish Cuisine*, ed. Arif Bilgin and Özge Samancı (Ankara: Ministry of Culture and Tourism, 2008), pp. 46–47.
9. Günay Kut, 'On the Additions by Shirwani (15th century) to His Translation of a Cookery-Book (13th century)', *First International Food Congress, Turkey 25–30 Sept. 1986* (Ankara: Ministry of Culture and Tourism, 1988), pp. 179.
10. Vağinag Pürad, *Mükemmel Yemek Kitabı–1926* (İstanbul: Aras Yayıncılık, 2010), p. 202.
11. Arto der Haroutunian, *Middle Eastern Cookery* (London: Pan Books, 1982), p. 113.
12. Sharon Hudgins, 'Feasting with the Buriats of Southern Siberia', *Food on the Move, Proceedings of the 1996 Oxford Symposium on Food and Cookery*, ed. Harlan Walker (Totnes: Prospect Books, 1997), pp. 142, 156.
13. Alan Davidson, *The Oxford Companion to Food* (Oxford: Oxford University Press, 2006), p. 594.
14. Margaret Shaida, *The Legendary Cuisine of Persia* (London: Grub Street, 2004), pp. 122–23.

Bibliography

Ahmedof, Ahmet Cabir. *Azerbaycan Mutfağı*. Ankara: Atatürk Kültür Merkezi Başkanlığı Yayınları, 2001.
Artun, Erman. 'Adana Mutfak Kültüründe Ekmekler ve Hamurişi Yemekler'. *Türk Mutfak Kültürü Üzerine Araştırmalar*. Ankara: 1994, pp. 17–39.
Barkan, Ömer Lütfi. *Belgeler IX*. Ankara: Türk Tarih Kurumu, 1979.
Berkok, Nimet, and Kamil Toygar. *Kardeş Mutfaklar-Türk Dünyası Yemeklerinden Örnekler-Azeri, Kazak, Kırgız, Özbek, Türkmen*. Ankara: [n.pub.], 1997.
Berkok, Nimet, and Kamil Toygar. *Kuzey Kafkas Mutfak Kültürü ve Yemekleri-Şapsığ, Abzah, Hatkoy, Kabartay, Besney, Abaza, Ubıh, Asetin, Çeçen, Dağıstan, Karaçay Malkar*. Ankara: [n.pub.], 1994.
Buell, Paul, and Eugene N. Andersen, Eugene N, *A Soup for the Qan: Chinese Dietary Medicine of the Mongol Era as Seen in Hu Szu-hui's Yinshan Zhengyao*. Appendix by Charles Perry. Henry Wellcome Asian Series. London: Kegan Paul International, 2000.
Davidson, Alan. *The Oxford Companion to Food*. Oxford: Oxford University Press, 2006.
Göktürk, Nur'ala. *Geleneksel Doğu Türkistan Uygur Mutfak Kültürü*. İstanbul: Mart Matbaa, 2005.
Haroutunian, Arto der. *Middle Eastern Cookery*. London: Pan Books, 1982.
Johnson, Maria-Kaneva. *The Melting Pot – Balkan Food and Cookery*. Totnes: Prospect Books, 1995.
Hudgins, Sharon. 'Feasting with the Buriats of Southern Siberia'. *Food on the Move, Proceedings of the 1996 Oxford Symposium on Food and Cookery*. Edited by Harlan Walker. Totnes: Prospect Books, 1997, pp. 136–56.
İsmayiloglu, Akhmed-Djabir. *Azer Baycan Xöræklæri/Azer Baijan Cookery.* Bakü: İşıq, 1997.
Kılıçeva, Şahsenem. *Şahsenem'den Orta Asya Kültürü ve Yemekleri*. İstanbul: Truva Yayınları, 2006.
Koşay, Hamit Zübeyir Koşay; Ülkücan, Akile. *Anadolu Yemekleri ve Türk Mutfağı (1961)*. İstanbul: Çiya Yayınları, 2011.

Kut, Günay. 'On the Additions by Shirwani (15th century) to His Translation of a Cookery-Book (13th century)'. *First International Food Congress, Turkey 25–30 Sept. 1986*. Ankara: Ministry of Culture and Tourism,1988, pp. 176–185.

Kut, Turgut. 'A Bibliography of Turkish Cookery Books up to 1927'. *Petits Propos Culinaires 36*. London, Prospect Books, 1990, pp. 29–48.

Mack, Glenn R.; Surina, Asele. *Food Culture in Russia and Central Asia*. Westport, CT: Greenwood Press, 2005.

Mahmud Al-Kāshgari; ed. and tr. Dankoff, Robert and Kelly, James. *Compendium of the Turkic Dialects (Dīwān Lugāt al-Turk)*. Cambridge, MA: Harvard University Press, 1984.

Perry, Charles. 'The Horseback Kitchen of Central Asia'. *Food on the Move; Proceedings of the 1996 Oxford Symposium on Food and Cookery*. Edited by Harlan Walker. Totnes: Prospect Books, 1997, pp. 243–248.

Peşteli, Selma. *Boşnak Yemekleri*. İstanbul: İnkilap Yayınevi, 2006.

Ramazanova, Zoya and Magomedkhan Magomedkhanov. 'Meat Foods of Mountain Jews of Daghestan'. Edited by Robert Chenciner. *Authenticity in the Kitchen, proceedings of the 2005 Oxford Symposium on Food and Cookery*. Edited by Richard Hosking. Totnes: Prospect Books, 2006, pp. 363–367.

Saberi, Helen, *Noshe Djan. Afgan Food and Cookery*. Totnes: Prospect Books, 2004.

Shaida, Margaret. *The Legendary Cuisine of Persia*. London: Grub Street, 2004.

Smith, R. E. F. 'Kazan Tatar Diet and Russia'. *First International Food Congress, Turkey 25–30 Sept. 1986*. Ankara: Ministry of Culture and Tourism, 1983, pp. 276–283.

Şahin, Haşim. 'Cuisine during the Turkish Seljuk and Principalities Eras'. *Turkish Cuisine*. Edited by Arif Bilgin and Özge Samancı. Ankara: Ministry of Culture and Tourism, 2008, pp: 39–55.

Pürad, Vağinag. *Mükemmel Yemek Kitabı–1926*. İstanbul: Aras Yayıncılık, 2010.

Uvezian, Sonia. *The Cuisine of Armenia*. New York: Hippocrene, 1996.

Ünver, Özgün; Saatçi, Can; Erelçin, H. Devin; Özer, Meltem. 'Geçmişten Günümüze Orta Asya'dan Anadolu'ya Mantı'. *Yemek ve Kültür–Sayı 8*. Istanbul: Çiya Yayınları, 2007, pp. 180–188.

A Knish is just a Knish – or is it? The Evolution of a Lowly Street Food to *Haute* Nosh

Elizabeth Field

Back in the days when tickets to a New York Yankees baseball game cost $5 – quite a while ago – my Bronx-born husband Bruce used to grab a pre-game bite from the hot dog vendor outside Yankee Stadium. It was invariably a knish, a leaden, yellow, deep-fried, square dumpling stuffed with tepid, barely seasoned mashed potatoes. At fifty cents with a squirt of mustard, it was cheap, filling and satisfying – the way a street snack should be. It also marked, in that moment in time, a confluence of personal identifiers: a Jewish boy cheering his hometown team while eating an ancestral food that had become a New York food.

Fast-forward thirty years and the ubiquitous New York City street-cart knish is alive and well. It is still leaden, lukewarm (a Giuliani administration edict specifying that knish carts carry a warming oven hasn't made much of a difference in serving temperature), filling, and affordable at $2.50. Most New York street-cart knishes are made by Gabila's Knishes, the first mechanized knish production facility, founded on the Coney Island boardwalk in 1921.[1] They are the quintessential 'Coney Island knish,' which means they are about three inches square, two inches deep, and fried. Some enthusiasts insist that the other major form of knish – an approximately three and a half inch round of pastry, stuffed with mashed potatoes, kasha (buckwheat groats), or other vegetables, its pastry edges folded over the filling, and baked – is more genteel.

There's a new knish in town, though, as well as in other towns including Boston, San Francisco, Washington, Toronto, and London. Unlike the humble originals, these are *haute*: handmade by a chef in a restaurant, food truck, or specialty deli, using luxurious or unorthodox ingredients such as wild mushrooms and caramelized onions, or sliced belly ham and Swiss cheese, or hazelnuts and chocolate. They run in price from around $3.50 to $17, and are meant to be savoured, not gobbled. These are considered, rather than utilitarian knishes.

How did the new *haute* knishes evolve? Do they represent a younger generation of Jewish-American chefs seeking comfort and stability in the idealized reinvention of their *bubbe's* (grandma's) food traditions? Are they a vehicle for culinary innovation? A fad? Or do they represent an entrepreneurial opportunity for purveyors of 'updated Jewish cuisine'? As Jennifer Jordan observes, dumplings are 'ripe for both powerful symbolism and changing meanings'.[2] This paper explores changing meanings in a knish.

A knish is basically poor man's food, dough wrapped around a filling to stretch it further. It originated as a medieval Slavic fried patty called *knysz* in Poland, a peasant dish made from a cooked vegetable, most notably mashed turnips, or kasha. Eastern European Jews adapted the *knysz* to the dictates of kosher laws and to their tastes, transforming it into the knish, a small, round, fried pastry filled with potatoes, kasha, cabbage, or curd cheese. In the mid-nineteenth century, with the popularization of the home oven, the baked knish emerged as the preeminent eastern Ashkenazic filled pastry.[3]

Knishes are closely identified with New York, having been brought to Manhattan's Lower East Side by the large-scale immigration of Ashkenazi Jews from Eastern Europe and Russia in the late nineteenth and early twentieth centuries.[4] Darra Goldstein described the teeming, turn-of-the-century square-mile ghetto on the Lower East Side as the 'most crowded place in the United States'.[5]

Within the rapidly expanding population of the city, the pushcart peddler became an important element in the food distribution system. Because peddling didn't require extensive capital or language skills, it was a favoured occupation among immigrants, predominantly Jews and Italians.[6] Where Italians tended to peddle greens, peppers, cheese, garlic, nuts, and olives, Jewish peddlers offered fresh and preserved fish, onions, potatoes, cabbage, carrots, pickles, sweet potatoes, soda water, halvah, hot chickpeas, knishes, hot corn, chestnuts, fruit, nuts, pretzels, ice cream, and chewing gum.[7] Women and children made up a large percentage of the pushcart workers.

Enterprising peddlers expanded their businesses into stores and restaurants. The stretch of Second Avenue between 14th Street and Houston Street, dotted with Yiddish theatres, became known as Knish Alley.[8] On 17 January 1916, the *New York Times* ran an article called 'Rivington Street Sees War, Rival Restaurant Men Cut Prices on Succulent Knish'. One of the most beloved and extant neighbourhood knisheries, Yonah Schimmel, opened in 1910 on East Houston Street, after relocating from Coney Island. It originally sold Mrs Schimmel's 'always baked' potato and kasha knishes to workers, students and businessmen as a warm, inexpensive snack or meal. It later broadened its selection to include red cabbage, spinach, mushroom, sweet potato, broccoli and blueberry-cheese, as well as some recent Hispanic-influenced hybrid combinations.

The importance of place in knish culture cannot be underestimated. Food historian Laura Silver, author of the forthcoming *Book of Knish: Loss, Longing and the Search for a Humble Hunk of Dough*, has concentrated much of her research on working-class and lower middle-class Ashkenazi Jewish enclaves in the Lower East Side and Brooklyn, New York. (Part performance artist and part scholar, Silver dressed up as a knish in a yellow foam rubber suit and paraded down Second Avenue during the Hester Street Fair of 2010.)[9]

Nostalgia permeates the memories of New York knish-lovers who grew up between the 1930s and 1970s. At a recent talk given by Silver at the Brooklyn Historical Society, audience members called out the names of their favourite childhood knisheries: Mrs Stahl's and Hirsch's in Brighton Beach, Shatzkin's of Coney Island, Jerry's in Far Rockaway. Knish-maker Noah Wildman recounts childhood visits to the Coney Island boardwalk in the 1970s: 'The hot fried knish eaten on the hot boardwalk, accompanied by a high-acid, sweet lime rickey was a perfect combination'. An entire website is devoted to memories of one seller, Ruby the Knishman, who plied his trade in Canarsie and Manhattan Beach, Brooklyn, as well as the bungalow colony villages in the 'mountains' of New York's Catskill region in the 1960s and 1970s.[10] In a typical post, Deborah Olin recounts:

> I remember Ruby and his great knishes. I'm also a chef and spent years trying to reproduce Ruby's Knishes and I finally did. It's a variation of a Russian Peirogie [sic], that's very popular in Russian Communities [sic] and sold for years and years in Russia in train stations, to workers, students. It's made with yeast-risen dough and Ruby must have had it rising all over his house (I just imagine Ruby made them at home to save money, rather than him having a separate kitchen to make them). Since he sold so many and not only in Canarsie ... he must have had buckets of dough rising. I imagine him using garbage containers (unused!) to rise all that dough in. I remember Ruby talked dirty, he would tell the kids, the boys that he bought his wife a negligie [sic] and he'd talk about her boobies, and how she'd slap him off of him. Just weird stuff I didn't quite get yet at that point. When I didn't have money he often gave me and sometimes a friend a free knish, usually broken ones, but who cared. I remember the salt tin and everyone putting their palm out to get some then we'd all stand around licking the salt and feeling so incredibly lucky...[11]

Cara De Silva has described urban fusion as a 'swap meet' of a growing number of available ingredients from around the globe, comingling of immigrant groups, creativity, globalization and commercial forces.[12]

Knishes have been affected by these factors. Adelman's Kosher Deli and Restaurant, located under the elevated subway on Kings Highway in Brooklyn, in a mixed Russian, Georgian, Ukrainian, and Hispanic neighbourhood, is a quintessential 'old New York' deli, with its storefront neon signage, faded linoleum floor, Formica tables, and aging, floor-to-ceiling memorabilia of New York sports teams. Its heavy, deeply satisfying potato, sweet potato, kasha, mushroom, and shredded pastrami knishes cost $2.95. Founded over 50 years ago in the Borough Park neighbourhood, it is now owned by Mohamed Salem, an Egyptian-born archaeologist who bought the present store in 2006 after working as a counterman there for 20 years. A Hispanic baker makes the knishes. Salem says that he has no reason to hide his faith, and in fact sees himself as living proof that peace between historically warring peoples ought to be made over a *gezunte* meal.[13]

Similarly, an anachronism among the hipster bars, whole foods market and designer clothing shops on East Houston Street, Yonah Schimmel is a throwback to the old Lower East Side. Amid faded family photos, news clips, handwritten signs in Yiddish and greasy display cases of potato knishes set under warming lights are some bilious, bright yellow knishes, stuffed with jalapeños and cheese and with garlic and jalapeños.

The new flavours were created in response to customer demand, according to the Puerto Rican counterman.

An emerging trend for 'updated Jewish cuisine' combines the worldly sophistication of fresh, wild, and organic ingredients (in Brooklyn, the Gefilteria's gefilte fish is made with whitefish, salmon, and pike sourced from the sustainable purveyor Wild Edibles), house-cured meats, and 'artisanal' breads with a nod to the humble origins of Ashkenazic cuisine. It speaks to a kind of interplay of nostalgia and heightened culinary standards – a linear, generational viewpoint, rather than a melding of different cultural strands. It also speaks to the usual criticisms about Jewish food that it is heavy, oily, a 'heart attack on the plate'.

In the last two years, the Mile End Delicatessen, Kutsher's Tribeca, Balaboosta, and Zucker Bakery (among other eateries) have opened in New York, while Wise Sons Jewish Delicatessen, Bubala's Rugelach, and Old World Food Truck have opened in San Francisco. Other similar establishments have appeared in Toronto, London, Washington and Portland, Oregon. Says Gefilteria's co-owner Jeffrey Yoskowitz: 'We're embracing our heritage but in a way my generation can relate to. Bring back the *schav*!'.[14] Somewhat more cynically, Jewish food historian Jenna Weisman Joselit sees the return to schmaltz as an expression of the current sixties zeitgeist expressed in television shows like *Mad Men*. 'It's almost a faux nostalgia for something they never experienced in the first place', she told *The Forward*.[15]

Haute knishes coincide with this movement. For a Boston event called 'Beyond Bubbie's Kitchen', held in January 2011, fifteen Jewish and non-Jewish local chefs created innovative dishes based on traditional Ashkenazi and Sephardic cuisine.[16] Chef Steven Brand created a luxurious knish stuffed with braised lamb, caramelized onions, and a syrupy reduction flavoured with lamb fat and smoked paprika. 'It was unctuous and rich enough so that a pesto made with cilantro, mint, and garlic really brightened it up', he told me. The impetus for creating delicious Jewish food arose out of childhood memories of 'awful' food encountered while eating in restaurants during Passover week. In Brand's case, his dish might have been a 'fantasy knish'.[17]

Lower East Side knish-maker Noah Wildman is not trying to reinvent the knish, he says, but rather to bring a greater culinary and technical awareness to his evolving roster of offerings.[18] 'Knishes have four walls, a floor, and a ceiling', he says. He tries to balance a dough's crisp and elastic textures with the chewy and crumbly properties of fillings. Keeping the right proportion of dough to filling is one of the most critical elements of a perfect knish, he believes. To that effect, his knishes are smaller than the softball-size dumplings sold at many delis.

His standard recipes include potato-onion, roasted garlic and spinach, and broccoli and cheese knishes, which he prepares in his home kitchen and sells at street fairs and at a neighbourhood craft beer and cheese store. He was unable to find lung when trying to recreate an old cookbook recipe – but is 'aching to go full-throttle' on a *gribenes* (crispy chicken fat) knish, a potato and Guinness knish, and a mushroom-quinoa knish. He uses a 'kind of Bubbe's pâté sucrée', for his sweet knishes filled with curd cheese and vanilla bean, and chocolate and hazelnuts. I ate one of Wildman's kasha and potato knishes ($4.50) for supper recently. It was a perfect combination of earthy, nutty and refined. 'The knish chose me', he told *Tablet* magazine. It is obviously his vehicle for personal expression, as canvas is for a painter.[19]

In San Francisco, chef Kenny Hockert recently launched his Old World Food Truck, from which he sells 'East European and Jewish soul food', including several varieties of knish ($5 to $7), home-smoked fish, and pierogis. Something of an iconoclast and visionary – 'my cooking is a self-narrative' – he also embraces the political aspects of mobile food distribution. By setting up his truck in various locations, he is able to 'bring food to a broader geographic and keep costs lower than in a restaurant'.[20]

On the opposite end of the spectrum are the deep-fried buckwheat-potato knishes with caviar, created by Mario Carbone and Rich Torrisi, chef-owners of Torrisi Italian Specialties in New York. A recipe suggesting the dish as a 'sophisticated appetizer' for New Year's Eve appeared in the December 2011 issue of *Food and Wine* magazine.[21] Complicated and expensive, and loaded with heavy cream, butter, cream cheese, sour cream and caviar, these knishes are also loaded with the sort of irony and *chutzpah* embodied by the 'beggar's purses' – miniature crepes filled with caviar, tied with a length of scallion, and dusted with gold leaf – made famous in 1980 at the former Manhattan restaurant, Quilted Giraffe. (Bryan Miller called the dish 'America's first profligate small plate'.[22])

I leave the discussion of the sour cream and chive knish enrobed in house-made 'pastrami-smoked' salmon, and surrounded by baby greens, capers, dill, and a mustardy vinaigrette, at Kutsher's Tribeca in New York, for last, because I am the most ambivalent about this knish. In keeping with the restaurant's concept of elevating the 'low' Ashkenazi cuisine and kitschy mid-century modern décor of the original Kutsher's Hotel & Country Club into something hip and modern (the restaurant's owners call it a 'modern Jewish-American bistro, not a deli'), the dish is rich with extra-virgin olive oil and *schmaltz*, elegantly composed using top-notch ingredients, and filling enough to comprise a full lunch.[23] But it is no on-the-run quick snack, and at $17 it is not for those on a budget. It has been accused by some of being 'too posh'.

I debated with myself about what really constitutes a knish, until I felt a familiar touch of the indigestion that often follows a 'traditional' Jewish meal. I thought to myself that knishes may be simple snacks or vehicles for aspiration and sophistication, but one thing they never are is light. Using that criteria, even Kutsher's counted as the real deal.

Notes

1. Gil Marks, *Encyclopedia of Jewish Food* (Hoboken, NJ: John Wiley and Sons, 2010), p. 323.
2. Jennifer Jordan, 'Elevating the Lowly Dumpling: From Peasant Kitchens to Press Conferences', Ethnology 47.2/3 (2008): p. 109.
3. Marks, p. 322.

4. The first Jews to arrive in America were Sephardim who had escaped the Spanish Inquisition and settled in Recife, Brazil around 1636. They subsequently founded communities along the East Coast, including Newport, Rhode Island, and Savannah, Georgia. The second wave of Jews to immigrate to the United States were Ashkenazi German Jews, who arrived between 1830 and 1880. Many of these became successful merchants and bankers; their priority was assimilation. The latest wave of Russian and Eastern European Jews were derided as 'kikes' not only by non-Jews but also by bourgeois German Jews.
5. Darra Goldstein, 'Will Matzoh Go Mainstream: Jewish Food in America', *The Jewish Role in American Life: An Annual Review*, vol. 4, eds. Barry Glassner and Hilary Taub Lachoff (Los Angeles: University of Southern California Casden Center for the Study of the Jewish Role in American Life, 2005): p. 7.
6. Suzanne Wasserman, 'Hawkers and Gawkers: Peddling and Markets in New York City', *Gastropolis: Food and New York City*, eds. Annie Hauck-Lawson and Jonathan Deutsch (New York: Columbia University Press, 2009), p. 158.
7. Wasserman, p. 155.
8. Sewell Chan, 'Something to Nosh On: Here's the Skinny on Jewish Delis', *The New York Times* 1 August 2007: p. 2.
9. Forthcoming from Brandeis University Press; Laura Silver, 'Knish Alley Revived for a Day', *The Lo-Down* 11 October 2010: http://www.thelodownny.com/leslog/2010/10/knish-alley-revived-for-a-day.html.
10. Bruce Brodinsky, 'Ruby the Knishman', Bruce's Useless Web Page: http://www.brucebrodinsky.com/ruby.html.
11. It should be noted that while knishes are generally associated with pushcarts, delis, and knish stores, and modern Jewish cookbooks generally only offer a few basic recipes for knishes (*The New York Times Jewish Cookbook*, ed. Linda Amster (New York: St. Martin's, 2003): p. 286; Sharon Lebewohl and Rena Bulkin, *The Second Avenue Deli Cookbook* (New York: Villard, 1999): pp. 172-73; Claudia Roden, *The Book of Jewish Food* (New York: Knopf, 1996), p. 75), knishes were regularly made at home prior to World War II. *Regina Frishwasser's Jewish American Cookbook: 1600 Selected Recipes* (New York: Forward Association, 1946) includes twenty recipes for knishes filled with cheese, potatoes, lima beans, peas, spinach, beets, carrots, cabbage, peppers, onions and farina, rice, chicken, liver, stewed veal and lung, apples, and nuts. (In other words, leftovers.) Five similar recipes for 'pockets' feature liver, apples, cherries, huckleberries, and jam versions. As noted in her preface, the English-language recipes in her book are directed toward the daughters of her readers who are unfamiliar with Yiddish print.
12. Cara De Silva, 'Fusion City From Mt. Olympus: Bagels to Puerto Rican Lasagna and Beyond', *Gastropolis: Food and New York City*, eds. Annie Hauck-Lawson and Jonathan Deutsch (New York: Columbia University, 2009): pp. 8,10.
13. Reuven Fenton, 'Arab Meets Chew' *New York Post* 9 October 2009.
14. Adeena Sussman, 'Haimish to Haute in New York' *The Forward* 6 April 2012.
15. Sussman.
16. Jane Dornbusch, 'Even Bubbie would have Eaten More', *Boston Globe* 2 February 2011.
17. Steven Brand, in conversation with the author, 15 April 2012.
18. Jeffrey Yoskowitz, 'Dough Boy' *Tablet* 1 December 2011.
19. Yoskowitz.
20. Kenny Hockert, in conversation with the author, 16 April 2012.
21. Mario Carbone and Rich Torrisi, 'Buckwheat-Potato Knishes with Caviar', *Food and Wine* December 2011.
22. Bryan Miller, 'From Caviar to Burgers: Reimagining Luxury', *Food and Wine* September 2008.
23. Molly Yeh, 'Kutsher's Tribeca Updates Jewish Classics', The Jew & the Carrot 27 October 2011: http://blogs.forward.com/the-jew-and-the-carrot. Kutsher's Hotel & Country Club was one of the classic 'Borscht Belt' resorts in New York's Catskill region, where lower- and middle-class urban Jews would decamp for trips to 'the mountains'. Its heyday was from the 1950s–1980s.

All Wrapped Up – A History of Mummy Eating

Len Fisher and Janet Clarkson

Let food be thy medicine, and medicine be thy food
Hippocrates[1]

When it comes to stuffing and wrapping, nobody did it better than the ancient Egyptians. Corpses were eviscerated and dried with a desiccating salt mixture known as *natron*. They were then stuffed with aromatic plant oils and spices, including cassia, cinnamon and occasionally one or more onions, before being carefully wrapped in linen that was then covered in a resinous paste.[2] The intention was to preserve the structure of the body in preparation for the return of the soul, and bodies so preserved could last for thousands of years. Wealthy medieval people, however, found another, more macabre use for these ancient stuffed and wrapped objects – they used them as food.

Why did they do this? The answer is simple. Just like the modern consumers of stuffed and wrapped foods who line the tables of Subway and Pret A Manger, these ancient consumers of *mummia*[3] believed that what they were eating was healthy.[4]

Stuffed and wrapped foods have come to be associated in many people's minds with a healthy diet[5] but the historical reasons for stuffing and wrapping foods had little to do with health. According to Rachel Laudan, winner of the Sophie Coe prize in 1998, the aims of stuffing and wrapping are 'to make handling and serving easier; to hold loose mixtures together until they consolidate during cooking; to create variety in taste and textures; and to create beauty or provoke astonishment.'[6]

It would certainly have astonished the ancient Egyptians if they had known that the carefully preserved corpses of their families and nobility were to be dug up in their thousands during medieval times to be ground up, suspended in spirits of wine, and consumed as *mummia*. The practice drew considerable criticism from the sixteenth century onwards,[7] although belief in the value of medical cannibalism, which has even influenced the works of Shakespeare,[8] continued in the West into the early twentieth century,[9] and continues in some countries even to this day.[10]

Mummia was the superfood of its day. Just as almonds, black beans, watermelon, and a host of other 'natural' foods are believed to have 'age-defying, disease-fighting, fat-blasting superpowers', so *mummia* was believed to have a literally incredible range of benefits.[11] Medieval noblemen carried tiny bags of mummy powder tucked into their clothing,[12] and François I of France always rode with a leather pouch of it attached to his horse.[13] This mummy powder was also used in the treatment of battlefield and other injuries, difficulties in childbirth, wasted limbs, consumptions, 'fluxes and rheums', apoplexy, 'pestilence and dropsey', 'joints that are out of place', 'flux of the semen and night pollutions', the 'falling sickness' and even nosebleeds.[14] The most impressive supposed benefit of *mummia*, however (at least for half of the human race), is celebrated in verse by Rupert Brooke in his 1916 poem 'Mummia':

> As those of old drank mummia
> To fire their limbs of lead,
> Making dead kings from Africa
> Stand pandar to their bed;
>
> Drunk on the dead, and medicined
> With spiced imperial dust,
> In a short night they reeled to find
> Ten centuries of lust.[15]

Perhaps this is why Shakespeare's Othello gives to his beloved Desdemona a handkerchief 'dyed in mummy, which the skilful | Conserved of maiden's hearts'. He tells her that handkerchief had been made for his mother by a witch, to 'make her amiable and subdue my father | Entirely to her love'.[16]

Mummia is no longer available commercially, but material that was probably collected for this purpose may still be found in museums. One example may be seen in the current 'Enlightenment' exhibition at the British Museum, which features a box of curious objects collected by Sir Hans Sloane, including a mummy's finger intended for grinding into a medicinal powder. More substantial specimens are to be found in the collection of the Royal Pharmaceutical Society, including a hand and a jawbone with teeth.[17] Both carry labels that they were used to 'treat bruises, wounds and epilepsy', while the jawbone label carries the additional information that it could be used to induce vomiting. Certainly this last use seems to be the most likely to work.

It is interesting to note that mummification is not a dead art. Torquay cabdriver Alan Billis, suffering from terminal lung cancer, volunteered to be mummified after his death by York University researcher Stephen Buckley. In January 2011 the event came to pass and was recorded in a Channel 4 documentary entitled *Mummifying Alan: Egypt's Last Secret*.[18] It is to be hoped that the packaged and preserved Alan will remain food for no more than thought.

The 'edible' packaging that became part of *mummia* consisted of the degraded linen wrappings and the bituminous substances with which they had been coated. Both were natural materials, even if somewhat indigestible. Stuffed and wrapped foods from many cultures have been encapsulated in rather more digestible natural materials, but only recently have we come to understand just how those materials function, and to expand their range through the selective use of natural polymers made from animal and vegetable proteins, gums and lipids.[19] These new materials can act as 'intelligent packagings' through their ability to control selectively the permeation of oxygen, water vapour and bacteria. Such packagings can also be used to separate several compartments within a food, offering new opportunities to expand the range of wrapped and stuffed foods.

These new foods may not last as long as the ancient Egyptian mummies, but they will be preserved at least as well in the short term – and will also be rather tastier and better for us than *mummia*.

Appendix 1: the uses of mummia
The following is a fairly random selection of indications for the use of *mummia*, taken from sixteenth- and seventeenth-century medical textbooks.

> A remedie for such as have out their fundament.
> To heale corrosive hurts called commonly the Wolfe ['Lupus' in today's jargon]
> To remedie the ioynts that are out of their place.
> An excellent preservative against the Pestilence and Dropsey.
> To remedie a rupture or breaking.
> A more excellent remedie against empoysments than is common Triacle.
> A very comfortable water, for all woundinge.
> For difficult parturione, or Childbirthe, When a woman hath noe travayle.
> When a woman can nether be deliverede of her Secondes, nor her deade Childe.
> A tried restriction of Bloode.
> Another vulnerarye when anye man is thruste, Shotte, or els hath fallen.
> If any Persone have fallen in peeces one of his Ribbes, which with the Handes we cannot restore agayne into his naturalle situation.
> For the coulde burninge, or Gangranation.
> A goode Salve for all woundes.
> A Pouder for such as are bruised by a Fall.
> For the falling down of the Fundament [Post natal prolapse of the womb.]
> An Experimented Vulnerary Potion or Wound-drink.
> Wounds in the Trachea, Arteria and Oesophagus.
> A fracture plaister for Fractures with wounds, after the bone is set.
> An Astringent medicine (external application) for gonorrhea.
> [It] dissolveth clotted Blood in the Body happening by any Fall or Bruise, and healeth Burstings and broken Parts as well inward as outward.
> Fluxes and rheums.
> Apoplexy.
> Flux of the semen and night pollutions.

Appendix 2: mummy recipes
Pieces of *mummia* were often simply broken into small pieces, or ground to a powder and taken with wine or food, but the mummy flesh was also distilled into 'elixir' or 'treacle' (or 'theriac' – a poison antidote and panacea.)

All Wrapped Up – A History of Mummy Eating

Elixir of Mummy is made thus

Take of mummy (viz., of man's flesh hardened), cut small four ounces, spirit of wine terebinthinated ten ounces, and put them into a glazed vessel (three parts of four being empty) which set in horse dung to digest for the space of a month. Then take it out and express it, and let the expression be circulated a month. Then let it run through manica hippocratis, and then evaporate the spirit until that which remains in the bottom be like an oil which is the true elixir of mummy.

This elixir is a wonderful preservative against all infections, also very balsamical.[20]

Treacle of Mummy

Chuse the Carcase of a red[-haired] Man, whole, clear without blemishes, of the age of twenty four years, that hath been Hanged, Broke upon a Wheel, or Thrust-through, having been for one day and night exposed to the open Air, in a serene time [ie to the influence of the sun and moon].

This Mumy … cut into small pieces or slices, and sprinkle on them Powder of Myrrh, and of Aloes, but a very little (otherwise it will be too bitter) afterward by Macerating, Imbibe them for certain days in Spirit of Wine, hang them up a little, an again Imbibe them, then hang them up to dry in the Air; this so dryed will be like Flesh hardened in Smoak, and be without stink. Afterward with Spirit of Wine, or Spirit of Elderflowers, according to art, extract a most red Tincture.

Also Oyle Olives may a part with the dryed Mumy (for the moisture in digestion causeth an intolerable Stinke) be Macerated for a Month, and so be Tinged therewith; this Tinged Oyle Olive, may afterward at pleasure be added to the Tincture of Mumy, before it be mixed with the Treacle.

Rx [measurements translated from the apothecary symbols] Therefore of the Tincture or Extract of Mumy made with Spirit of Wine, from which the Spirit is afterward abstracted, half a pound.

Oyle Olives mumia 2 oz
Salt of Pearls and Corals, of each 2 drachms
Terra sigillata 2 oz.
Musk 1 drachm (15)
Mix and digest these by Circulating for a Month.[21]

An excellent preservative against the Pestilence and Dropsey.

Take one ounce of the juyce of greene nuttes, of the juyce of Agrimony half an ounce, of the juice of Rew three drams, of the juice of [?] three ounces, of the juice of Hempe foure ounces. meddle them together, then take of the saide mixture half an ounce, of *Mumia* half a dramme, of Sugar Candy halfe an ounce, of Sugar Rosate one dramme, make a lectuary, of the which, dissolve in good wine the quantitie of a Chestnut. or else in Buglosse water, or of the flowers of Marygolds, and many nights when you go to bed, use to drinke thereof.[22]

For difficult parturione, or Childbirthe
When a woman hath noe travayle.
Give unto her Mummye, the quantitye of a Pease, with wine to drincke.[23]

When a woman can nether be deliverede of her Secondes, nor her deade Childe.
Take Mummye, *Viscus quersinus* [mistletoe of the oak], white Ambre, & the spermaticks of a Hinde of each the biggenes of a pease contunde it smalle & give it to her to drincke ether with wine, or Lillywater.[24]

A tried restriction of Bloode.
Take Mummia ... Deade mans bone, ... beate it small, & drincke that poudre with coulde water, & it will stenche the bloode.[25]

A very comfortable water, for all wounding.
Take *Mummie*, & Mace ana .... *Castereum*, 12. Graynes, add thereunto *Aquavitae*, Cinnamome water, or Malmasye, & reserve the same in a glasse closely occluded: & when you administer the same to anye bodye which is halfe deade ... he shall be agayne revidede.[26]

An Experimented Vulnerary Potion or Wound Drink.
Take leaves of the large Comfrey, Agrimony, Armoise Mugwort, of each two handfuls; herb Robert 3 handfuls, *Mumia* half an ounce, *Pauls* Betony or Speedwell six handfuls; make a Decoction of this with White-wine and Water in a Vessel close stopt. Then pour off as much as you can of the clear; then distil the remaining matter. Then add the distilled water to the Decoction. Take of this a little Glassful in the morning fasting, and as much at four of the clock in the afternoon.

This hath cured a Gentlewoman of an Ulcer in the Reins, in six weeks space.

This cured also a Frier, who being Cut of the Stone, could not be healed.[27]

A Pouder for such as are bruised by a Fall.
Take of *Terra sigillata* (a new name for earth of Lemnos) a *Sanguis Draconis* (Dragons blood, so called, although it be noghin less, but only the gum of a tree), Mummy, of each two drachms, Sperma Ceti one drachm, Rhubarb half a drachm, beat them to pouder according to art.

You must beat the rest into a pouder and then add the Sperma Ceti to them afterwards, for if you put the Sperma Ceti and the rest altogether, and go to beat them in that fashion, you may as soone beat the mortar into pouder as the Simples. Indeed your best way is to beat them severally, and then mix them altogether, which being done, makes you a gallant medicine for the infirmity specified in the title, a drachm of it being taken in Muskadel, and sweating after it.[28]

All Wrapped Up – A History of Mummy Eating

Postscript
For a nice selection of modern recipes for human body parts we can do no better than refer to *Human Cuisine*, by Ken Albala and Gary Allen (Booksurge, 2008), which includes an enticing selection of ideas at the end of each chapter.

Notes
1. This well-known phrase, attributed to Hippocrates, is frequently quoted in well-respected journals, without it actually appearing in his collected works. It is, however, a distillation of the beliefs of Hippocrates and his followers on the topic of food as medicine and medicine as food. See Hippocrates, 'The Art Of Medicine In Former Times', *The Writings of Hippocrates and Galen. Epitomized from the original Latin Translations*, by John Redman Coxe (Philadelphia: Lindsay and Blakiston, 1846): http://oll.libertyfund.org/title/1988/128089.
2. Gomaa Abdel-Maksoud and Abdel_Rahman El-Amin, 'A Review on the Materials Used During the Mummification Processes in Ancient Egypt', *Mediterranean Archaeology and Archaeometry* 11 (2011), pp. 129–50.
3. *Mummia* (various spellings) was a 'sovereign remedy' or panacea prepared for medicinal use from mummified human flesh – a belief that goes back to Paracelsus (Howard Bayles 'Mummy in Paracelsian Pharmacy', *The Chemist and Druggist* (20 August 1949), pp. 254–56). The word derives ultimately from the Arabic *mūmiyā* (and/or the related Persian *mūmiyā'ī*) indicating a rare, naturally occurring bituminous material believed to have powerful medicinal properties. By the mid-fifteenth century in Europe, it was incorrectly believed that this substance was used by ancient Egyptians to embalm corpses. Hence these bodies became mummies, and a new source of *mummia*. Eventually the medicinal properties became attributed to the mummified flesh itself.
   A belief in the healing and restorative powers of human flesh was quite logical in the context of the prevailing medical beliefs of the time. It fitted perfectly with the concepts embodied in the Doctrine of Humours and the Doctrine of Signatures, and the idea of the physical body being preserved indefinitely by mummification no doubt added another layer of authenticity. The belief was that the flesh contained the 'essence' – the spirit, or life-force, if you will – which could then be transferred (by ingestion) to the recipient. *Mummy* was listed in many pharmacopoeias, such as Edward Taylor's 'Dispensatory' in Puritan New England (Karen Gordon-Grube, 'Evidence of Medical Cannibalism in Puritan New England: "Mummy" and Related Remedies in Edward Taylor's "Dispensatory"', *Early American Literature* 28 (1993), pp. 185–221). 'Anthropophagy in Post-Renaissance Europe: The Tradition of Medical Cannibalism', *American Anthropologist* (New Series) 90 (1988), pp. 405–09. *Mummia* was not only used as a medicinal food. In the nineteenth century, it even featured in a recipe for fish bait that 'prodigiously causes fish to bite' (*The Angler's Vade Mecum* (1863), qtd. 'A Sportsman's Experience Fishing and Shooting in England' *New York Times* (7 March 1903)). Even more bizarrely, the linen rags in which mummies were wrapped found their way into American newspapers in the mid-nineteenth century – not just as a story, but as a physical component of the paper itself! Among the 'millions of pounds of rags' imported from Alexandria to make paper a correspondent of the *Journal of Commerce* in Gardiner, Maine observed 'the plundered wrappings of men, bulls, crocodiles and cats, torn from the respectable defunct members of the same' ('Egyptian Mummy Rags in a Yankee paper Mill', *Pioneer and Democrat* (Olympia, Washington Territory) 5 November 1858). The scale of this importation of Egyptian rags (some of which came from mummies) into the United States in the second half of the nineteenth century appears to have been significant (see J. Munsell, *Chronology of the Origin and Progress of Paper and Paper-Making*, Albany (1876), p. 142, p. 198: http://archive.org/stream/chro-

nologyorigi00munsgoog/chronologyorigi00munsgoog_djvu.txt). It is not inconceivable that some of this 'mummy paper' found its way into grocery stores, and ended up as wrapping for various foodstuffs! For an excellent account of the history of *mummia* and its medical uses, see Sarah Bakewell, 'Cooking with Mummy', *Fortean Times* 124 (1999): http://www.sarahbakewell.com/Other%20Writing.html#Cookingwithmummy.

4. Janet Clarkson, 'The Mother of All Medicines', *Focus* magazine (Suppl. to *Australian Doctor Weekly*), December 2003; Karl H. Dannenfeldt, 'Egypt and Egyptian Antiquities in the Renaissance', *Studies in the Renaissance* 6 (1959), pp. 7–27.

5. The claimed 'healthiness' of stuffed and wrapped foods, as purveyed in some major chains (e.g. Pret a Manger, 'Healthy Food' (http://www.pret.com/sustainability/healthy_food.htm)) has been questioned (see, for example, Anne Shooter, 'The Alarming Truth about Your "Fresh and Healthy" Pret a Manger Lunch', *Daily Mail* (11 April 2011): http://www.dailymail.co.uk/femail/article-1375525/Pret-A-Manger-The-alarming-truth-fresh-healthy-lunch.html). Readers must make up their own minds.

6. Rachel Laudan, 'Wrapped Foods', *Food Encyclopedia*: http://www.huffingtonpost.com/encyclopedia/definition/wrapped-foods/2678/.

7. Karl H. Dannenfeldt, 'Egyptian Mumia: The Sixteenth Century Experience and Debate', *The Sixteenth Century Journal* 16 (1985), pp. 163–80.

8. According to literary analyst Louise Noble, the belief that eating human flesh can be good for you forms an implicit theme in Shakespeare's *Titus Andronicus* ('"And Make Two Pasties of Your Shameful Heads": Medical Cannibalism and Healing the Body Politic in *Titus Andronicus*', *English Literary History* 70 (Fall 2003), pp. 677–708). Unlike the far-from-fresh mummia, however, the flesh of Tamora's sons Demetrius and Chiron was all-too-fresh, being wrapped in pastry immediately after their slaughter and served up to their parents in a pie, in what is surely one of the most grisly and blood-soaked ends to any stage drama, Sweeney Todd notwithstanding.

9. 'Mummy' was featured as a therapeutic substance in the first American edition of *Merck's Index*, published in 1889, where it was priced at $5 per pound, and in the German Merck Index as late as 1909, being described as 'genuine Egyptian mummy, as long as the supply lasts, 17 marks 50 per kilogramme' (Karen Gordon-Grube, 'Anthropophagy in Post-Renaissance Europe: The Tradition of Medical Cannibalism', op. cit.). For the use of mummia as a therapeutic 'food' up until the nineteenth century, see Richard Sugg, '"Good Physic but Bad Food": Early Modern Attitudes to Medical Cannibalism and its Suppliers', *Social History of Medicine* 19 (2006), pp. 225–40. It has been argued that pathogen transmission is an important cost of cannibalism, and that this explains why it is infrequent in most species (D.W. Pfennig, S.G. Ho and E.A. Hoffman, 'Pathogen transmission as a selective force against cannibalism' *Animal Behaviour* 55 (1998), pp. 1255–61). When cannibalism occurs out of necessity (with the survivors of a shipwreck or an air crash, for example, the survivors often swear that a fair lottery was led. However, as pointed out by Lewis Petrinovich in *The Cannibal Within*, 'the loser is usually an obvious choice: a boy, … a foreigner, or a slave, never an officer and seldom a cook' ((Piscataway, NJ: Transaction, 2000), p. 3.)

10. One of the more gruesome manifestations of this belief was the discovery in 2012 of thousands of pills, made from dried, crushed foetuses, that were being smuggled from China to South Korea, and bought by people who believed that they could act as a universal panacea (Richard Shears and Rob Cooper, 'Thousands of Pills Filled with Powdered Human Baby Flesh Discovered by Customs Officials in South Korea', *The Daily Mail* 7 May 2012: http://www.dailymail.co.uk/news/article-2140702/South-Korea-customs-officials-thousands-pills-filled-powdered-human-baby-flesh.html).

11. 'Cancer', MSNBC: http://www.msnbc.msn.com/id/38311826/ns/health-cancer/t/disease-fighting-superfoods/#.T8HYh793Q7A. Some of the latest candidates for this less-than-exclusive club include goji berries ('Goji Berries and Goji Juice': http://www.naturaltherapypages.com.au/article/goji_berries_and_goji_juice) and folic acid (Mark Lucock, 'Is Folic Acid the Ultimate Functional Food Component for Disease Prevention?' *British Medical Journal* 328 (2004), pp. 211-14).

12. R. Pitt, *The Crafts and Frauds of Physick Expos'd*. 2nd ed. (London: T. Childe, 1703), p. 42.

13. A.-P. Leca, tr. L. Asmal, *The Cult of the Immortal* (London: Souvenir Press, 1980), p. 234.
14. Janet Clarkson, 'The Human Remedy' in Ken Albala and Gary Allen, *Human Cuisine* (BookSurge, 2008), pp. 187–202.
15. Rupert Brooke, *The Collected Poems of Rupert Brooke*: http://www.gutenberg.org/cache/epub/262/pg262.txt.
16. William Shakespeare, *Othello* 3.4.75–76. It may be that some of Shakespeare's knowledge of the medicinal use of mummia was acquired close to home. His son-in-law, John Hall, was a physician, and his case notes from 1611–35 show that mummy powder was part of his therapeutic armamentarium. One patient, 'Mr. P' was 'afflicted with a Flux of Semen, and Night-pollutions, by which he was much weakned'. For this serious problem (his 'life force' visibly ebbing away), Dr Hall prescribed a pill containing gum arabic, gum tragacanth, Armenian bole, carabe (amber), mummy powder and Mandibule Lucii piscis (jaw of pike.) See Joan Lane (ed.), *John Hall and his Patients. The Medical Practice of Shakespeare's Son-in-Law* (Stroud, UK: Sutton, 1996), p. 196.
17. Nigel Tallis, 'Pharmaceutical Society Holds Mummy's Hand', *The Pharmaceutical Journal* Dec. 24 & 31 (1988), p. 809.
18. Alexander H. Tullo 'Mummy Preservation, When Frankenstein Came To Life', *Chemical and Engineering News* 89 (2011), p. 64.
19. Frédéric Debeaufort, Jesùs-Alberto Quezada-Gallo and Andrée Voilley: 'Edible Films and Coatings: Tomorrow's Packagings: A Review', *Critical Reviews in Food Science and Nutrition 38* (1998), pp. 299-313.
20. John French, *The Art of Distillation: Book 4* (1651): http://levity.com/alchemy/jfren_4.html.
21. Oswald Crollius, *Basilica Chymica* trans. John Hartman (1670): accessed via Early English Books Online (http://eebo.chadwyck.com/home).
22. *A Very excellent and profitable Booke conteining six hundred foure score and odd experienced Medicines* ... Mayster Alexis [of Piemont], trans. from Italian Richard Androse (1569): accessed via Early English Books Online (http://eebo.chadwyck.com/home).
23. Gabelhouer, Oswald, *Boock of Physicke* (1599): accessed via Early English Books Online (http://eebo.chadwyck.com/home).
24. Gabelhouer.
25. Gabelhouer.
26. Gabelhouer.
27. Kenelm Digby, *The Closet of the Eminently Learned Sir Kenelm Digby Kt* (1669): accessed via Early English Books Online (http://eebo.chadwyck.com/home).
28. Nich. Culpeper, *A Physical Directory, or a Translation of the London Directory* (1649): accessed via Early English Books Online (http://eebo.chadwyck.com/home).

Rich Man's Fowl, Poor Man's Fowl: What's under the Wrapper?

Alexandra Grigorieva

Hunting has meant nutritional freedom from times immemorial – freedom and certain gastronomic luxuries that could hardly be obtained any other way. Small game such as fowl (larks, ortolans, warblers, blackbirds, pigeons, etc.) was especially appreciated and often accessible to all levels of society from aristocratic hunters to crafty peasants. But as there was not much delicate meat to be had from such birds, they were often wrapped in some kind of protective layer to keep them from drying out and to make them more palatable, appetizing and alluring.

In Roman times, flour and olive oil were mixed into dough 'to make the bird more flavourful and rich and to preserve its natural fattiness' in the oven.[1] In the fifteenth century, Maestro Martino preferred wrapping warblers in vine leaves with a little salt, fennel and fat before roasting.[2] For the last several centuries, warblers have often been barded, or wrapped in fat plain and proper, cured or not. And sometimes, bird size allowing, wrapping was achieved by even humbler means, as in Sicily, where one of the prized regional recipes (*beccaficu 'nna a cipudda*) specifies placing warblers inside hollowed onions and then baking them in hot ash.[3] More elegantly, Escoffier topped halved damson plums, baked with a little butter, with ortolans wrapped in vine leaves into each half before roasting them for four minutes (*ortolans aux quetsches*).[4] The ortolan was served with a sprinkle of verjuice and salt, but Escoffier insists that the damson plum is to be left uneaten; the Sicilian recipe recommends eating the onion (at least the part free of ash).

Unlike either onion or plum, presentation fowl 'wrappers' aim to captivate the rich diners' eyes and imaginations, not their palates. In the first century AD, Petronius described such gastronomic surprises at Trimalchio's feast.[5] Imitation peahen eggs made of pastry were placed under a wooden hen and made 'fertile' by stuffing fat warblers in peppered yolk inside them. Even more impressive was a boar that, when carved, released a flock of live blackbirds that were then caught and handed over to diners as a take-away present, along with two kinds of dates from baskets hanging from the boar's mouth and a litter of imitation piglets (also of pastry) that indicated that the boar was female. That no such recipes survive in *Apicius* (book 6 on fowl is, alas, sadly mutilated) does not mean that such things were not done. 'Four and twenty blackbirds baked in a pie' might be just a nursery rhyme, but we do find *pastello volativo*, a glorious pie with an inner section reserved for live birds to be released at the feast in Maestro Martino's cookbook, and various references to live birds in festive dishes in late medieval and Renaissance times.[6]

Rich Man's Fowl, Poor Man's Fowl

Another 'wrapper' prized for the rich feasts through the centuries was birds' own plumage. Around the end of the fourteenth century, even the relatively homely and bourgeois Menagier de Paris gives a recipe for a swan served in its plumage.[7] Similarly, Maestro Martino details how to serve peacocks and other spectacular looking birds in full plumage and even how to make them breathe fire.[8] Many centuries later almost the same thing was fashionable at the special hunting-themed banquets for the select few in Soviet restaurants in the 1970s and 1980s. Alexander Filin, one of the great Soviet and Russian chefs, once told me that he kept several reusable plumages of game birds (grouse, partridge, etc.) for such occasions and that the cooks poured vodka into birds' beaks and ignited it when serving.

Although these are all fascinating examples of fowl 'wrappers' for the rich, the humbler part of our gastronomic story involves small game – or the lack of it – among bourgeois town dwellers, who relied on butchers and could not get such dainties too often. As a result, they devised a kind of poor man's fowl: wrapped and stuffed bundles of some other kind of meat named after a bird, often with a sly reference to inauthenticity. Such wrapped and stuffed 'birds' can be found in many cuisines of Europe. In fact I have found at least three families of such dishes.

The first family of false fowl is the most numerous and spreads from France and Italy to Switzerland, the Czech Republic, Austria, Germany (especially in the south), Belgium, the Netherlands, Latvia and even England, although it is harder to recognize there. The oldest examples, called *aloes*, or 'larks', come from late medieval France and England of the fourteenth and fifteenth centuries. They are in fact little steaks wrapped around some highly seasoned stuffing and then skewered and roasted. This dish is the source of the English expression 'beef olives' and also of the French word *aloyau* (or *bavette d'aloyau*), a French beef cut (the part of flank that borders the British rump, or the American bottom sirloin) especially suitable for making imitation larks.[9] In modern France, delicate *alouettes sans tête* ('headless larks'), beef rolls stuffed with *petit salé* (salted pork and herbs) and stewed in a rich wine and tomato sauce, are a regional specialty of Provence that are often available in local butcher's shops.

French cooking websites (such as www.marmiton.org) include quite a few variations of *alouettes* (sometimes even called *alouettes de boeuf*, including one *alouettes sans tête* recipe that stuffs a veal and ham roll with a whole hard-boiled egg: one of the comments accuses the recipe's author of giving a recipe for *paupiette* – a general term for a meat roll in French – under the name of *alouette*. Others say that this is similar to the recipe they know as *nid de pigeon* ('pigeon's nest') or *nid d'hirondelle* ('swallow's nest'), and indeed these recipes, presented at the same website, are pretty close. Still another recipe is called *moineau sans tête* ('headless sparrow') which indicates its provenance not from Provence but from Flanders, northern France, or francophone Belgium where such beef rolls, also called 'headless birds' (*oiseaux sans tête*), are usually stuffed with ground meat and stewed in a beer-based sauce, but many other variations are also popular.[10]

In the Flemish part of Belgium and in the Netherlands, such meat rolls are called *blinde vinken* ('blind finches', probably because they obviously have no heads).[11] Another Belgian specialty called *loose vinken* ('escaped or crazy finches'), is beef rolled around a strip of bacon. And *slavinken* (a mystery word again involving 'finches') in the Netherlands dispenses with the beef roll itself, replacing it with ground meat stuffing wrapped in bacon.[12] One of my Dutch friends, Loet Vos, who was born in the Netherlands in 1933, insisted that that was the way *blinde vinken* were made and sold by the butchers in her time.

Quite a few similar recipes exist in Scandinavian culinary cultures. Norwegian cuisine has *benløse fugler* ('boneless birds' from beef), which remains popular with US families of Norwegian descent. The original way of making *benløse fugler* was to roll thin slices of well-pounded beef around bits of bone marrow or chopped lard, to tie the bundles up with a string and to braise them with some stock; that is how they are still usually made in the US, often with a bacon stuffing. However, in modern Norway, beef slices have been mostly replaced with ground beef, so that the 'boneless birds' in question have in fact turned into elongated meatballs stuffed with marrow or chopped lard.[13] This transition parallels the similar shift in the Netherlands.

Denmark has a splendid plethora of false fowl: *benløse fugle* ('boneless birds'), *forloren kylling* ('fake chicken') and *forloren and* ('fake duck').[14] 'Boneless birds' are usually meat rolls made from thin slices of beef wrapped around a thin piece of carrot with some bacon or solid lard. They are braised with stock, which is then made into a classic Danish thick brown sauce to accompany them and their usual side-dish of mashed potatoes. 'Fake chicken' is made from light-coloured veal stuffed with parsley and a little bit of butter, the usual summer stuffing for roast chicken. Like summer chicken, it is served with a sweet and sour fresh cucumber salad and new potatoes, the sauce lighter in colour but of the same type as for 'boneless birds' with maybe a dash of cream added. 'Fake duck' is made from pork stuffed with apples and prunes and served with brown sauce, potatoes and braised sweet and sour red cabbage, a classic Danish side-dish for the duck.

Icelandic cookbooks include both *beinlausir fuglar* ('boneless birds') and *fölsk önd* or *gerviönd* ('fake duck' or 'pretend duck') and also *fölsk gæs* or *gervigæs* ('fake goose' or 'pretend goose').[15] Considered old-fashioned, such dishes are not well-known in modern Iceland. 'Boneless birds' are rolled with slices of lard, tied up and braised; they could be made with almost any meat: lamb, beef, veal, and yes, horse (very popular in Iceland), although never pork, which used to be rare. 'Fake duck' was made with beef or horse tenderloin stuffed with prunes and sometimes also apples, browned and braised and served with more prunes and apples and vegetables. 'Fake goose' was a kind of meatloaf stuffed with dried apples and prunes and then baked.

In Latvia there is a similar dish called 'false partridge', a veal roll stuffed (and held in place) with a strip of smoked lard, braised with root vegetables and served with a sour cream sauce enriched with the braising stock.[16] In Germany such 'birds' are mostly unspecified, although I have found recipes for 'Spanish birds' (all kinds of beef or veal rolls that may be stuffed with Czech-style fatty sausage and dill pickles, ham and dill pickles or even anchovies) that are traditional in the Czech Republic as *španělské ptáčky* and appear in German sources as *Spanische Vogel/Vögerl*. There are also some German *Vogelnest* ('bird nest') recipes of meat rolls with eggs, but mostly this name is reserved for cookies. Otherwise the most popular name in Germany for such dishes seems to be *Kalbsvögel* ('veal birds'), veal rolls stuffed with anything from bacon, onions and herbs to whole, hard-boiled eggs and ham or even spinach and ricotta. *Kalbsvögel* are generally recognized as a regional specialty of Swabia.

'Birds', veal and beef rolls, are also quite popular in Austria. In his comprehensive work on Austrian food, Heinz-Dieter Pohl lists *Vögerl* ('little birds'), *Kalbsvögerl* ('veal little birds') and *Rindsvögerl* ('beef little birds') as separate entries although cross-referencing them as 'a kind of roll' (*Art Roulade*).[17] However, the two *Kalbsvögerl* recipes present in a classic book on Viennese cuisine are actually not rolls at all but liberally-larded, thin slices of veal either cooked with aromatic vegetables and tomato sauce, or braised separately and then finished with buttered mushrooms, so they are not necessarily stuffed or wrapped.[18]

In Switzerland, the name of such veal rolls changes to *Fleischvögel* ('meat birds'), which are popular in many Swiss cantons. In Valais, the south-west Swiss canton that borders Italy, people have been eating this dish for centuries: there is a recipe for it from 1581 in the archives of the town of Brig.[19] Its title is *Vögell auss kelberem flaisch zue braten* ('To roast "birds" out of veal meat'), and it recommends beating a piece of veal until tender with a knife, spicing it with cinnamon and ginger and stuffing it with a bit of kidney and a sprig of rosemary. Nowadays there are countless regional variations: Appenzell canton's stuffing may include *Mostbröckli* (cured beef filet) and stinky Appenzeller cheese; Glarus canton goes for goat cheese, carrot and celery; modern Valais canton stuffing often includes ham, sausage and asparagus. One of the most popular stuffings, regional differences notwithstanding, includes bacon, white bread, parsley and carrots, but new variations include many vegetables and even fruit.

In Italy (at least since the seventeenth century), the common name for false-fowl meat-rolls has been *uccelli/uccellini/ucelletti scappati* ('runaway birds').[20] They are made with veal or pork, often wrapped in bacon and sage leaves, and the stuffing may include bacon, mortadella and liver (and other kinds of offal); the rolls are then fried with butter and deglazed with white wine, stock or just water. Contrary to the 'birds' described earlier, these are often cooked and served several 'birds' per skewer like real game birds. Such 'birds' are especially popular in Lombardy and Emilia-Romagna.[21] A more unusual recipe may be found in the *fin-de-siècle* culinary masterpiece by Pellegrino Artusi, the first grand cookbook of a truly united Italy: called *tordi finti* ('imitation blackbirds'), it describes exquisite milk-veal rolls stuffed with finely minced chicken livers, anchovies, lardo and juniper berries (to enhance 'blackbird' flavour), wrapped in sage leaves and lardo and fried till golden, then finished with a little stock and served hot or cold on toast.[22]

Rich Man's Fowl, Poor Man's Fowl

The second family of imitation bird meat rolls is much smaller, more uniform and predominantly Slavic. Central and east European cabbage rolls are called 'little pigeons' (*golubtsy/halubcy/gołąbki* etc. – the origin of Ashkenazi Jewish *holishkes* and Canadian Mennonite *halupkes*). These are old words, and many people, for instance Russians who eat *golubtsy* cabbage rolls, may not realize that their name is related to the Russian word for pigeon, *golub'*. Apart from Russia, one can find such meat-and-rice stuffed cabbage 'pigeons' in Poland, Belorussia, Ukraine and eastern Slovakia; they are popular with local gypsies too. Such cabbage rolls are also present in Lithuanian cuisine as *balandėliai* (which also means 'little pigeons'). Unlike the cabbage rolls of Hungary, Romania and the Balkans, 'little pigeons' are mostly made with blanched leaves of fresh cabbage, not sauerkraut leaves. Stuffings may include buckwheat or pearl barley instead of rice, and mushrooms and herbs may be added; stewing liquids range from stock and sour cream to tomato sauce.

While looking in a desultory way for more 'pigeon' cabbage rolls and other false fowl in the Balkans, I stumbled on Dalmatian sauerkraut cabbage rolls called *arambašići*, which are quite unusual because the stuffing does not include rice, just lots of rich meat (diced, not minced); spiced with cinnamon, nutmeg and cloves; and stewed with more smoked meat or sausages. I was so excited to find something not called *dolma*, *sarma*, *yaprak* (and their translations and derivatives) in the Balkans that I rushed on an enthusiastic etymological wild-goose chase only to discover that in Croatian *arambašići* are supposed to mean 'bandit/partisan leaders'.[23] However I was slightly mollified when I discovered that a variation of the Croatian *arambašići* recipe is popular in Friuli in Italy on the Croatian border. There the official name of the dish is *rambasicci,* but it is usually called by a more familiar name, just *uccelli scappati nella verza* ('runaway birds' in Savoy cabbage).[24] And this dish seems a far cry from the military Dalmatian cabbage rolls: the meat stuffing is minced, no spices are added, the cabbage is fresh (and a different variety to boot) and after the cabbage rolls are stewed with some stock they are even (unthinkable!) sprinkled with grated grana cheese and breadcrumbs.

Another fowl-related cabbage-roll curiosity is called *cuiburi de cinci*, 'a nest of five', which is a truly regal dish from a poor Romanian household in Carlibaba described at length by the Romanian gourmet and food writer, Radu Anton Roman.[25] It consists of five different sauerkraut cabbage rolls cooked with a rich sauce in a whole sauerkraut leaf like in a nest and presented, one nest each, to diners at the feast. Stuffings include 1) poultry, smoked goose *pastrama*, bread and goose fat; 2) pork, smoked lard and rice; 3) veal, cured lard and rice; 4) mutton, bread and butter; and 5) mushrooms, rice and tomato coulis. All are delicately spiced and enriched with different herbs and vegetables. While these complex combinations are not referred to as 'little pigeons', the idea of making them into a nest continues that old association.

In addition to these predominantly Slavic instances of false fowl stuffed cabbage rolls, there exists a surprising *poule verte* ('green chicken') recipe for stuffed cabbage from Gascony, France.[26] This dish imitates the famous *poule-au-pot* ('chicken in the pot'), designed to provide both a savoury soup and main course in one go when there is no real chicken available. A big Savoy cabbage is blanched, its heart taken out and the resulting hollow stuffed with aromatic vegetables browned in duck fat, mixed with moistened stale bread, eggs, chopped leftover dry-cured ham or bacon, herbs and spices. Then it is wrapped and cooked in simmering vegetable broth with lots of vegetables cut in big chunks until the cabbage is ready and the flavours marry well. The broth is served first, then '*green chicken*' cut into wedges is served as a main course accompanied by vegetables from the soup and a tangy tomato sauce, or just mustard and cornichons. Unlike this authentic recipe from rural Gascony, other recipes for 'green chicken' I have found on the Internet are rather different. One involves cabbage rolls stuffed with pork and stale bread and cooked with cured lard (which rather undermines the whole idea of economy) in a similar soup; another seems a bizarre cold meatloaf made with sausage meat, eggs and chopped sorrel. Still, pork replaces chicken at every occasion, so there is a kind of continuity to all three.[27] This 'green chicken' seems to be a stand-alone tradition, or at least I have not yet discovered any links to neighbouring culinary cultures.

The last false fowl family is, I confess, not a family at all, as I have managed to find only one proper word to represent it. It is a recipe from Piedmont called *flisse o grive* ('flisse or blackbirds')[28] and consists of pig liver and calf brains minced together with juniper berries, nutmeg, eggs and a little Parmesan, wrapped in caul and fried. The word *flisse* is problematic, maybe a corruption of Swiss German *Fleischvögel* across the border or perhaps somehow related to the old Frankish word *flikka* that means side of bacon (i.e. the flitch). Still, similar recipes of offal bundles wrapped in caul (*caillette*, *attriaux* etc.) are very numerous in the regions of Switzerland and south-eastern France that once belonged to the Duchy of Savoy.[29] There may well be some other fowl-related dialectal words for these plump parcels.

In short, what we have found out is that any wrapper will do, any stuffing will do – our gastronomic imagination transforms the result into a delicious 'bird'. These days, it seems unlikely that what's hidden under the wrapper and masquerading as a fowl ever sang for its supper.

Rich Man's Fowl, Poor Man's Fowl

Notes

1. As recommended in *Apicius* 6.5.6, ed. M. E. Milham (Leipzig: Teubner, 1969): 'avem sapidiorem et altiliorem facies et ei pinguedinem servabis, si eam farina oleo subacta contextam in furnum miseris'.
2. Maestro Martino da Como, *Libro de Arte Coquinaria* (Terziaria: Milano, 1990): capitolo 1, p. 20.
3. Anna Gosetti della Salda, *Le ricette regionali italiane* (Milano, Solares, 2003), p. 1015.
4. Auguste Escoffier, *Le Guide Culinaire* (Paris: Flammarion, 1993), p. 687.
5. Petronius, *Satyricon* (Paris: Les Belles Lettres, 1993), p. 33 and p. 40.
6. Op.cit., capitolo 6, p. 126–127. See also David Sutton's '"Four and Twenty Blackbirds Baked in a Pie": A History of Surprise Stuffings' later in this volume.
7. See Terence Scully, *The Art of Cookery in the Middle Ages* (Woodbridge: Boydell, 2002); *Le Menagier de Paris* (Paris: Le Livre de Poche, 1994): 2.5.158.
8. Op.cit., capitolo 1, p. 11.
9. See Peter Brears, *Cooking and Dining in Medieval England* (Totnes, prospect Books, 2008), p. 314; Ernst Gamillscheg, *Etymologisches Wörterbuch der Französischen Sprache* (Heidelberg: Carl Winter, 1928).
10. http://fr.wikipedia.org/wiki/Oiseau_sans_t%C3%AAte (accessed June 6, 2012); see also recipes provided by the eponymous Belgian retail group and supermarket chain: http://www.colruyt.be/colruyt/static/culinair/search-fr.shtml?key=oiseaux%20sans%20t%C3%AAte (accessed 14 March 2013).
11. In contrast, a meatless version of the usually meaty scouse stew from Liverpool is called 'blind scouse' in the eponymous English dialect (*Scouse English*, compiled by Fred Fazakerley (London: Abson, 2012), p.10) so the blindness here might also express an idea of something being not as it should be, being a travesty of the real thing.
12. http://www.thedutchtable.com/2011/11/slavinken.html.
13. Many thanks to Ove Fosså, an Oxford Symposium veteran and Slow Food activist for information on 'boneless birds' in Norway.
14. Louise Sophie Thora Nimb (1842–1903), *Fru Nimbs Kogebog* (Copenhagen: Christian Ejlers Forlag, 1996), p. 313 recipe 681: forlorne kyllinger (dubbed also veau à la Trianon)' Many thanks to Katrine Klinken, Danish food writer, professional cook, Slow Food activist and Oxford Symposium regular, who provided me with detailed information on these Danish culinary classics.
15. Many thanks to Nanna Rögnvaldardóttir, Icelandic food writer and Oxford Symposiast for all the information on Icelandic false fowl; one of the cookbooks even has a recipe for beinlausir fuglar úr lifer, that is, 'boneless birds' made from lamb's liver.
16. N. Masiliune and A. Pasopa. *Latyshskaya kuhnia* (Riga: Avots, 1987).
17. Heinz Dieter Pohl. *Die österreichische Küchensprache: Ein Lexikon der typisch österreichischen kulinarischen Besonderheiten (mit sprachwissenschaftlichen Erläuterungen)*, (Vienna, praesens Verlag, 2007), p. 151, p. 122, p. 84. I am particularly grateful to Austrian lexicographers Hubert Bergmann and Helmut Klug for bringing this wonderful work to my attention.
18. Franz Ruhm, 'Champignon-Kalbsvögerl' and 'Tomaten-Kalbsvögerl', *Das Franz Ruhm Kochbuch. Das Standardwerk der Wiener und österreichischen Küche von heute mit über 1000 Rezepten* (Vienna: Orac, 1994), p .236.
19. http://www.bettybossi.ch/de/schwerpunkt/2626_iwb_spkt_tdsu.aspx.
20. DEVOTO-OLI, *Vocabolario della lingua italiana*, Le Monnier, 2009.
21. Anna Gosetti della Salda, op.cit. uccellini scappati (Lombardy), p. 244; uccelletti scappati alla reggiana p. 514.
22. Pellegrino Artusi, *La scienza in cucina e l'arte di mangiar bene* (Florence: Agnelli, 1993), p. 170 (ricetta # 281).
23. http://hr.wikipedia.org/wiki/Sinjski_aramba%C5%A1i%C4%87i (accessed 28 May 2012); http://www.coolinarika.com/recept/arambasici/ (accessed 14 March 2013); http://www.crochef.com/index.

php?page=recepti&id=451 (accessed 14 March 2013); http://en.wikibooks.org/wiki/Cookbook:Aramba%C5%A1i%C4%87i (accessed 14 March 2013).
24. Anna Gosetti della Salda, op.cit., p. 347.
25. Radu Anton Roman, *Savoureuse Romanie* (Montricher: Noir sur Blanc, 2001), p. 446.
26. I am deeply grateful for this information to Kate Hill, professional cook, culinary educator and founder of Camont cooking school and retreat in Gascony.
27. http://kitchen-at-camont.com/2009/10/21/945/; http://www.elle.fr/Elle-a-Table/Recettes-de-cuisine/poule-verte-552398; http://www.750g.com/fiche_de_cuisine_complete.htm?recettes_id=41553 .
28. Anna Gosetti della Salda, op.cit., p. 58.
29. L'Inventaire du Patrimoine Culinaire de la France series, *Rhône-Alpes, produits du Terroir et Recettes Traditionnelles* (Albin Michel/Conseil National des Arts Culinaires, Paris, 1995); Marie-Thérèse Hermann, *La cuisine paysanne de Savoie. La vie des fermes et des chalets racontée par une enfant du pays* (La Fontaine de Siloé, 2006); Marie-Thérèse Hermann, *Dictionnaire de la Cuisine de Savoie* (Bonneton, 1992); http://fr.wikipedia.org/wiki/Attriaux (accessed 28 May 2012).

The Magic of Dumplings: Bringing *Pierogi* into the (New) World

Naomi Guttman and Franklin Sciacca

> Flour on my fingers, I crimp your tiny pillows
> of plum and cheese, watch them bob
> and float in the salty water, and rescue them
> again and again.
>
> Karen Kovacik, 'Making *Pierogi*'[1]

The origin of *varenyky-pierogi*

The half-moon-shaped stuffed boiled dumpling of Ukraine-Poland is called by a variety of names: *varenyky* and *pyrohy* in Ukrainian, *pierogi* in Polish, *kolduny* in Belarusian. If one were to map the numerous stuffed dishes wrapped in unleavened dough across the vast Eurasian plain, the *varenyky-pierogi* zone would appear at a boiled-dumpling crossroads between the *ravioli-tortelloni* region of the Mediterranean, the Russian-Siberian territory of *pel'meni*, and the vast territory of various Central Asian-Turkic and East Asian steamed and boiled dumplings (*manty, kundumy, shiu mai, jiaozi*). Some cookbooks suggest that *varenyky-pierogi* are adaptations or borrowings from these culinary traditions. However, studies of the earliest Western cuisines, those of the Fertile Crescent, where wheat cultivation arose some 10,000 years ago, as well as of Egypt, Greece and Rome, suggest no evidence of an ancient prototypical boiled dumpling of any sort. Needless to say, the innovation of the stuffed dumpling must post-date the invention and spread of fresh pasta. By way of helping to establish a chronology, it is worth noting that *jiaozi* that date to the Tang dynasty (*ca.* AD 700) have been unearthed in a tomb in Turpan, Xinjiang, China.[2]

The literature of dumpling origins and possible migratory paths yields multiple theories. Zanini de Vita has collated information concerning the origin of the *raviolo*. She notes that while stuffed pastas are associated with the kitchens of the courts of northern Italy of the 1500s, it is the late thirteenth-century *Liber de ferculis* of Giambonino da Cremona, which includes a *ca.* 1100 Arabic recipe that 'may be the first description of the *raviolo*, which Giambonino calls *sambusaj*, the term for a triangular piece of pasta (hence the Arabic name, itself probably of Persian origin) filled with ground meat', and suggests an origin in Arab-dominated Sicily at an even earlier date.[3] This description recalls the Middle Eastern/Central Asian *manty*. Belarusian food historians suggest that the Belarusian variant of the *varenyk*, called *koldun*, is directly borrowed from the Tatars, who settled in Belarus in the late fourteenth century. Their dish is a lamb-stuffed dumpling called *kunduny*, typically prepared for Muslim feasts (although they are sometimes deep-fried in melted sheep fat, not boiled).[4] Compelling as these proposed routes of dumpling migration are, it is not likely we can resolve the complex issue of inter-ethnic migration in any definitive way.

Given that *varenyky* and *pierogi* are words of purely Slavic origin, and are not, as some have suggested, linguistic borrowings, our focus here is the Proto-Slavic zone. Unfortunately there is precious little documentary evidence from medieval times from the historic territory of the '*pirog*', that is Rus', the progenitor state of modern-day Ukraine, Belarus, and Russia. The search for origins is complicated by the fact that the term *pirog* refers to two distinct dishes, depending on region – a baked or fried stuffed pie made of a leavened or sourdough crust typical in Russia, or the boiled, stuffed dumpling made of unleavened pasta-type dough throughout Ukraine and Belarus. The earliest attestations of the word *pirog* appear in Kievan documents of the late twelfth century, derived from *pyro* (wheat, spelt; an Indo-European root), and refers to a bread baked from sifted wheat flour, with spelling variation under the influence of *pir* – a word used to refer to food in a general sense, but more specifically to food that is shared at a feast or banquet, and to the feast itself.[5] Certain specific types of baked *pirogi* were common at peasant feasts, for example the ornamented *kurnik* (chicken *pirog*) that was typically served at weddings. Indeed the *pirog* functions as ceremonial fare. Sharing a communal dish of this sort functions as a magic act to bind the participants during life-rituals and on feast days, not unlike the sharing of Eucharistic bread during the Divine Liturgy.

In Russia proper, the earliest testimony that *pirog* signifies a stuffed pastry/pie, attested in a variety of shapes and sizes, either baked or deep-fried, is from monastic documents and the so-called *Domostroi* ('Rules for Russian Households'), both of the sixteenth century, in which its typical current meaning in Russian is indicated. For example, the *Domostroi* catalogues a variety of fillings appropriate for fast days: 'kasha, peas,.. turnips, mushrooms, cabbage,' and elsewhere mentions 'pies [*pirogi*] – little turnovers [*pirozhki*; the diminutive form of *pirogi*] cooked in nut oil with dried peas... sourdough pies, stuffed with peas and cooked in the same nut oil... pies stuffed with hempseed cakes, fish spines, pink salmon, sheatfish, and herring (in other words, varieties of *kulebiaka/ coulibiac*)'.[6] It is thought that baking the *pirog* was the original technique employed in ancient Rus', while shallow-frying (the technique called *priazhenie)* is a borrowing from the Tatars in the sixteenth century.

But in what is now Ukraine (formerly 'Little Rus'), *pirog* (Ukrainian form *pyrih*) refers to a semi-circle-shaped boiled dumpling made of unleavened dough, although it is more often referred to by a synonymous term, *varenyky* (one must note that the term *pirog/pyrih* in its singular form, can also refer to the baked stuffed pastry in some regions of Ukraine). At what time and in what manner the term *pirog* undergoes a dramatic shift in meaning – preserving the concept of a filling stuffed in dough, but with complete variance in the type of dough, shape, and method of cooking – is unknown. But there is a curious analogy to the history of the term *raviolo*. Redon, Sabban and Serventi note that 'in medieval Italian cooking sources these are nearly thirty recipes entitled Ravioli'. However, the preparations are variable: the evolution of ravioli 'took two divergent paths in the fifteenth century: stuffed dough cooked in moist heat and served at the beginning of the meal sprinkled with grated cheese and spices; and stuffed dough deep-fried and served at the end of the meal sprinkled with sugar or drizzled with honey'.[7]

It is from this adapted meaning of East Slavic *pirog* that the Polish form *pierog* derives. The earliest Polish documents suggest that the dish originally called *pierogi ruskie* (*Rus' pirogi*), and originally made from buckwheat flour, derives from 'Russia,' more precisely from the East Slavic territory known as Red Rus' (Czerwona Rus', that is Galicia or Ruthenia) – and only in the nineteenth century.[8]

The etymology of *varenyky* is far less complex. It derives from the verb *varyty*, originally meaning simply to cook, equivalent to Latin *coquere*. Sreznevskii suggests that the root in the substantive form *varenie* was a generic term for 'food' in medieval East Slavic, the equivalent of Latin *coctio*, 'cooking' or 'digestion'.[9] The stem in this meaning is preserved in the word *povar*, cook. In modern Russian and Ukrainian the verb with this stem now more specifically specifies cooking with moist heat, by boiling, steaming, poaching, or brewing. Thus *varenyky* means broadly food that is cooked by boiling or steaming, and thus focuses on the method of cooking rather than on any specific ingredients. Be that as it may, in modern Ukrainian the term refers exclusively to stuffed dumplings so cooked.

Given the Slavic roots of *varenyky* and *pierogi*, we would posit that we are dealing with a uniquely indigenous innovation/adaptation of a concept that is most probably eastern in origin and which entered East Slavic territory under the influence of Tatar and Turkic nomads. Evidence is provided by the Ukrainian word for noodles, *lokshina*, which is derived from Turkic *laqsha*, and points to the introduction of a type of pasta dough from Central Asia.[10] Likewise, the nomenclature for Siberian meat-filled dumplings, *pel'meni*, originates in the Finno-Ugric Komi and Mansi term *pel'nyan'* (from *pel'*=ear and *nan'*=bread, which refers to the auricular shape; in Tatar, *pilmän*).[11]

Mimetic pregnancy: stuffed dumplings as magic food

By the nineteenth century, *varenyky* and *pierogi* emerge as a signifier of ethnic identity and memory. They are identified with these Slavic peoples the way pasta is identified with Italians. In the popular imagination, literary works and ethnographic studies, these dumplings serve as a marker of authentic nationality. Slavic ethnographers began their first serious efforts to isolate the distinguishing ethnic features of Ukrainians ('Little Russians') and Poles, and in their studies paid particular attention to unique foodways. Among the earliest was Markevich's *Customs, Beliefs, Cuisine and Drinks of the Little Russians* (Kiev, 1860), which provides a description of the various typical fillings of *varenyky*, and notes that the dough was made of wheat or buckwheat flour and shaped in a triangle.[12] *Varenyky* were considered festival fare because they were believed to possess magical significance and functioned as invocations of fertility and life, and as such played a ritual role in weddings, baptisms, funerals, as well as Christmas, Epiphany, *Masliana* (a pre-Lenten celebration equivalent to Mardi Gras), and Lenten fast periods.[13] In ancient days *varenyky* were consumed as a ritual dish during the harvest season and were prepared in the household whenever a woman gave birth, or when calves or lambs were born.[14] The act of forming *varenyky* took on a sacred character and gave rise to a variety of superstitions. 'If one counts [*varenyky*] as one makes them, they will overcook and the filling seep out'.[15] One informant of Ukrainian background noted that when making *varenyky*, the women should never gossip or speak in a frivolous manner to avoid infecting the food with negative emotion. Handling wheat flour in general demands respect for the staff of life.

Because they are stuffed and thus mime pregnancy and invoke bounty, *varenyky* were considered an auspicious dish. A host of folk proverbs, rituals, and songs invoke *varenyky* as harbingers of hyperbolic plenty and protectors of home, hearth, and family. For example, 'during the traditional Christmas Eve Supper, a bowl of *varenyky* is placed before the father. He play-hides behind it, asking, "Can you see me, children?" "Oh no, we cannot!" they shout. "May God grant us such bounty throughout the coming years, he responds".'[16] The magical function ascribed to *varenyky* is further evident from ritual behaviour observed in the Podillia region: 'The head of the household would clasp a loaf of bread under his arm, sprinkle the courtyard and cattle with water blessed during the Feast of the Baptism of Christ, and then inscribe a small cross on all the doors with chalk, while the children followed him carrying a bowl filled with pear *varenyky* – "to insure that the cattle would be as full as these *varenyky*".'[17] The plump dumplings function as sympathetic magic, imitating the hoped-for pregnancy of domestic animals and women of the household. The pregnant or full-hipped shape of pears would seem to explain the specific use of this filling in this context. Of all the fruits, the pear resembles most remarkably the wide-hipped goddess figurines typical throughout much of eastern Europe in the Paleolithic and Neolithic ages, and which Gimbutas associates with earth fertility rituals.[18]

Further evidence of this association exists in a harvest song (rhymed in the original) from the Kiev region that seems to reference the half-moon shape of *varenyky* in the context of reaping:

> The moon is already waning…
> Oh, let's hurry and complete the harvest!
> It's not far 'til we reach the edge of the field,
> *Varenyky* are already in the dough-trough!
> Let's not tarry in the field—
> *Varenyky* are already in sour cream![19]

Clearly the singers look forward to consuming *varenyky* as a communal ritual repast after the day's collective labour.

The Magic of Dumplings

In literature the *varenyk*'s debut is featured in a passage from Nikolai Gogol's 1832 tale, 'Christmas Eve', in which a sorcerer enchants a bowl of *varenyky*:

> Patsiuk opened his mouth wide, looked at the *varenyky*, and opened his mouth still wider. Just then a varenyk flipped out of the bowl, plopped into the sour cream, turned over on the other side, jumped up, and went straight into Patsiuk's mouth. Patsiuk ate it and again opened his mouth, and in went another varenyk in the same way. He was left only with the work of chewing and swallowing.[20]

Here, Gogol fully comprehends the supernatural quality of the dumpling.

Fillings and shapes

The vast array of stuffings (savoury and sweet; meat and fish; dairy, vegetable and fruit) indicates that the dumpling became a handy container to encapsulate any food at hand, whether leftovers or seasonal bounty, orchestrated to conform to Lenten restrictions or to reflect holiday particulars. The earliest ethnographic studies enumerate the typical traditional types of fillings: cheese (usually quark, a fresh cheese made from soured milk), fried sauerkraut or cabbage, boiled and mashed potato, poppy seed, boiled dried fruits, fresh berries, boiled dried berries, mushrooms and in some regions meat or fish.[21] Meat fillings are typical in Lithuanian and Belarusian *kolduny*. The so-called *pierogi ruskie*, popular in Polish territories that border western Ukraine, are typically a mixture of potato and cheese. All these fillings are the products of farm and forest, and most are undoubtedly of ancient and indigenous discovery. The potato is attested in eastern Europe by the late seventeenth century, introduced by King Jan III Sobieski, who planted them in the 1680s at Wilanow Palace near Warsaw, and in the Russian Empire in the mid-eighteenth century in the reign of Catherine the Great, although 'Russia didn't truly become potato territory until 1850'.[22]

While the generic practice of stuffing (or farcing) dough is rather monotone, the variety of dumpling shapes is astonishing and clearly reflects highly localized and idiosyncratic tastes and traditions. As Camporesi remarks about the variability of pasta, 'Each variety of pasta has its own particular shape and its own descriptive name, which is almost always metaphorical or analogical. All of them are made with the same simple ingredients, but, surprisingly, they have different flavours depending on their shapes (a sort of absolute formalism that decisively conditions their inner essence)'.[23] The shape of *pierogi-varenyky* are remarkably simple, yet unlike most other dumplings in the surrounding zones. While Markevich (and some cookbooks) observed that they could be triangular in shape (a square cut from rolled out dough folded along the diagonal), *varenyky* are nearly universally half-moon-shaped when formed by hand.[24] The oldest tradition would seem to be the rolling of the dough into a log, which was subsequently cut into one-inch chunks that were each rolled separately into a round. More common nowadays is rolling out a sheet of dough, then using some circle-shaped cutter or glass rim to form rounds. Starting in the twentieth century, in an attempt to simplify home production and make the dumplings uniform in shape, ridged templates were developed in the Soviet Union (similar to forms available for ravioli production) that simplified the making of the dumplings, but they tend to square off the corners in order to use a sheet of rolled out dough more efficiently. In urban centres with Asian communities in the USA, mass-produced wonton skins are sometimes used to avoid making the dough, although the final result offers a very different texture and mouth-feel. After boiling, the *varenyky* are placed in a bowl with butter to prevent sticking. Often *varenyky* are fried after boiling and are topped with additional butter, fried onions or pork cracklings (*shvarky*), and sour cream.

Bringing dumplings to the new world: the case study of Utica, New York

From the late nineteenth century through the post-war period, *pierogi/varenyky* arrived in North America with waves of Slavic immigrants. Devotion to food traditions continues even as the descendants of those immigrants may neither speak their ancestral languages nor visit the homeland. As Deborah Silverman writes in her book *Polish American Folklore*, 'foodways are among the most durable folkways', keeping alive the original food terminology and traditions of a culture even when, in some cases, the meanings and origins of these traditions have been lost.[25]

Ann Marie Jenkins (née Kaminski) of Clinton, NY, grew up on a dairy farm in Barneveld, a rural community in the southern foothills of the Adirondacks. Grandparents on both sides had emigrated from Poland in the early twentieth century, and while her own mother was too busy with a dairy farm to make *pierogi*, Ann Marie remembers helping her grandmothers make them for the holidays. These days, Ann Marie, her siblings and her cousins keep the *pierogi*-making tradition alive by convening at a cousin's home in New Hampshire one weekend each October. The families, now spread out from New York to

Connecticut, bring their own potato, cheese, and sauerkraut fillings. While the cousin's husband rolls the dough she has prepared ahead of time, Ann Marie cuts the circles and others shape the dumplings. They eat, drink and catch up with each other as they prepare 700 or so *pierogi* to boil, brush with butter and put in plastic bags for everyone to take home and freeze to eat during the Christmas holidays.[26]

Along with *pierogi,* certain other Polish words persist in Ann Marie's vocabulary, mostly having to do with food, though Ann Marie also refers to herself as the *Chachi* (*ciocia*) or Auntie in her family. Her uncle used to make blood sausage (*kiszka*) with pig blood and buckwheat. At Christmas, Ann Marie makes *chrusciki* – angel wings – which are strips of bow-tied fried dough dusted with powdered sugar. When asked why she participates in the preservation of these food traditions, Ann Marie replied, 'It's the labour – giving something to the family and keeping the tradition alive. So many things have gone by the wayside. Families aren't as close as they used to be'. Clearly, for Ann Marie, this process of cooking with family represents a concrete means of keeping family ties alive across distances and generations, and lately she has decided that she wants to bring this tradition of *pierogi*-making closer to home with nearby relatives.

In local communities, churches were and continue to be important in defining ethnic and community identity and also in contributing to the persistence of *pierogi/varenyky* as a cultural marker – as well as a significant source of income. Though not exclusively the domain of women, women are often the vital source of labour in these enterprises. Evidence of the importance and value of female labour is revealed in Goldstein and Green's study of women parishioners at St Mary's Church in New York Mills (a Utica suburb), who participated in making and selling traditional Polish foods in anticipation of Christmas and Easter holidays. At the time of the interviews, these first-generation Polish immigrant women were already grandmothers and had endured hard lives of blue-collar labour. As the writers observe, 'work was an unquestioned part of their existence', but it was also tied to family, for to have a family meant to work for the family: 'For these women, work and family are a single concept'.[27] The authors concluded that 'the value of *pierogi* and *babka* lies beyond their palatability. These foods carry cultural and ethnic associations. Likewise, the work itself is an act of symbolic as well as culinary significance for these ladies. Through their labour they express and affirm the values that have shaped their lives'.[28] This symbolic significance matches with Ann Marie's current attitude toward the importance of 'labour', as she put it, in keeping families close through a tradition of giving.

While *pierogi*-making dropped off at St Mary's, over the past two decades it has been taken up by other area churches serving parishioners from Polish and Ukrainian backgrounds. Congregants at two Utica Catholic churches, Holy Trinity (Polish) and St Volodymyr's (Ukrainian), make *varenyky* year-round to raise money. At St Volodymyr's this brings in approximately $800 a week during the year and about twice as much in anticipation of Holy Days, especially during Lent. On a recent visit to St Volodymyr's we found mostly men in the kitchen, drinking beer as they machine-rolled and cut the dough, while a group of women, speaking Ukrainian, sat at a long table in the hall shaping the *varenyky* by hand. Taras Zenczak, a parishioner at St Volodymyr's who was born in the US into an immigrant Ukrainian family, answered some of our questions and emphasized the 'agrarian environment' from whence *varenyky* come. They make large amounts of dough using an industrial mixer in the basement, then put it into plastic pails and bring it upstairs to the kitchen to the dough-rolling machine. He pointed out that the dough is set to press thinner for potato and cheese *varenyky* and thicker for cabbage, because of the water content. When asked who buys the *varenyky*, Mr Zenczak says that although it's mainly people from Slavic backgrounds, everyone in the area knows about and enjoys *pierogi*. The church advertises the sale in the city paper on Fridays, and word of mouth also creates a clientele. People from fifty and ninety miles away phone in orders of forty dozen to pick up.

Many of the fourteen ladies who were stuffing *pierogi* had arrived in the US as newlyweds after World War II, and several of them are now widows. When asked whether they still make *pierogi* at home, they all said yes, but they make them a little differently, not exactly according to the same recipe as used by the church. They make their own because the grandchildren love them, and when there is interest in the younger generation, they teach their granddaughters the recipe. Thus the habit and technique of *varenyky*-making is being passed down within families.

The importance of labour in the making of *pierogi*, the way it glues both families and communities together, is a continual theme in all ethnographic literature and interviews. While in the case of Ann Marie Jenkins and her cousins the tradition of gathering to make *pierogi* is relatively new, it harkens back to nostalgia for the grandmother's kitchen and the stability of large and extended families participating in ritual festival activities. It seems to be a way of keeping mothers and fragments of the mother-tongue alive as well as keeping up relationships between siblings and cousins, parents and children, who are dispersed across the north-eastern US and beyond. The largely female labour required to make these stuffed dumplings and their relevance to religious festivals that celebrate the birth and resurrection of Christ, as well as other life-cycle family celebrations, arguably return us to the ancient and arcane cultural connection with the mysterious 'magic' of pregnancy. Given the importance of *labour* in their creation, perhaps a link between this humble dumpling and fecundity, the gift of female labour, is not far-fetched.

Buying nostalgia: *pierogi* for the dumpling proletariat

While churches provide a means for smaller pockets of people to enjoy *pierogi*, Polish and Ukrainian dumplings also have a presence in the world of restaurants and supermarkets across North America. One of the most famous and longest-lived Ukrainian restaurants in the US is Veselka on New York's Lower East Side. *Varenyky* are one of their signature dishes, and recently they published a recipe book with a cover blurb by political comedian Jon Stewart who attests that 'Veselka is always there whenever [he's] had a three a.m. *pierogi* emergency'.²⁹ Along with the expected stuffings of potato, cheese, meat and sauerkraut-mushroom, Veselka also offers stuffings that seem designed to appeal to an upscale, health conscious and diet-restricted clientele: sweet potato, arugula and goat cheese, and broccoli and Vermont cheddar were recent offerings.

Varenyky-making in Ukraine was and still is ubiquitous. As one woman from St Volodymyr's pointed out, Ukraine has rich soil, perfect for potatoes, and potato *varenyky* are 'a poor man's meal', one with few ingredients, easily put together, and satisfying besides. Olesia Lew, a chef at Veselka who grew up in western Ukraine, says that it's probable that in every household someone knew how to make *varenyky*, but that in the Soviet period, when most people lived in communal households with a single kitchen, some of that knowledge got lost. During that era, food production became the domain of a few women working together to produce mass amounts that would feed the whole building. Because of this practice, many women grew up not knowing how to make *varenyky*, including Ms Lew's grandmothers. One did not learn because she came from a privileged family that had a cook; the other didn't learn until she came to the US because she spent her formative years in a DP camp. Traditionally, however, Ms Lew believes that for weddings, holidays, names days, and other celebrations – any time when there would be a need for large amounts – *varenyky* would have been made by a group of people, and they were so ubiquitous on restaurant menus that people would regularly eat them, as they do to this day.³⁰

During the course of the twentieth century, in their homelands *pierogi/varenyky* shifted from regional village to national cuisine. The process began in the Soviet period – when '*varenychnaia*' or *varenyky*-cafeterias served up hearty and cheap plates of mass-produced dumplings for the working class in cities of the Ukrainian SSR. With the end of Soviet rule over twenty years ago, the population of eastern Europe initially rejected much of the food associated with rural life and provincialism. With rising political and economic freedom came interest in 'Western' and luxury cuisine, (e.g. sushi and pizza). Recently, however, there is a resurgence in indigenous foods. A *New York Times* article reports on Polish nostalgia for restaurants serving simple traditional fare, and Veselka's Ms Lew comments that while restaurants in Ukraine still serve the usual toppings of browned onions and sour cream, other traditional toppings are making a comeback: 'sauces such as mushroom, bacon, or *brinza*, a brined sheep cheese'.³¹ Ukrainian cities are now crowded with upscale restaurants that feature authentic national cuisine. Often the interiors are constructed to resemble idealized peasant huts, where urban Ukrainians can play-act at living the way their ancestors did. One notable example is Kiev's O'Panas where *varenyky* are categorized according to Western menu norms – listed under appetizers (savoury types) and desserts (sweet).³²

Pierogi likewise figure in the high-status restaurants of post-Soviet Poland, for example the renowned Wierzynek Restaurant in Krakow (which traces its origin to the year 1364), where 'Home-made Dumplings Two Flavours', cottage cheese with potatoes and mushroom with cabbage, are featured on one of their traditional menus. The more elegant 'Home-made Dumplings with Morels and Fried Young Cabbage' figure among their 'Starters' and 'Home-made Polish Potato Dumplings with Fresh Boletus Sauce' among the vegetarian dishes.[33] Polish cities also feature *pierog* cafeterias, the *pierogarnia*.

At Veselka and its second venue, Veselka Bowery, *pierogi/varenyky* have never gone out of style because there is a steady clientele for the dumplings. In fact, certain customers come for their weekly 'fix' on the same day each week. Staff begin preparing stuffings as early as 6:00 a.m., with the roasting of the meat for the meat filling. By 2:00 p.m. each day, the stuffings are ready for the two women who work full time five–six days a week to hand-shape the approximately 700 dumplings consumed daily. That's over one hundred customers ordering hand-made *pierogi* per day in the main restaurant.

For those who don't live in New York City, other Slavic restaurants across the country are prepared to fill the gap: Pierogi Heaven, in downtown Chicago, Pierogi Grill, in Clearwater, Florida, and Babushka's Kitchen, a chain of 'Polish Heritage' restaurants across Ohio, are examples of the many restaurants in the US and Canada that serve *pierogi* regularly. But for those who don't live anywhere near such establishments, there is always 'Mrs T's,' a family-run factory established 60 years ago that claims to produce over a billion *pierogi* a year that are sold nation-wide in the frozen-food sections of large supermarkets.[34]

It could be said that *pierogi/varenyky* is Slavic soul-food, a comforting reminder of family traditions and ethnic identity that delivers to both diasporic and post-Soviet Slavs a dose of nostalgia for lost village and folk culture, binding individuals to each other and to the past. Whether they are home-made or bought from churches or supermarket freezer cases, this stuffed dumpling's longevity indicates that it will find its place on tables around the world for years to come.

Notes

1. Karen Kovacik, *Beyond the Velvet Curtain, poems* (Kent, Ohio: Kent State University Press, 1999).
2. Fuchsia Dunlop, *Land of Plenty* (New York: W. W. Norton, 2003), p. 101. For a summary of recent thinking on the origin of pasta see Barberis's introduction to Oretta Zanini de Vita, *Encyclopedia of Pasta* (Berkeley: University of California Press, 2009), pp. 13-18.
3. Zanini de Vita, pp. 223-24.
4. Alexander Bely, *The Belarusian Cookbook* (New York: Hippocrene Books, 2009), p. 140.
5. A. G. Preobrazhenskii, *Etymological Dictionary of the Russian Language* (New York: Columbia University Press, 1951), p. 60; I. I. Sreznevskii, *Materialy dlia slovaria drevenerusskogo iazyka* (Moskva : Gos. izd-vo inostrannykh i natsional'nykh slovarei, 1958): vol. II, col. 933; *Slovar' russkogo iazyka XI-XVII vv.*, vyp. 15 (Moskva: 'Nauka', 1989), p. 49.
6. Caroline Pouncy, ed., *The Domostroi. Rules for Russian Households in the Time of Ivan the Terrible* (Ithaca: Cornell University Press, 1994), p. 125, p. 192. For a discussion of pirogi and 'Russianess,' see

Alison K. Smith, *Recipes for Russia. Food and Nationhood under the Tsars* (Dekalb: Northern Illinois University Press, 2008), p. 88; and on comparable stuffed pastries in Western Europe, see Ken Albala, *The Banquet. Dining in the Great Courts of Late Renaissance Europe* (Chicago: University of Chicago Press, 2007), pp. 90–100.

7. Odile Redon, Francoise Sabban and Silvano Serventi. *The Medieval Kitchen. Recipes from France and Italy* (Chicago: University of Chicago Press, 1998), p. 62.
8. Maria Dembinska, *Food and Drink in Medieval Poland. Rediscovering and Cuisine of the Past* (Philadelphia: University of Pennsylvania Press, 1999), p. 112.
9. Sreznevskii, I, cols. 227-28.
10. Alla Sacharow, *Classic Russian Cuisine* (New York: Arcade, 1993), p. 178.
11. Vladimir Dal', *Tolkovyi slovar' zhivogo velikorusskogo iazyka* (Moskva: 'Univers', 1994).
12. Nikolai Markevich, *Obychai, pover'ia, kukhnia i napitki malorossiian* (Kiev: Tip. Davidenko, 1860), p. 151.
13. Petro Zvarich, *Varenyky, mlyntsi, pampushky* (Kyiv: 'Tekhnika', 1995), p. 3; *Encyclopedia of Ukraine* (Toronto: University of Toronto Press, 1984): V, p. 556.
14. L. Sokolenko, *Z narodnoji krynytsi*. 'Personal plius' 30 (233), 8–14 serpnia 2007: http://www.personal-plus.net/233/2363.html.
15. Marta Pisetska Farley, *Festive Ukrainian Cooking* (Pittsburgh, Pa.: University of Pittsburgh Press, 1990), p. 18.
16. 'Varenyky' recipe card by Yaroslava Surmach-Mills.
17. A. P. Ponamar'ov, *Podillia: istoryko-etnohrafichne doslidzhennia* (Kyïv: Vyd-vo Nezalezhnoho kul'turnoho tsentru 'Dolia', 1994), pp. 289-90.
18. Marija Gimbutas, *The Language of the Goddess* (NY: Thames and Hudson, 1989).
19. Sokolenko.
20. Nikolai Gogol, *The Collected Tales* (New York: Vintage, 2011), p. 42.
21. Ponamar'ov, p. 289; Elena Molokhovets, *Classic Russian Cooking. Elena Molokhovets' A Gift to Young Housewives*, trans. Joyce Toomre (Bloomington: Indiana University Press, 1992), pp. 326-28.
22. Dembinska 116; A. Smith 26-35, Larry Zuckerman, *The Potato: How the Humble Spud Rescued the Western World* (New York: North Point Press, 1999), p. 82, R.E.F. Smith and David Christian, *Bread and Salt: a Social and Economic History of Food and Drink in Russia* (Cambridge: Cambridge University Press, 1984), pp. 278-87.
23. Piero Camporesi, *The Magic Harvest: Food, Folklore, and Society* (Cambridge, polity Press, 1993), p. 106
24. Markevich, p. 151.
25. Deborah Anders Silverman, *Polish-American Folklore* (Chicago: University of Illinois Press, 2000), p. 159.
26. Ann Marie Jenkins, Interview, 15 May 2012. Clinton, NY.
27. Elizabeth Goldstein and Gail Green, 'Pierogi- and Babka-Making at St Mary's', *New York Folklore*, 4 (Summer-Winter 1978), p. 77.
28. Goldstein and Green, p. 71.
29. Tom Birchard and Natalie Danford, *The Veselka Cookbook: Recipes and Stories from the Landmark Restaurant in New York's East Village* (New York: Thomas Dunne Books/St Martin's Press, 2009).
30. Olesia Lew, Interview 22 and 23 May 2012, over e-mail and by phone.
31. Joanna Berendt, 'Flavor of Nostalgia Grows More Appealing to Poles Brimming With Pride', *New York Times International*, 19 April 2012: A7.
32. O'Panas Restaurant, Kiev: http://www.opanas.com.ua/en/.
33. Restauracja Wierzynek, Krakow: http://www.wierzynek.com.pl/en/wierzynek/starters.html.
34. Ateeco, Inc., Mrs. T's Pierogies: http://www.pierogies.com/retail/products/products.asp.

Modernist Stuffing and Wrapping Techniques and Applications

Peter Hertzmann

To paraphrase Potter Stewart, 'I don't know how to define Modernist cuisine, but I know it when I see it.' Like pornography, Modernist cuisine is many things to many people. It is difficult to define with a simple phrase or statement.[1]

Nathan Myhrvold, who codified the Modernist cuisine genre in his five-volume tome of the same name, never provides a succinct definition. He provides hundreds of formal and informal prescriptions for dishes that seemingly fit the genre, but not a definition. The closest Myhrvold comes is when he provides his *Ten Principles of Modernist Cuisine* as his homage to Gault and Millau's *Ten Commandments of Nouvelle Cuisine*.[2]

No significant restaurant in the world places its offerings into the Modernist cuisine genre. When forced to categorize their menus, these restaurants generally prefer labels based on regional or political descriptions. This is partly a function of good marketing and partly the reality that the restaurant-going public is also confused by the Modernist-cuisine moniker. Some diners embrace the technological and or chemical reputation of Modernist cuisine, just as some people were able to cuddle up with the previously ill-conceived label of molecular gastronomy. Other diners are adverse to Modernist cuisine because of its avant-garde reputation. In the end, most avant-garde restaurants do embrace Myhrvold's fifth principle: The food should evoke an emotional response. The principle concludes, 'The repertoire of the Modernist chef isn't just flavour and texture; it is also the range of emotional and intellectual reactions that food can inspire in the diner'.[3] In this statement, Myhrvold doesn't go as far as Ferran Adria who says, 'At the end of a four-hour meal the more bewilderment the better', or 'It's not just about, "Man, this tastes good." You feel something. You think, "Killer!"'.[4]

Like several other current cuisines, Modernist cuisine's plated dishes are comprised of a number of items, often of equal importance. This approach stands in opposition to traditional cuisines which tend to present a plated dish based on a primary item, usually a protein, accompanied by one or two secondary items, what Escoffier would have termed garnishes. Each of the many items on a Modernist plate may involve hours of preparation and a high degree of complexity although sometimes they can be quick and simple.

Upon reading the recipes in the *Modernist Cuisine*, it is easy to get the impression that if a process can be completed with an expensive piece of equipment or an inexpensive piece or by hand, the most expensive one will be chosen. A partial list of

Modernist Stuffing and Wrapping Techniques and Applications

the equipment featured in the book includes an Aerolatte wand, an autoclave, a blast chiller, a CVap oven, a centrifuge, a chamber vacuum sealer, a Champion-style juicer, a cold smoker, a colloid mill, a Combi oven, a dehydrator, a Dewar flask, a fermentation chamber, a freeze dryer, a Genevac Rocket, a hydrometer, a Jaccard tenderizer, a Pacojet, a pressure filter, a proofing cabinet, a refractometer, a rotary slicer, a Rotavap, a rotor-stator homogenizer, a smoke gun, a spray dryer, a Thermomix, an ultrasonic cleaning bath, a vacuum dryer, a vacuum evaporator, a vacuum oven, a vacuum sealer, and a water-vapour oven. Prices for these devices ranges from a few dollars to $50,000 before installation. Many tools require custom utility hook-ups and venting. Much of this equipment is too expensive for the average restaurant. Alternative methods have been developed by many to achieve results similar to what could be achieved with the high-end equipment. For the home cook, many Modernist recipes, as presented in the book, are out of reach because of the lack of vital equipment.

Average diners are ignorant of the equipment used to prepare the Modernist meals set before them, but many have heard that chemicals are involved in the preparation. The terms 'alginate', 'liquid nitrogen' and 'meat glue' have been sensationalized in the lay press. Since these items are commonly used in demonstrations to give the cuisine a 'wow' factor, a misrepresentation of their importance seems commonplace. Diners may even get the impression that they are partaking in 'artificial' meals. In reality, most of the so-called chemicals used in Modernist cuisine are either naturally occurring or derivatives of naturally occurring items.

Applying the filter of 'wrapped' and 'stuffed' to Modernist cuisine presents a challenge. The traditional reasons for wrapping or stuffing foods, such as to make them portable, to add flavour to a bland item, or to hold loose items together, don't come into play much in Modernist cuisine. For example, why should ground meat need to be stuffed into a piece of intestine when you can glue it together with an enzyme and achieve the same shape? Wrapping and stuffing are simply two more ways of the many that foods can be combined in a Modernist way. Also, since plated Modernist dishes tend to be an assortment of many seemingly disparate preparations, it is unlikely that wrapping or stuffing would be used for all items on a plate. For the examples delineated in this paper, I've stayed with single-item preparations. These dishes are designed to be suitable as an *amuse-bouche*[5] or *mignardise*[6] rather than as a full course in a meal.

Although 'wrapping' and 'stuffing', when used as verbs, are generally clear and require no definition, there are other terms common to Modernist cuisine that may be thought as equivalent when 'wrapped' and 'stuffed' are treated as adjectives. If a food is encapsulated in a hydrocolloid, is it wrapped in that material? How about enrobed? If one food is infused into another by changing the surrounding atmospheric pressure, has the first item been stuffed into the second? I've decided to split hairs in these situations. I don't consider spherification performed by dribbling droplets of one material into another to be wrapping, but I consider spherification performed by laying a glob of material into another and rolling the glob around so a chemical reaction occurs, to be a form of wrapping. The difference is that a wrapping-like physical action by the cook, to form the final shell around the glob, has occurred.[7]

The naming of dishes in restaurants serving Modernist cuisine, or the like, seem to fall into one of two forms: a simple listing of the main ingredients on the plate or the name of the dish that was the inspiration for the modern version. Thus, Wylie Dufresne's Eggs Benedict would be a disappointment for a patron expecting something close to the classic version. In his, the elements are cylinders of slow-cooked egg yolk, very thin slices of frozen and deep-fried Canadian bacon, deep-fried hollandaise cubes,[8] a couple of chive sprigs, and a sprinkling of black salt. Another restaurant serving the same dish may simply list egg yolk, Canadian bacon, butter, English muffin, chive, and salt on the menu. For the preparations used as examples in this paper, more conventional names have been selected.

Macaroni and cheese: Rigatoni, or other large, tubular pasta shape, is cooked in heavily salted, boiling water for about three times longer than normal.[9] The pasta is drained briefly and placed in a dehydrator at 55 °C (130 °F) until dry but still slightly pliable. During drying, dowels are inserted into the pasta tubes to prevent them from collapsing. For service, oil is heated to between 175 °C (350 °F) and 190 °C (375 °F). Each pasta shape is placed in the oil with a bamboo chopstick inserted into it so that once the shape puffs up, there will be a passage for the cheese to flow through from one end to the other. The pasta is drained and stuffed with *fromage blanc*.

Pig's feet lollipops: A pig's foot and hock is injected and then soaked for three days in a brine consisting of 5% salt, 2% sugar, and an appropriate amount of sodium nitrite. The drained pork pieces are simmered with a few vegetables until the meat is tender and the skin is soft. The skin and meat are separated. The stock is strained and reduced to a syrup. A few shiitake-mushroom slices are salted and cooked in butter. A piece of plastic wrap is laid directly on a countertop. A rectangular piece of pig skin from the hock is arranged on the plastic. The meat pieces are torn into strips. The warm meat and mushroom slices are moistened with the reduced stock and arranged along the near edge of the pork skin. The whole assembly is formed into a cylinder by wrapping the skin around the meat and mushrooms. It is refrigerated overnight. For service, the 'sausage' is sliced into 8-mm ($^1/_3$-in) thick slices. Each slice is mounted on a lollipop stick, and garnished with whole-grain mustard and a strip of green onion.

Broccoli soup: Chicken broth is prepared from breast carcass portions with the pectoral minor muscle still attached, onions, carrots, and black peppercorns. The completed broth is strained and combined with 0.9%, by weight, agar before cooling. After cooling, the broth is mixed with egg whites and shredded cabbage, and clarified in the normal manner. The clarified broth is further reduced by about half, thus intensifying its colour and increasing the proportions of gelatin and agar. The floral apices of a lateral shoot from a head of broccoli are separated into pieces no larger than 5 to 7 mm ($^3/_{16}$ – $^1/_4$ in). These are blanched in the hot soup until almost tender. The most symmetrical examples are stuffed into the apexes of pyramid-shaped silicone moulds so their stems are pointed outward. Enough hot soup is spooned over the broccoli pieces to stabilize them, but not enough so they float. When this soup begins to gel, but before it is hard, four more pieces of broccoli are arranged (stuffed) on each side of the pyramids. More hot soup is then spooned over these to hold them in place. When that soup begins to gel, the moulds are completely filled. The moulds are placed in the refrigerator to fully harden the gelatin. For service, the soup pyramids are removed from the moulds and set in 60 °C (140 °F) water for 7 minutes to reheat the soup. The pyramids are served warm.

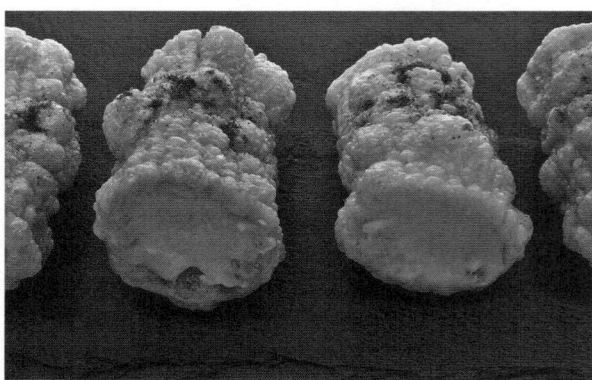

Figure 1. Macaroni and cheese.

Figure 2. Pigs feet lollipops.

Figure 3. Broccoli soup.

Modernist Stuffing and Wrapping Techniques and Applications

Crab-apple napoleon: A Red Delicious apple is cut crosswise into 1-mm ($\frac{1}{25}$-in) thick slices. The slices are dehydrated to produce ¼-mm ($\frac{1}{100}$-in) thick pieces that are both dry and flexible. A crab salad is prepared using canned white-crab meat. The crab is very well drained and combined with a little mayonnaise and salt. A single jalapeño pepper is cored, seeded, and skinned, and then diced into 2-mm ($\frac{1}{12}$-in) cubes. Some of the pepper cubes are mixed into the salad. Three apple slices are selected. A small portion of the crab salad is spooned onto the centre of the largest slice and placed on the plate. The same is done for the other two slices with the smallest slice on top. Some additional pepper cubes are sprinkled on top of the stack. When eaten, the diner wraps an apple slice around the salad and eats the whole piece at once.

Stuffed chicken wings: A simple sausage meat is prepared from ground pork, salt, pepper, nutmeg, and transglutaminase (Activa RM). The upper wings of a chicken are boned out leaving the skin and muscle intact. The sausage meat is stuffed into the space where the humerus bone was. The muscles are realigned. The portion is reshaped and formed into a cylinder by wrapping tightly with plastic wrap. This is refrigerated for at least four hours to give the transglutaminase time to work. The package is cooked in 60 °C (141 °F) water for the time required for a 6D bacteria kill. After cooking, the wings are browned in very hot oil. Each wing produces two portions. A simple sauce is prepared by thinning chicken demi-glace with Madeira wine. A sprinkle of some minced herbs finishes the dish.

Caprese salad: Whole-milk mozzarella curds, whole milk, fine salt, and citric-acid powder are combined together in a food processor and puréed. The mixture is packed into hemispherical moulds and frozen. At the same time tomato essence[10] is loaded with 2% calcium lactate gluconate, similarly moulded, and frozen. When frozen, the hemispherical pucks are removed from the moulds and stored in the freezer until needed. Shortly before service, the frozen pucks are dropped into a room temperature 0.5% sodium alginate solution. Once in the solution, the pucks are rolled with a finger so calcium alginate wraps around each puck as it forms. The tomato essence is manipulated in the algirate solution for about three minutes and the mozzarella mixture for about ten minutes. Both are placed in plain water until the centres are fully thawed, and then drained. One puck of each flavour, now shaped like a round pillow, is placed on a serving spoon along with a similarly sized basil leaf.

Kumquats stuffed with beef foam: Kumquats are selected for their shape and size. A small portion is cut from the stem end exposing the interior. All the juice vesicles and most of the albedo is removed with a small baller. The last of the albedo is curetted from the flavedo. Alternatively, the flavedo can be cleaned with a short soaking in a 0.4% Pectinex SPL solution. Strong-flavoured beef broth is blended together with VersaWhip 600 and xanthan gum, and then whisked in a stand mixer until a firm foam is achieved. The foam is frozen. Just prior to service, some of the foam is stuffed into the kumquat shell and the top levelled. Additional foam is spooned into the serving glass to support the kumquat for presentation.

Modernist Stuffing and Wrapping Techniques and Applications

Figure 4. Crap apple napoleon.

Figure 5. Stuffed chicken wings.

Figure 6. Caprese salad.

Figure 7. Kumquats stuffed with beef foam.

Carbonated grape: Large, firm grapes are selected. Each is peeled and placed in the jar of a half-litre siphon. The jar is closed and charged with 16 g (½ oz) of carbon-dioxide gas. The jar is given a few shakes and set aside for a while. After another shake, the gas is released and the jar opened. The grapes stuffed with gas are served with a few drops of an appropriate sweet wine.

Egg in its nest: Quail eggs are placed in a non-reactive bowl and covered with 6% acetic acid. On the following day, the eggs are rubbed with a finger to remove any loose shell. If some of the shell is still attached, the spent acid is replaced with fresh acid and the bowl is set aside for another day. When all the shell is gone, the eggs are rinsed in plain water. The shell-less eggs are submerged in *shiro miso* and placed in a refrigerator for two weeks. The eggs are removed from the miso and rinsed. The double membrane surrounding each egg is carefully pierced and the liquid white collected in a bowl. The gelatinous yolk is extracted from the membrane and rinsed prior to collecting in a separate bowl. The bowl with the whites is covered tightly with plastic wrap and set in simmering water until the whites become opaque. The cooked whites are set aside to cool. For service, a small spoonful of whites is placed in a serving spoon, and a yolk is stuffed into the whites.

Shrimp cocktail: A simple sauce is made from diced onions and cored, peeled and seeded tomatoes. The sauce is flavoured with fresh oregano, ancho-chilli powder, prepared horseradish, and salt. Agar is added to the sauce at a rate of 1% by weight. The sauce is boiled for 4 minutes to fully hydrate the agar. The cavities of silicone-rubber parfait moulds are filled about half full with the sauce. Precooked cocktail shrimp are stuffed in the sauce until the cavities are filled. The moulds are refrigerated until the 'cocktails' are cool. The individual servings are removed from the moulds. For serving, the cocktails are garnished with finely slivered, fresh oregano.

Oil-Cured olive ravioli: Oil-cured olives are seeded, puréed, and thinned with a little olive oil. The purée is forced through a fine sieve and placed in a syringe fitted with a blunt, 14-ga. needle. Small potato-starch bags (オブラート) are filled with the purée and heated, sealed, for serving.

Dried-pork rolls: A pork loin is placed in a non-reactive container and coated all over with a thick layer of coarse salt. The container is placed in a refrigerator for 24 hours. The loin is rinsed to remove all the surface salt and sewn into a muslin bag. The bag is hung in the refrigerator until the meat is dry, which is determined by squeezing the meat through its shroud. The dried meat is cut very, very thin with a rotary meat slicer. For service, two immature romaine (cos) lettuce leaves are stacked together. Some *okonomi* sauce (おこのみ ソース) is brushed on a slice of the meat, and the slice is wrapped around the lettuce, sauce side in. The 'package' is tied with a chive sprig and garnished with two petals from an edible flower.

Pulled-pork ravioli: A whole pork shoulder (butt) is heavily coated with a spice mixture[11] and set in the refrigerator overnight. The following day, the meat is placed in a tight-fitting pot, covered, and placed in a 160 °C (320 °F) oven. The meat cooks until

Figure 8. Carbonated grape.

Figure 9. Egg in its nest.

Figure 10. Shrimp cocktail.

Figure 11. Dried pork rolls.

it shreds easily with a fork, about three to six hours. When cool enough to handle, any bones, cartilage, or large pieces of fat are removed and discarded. The rendered juices are collected and reduced by half to serve as a sauce. The meat is shredded by hand. Some of the meat is packed into a loaf pan to a depth of about 4 cm (1½ in) and pressed under weight overnight in the refrigerator. The resulting solid block is cut into squares. Each square is wrapped with a small piece of *brik*. For service, each square is pan-fried in vegetable oil and served with a little warmed sauce.

Beets, caviar and cream: Cooked beets are puréed in a high-speed blender along with some water, prepared horseradish and wine vinegar. An amount of water equal to about a quarter of the purée is combined with agar, calculated to be 0.9% by weight of the entire mixture, in a small saucepan and set over high heat. Once the agar is totally hydrated, the mixture is combined with the purée. The cavities of a silicone mould are filled with the new mixture and set in the refrigerator to gel. When firm, each moulded beet purée is hollowed out with the aid of a small baller. Each cavity is stuffed level with caviar. Heavy cream is whipped lightly and a small dollop is added to hide the caviar. A smaller dollop of caviar is placed on top of the cream. A sliver of scallion green is added for decoration.

Meatloaf and gravy: The meatloaf is prepared by combining ground beef (20% fat) with salt, pepper, white wine, onion powder, sodium nitrite and transglutaminase (Activa RM). The mixture is formed into a long-sausage shape, about 27 mm (1¹/₁₆ in) diameter, using plastic film. The package is frozen, vacuum-packed, thawed and cooked in 63 °C (146 °F) water until the internal temperature of the meat is about the same. The hot meat is chilled thoroughly in an water-ice bath, unwrapped, and cut into 2-cm (²⁵/₃₂-in) long cylinders. A cylindrical plug is cut from the centre of each cylinder. The hole is stuffed with strong-flavoured beef broth that has been combined with 0.9%, by weight, agar. The combination is chilled thoroughly, vacuum-packed, and reheated for service in 60 °C (140 °C) water for 10 minutes.

Raw beef sushi: Medium-grain white rice is cooked in the normal manner for sushi. The hot rice is cooled by a combination of fanning and 'cutting' with a wooden spatula. During the cooling, commercial *katsu* sauce (カツソース) is sprinkled over the rice instead of the normal flavoured vinegar. The cold rice is formed as for *nigirizushi* (握り寿司), but with the shape more rectangular. A dab of prepared *wasabi* (わさび) is smeared on the top of the rice. A thin slice of raw beef is sprinkled with salt and black pepper, and wrapped over the sides and top of the rice. The ends are left uncovered. Each piece is sliced crosswise into two servings.

Salmon wheels: Raw shrimp, scallops and catfish are finely ground and mixed with salt, white pepper, transglutaminase (Activa RM) and finely sliced fresh sage. The paste is mixed until it becomes sticky. It is then rolled into a 12-mm (½-in) diameter 'log'. The log is placed in the freezer until frozen. Fresh salmon is sliced very thin and arranged on a plastic sheet. Where the pieces overlap, a light coating of transglutaminase is sprinkled. The whole salmon layer is sprinkled with transglutaminase and wrapped tightly around

Modernist Stuffing and Wrapping Techniques and Applications

Figure 12. Pulled pork ravioli.

Figure 13. Beets, caviar and cream.

Figure 14. Meatloaf and gravy.

Figure 15. Raw beef sushi.

Modernist Stuffing and Wrapping Techniques and Applications

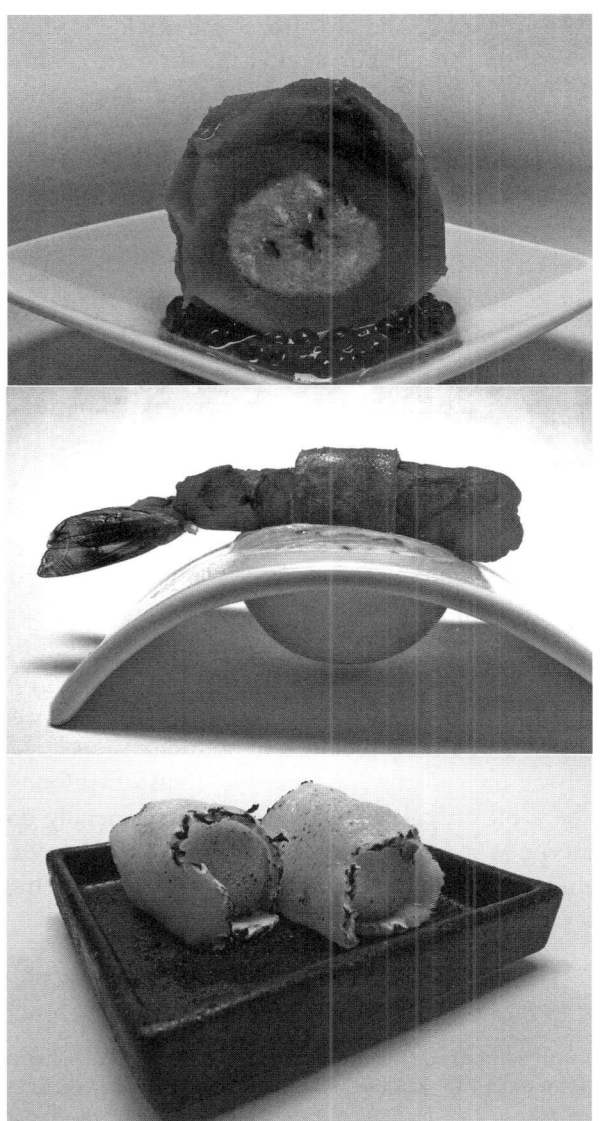

Figure 16. Salmon wheels.

Figure 17. Pickled prawn.

Figure 18. Three-cheese gnocchi.

the white-fish log. The resulting log is frozen until solid. The frozen salmon log is sliced into 1.8-cm (7/10-in) thick slices and vacuum packed. For service, the slices are cooked in a water bath set to 41 °C (106 °F) until warmed all the way through, about thirty minutes. The disks are served on a layer of salmon caviar.

Pickled prawn: Headless tiger prawns (26–30 count) are deveined with scissors by cutting along the back through the shell covering the abdominal segments and finishing with the telson. The shell is left in place. A thick wooden skewer if inserted into the flesh for the entire length. The skewered prawn is immersed in *shiro miso* (史郎味噌), under refrigeration, for 3 days. At the end of the pickling, the prawn is rinsed of any clinging *miso,* and the skewer is removed. The shell is removed. *Kizami shoga* (きざみしょうが), red pickled ginger, is stuffed into the opening created by the skewer. A strip of pickled egg yolk is wrapped around the prawn.[12] A dipping sauce is prepared by combining powdered *wasabi* (わさび) and *ao-nori* (青海苔) with mayonnaise prepared from an egg white, rice vinegar, salt and canola oil.

Three-cheese gnocchi: Whole-milk ricotta, heavy cream, salt and pepper are mixed together until smooth. This mixture is blended with modified food starch (Ultra-Tex 4) until a dough-like texture is achieved. The mixture is rolled into 2.5-cm (1-in) long by 2-cm (25/32-in) round cylinders. A 2.5-cm (1-in) long piece of pecorino-Romano cheese is stuffed into the centre of each cylinder. The cylinders are individually frozen. For service, the requisite number of ricotta cylinders are thawed and heavily coated with tapioca starch. These are quickly deep-fried in oil at 210 °C (410 °F). Each is then rapidly wrapped in a thin slice of Brie that has been partially melted with a torch.

As the above examples show, applying the construct of 'wrapped and stuffed foods' to Modernist cuisine turns out to be a bit artificial. Such preparations generally do not require wrapping or stuffing except as a way of introducing additional flavour. Wrapping and stuffing helps Modernist dishes fit Adrià's criteria of 'whether something is magical, whether it opens up new tastes'.[13]

Notes

1. Stewart's words about obscenity were: 'I shall not today attempt further to define the kinds of material I understand to be embraced within that shorthand description; and perhaps I could never succeed in intelligibly doing so. But I know it when I see it, and the motion picture involved in this case is not that.' Jacobellis v. Ohio 378 U.S. 184 (1964) (Stewart, J., concurring).
2. Myhrvold's ten principles of Modernist cuisine (Nathan Myhrvold with Chris Young and Maxime Bilet, *Modernist Cuisine: The Art and Science of Cooking,* 5 vols & supp (Bellevue, WA: The Cooking Lab, 2011): v. 1, p. 56):
   1. Cuisine is a creative art in which the chef and diner are in dialogue. Food is the primary medium for this dialogue, but all sensory aspects of the dining experience contribute to it.
   2. Culinary rules, conventions, and traditions must be understood, but they should not be allowed to hinder the development of creative new dishes.
   3. Creatively breaking culinary rules and traditions is a powerful way to engage diners and make them think about the dining experience.

4. Diners have expectations – some explicit, some implicit – of what sort of food is possible. Surprising them with food that defies their expectations is another way to engage them intellectually. This includes putting familiar flavours in unfamiliar forms or the converse.

5. In addition to surprise, many other emotions, reactions, feelings, and thoughts can be elicited by cuisine. These include humour, whimsy, satire, and nostalgia, among others. The repertoire of the Modernist chef isn't just flavour and texture; it is also the range of emotional and intellectual reactions that food can inspire in the diner.

6. Creativity, novelty, and invention are intrinsic to the chef's role. When one borrows techniques and ideas or gains inspiration from other chefs or other sources, that should be acknowledged.

7. Science and technology are sources that can be tapped to enable new culinary inventions, but they are a means to an end rather than the final goal.

8. First-rate ingredients are the foundation on which cuisine is built. Expensive ingredients such as caviar or truffles are part of the repertoire but have no greater intrinsic value than other high-quality ingredients.

9. Ingredients originating in food science and technology, such as hydrocolloids, enzymes, and emulsifiers, are powerful tools in helping to produce dishes that would otherwise be impossible.

10. Diners and chefs should be sensitive to the conditions under which food is harvested and grown. Whenever possible, they should support humane methods of slaughter and sustainable harvesting of wild foods such as fish.

3. Myhrvold, v. 1, p. 56.
4. *El Bulli: Cooking in Progress*, dir. by Gereon Wetzel (if... Productions, 2011).
5. A small dish served before the start of a sit-down meal, often presented as 'a gift from the chef.'
6. Small sweet items, sometimes referred to as petits fours, served at the end of the meal. These are often presented with the coffee, if ordered, or with the bill.
7. Dave Arnold, *Course Notes, Magic Potions: Hydrocolloids* (New York: French Culinary Institute, 2011): loose-leaf handout.
8. For the deep-fried hollandaise cubes: 'Dissolve gelatin into melted butter and reserve. Blend Hexaphosphate, citric acid, gellan gum, and water together and bring to a boil in a small pot. Pour into a container and cool until completely set. Place in a blender with the 100 grams of egg yolks and mix well. Pour half of the gelatin/butter mix into the blender as you would with a classic hollandaise. Combine water and Ultrasperse M, mixing well, and then combine with the remaining half of the gelatin/butter mixture. Add to the mixture in the blender (the blender should be running throughout all of these steps). At this point a thick and creamy sauce should have formed. Adjust the seasoning with salt and lemon juice. Pour sauce into a shallow baking tray lined with plastic and allow to chill 8 hours (or overnight). The next day, cut the hollandaise into cubes and bread them using a classic three step process: flour, egg wash, and English muffin crumbs. Reserve the breaded cubes in the freezer.' When needed: 'Pan-fry the hollandaise cubes and then place in oven to warm through.' (Wylie Dufrense, Course Description, Innovations at wd-50: http://www.starchefs.com/cooking/?q=node/91).
9. Dave Arnold, *Cooking Issues*, 27 October 2009: http://www.cookingissues.com/2009/10/27/puffed-snacks-1-wherefore-the-puff/.
10. Tomato essence is prepared by separating the clear liquid that surrounds the seeds from the rest of the tomato. It has an intense tomato flavour, but no visual clue that it is from a tomato.
11. The spice mixture consists of juniper berries, cumin seeds, coriander seeds, fennel seeds, cloves, red pepper flakes, cinnamon, ancho chilli powder, and sweet paprika; roasted, ground, and mixed about two-to-one with fine salt.
12. Pickled egg yolk is the result of preparing an egg as in the 'egg in its nest' description above except a chicken egg is used, and the time covered with miso is extended to 21 days. Once the yolk is harvested from the pickled egg, it is pressed very thin, frozen, and cut into strips. The strips are kept frozen until needed.
13. *El Bulli: Cooking in Progress*.

Siberian Stuffed: A Profusion of *Pel'meni*

Sharon Hudgins

Known as 'the national dish of Siberia', *pel'meni* are a type of boiled dumpling made of pasta dough enclosing a filling of minced meat, fish, vegetables or other ingredients. Similar in size and shape to Italian *cappelletti* and *tortelloni*, they belong to the large family of filled, boiled pastas found in many parts of the world, including Japanese *gyoza*; Korean *mandu*; Chinese *jiaozi*, *wontons* and many other varieties of filled-and-boiled dumplings; central Asian, Caucasian, and Turkish *manti*; Uzbek *chuchvara*; Ukrainian *vareniki*; Polish *pierogi*; Baltic and East European *kaldunyǀkolduny*ǀ*koldūnai* and *ushki*ǀ *vushki*; Czech and Slovak filled *knedlíky*; Slovak *pirohy*; Italian *ravioli* and many other Italian filled pastas; German-Schwabian *Maultaschen*; and Jewish *kreplach*. Of the cooked dishes that came into Russian cuisine from the Ural Mountains and the territory east of there, *pel'meni* is the Siberian dish most popular throughout all of Russia today.[1]

I first learned how to make Siberian *pel'meni* in the city of Vladivostok, in Russia's far east. It was 1 January 1994, a snowy, blustery night when the wind-chill was well below zero. My husband, Tom, and I were living in an apartment in one of those ugly, gray, prefab-concrete, Soviet-era high-rise buildings that encircle every major Russian city. Alla, a Russian neighbor in the same building, had invited us for a festive New Year's Day dinner, a follow-up to the feast we'd shared on New Year's Eve with Alla's family and other Russian friends, when the triple-whammy cut-off of electricity, water and heating in our building had shaped the traditional holiday meal into an improvised smorgasbord of cold dishes assembled and eaten by candlelight.

For the 1 January follow-up dinner, after the electricity and water came back on, Alla laid out a tempting array of several hot home-cooked dishes, elaborate cold vegetable salads, a few desserts and plenty of drinks, more than enough for the six adults and four children gathered around the table. Two hours later, around 11 p.m., when we all felt so full we couldn't take another bite, Alla announced that it was time to go into the kitchen to make *pel'meni*! I thought she was joking, until Alla explained that Siberian *pel'meni* were a traditional Russian food for New Year's Day, and we had to start making them before 1 January ended at midnight. Alla had prepared the dumpling dough in advance, along with the filling of minced beef, pork and onions. Working together in her small kitchen, we women rolled out the dough, cut it into two-inch circles with a crystal wineglass, spooned some filling onto the dough and formed it by hand into ear-shaped pockets of pasta about the size of a walnut shell. Then Alla put a large pot of water on the stove to boil, tossed in some spices and told us to leave the kitchen so the men could come in to do their part.

Siberian Stuffed: A Profusion of Pel'meni

We retired to the adjacent living room, where we sat around drinking goblets of white wine and listening to the men singing lustily in the kitchen as they rolled, filled and formed their own portions of *pel'meni*. After the men had cooked all the *pel'meni* that both groups had made, they served the dumplings with a choice of garnishes: butter; sour cream; Russian hot, spicy mustard; soy sauce; and Russian brown ketchup. While the men knocked back shots of vodka, Alla showed Tom and me the proper way to eat *pel'meni* by popping each one whole into our mouths. She explained that Russians consider it uncouth to cut their *pel'meni* into pieces.[2]

Origin and history

The exact origin of Russian *pel'meni* is probably lost in the mists of Siberia's swamps. Many historians think that *pel'meni* came to Russia with the Mongols, who had learned to make filled dumplings from the Chinese when different Mongol tribes conquered Chinese territories during the tenth to thirteenth centuries. In 1959, archaeologists discovered a tomb from the Tang Dynasty era in China (AD 618–907) containing the fossilized remains of filled dumplings that look exactly like *pel'meni*.[3] According to this version of culinary history, the Mongols then brought the technique of making *pel'meni* with them when they expanded into Siberia and parts of eastern Europe in the thirteenth century, subjugating large swaths of that territory for the next 250 years. Part of this hypothesis is based on the Siberian tradition of using black pepper to season the *pel'meni* filling; black pepper was a spice introduced into Siberia by the Mongols, who had re-opened the old spice routes from Asia to the West during the thirteenth and fourteenth centuries.[4]

Some linguists suggest that *pel'meni*'s roots might be found in the Russian name of this dish, which supposedly comes from the ancient Finno-Ugric Komi people's word *pel'nian*, derived from their words *pel'* (ear) and *nian* (bread, or anything made from flour).[5] The German linguist Max Fasmer dates the origin of this word back to the tenth century, long before the Mongols arrived, to the Komis living in the Kama River basin just west of the Ural Mountains (the geographic divide between European Russia and Siberia), in the regions of the present-day Komi Republic and Perm Territory in the Russian Federation, and to the Udmurts, another Finno-Ugric people living just south of there in today's Republic of Udmurtia. One hypothesis holds that the Udmurts might have learned how to make *pel'meni* from the Persians, from whom they also learned about flour and whose word for bread is *nan*.[6] Although lacking archaeological evidence of pre-Mongol, ear-shaped, filled pastas in this region (like those found in the Chinese tomb), the Udmurts still claim that *pel'meni* were born in Udmurtia. In 2004 in Izhevsk, the regional capital of Udmurtia, they even erected the world's only public monument to *pel'meni* – a 3-meter-tall silver-gray fork holding a giant white *pel'men'*.[7]

Instead of faraway China, some linguists and culinary historians have suggested that these dumplings came from Central Asia and spread from there into Siberia and eastern parts of European Russia during the thirteenth and fourteenth centuries. They also base their hypothesis on the term *pel'nian*, citing *nan* as a common central Asian word for 'bread', and on the shape of *pel'meni*, which resembles other filled pasta made in central Asia.[8] And since the Tatars did move into parts of Udmurtia in the thirteenth and fourteenth centuries, it is possible that the local Udmurts learned to make filled pastas during that time from those central Asian people.[9]

From the late 1400s to late 1500s, the Russians slowly regained power over their eastern European territories that had been lost to the Mongols and began pushing their borders southward toward the Caucasus and eastward toward, and beyond, the Ural Mountains into Siberia. As a result, they also began to adopt some of the foods and cooking techniques of the Asians they conquered along the way (or of the Finno-Ugric Udmurts and Komis they encountered there, depending on which hypothesis you believe). Thus in the late sixteenth century, Russians began learning how to make pasta – including *pel'meni* – from their subjects living in the European and Siberian regions formerly controlled by the Mongol/Tatar Golden Horde.[10]

Whatever its origins, *pel'meni* ultimately became a Siberian/Russian dish. By the end of the nineteenth century some previously 'foreign' foods, such as *pel'meni*, had become so assimilated into Russian cuisine that they were considered 'Russian' or 'Siberian', not German, Dutch, French, Chinese, Mongol or Tatar.[11] *Pel'meni* were considered the original Siberian 'convenience food', which could be prepared in advance, frozen for storage, and then easily cooked for a quick meal at home. In winter, hunters and fishermen carried frozen *pel'meni* with them into the *taiga* (forest), where they boiled the dumplings in pots of melted snow over an open fire. Travelers, explorers, soldiers and settlers carried stocks of *pel'meni* on winter journeys. Today, frozen *pel'meni* are still a favorite convenience food for hikers, students, bachelors and busy mothers.

Traditions and rituals

An old, Siberian village tradition was for large groups of people to gather after the first frost for communal *pel'meni*-making sessions, where the labor-intensive work was shared by family, friends and neighbors, sometimes over the course of several days. The dumplings were mass produced in assembly-line fashion: the women made the pasta dough and chopped the filling meat in big wooden troughs (sometimes the men took on this harder job), and the men stuffed and shaped the little dumplings, while songs were sung and stories told.[12] Even in today's urban high-rise apartment buildings, modern Siberian cooks still enjoy getting together with their friends to produce large quantities of home-made *pel'meni* for their families. Thousands of *pel'meni* can be made this way in one day, the work punctuated by shots of cold vodka every time another 100 dumplings are completed.

In the villages these gatherings often ended with *pel'meni*-eating contests, much like hot-dog or jalapeño-eating contests in America. The Siberians let the remaining uncooked dumplings freeze solid outdoors in the open air, then stored them in bags or boxes in their cellars; outdoors on racks above ground, away from hungry animals; or buried in sealed containers in the snow. The *pel'meni* stayed frozen throughout the long winter, for cooking later as needed. Modern urban Russians store them on the balconies of their apartment buildings or hang bags of *pel'meni* outside their windows in winter. Many Russians still believe that *pel'meni* taste better if frozen for at least twenty-four hours before they are cooked.

Several rituals and traditions are associated with the making and eating of *pel'meni*. In many parts of Russia, *pel'meni* are a traditional food for New Year's Day. In the Perm region, families get together on the first day of Easter, after their morning prayers, to make *pel'meni*.[13] In nineteenth-century Perm, it was also customary to serve these dumplings to a bride at her 'farewell feast', a female-only dinner, before the wedding day. And today *pel'meni* are still sometimes featured at wedding dinners and other celebrations.[14]

Whenever some of the dumpling dough is left over, many cooks make a 'surprise' *pel'men'* or two, with a totally different filling (cheese, mushrooms, whatever), which is cooked in the same pot with the regular *pel'meni*. Whoever finds a 'surprise' dumpling in his or her portion of *pel'meni* at the table will have good luck. It is even said that in tsarist times the royal cooks were instructed to hide precious stones within certain *pel'meni* served to the tsar's guests.[15] What a surprise indeed!

Similarly, some cooks hide a button, a ring, a coin or a garlic clove inside a *pel'men'*, along with the regular filling – again, as a predictor of good luck for whoever finds it. Certain 'surprise' *pel'meni* fillings supposedly predict specific futures, too: a coin means wealth, sugar means a successful year, greens bring you joy and a dumpling of solid dough brings you luck. In the region of Perm, young maidens would get together to make *pel'meni* with a variety of different fillings, which were all then cooked together in the same pot. Each *pel'men'* filling carried its own prediction about the future: a *pel'men'* filled with flour foretold marriage to a rich husband; a meat filling meant an easy life, whereas a black pepper filling meant a hard one; and a *pel'men'* stuffed with wool predicted a happy life sometime much later in the future.[16]

Pel'meni dreams have their own meanings, too. Before going to sleep, Tatar girls in the Perm region would eat *pel'meni* filled with salt; whoever appeared in their dreams to drink water would become that girl's fiancé.[17] If someone dreams that he is sitting at a table set with a large portion of *pel'meni*, then he'll soon meet old friends. If a person dreams of making *pel'meni* himself, it means that he is alone in life or lacking the comfort of a family. If a young woman dreams that she has made bad dumplings that stick together or fall apart, it means that her boyfriend has picky eating habits and will criticize her cooking.[18]

The *Pel'meni*-making process

When Siberians speak of the process of making *pel'meni*, they don't use the common cooking term *gotovit'* (to prepare, to make, to cook), but instead say *striapat'* (to cook up, to concoct), or more specifically *lepit'* (to sculpt, to build, to model).[19] The process

Siberian Stuffed: A Profusion of *Pel'meni*

of 'sculpting' *pel'meni* begins with the dough, most often made from white flour, eggs, cold water, and salt; in varying proportions depending on the type of wheat the flour was milled from; the humidity of the day and the preference of the cook. Recipe variations include adding butter, vegetable oil or sour cream to the dough; omitting the eggs; using whole wheat or buckwheat flour; and substituting milk or hot water for the cold water.

Some very old recipes are said to have used sourdough composed of soft winter wheat mixed with buttermilk or whey, then allowed to slowly ferment over several days.[20] In earlier times, *pel'meni* dough in the Urals was often made with partridge eggs; in the steppes south of there, quail and bustard eggs were used.[21] Although classic *pel'meni* are always creamy white, creative modern cooks sometimes color the dough by adding cooked, puréed carrots (pale orange), beets (pink), spinach or other greens (pale green) and even squid ink (black). However the dough is concocted, it must be flexible yet tough – elastic enough to be rolled thin so the filling can cook quickly, but also strong enough not to break apart during cooking.

A characteristic of Siberian *pel'meni* is that their fillings are savory, not sweet. Traditional *pel'meni* are filled with a mixture of minced raw meats (preferably two or three kinds combined) seasoned with onion, salt and black pepper. Some cooks also spice them up with a bit of fresh garlic or a hint of hot red pepper. Beef and pork are the meats found in most *pel'meni* today, although veal, lamb, mutton, poultry, horsemeat, reindeer and wild game (deer, elk, moose, boar, bear, grouse, etc.) are used in Siberian *pel'meni*, too, as are a variety of fish and shellfish from Siberia's rivers, lakes and seas. The ingredients are finely chopped by hand, or put through a meat grinder twice. Crushed ice, meat broth, milk or berry juice is sometimes added to the meat mixture to enhance the flavor and texture.

Non-meat versions of *pel'meni* are stuffed with cooked potatoes, rice, buckwheat groats, mushrooms, chopped hard-boiled eggs, pumpkin, turnips, cabbage, sauerkraut, radishes – singularly or in combinations of two or three – or with finely chopped fresh greens that grow in Siberia, such as wild garlic, onion, horseradish, dandelion, sorrel, young nettles and goosefoot. Vegetarian versions are also made for Lent and other fasting days on the Russian Orthodox Church calendar. Sometimes vegetables other than, or in addition to, onions are combined with meats for *pel'meni* fillings, as are wild berries such as cranberries and blueberries.

After the dough ingredients have been mixed together, kneaded lightly and set aside to rest for a while, the dough is rolled out to a thickness of $\frac{1}{16}$ inch and cut with a water glass, wine glass, or cookie cutter into 2–2½-inch diameter rounds. (Only rarely is the dough cut into squares, like *wonton* wrappers; this is considered a lazy way of making *pel'meni*, as is using store-bought *wonton* wrappers.) Each circle of dough is then rolled a bit thinner before the filling is placed in the center. Alternatively, the dough is rolled by hand into a long rope, then half-inch pieces are pinched or cut off it and patted by hand, or rolled out, into very thin, individual rounds.

Siberian Stuffed: A Profusion of Pel'meni

A small amount of filling is placed in the center of each dough circle, which is then folded in half to make a semi-circle; sometimes the edges are moistened with water or beaten egg white before being pressed together firmly to seal in the filling. Then the pointed ends of the semi-circle are brought together, slightly overlapping, and pinched together to make an ear-shaped pocket of filled pasta.[22] These dumplings can also be made more quickly with a *pel'menitsa*, a cast-aluminum or hard-plastic utensil that functions like an Italian ravioli mold and produces small, hexagonal-shaped *pel'meni*, not the traditional ear-shaped dumplings.[23] Although *pel'meni* can be large or small – such as the smaller ear-shaped *ushki*, or the gimmicky saucer-size *pel'meni* served at some contemporary restaurants – handmade *pel'meni* (always considered the best) are generally the size of a large walnut shell.

Raw (fresh or frozen) *pel'meni* are dropped into a large pot of boiling water or broth (beef, chicken or fish) seasoned with salt and other spices and herbs (often black peppercorns, whole cloves and bay leaves), simmered for a few minutes until they float to the top, then removed with a slotted spoon and drained thoroughly. In the past, raw *pel'meni* were also combined with sour cream in a *gorshok* (an earthenware pot shaped much like a Spanish *puchero* pot), the top completely covered and sealed with bread dough; the *pel'meni* were then slowly baked for several hours inside a traditional Russian masonry stove, before being served hot in their hermetically sealed cooking pot. Raw *pel'meni* can also be deep-fried in oil, sautéed in butter or even strung onto skewers with tomatoes and onions and cooked on a grill, but these methods of cooking *pel'meni* are not traditional. However, leftover cooked *pel'meni* are often reheated by being sautéed in butter, or added to omelets, or baked in sour cream or tomato sauce under a layer of cheese in a gratin pan.

Boiled, hot, drained *pel'meni* are usually tossed with butter before being served in a bowl or on a plate as a main dish for lunch or dinner (15 or 20 *pel'meni* per person). A smaller number can also be served in meat broth, at the start of a meal. In modern times, individual *pel'meni* have even found a place on buffet tables as cocktail tidbits or served in small portions, artfully plated, as appetizers at the beginning of a restaurant meal.[24]

Pristine *pel'meni*, straight from the pot and tossed with butter, are usually also served with one or more garnishes on top or on the side. Traditional Siberian garnishes include rich, nutty-flavored Russian sour cream; white or black vinegar, alone or with coarsely ground black pepper; and hot, spicy Russian mustard, alone or mixed with white or fruit vinegar. Other popular Russian garnishes include mayonnaise, grated cheese, fried bread crumbs, finely chopped fresh greens (green onion tops, chives, parsley, dill, chervil, marjoram, sometimes even cilantro), grated fresh horseradish or prepared horseradish sauce, ketchup or spicy tomato sauce, soy sauce, toasted pine nuts, or, more recently, Thai Sriracha sauce, American Tabasco sauce and various other foreign-made hot, spicy chilli sauces.

And what do Russians drink with their *pel'meni*? A Russian culinary website suggests, not surprisingly, ice-cold vodka, with chilled beer a distant, but acceptable, second choice. This website also counsels, '...it is worth understanding that wine and brandy with *pel'meni* are incompatible. However, if you want to impress guests or yourself, you can try such an extreme option'.²⁵

Commercial *pel'meni* production

All Russians know that the best *pel'meni* are made at home. Children traditionally learned *pelmeni*-making from their mothers, grandmothers and other elders in the community, not from cookbooks, television or the Internet. But times have changed. Sixty years ago, the classic Soviet cookbook, *Kniga o vkusnoi i zdorovoi pishche* (Book of Tasty and Healthy Food), contained only three recipes for *pel'meni*.²⁶ Today, home cooks can learn how to make *pel'meni* from many Russian cookbooks, several of them devoted solely to recipes for *pel'meni* and other Slavic and central Asian dumplings.²⁷ Russian culinary websites have dozens of recipes for different varieties of these dumplings, and television cooking shows, commercial videos and YouTube postings all offer demonstrations on how to make *pel'meni*.²⁸

But the easiest way to obtain *pel'meni* is to buy them, packaged or in bulk, in the frozen-foods section of a grocery store. Commercial *pel'meni* are popular with consumers, especially in urban areas, because they are inexpensive to buy and simple to cook at home for a quick and filling meal.

Commercial production of frozen *pel'meni* began in the Soviet Union in the mid-1930s.²⁹ Today *pel'meni* are the most popular 'semi-finished' (meaning you still need to cook them) commercial food product in Russia.³⁰ *Pel'meni* factories turn out two types of these dumplings, with a number of different fillings: totally machine-made *pel'meni* and 'handmade' *pel'meni*. The latter are dumplings filled and shaped into semi-circles by machine, then formed into the classic 'ear' shape by hand. The quality of these products varies, depending on quality (and quantity) of meats and other ingredients used in the fillings.³¹

Many brands of commercial *pel'meni* are available in Russia today, usually packaged in 500-gram boxes or plastic bags often decorated with folk-art designs that evoke 'Siberia' or rural Russia. 'Siberian Gourmet' brand, which claims to be the leading seller of *pel'meni*, in volume, from the Urals to the Russian far east, says that they make eighty tons of dumplings a day, of which ten tons are 'handmade'.³²

Pel'meni venues

Pel'meni are so popular that many Russian cities have *pel'mennye*, small cafés that specialize in these boiled dumplings – warm, steamy, little eateries where *pel'meni* can be consumed on the premises or purchased (fresh or frozen) to take home. Popular post-Soviet *pel'meni* restaurants, more glitzy and modern than the plain-but-cozy old Soviet cafés, include the Pel'meshka dumpling chain in Moscow and Beerman & Pel'meni, an award-winning restaurant in Novosibirsk, Siberia. *Pel'meni* parlors can also be found in Russia's neighboring Baltic states, and in such other locations such as Alaska, where Russians have settled, and Egypt, where Russians have settled or like to travel.

Siberian Stuffed: A Profusion of *Pel'meni*

In the winter, Russian vendors sell plastic bags of purportedly home-made frozen *pel'meni* at street stalls and farmers' markets. Cooked *pel'meni*, for take-out or to eat on site, are also sold at some street stands and at public festivals. And vendors on the station platforms along the Trans-Siberian Railroad tracks sell ready-made *pel'meni* to hungry passengers on the trains.

Pel'meni in advertising and the arts

Pel'meni appear not only on the table, but also in advertising and many of the arts, including music, literature, theater, television, painting, sculpture, photography, postage stamps, wallpaper design and textile arts.

In addition to the world's only *pel'meni* monument in Udmurtia, *pel'meni* have been depicted in felt sculptures and other three-dimensional forms. In 2008, models of a Russian Orthodox chapel and Mount Olympus, each made from hundreds of *pel'meni*, won the top awards at the Festival of Siberian Pel'meni in Krasnoiarsk, Siberia.[33]

Satiric songs have been composed about *pel'meni*, and *Pel'meni* is the title of a play by Vladimir Sorokin, Russia's most famous contemporary avant-garde writer. A popular Russian comedy group, Ural'skie Pel'meni, took its name from these dumplings and features them in its advertising posters.[34] *Pel'meni* appear in humorous Russian TV commercials and in several Russian jokes. In 2005 a billboard advertising campaign for Dar'ia-brand *pel'meni* featured a black-and-white photo of a naked woman's buttocks dusted with flour, with the printed tag line 'Your Favorite Little Pel'meni!'. The billboard was deemed so scandalous that local authorities banned it in St. Petersburg the day after it appeared, and in Moscow a week later.[35]

And, last but not least, an American telephone engineer who won the 'Audience Favorite' award at the 2010 Karaoke World Championship in Moscow went home with a voucher for one million *pel'meni*, enough to last for 27 years if he eats 100 *pel'meni* a day from now on.[36] *Priiatnogo appetita*! (Enjoy your meal!)

Siberian Stuffed: A Profusion of Pel'meni

Notes

1. Two other popular, non-cooked dishes that entered the Russian culinary repertoire from east of the Urals are sauerkraut (*kvashenaia kapusta* and its less strongly soured cousin, *kislaia kapusta*), which the Russians learned from the Mongols who ruled parts of Russian territory from the thirteenth to the sixteenth centuries; and hot, spicy Korean carrot salad (*morkovi po koreiski*), which the Russians learned from Koreans who Stalin deported from the Soviet far East to Uzbekistan (then part of the Soviet Union) in the late 1930s.
2. Adapted from Sharon Hudgins, *The Other Side of Russia: A Slice of Life in Siberia and the Russian Far East* (College Station, TX: Texas A & M University Press, 2003), pp. 193–94. For a full description of the two-week-long New Year's holiday season in Vladivostok, see pp. 186–96.
3. Silvano Serventi and Françoise Sabban, *Pasta: The Story of a Universal Food* (New York: Columbia University Press, 2002), p. 275, pp. 314–16. The photograph on p. 316 shows four fossilized Tang-era dumplings shaped exactly like Russian pel'meni of today.
4. Lesley Chamberlain, *The Food and Cooking of Russia* (London: Allen Lane, 1982), p. 12, pp. 228–29; 'Pelmeni,' http://www.enotes.com/topic/Pelmeni.
5. Alan Davidson, *The Oxford Companion to Food* (Oxford: Oxford University Press, 1999), p. 593.
6. Davidson, p. 593.
7. RIA Novosti Online News 2004: 'Monument to Pelmen Unveiled in Udmurtia', http://en.rian.ru/onlinenews/20041209/39775292.html (9 December 2004).
8. N. I. Kovalev, *Rasskazy o russkoi kukhne* [Tales of the Russian Kitchen] (Moscow: Ekonomika, 1984), p. 128.
9. See also V. V. Pokhlebkin, *Bol'shaia entsiklopediia kulinarnogo iskusstva* [Great Encyclopedia of Culinary Arts] (Moscow: Tsentrpoligraf, 2006), pp. 871–72. Another source (with Russian nationalist overtones) claims that *pel'meni* originated in the Urals where, as a part of ancient pagan rituals, they served as symbols of sacrificial animals, then later traveled eastward from the Urals to Siberia prior to the Mongol conquest, before coming back westward to European Russia and central Asia with the Mongols in the fourteenth century (Anna Vinner, Russian-language website, Pel'meshki ne terpiat speshki, 'Dumplings Take Patience', or 'Dumplings Can't Be Rushed' [literally, 'Dumplings Do Not Tolerate Haste']: History of Dumplings', http://pelemeni.ru/history.html [30 April 2009]). This same source does make a valid point that 'Many peoples invent their own kinds of dumplings, and there is nothing unusual in the assumption that the occurrence of dumplings in this or that tradition took place naturally, as a result of the culinary and nutritional needs of those people'. Another hypothesis suggests that although the Komi's recipe for *pel'meni* might have originated in China, *pel'meni* were carried from the Urals into Siberia by Russian settlers moving eastward into the lands of Asian Russia beginning in the late sixteenth century (Illya V. Loysha, 'Siberia: Cooking of the Chaldony': http://www.enotes.com/siberia-reference/siberia).
10. Joyce Toomre, *Classic Russian Cooking: Elena Molokhovets' A Gift to Young Housewives* (Bloomington, IN: Indiana University Press, 1992), pp. 16–17.
11. Alison Smith, *Recipes for Russia: Food and Nationhood Under the Tsars* (DeKalb, IL: Northern Illinois University Press, 2008), p. 91.
12. Chamberlain, pp. 228–29. See also Stephanie Williams, *Olga's Story: Three Continents, Two World Wars and Revolution—One Woman's Epic Journey through the Twentieth Century* (New York: Random House Digital, 2011), Chapter 4, first two pages (n.p.), which describes communal *pel'meni*-making in a Siberian village just north of the Chinese border, in 1905. Katherine Czapp, in 'Sourdough Egg Noodles', http://www.westonaprice.org/food-features/sourdough-egg-noodles (July 6, 2004), cites her own translation of *Russian Cuisine*, by V. Mikhailov and Riurikova (1998), which describes rituals surrounding the communal preparation of *pel'meni* in Siberia: 'Only women who had borne children were permitted to make them, and they wore particular garments with ornamentation propitious to the success of their endeavor'.
13. Marian Trotter (ed.), *Culinaria Russia* (Hagen, Germany: Könemann, 2006), p. 60.
14. Catherine Cheremeteff Jones, *A Year of Russian Feasts* (Bethesda, MD: Jellyroll Press, 2002), pp. 164–65.

15. Trotter, p. 52.
16. http://visitperm.ru/en/kray/perm_cuisine/146.
17. http://visitperm.ru/en/kray/perm_cuisine/146.
18. Vinner, 'Dumplings Take Patience: History of Dumplings'.
19. Kovalev, p. 131; Josh Wilson with Andrei Nestorov, 'Pelmeni: A Tasty History', www.sras.org/pelmeni_history (1 January 2010).
20. Czapp. Although it might seem counterintuitive to make pasta out of sourdough, French pasta makers in the Middle Ages, and Italians in the sixteenth and seventeenth centuries, made pasta from fermented doughs, which were considered more flavorful and easier to digest. See Serventi, p. 178.
21. Anna Vinner, 'Dumplings Take Patience: Ural Pel'meni', http://pelemeni.ru/ural.html (28 August 2009).
22. See YouTube video of making pel'meni by hand http://www.youtube.com/watch?v=qAtdN1M1VFA (in English).
23. See YouTube video of making pel'meni with a pel'menitsa http://www.youtube.com/watch?v=8eq-jmFGp4o&feature=related (in Russian).
24. Siberian traditions included serving pel'meni in a large bowl, to honor their guests and welcome them to stay as long as they wanted; a small bowl meant that the host preferred them to leave (Vinner, 'Dumplings Take Patience: History of Dumplings'). In earlier times in Siberia, pel'meni served in broth were also considered an insult to guests, although this is no longer the case (Anna Vinner, 'Dumplings Take Patience: Siberian Pel'meni', http://pelemeni.ru/siberian.html [15 November 2009]).
25. Anna Vinner, 'Dumplings Take Patience: How to Serve Pel'meni', http://pelemeni.ru/how.html (15 April 2009).
26. *Kniga o vkusnoi i zdorovoi pishche* [Book of Tasty and Healthy Food] (Moscow, pishchepromizdat, 1955 edition), p. 103, p. 180, p. 241. Later editions, in 1984 and 1990, contained more recipes for *pel'meni*.
27. For example, E. V. Usacheva, *Sibirskaia Kukhnia* [Siberian Cooking] (Rostov-on-the-Don: Feniks, 2000) has more than 80 recipes for *pel'meni*, including *pel'meni* dough, *pel'meni* fillings, and *pel'meni* salads, omelets, casseroles and soups. Czapp, referencing *Russian Cuisine* by Mikhailov and Riurikova, notes that the first chapter, 'Siberia: Motherland of Pel'meni', has 20 pages of recipes for *pel'meni* fillings. Amazon.com currently lists 10 cookbooks, published in Russian since 2008, with '*pel'meni*' in their title.
28. The websites http://pelemeni.ru and http://www.ruspelmeni.ru contain dozens of recipes for *pel'meni*. Use Google Translate to convert them from Russian to English (note that Google translates 'pel'meni' as 'ravioli').
29. Jukka Gronow, *Caviar with Champagne: Common Luxury and the Ideals of the Good Life in Stalin's Russia* (Oxford: Berg, 2003), p. 55.
30. Anna Vinner, 'Dumplings Take Patience: Semi-finished Products', http://pelemeni.ru/semi_product.html (10 December 2009).
31. English Russia, 'How Pel'meni Are Made', http://englishrussia.com/2011/09/13/how-pelmeni-are-made/ (13 September 2011), with good photographs and descriptions of the industrial production of pel'meni in Russia. See also the YouTube video http://www.youtube.com/watch?NR=1&feature=endscreen&v=oUqjP8wog5w (in Russian).
32. English Russia: 'How Pel'meni Are Made'.
33. Interfax, 'Model of Chapel Made of Pel'meni in Krasnoiarsk', http://www.interfax-religion.ru/?act=mosaic&div=254 (28 March 2008).
34. See Ural'skie Pel'meni video on YouTube http://www.youtube.com/watch?v=ptBSqO1qTOs (in Russian, one of several videos of this popular comedy group posted on YouTube).
35. David Burn, 'Sex Sells "Your Favorite Little Pel'meni"': http://www.adpulp.com/sex_sells_your/ (5 October 2005), with a photo of this billboard. The sexual symbolism of the shape of pel'meni has long been noted by many commentators.
36. BBC News Europe 2010: 'Karaoke Champion Wins One Million Russian Dumplings', http://www.bbc.co.uk/news/world-europe-11413500#story_continues_1 (26 September 2010).

Yufka: Food For The Cook's Imagination

Priscilla Mary Işın

In 1433 a young pilgrim from Burgundy, Bertrandon de la Brocquière (1400–1459), separated from his companions in order to journey through Ottoman Turkey and visit Constantinople. In the mountains near Antakya, the ancient Antioch, he came across an encampment of Turcoman nomads, where he watched the women rolling out *yufka*:

> We halted among them; they placed before us one of the table-cloths before-mentioned, in which there remained fragments of bread, cheese, and grapes. They then brought us a dozen of thin cakes of bread, with a large jug of curdled milk, called by them *yogort*. The cakes are a foot broad, round, and thinner than wafers; they fold them up as grocers do their papers for spices, and eat them filled with the curdled milk... It was here I saw women make those thin cakes I spoke of. This is their manner of making them; they have a small round table, very smooth, on which they throw some flour, and mix it with water to a paste, softer than that for bread. This paste they divide into round pieces, which they flatten as much as possible, with a wooden roller of a smaller diameter than an egg, until they make them as thin as I have mentioned. During this operation they have a convex plate of iron placed on a tripod, and heated by a gentle fire underneath, on which they spread the cake and instantly turn it, so that they make two of their cakes sooner than a waferman can make one wafer.
>
> (Brocquière n.d.: 314–5)

Yufka is a circle of paper-thin pastry, rolled out using a long, thin rolling pin called an *oklava*. It belongs to a family of thin flatbreads whose roots go back thousands of years in western Asia. According to Anderson and Buell, most of the 'thin, tough sheets, suitable for wrapping food as dumplings or for cutting and cooking as phyllo dough, noodles, and pastas of all kinds... seem to date back at least to Greek Classical times, and may be older. Only phyllo is a relatively recent Turkic innovation, although one based upon much older precedents' (Anderson, Buell and Perry 2000: 67). It was in western Asia that hard wheat varieties rich in gluten developed, allowing dough to be rolled or stretched into thin sheets. Ibn Sayyâr al-Warrâq's tenth-century cookery book, written in Baghdad, lists an ordinary rolling pin for regular bread (*raghif*) and a special big rolling pin for the thin bread called *ruqaq* baked in a tandoor oven (Nasrallah 2007: 88). The wrapped *yufka* filled with yoghurt offered to Brocquière by his Turcoman hosts is a version of today's popular fast-food, bread wraps, known as *dürüm* in Turkey, that also go back at least a thousand years. Ibn Sayyâr al-Warrâq describes a filling of ground meat, spices, eggs and onion (Nasrallah 2007: 149–50).

Yufka: Food For The Cook's Imagination

Yufka is closely related to *ruqaq*, but is not baked on the walls of a tandır. *Yufka*s made at home for immediate consumption are not cooked at all until incorporated into the final dish for baking or frying, but if made for sale by professional *yufka*-makers they are briefly half-cooked on a domed griddle so that they can be piled up and kept in the shop for several hours without sticking together, then folded up and wrapped for customers to take home. In rural areas *yufka* is prepared as winter provisions by cooking on a griddle until dried out. These are stacked up in towers in a corner of the house, and, when needed, dampened to soften them.

Yufka is recorded in central Asia in the 1074 Turkish Arabic dictionary by the Turkish writer Mahmud of Kashgar, who mentions one variety of *yufka* (*yalaci yuga*) so fragile it crumbled at a touch (Mahmud al-Kāshgari 1984: vol. 2, 159, 165). The same author quotes a Turkish proverb about two crafty people up against one another: 'The mother is tricky she makes *yufka*; her son is clever, he steals them two by two' (Mahmud al-Kāshgari 1984: vol. 2, 164). Clearly *yufka* rolling has always been recognized as a feat of dexterity. In the seventeenth century the people of Urfa excelled at making *yufka*, and Evliya Çelebi likens their *yufka* cooked on a griddle to rose petals (Evliya Çelebi 1996–2007: vol. 3, 94).

In villages, rolling out *yufka* is an almost universal art, and in the old days most country boys were as adept at the task as their mothers. The nineteenth-century cookery book writer Mahmud Nedim, an infantry officer who was writing for fellow bachelors, told his readers that if they do not know how to roll out *yufka* themselves they should ask one of the private soldiers, 'most of whom know how to make *yufka*' (Işın 1999: 31; Mahmud Nedim 1998: 28). Rolling a dough of wheat flour and water to semi-transparent thinness and in a precise circle is one of the ultimate culinary skills that no machine can beat. Hacettepe University Hospital in Ankara specifies that the *yufka* must be hand-rolled in its purchasing regulations (*Yufka Hazır Teknik Şartnamesi*), and most Turkish housewives would rather change their menu than use the machine-rolled variety sold in some city supermarkets. Instead city dwellers who cannot be bothered or don't know how to roll their own rely on the local *yufkacı* (*yufka*-maker) shop, where they are rolled freshly every day.

The even thinner *yufka* for baklava used to be sold in local *yufka* shops in Istanbul (Mehmed Reşad 1921: vol. 3, 17); now, alas, you either have to make your own or use the much inferior factory-made variety. Rolling these out one by one is a task that takes time and experience. However, there is an easier method, developed by Ottoman pastry chefs and first recorded in 1838 by Friedrich Unger (Unger 2003: 103), by which each walnut-sized ball of pastry is first rolled to a saucer-sized circle, then piled up, sprinkling starch between each, and the whole pile rolled out simultaneously, producing 10–20 tissue-like sheets. This method is the one mainly used by professional baklava-makers today, and sometimes by home cooks. For this an ordinary thick rolling pin is used.

Rolling out with a long slender *oklava* is very different from using a short thick rolling pin. To create thin sheets of dough 50–90 cm in diameter, a small ball of dough (about the size of a walnut in its shell) is first pressed out into a circle. The pin is placed near the edge of the circle and the dough rolled up around it. The pin is rolled backwards and forwards a few times with the flat of the hand, applying gentle pressure, then the circle is unrolled with a flipping movement. This process is repeated about ten to fifteen times, each time turning the circle about 45 degrees clockwise or anticlockwise. Because the circle of dough is turned each time, a perfect circle is produced, and because the sheet is repeatedly rolled up around the pin, the thickness is even.

The joy of *yufka* lies in its endless versatility, which has fuelled the cook's imagination. Consequently the diversity of savoury *börek*s and baklava-style desserts, the two main categories of dishes made with *yufka*, has steadily increased over the centuries. It can be wrapped, rolled, spiralled and layered in a seemingly endless variety of shapes, around an equally endless variety of fillings, savoury and sweet. Hardly a meal can be had in Turkey that does not include *yufka* in some form or other, and to varying degree it features in cuisines throughout the Middle East and the Balkans.

Börek

The word *börek* derives from the Turkish verb *bürmek*, to roll or twist (Tietze 2002: 381). The earliest mention of *börek* is by Mevlana in the thirteenth century (Mevlânâ Celâleddin 1957: vol. 1, 379). Although it is not mentioned in Mahmud of Kashgar's eleventh-century dictionary, we know that the term was current in central Asia because of two recipes in fourteenth-century Chinese sources. The first of these, titled *Pärâk*, is in a Chinese dietary manual, the *Yin-Shan Cheng-Yao*, written by a Turkic physician, probably a Uighur, and presented to the emperor in 1330 (Anderson, Buell and Perry 2000: 3–4, 315). This *börek* is filled with a mixture of chopped mutton, sheep's fat, leeks and spices, and baked on a griddle. The recipe suggests bottle gourd as an alternative filling. A sweet version called *Chäkärli Piräk* (*şekerli börek*, i.e. börek with sugar) is found in another fourteenth-century Chinese source (Buell 1999: 219). Here the pastry is stuffed with ground walnuts, honey and an unidentifiable roasted ingredient, and cooked on the wall of a tandoor oven. The recipe specifies that the pastries should be shaped like *sanbusak*, suggesting that *börek*'s roots may lie in the *sanbusak* (triangular, filled pastries) of Safavid Iranian cuisine. *Sanbusak* passed into Abbasid-period Arab cuisine under the name the *sanbusaj* (Perry 2001, 151, 379; Nasrallah 2007: 190–2), into Indian cuisine as *samosa* and into Anatolian Turkish cuisine as *senbuse*, corrupted in the vernacular to *samsa*. As *senbuse*, it is first recorded in an early fourteenth-century Turkish source (Tutmacı 1960, s. 35) and the Turkish physician İbn-i Şerif, writing in the 1420s, explains that it is what is known as *samsa* in Turkish (2004, s. 445). *Samsa* with a sweet filling is still made in Turkey today. In the province of İsparta, for example, *samsa* filled with pistachios, walnuts and roasted chickpeas, fried and soaked in syrup are sent to in-laws on feast days (Koşay and Ülkücan 1961: 138). The triangular fried pastry made with savoury fillings and known today as *muska böreği*, after triangular shaped charms known as *muska*, is a kind of *senbuse*, but made by folding a long strip of thin *yufka* diagonally eight to ten times.

The Turkish *börek* has thrived, spawning a multitude of varieties. Sources dating from the sixteenth and seventeenth centuries, when Ottoman *haute cuisine* flowered, record *böreks* filled with minced meat, cheese, *kaymak* (clotted cream), anchovies, chicken, sheep's feet and all kinds of vegetables from foxtail lily (*Eremurus spectabilis*) to turnips. A *börek* made by palace cooks in the seventeenth century contained a filling of minced meat, onion, dried apricots, currants, dates, chestnuts and apple (Reindl-Kiel 2006: 74). In regional Turkish cuisines there are scores, if not hundreds, of different fillings. Shapes are almost as numerous: layered in huge circular baking tins or wrapped into crescents, bundles, triangles, rolls, and spirals. *Böreks* made with *yufka* became a part of the shared culinary heritage of peoples throughout the former Ottoman Empire and beyond, and the word has entered around twenty languages, including Arabic, Persian, Greek, Armenian, Russian and all the Balkan languages: 'Syrian and Egyptian *burak/bureik*, Tunisian *brik*, Algerian *braka*, Persian (from the fourteenth century), Greek, Armenian and Kalmuk Mongol' (Anderson, Buell and Perry 2000: 113).

Baklava and related sweet pastries

The earliest recipe for a desert recognizable as baklava is in the thirteenth-century Arabic cookery book *Kitab al Wusla ila al Habîb*, which gives the pastry both a Turkish name, *karnı yarık* ('split belly'), and an Arabic name *kul wa-shkur* ('eat and give thanks') (Perry 1993: 242). The Turkish term *tutmaç* is used for the thinly rolled pastry, a second indication of the recipe's Turkish origin. Each pastry sheet is wrapped around the rolling pin then pushed down the pin so that it concertinas into a wrinkled hollow roll; the method still used today for the baklava types known as *sarığı burma* (coiled turban), *bülbül yuvası* (nightingale's nest) and *tırtıl baklavası* (caterpillar baklava) or *vezir parmağı* (vizier's finger) (Ayşe Fahriye 1882: 213; Mahmud Nedim 1900: 159; Ertürk 1994: 32–48). One of the earliest Ottoman recipes for baklava, dating from the sixteenth or seventeenth centuries, uses this technique, arranging the ground-almond-filled rolls in the baking tin to form a spiral (Bayramoğlu 1988: 43). Probably because of the ground almond filling, this is called *baklava-ı acemi* (Persian-style baklava).

Folding and layering the tissue-thin pastry leaves is reflected in the terms *katlama* ('folded') and *katmer* ('layered') for sweet and savoury pastries in central Asia and Turkey. According to Perry, 'A pastry called *qatlama* is known among the Uzbeks, Kazakhs, Tatars, Bashkirs, Azarbayjanis and Turkmens, and the Uyghurs of Xinjiang Province, China' (Perry 1994: 89). As well as simple layering, the dough sheets may be piled up (brushing each with melted butter), then folded up, so multiplying the number of layers, and rolled out again (*katmerli* as made in Ardahan, described by Hanım Özdağ on 5 May 2012). Or a single dough-sheet may be folded lengthwise several times to form a long narrow rectangle, formed into a spiral, and rolled or pressed out again (*fesili* as made in Ardahan, described by Hanım Özdağ on 5 May 2012). An Ottoman recipe for a sweet pastry called *katmerli* again involves wrapping each *yufka* (made with a paste of flour, eggs and ash water) around the thin rolling pin and pushing it down to produce a corrugated roll (Mahmud Nedim 1998: 86). The roll is then removed from the pin, pressed with the fingers at the centre to form a small circle, rolled out again to the size of a medium plate, deep-fried and sprinkled with icing sugar or syrup.

The earliest recipes by the name 'baklava' are recorded in the above-mentioned Ottoman manuscript (Bayramoğlu 1988: 43–4). Two of these are made with individually rolled *yufka* and one with a type of puff pastry. One of the variations consists of the corrugated rolls described in the thirteenth-century *karnı yarık* recipe, again arranged in a spiral in the tray. The layered baklava is made with just eight *yufka*, whereas later recipes called for anything from sixteen to sixty layers (e.g. an eighteenth-century cookery book specifies forty layers, see Sefercioğlu 1985: 21; Mehmed Kâmil's 1844 cookery book 35–60 layers, see Mehmed Kâmil 1997: 47; and Türâbî Efendi 50 layers, see Türâbî Efendi 1864: 47).

From the late sixteenth century onwards the race was on among élite pastry chefs to create as many layers as possible. At the celebrations for the circumcision of Murad III's son, the future Mehmed III, in 1582, 'trays of many-layered baklava' were prepared (Prochazka-Eisl 1995: 85), and in the mid-seventeenth century Evliyâ Çelebi reported – with a generous measure of poetic hyperbole – that baklavas the size of cartwheels with a thousand layers each were baked in *tandır* (tandoor) ovens for wedding feasts in Belgrade (Evliyâ Çelebi 1996–2007: vol. 5, 199). Although the thousand layers must be a gross exaggeration, the importance attached to the number of layers is evident.

As the number of layers multiplied, baklava had to remain as light and crisp as ever, which was no mean feat. Baklava became a measure of culinary skill, tested by dropping a coin from a height onto the baklava, a test that is first mentioned by Evliyâ Çelebi in the mid-seventeenth century (Evliyâ Çelebi 1996–2007: vol. 5, 268). Only if the coin pierced every layer and struck the bottom of the baking tray did the baklava pass muster (Mahmud Nedim 1998: 165).

Some of the baklava types recorded in Ottoman cookery books have been forgotten today. Unusual fillings include puréed beans, musk melon and unsalted cheese (Sefercioğlu 1985: 31; Mehmed Kâmil 1997: 47). Although hot baklava with a fresh cheese filling has been forgotten in Istanbul, it is still made in other places, such as the south-eastern Turkish city of Urfa, where it is known as *katmer*, and in the town of Yalvaç in central Turkey, where it is known as *peynir baklavası* (cheese baklava) (*Yöresel Yalvaç Yemekleri* 2011: 183). The old fashioned method of cooking baklava over a charcoal fire rather than an oven has also been preserved in Yalvaç and is said to give a finer flavour. Ordinary baklava may be eaten hot or cold, hot being more usual in the past, but when made with cheese it has to be eaten hot, since if allowed to cool the cheese becomes leathery.

Gaziantep-style *katmer* is made by rolling out a sheet of dough to 30–40 cm in diameter, then stretching it by holding the edge of the dough and throwing it to left and then right in a swinging movement. Holding the edge at different points each time, the dough is swung until it is almost transparent, a process called *savrulma* (Tokuz 2002:

273). The individual *yufka* are then folded envelope-fashion over a filling of clotted cream or ground pistachios and semolina custard. The former is fried, while the latter is baked.

The method of stretching dough over a sheet as used for strudel and Greek phyllo does not appear to have been used in Turkey until the late Ottoman period (Mehmed Reşad 1921: III 17).

Ingredients of the dough

Yufka for *börek* is basically made of flour, water and salt alone, which are the ingredients of shop-made *yufka*. However, historical and regional recipes often include eggs and/or 'ash water' (*küllü su*) (as for example Mehmed Reşad 1921: III 25 and Mahmud Nedim 1998: 87). Ash water, which used to be used as a rising agent but has now largely been replaced by baking powder, was made by stirring some clean wood ash (preferably oak) into water (about 1 part in 10, but recipes vary wildly) and leaving it until the ash settles. Then the clear water is carefully poured off so as not to disturb the sediment. Since it contains potassium carbonate rather than sodium carbonate, ash water is said to result in a pleasanter flavour (Üçer 2006: 212). For baklava the basic dough is made of flour, eggs and sometimes yoghurt. In the past ash water was occasionally added (Mahmud Nedim 1998: 159, 164).

Bibliography

Anderson, E.N., Paul D. Buell and Charles Perry, 2000. *A Soup for the Qan: Chinese Dietary Medicine of the Mongol Era as Seen in Hu Sihui's Yinshan Zhengyao*. Sir Henry Wellcome Asian Series. London: Kegan Paul International.

Ayşe, Fahriye, 1882. *Ev Kadını*. Istanbul, AH 1300/1882–83.

Bayramoğlu, Fuat, 1988. 'Türk Mutfağı ve Yazılı Kaynaklar', *Birinci Milletlerarasi Yemek Kongresi, Türkiye, 25–30 Eylül 1986* (Ankara): pp. 38–49.

de la Brocquière, Bertrandon. n.d. 'The Travels of Bertrandon de la Brocquière 1432, 1433', in Thomas Wright (ed.), *Early Travels in Palestine*, London.

Buell, Paul D, 1999. 'Mongol Empire and Turkicization: The Evidence of Food and Foodways', in Reuven Amitai-Preiss and David O. Morgan (eds.), *The Mongol Empire and its Legacy*. Leiden, Boston and Köln.

Ertaylan, İsmail Hikmet (ed.), 1960. *Tabiatnâme*. Istanbul.

Ertürk, Necip, 1994. *Türk Tatlı Sanatı*, 4th edn. Istanbul: Remzi Kitabevi.

Evliyâ, Çelebi, 1996–2007. *Evliyâ Çelebi Seyahatnâmesi*, 10 vols., eds. Seyit Ali Kahraman, Yücel Dağlı, Robert Dankoff *et al.* Istanbul.

İbn-i Şerif, 2003. *Yâdigâr, 15. Yüzyıl Türkçe Tıp Kitabı*, 2 vols, eds. Ayten Altıntaş, Yahya Okutan, Doğan Koçer and Mecit Yıldız. Istanbul, 2003–2004.

Işın, Priscilla Mary, 1999. 'A Nineteenth Century Ottoman Gentleman's Cookbook', *Petits Propos Culinaires*, 61.

Koşay, Hâmit, and Akile Ülkücan, 1961. *Anadolu Yemekleri ve Türk Mutfağı*. Ankara.

Mahmud Nedim bin Tosun, 1998. *Aşçıbaşı*, ed. Priscilla Mary Işın. Istanbul: 1998.

Mahmud al-Kāshgari, 1984. *Compendium of the Turkic Dialects (Dīwān Luγāt at-Turk)*, 3 vols, ed. and transl. Robert Dankoff in collaboration with James Kelly. Cambridge, MA: Harvard University Press.

Mevlânâ Celâleddin, 1957. *Dîvân-ı Kebîr*, transl. Abdülbâki Gölpınarlı. İstanbul: Remzi Kitabevi.

Mehmed Kâmil, 1997. *Melceü't-Tabbâhîn (Aşçıların Sığınağı)*, ed. Cüneyt Kut. Istanbul.

Mehmed Reşad, 1921. *Fenn-i Tabâhat*, 4 vols. Istanbul: H. 1340/1921–22.

Nasrallah, Nawal, 2007. *Annals of the Caliphs' Kitchens: Ibn Sayyâr al-Warrâq's Tenth Century Baghdadi Cookbook*. Leiden and Boston: Brill.

Perry, Charles, 1992. 'Early Turkish Influence on Arab and Iranian Cuisine', *Dördüncü Milletlerarası Yemek Kongresi*. Konya, 1993. pp. 241–244

Perry, Charles, 1994. 'The Taste for Layered Bread among the Nomadic Turks and the Central Asian Origins of Baklava', in Sami Zubaida and Richard Tapper (eds.), *Culinary Cultures of the Middle East*. London: I.B. Tauris.

Prochazka-Eisl, Gisela, 1995. *Das Surnâme-i Hümâyûn*. Istanbul.

Reindel-Kiel, Hedda, 2006. 'Cennet Taamları', *Soframiz Nur Hanemiz Mamur*, eds. Suraiya Faroqhi and Christoph K. Neumann. Istanbul. pp. 55–110.

Sefercioğlu, M. Nejat, 1985. *Türk Yemekleri XVIII. Yüzyıla Ait Yazma Bir Yemek Risalesi*. Ankara.

Tietze, Andreas, 2002. *Tarihi ve Etimolojik Türkiye Türkçesi Lugatı / Sprachgeschichtliches und Etymologisches Wörterbuch des Türkei-Türkischen*, vol. 1 (A-E). Istanbul and Wien.

Tokuz, Gonca, 2002. *Gaziantep ve Kilis Mutfak Kültürü*. Gaziantep.

Türâbî Efendi 1864. *Turkish Cookery Book*. London, n.d. [1864].

Unger, Friedrich, 2003. *A King's Confectioner in the Orient*, ed. Priscilla Mary Işın, tr. Merete Çakmak and Renate Ömeroğulları. London.

Üçer, Müjgân, 2006. *Anamın Aşı Tandırın Başı - Sivas Mutfağı*. Istanbul.

Yöresel, Yalvaç, 2011. *Yemekleri*, Yalvaç Belediyesi. Isparta.

Yufka Hazır Teknik Şartnamesi 2012: http://www.hastane.hacettepe.edu.tr/Satinalma/ihaleler%28pazarlik%29/2012–114.htm [accessed 24 September 2012]

From Lettuce to Fish Skin: Koreans' Appetite for Wrapped and Stuffed Foods

Jin Kyung Kim

Wrapping is one of the best loved and most enjoyed practices in Korean cuisine, and wrapping with raw vegetables is an eating habit that has long been a part of Korean food culture. The most common kind of wrapping as an eating method is called *ssam* (wrap). Basic *ssam* is made by placing a wide piece of raw, leafy green vegetable, for example lettuce, on your palm, putting some cooked rice and sauce onto the lettuce and folding the leaf into a small parcel. This wrapped food is then eaten in one delicious mouthful.

This paper will describe the ingredients and methods most commonly used in Korean cuisine for wrapped and stuffed food. It will also explore regional, seasonal and traditional methods of wrapping and stuffing that have long been used in Korea. The appendix includes a glossary of Korean culinary words and terms used in this paper.

As mentioned before, *ssam* loosely translates as 'wrap'. So when a word contains *ssam*, it means that the dish is wrapped one way or another. For example, persimmon *ssam* is semi-dried persimmon with walnuts, either stuffed or wrapped, and then sliced and served with tea as a snack, or placed into the traditional *SuJungGua*, a sweet ginger and cinnamon drink, or into alcoholic beverages.

Ssam is not an accidental way of eating rice and vegetables together. In the olden days, Koreans believed good fortune could be wrapped, hence the common use of *BoJaGi*, which is a piece of squared cloth made to wrap anything from food to gifts. *BoJaGi* comes in various sizes and various fabrics are used, from cotton to silk; it is widely used by all social classes. This wrapping in cloth symbolizes a traditional belief in wrapping blessings and wrapping good fortune. *BoJaGi* is also called *Bo*, which sounds similar to the Korean word *Bok* (luck). Wrapped foods are believed to have their origins in this belief system, which was extensively practiced in Korean culture. Koreans once had faith that consuming wrapped food, i.e. eating good fortune, would actually bring good luck. The *ssam* marriage of cooked rice, the staple food of Korea, and wrapping was perhaps inevitable. Edible plants have long been used as one medium to fulfil people's desires to bring luck, blessings and wealth to their household.

On *DaeBoReum*, the first full moon of the year (15 January, according to the lunar calendar), Koreans celebrate the full moon and prepare special dishes to eat. *O-KokBap* (cooked five grains with rice) is one of the signature dishes eaten on this particular day (literally Great Full Moon).[1] Along with *O-KokBap*, another special treat of the day is *bokssam*, which literally means 'good fortune wrap'. Traditionally, *bokssam* is made with

Koreans' Appetite for Wrapped and Stuffed Foods

Chinese cabbage leaves, *Chwi* (a plant from the wild aster family) and/or wild sesame leaves. In coastal areas, *Gim* (dried laver sheet) is used to make *bokssam* as well. On the morning of the full moon, *bokssam* wraps are prepared and stacked up so they resemble rice sheaves. The piled *bokssam* is first offered to the Household God, asking her to bless the family with good harvests that year, and then those wraps are eaten for breakfast. *Bokssam* is also called *MyungSsam* ('live long wrap') as people believed it would extend life.[2] Although modern Koreans no longer depend on agriculture as much as in the past and thus may no longer be as interested in such symbolic meanings and belief rituals, Great Full Moon Day food traditions are still practised.

In the early 1900s poem, 'Lettuce *Ssam*', the poet Yoon Choi humorously describes the physical feeling of eating *ssam* everyday. He describes *ssam* as a wrapped food that is consumed in one mouthful with the eyes half-closed to help open one's mouth wider. Contemporary Koreans would understand what he means, as everyone has this experience when eating *ssam*. However, during the *ChoSun* period (from the fourteenth to nineteenth centuries), the upper class considered it 'improper' to make *ssam* too big and to open one's mouth overly wide to consume it. It is still considered ill-mannered to stuff yourself with *ssam*. However, sometimes friends will make and offer each other super-sized *ssam* as a prank.

Ssam is a popular dish all year around but especially in spring and summer when there is an abundance of young tender leaves that can be eaten raw. During the summer, when it is hot and humid, lettuce is the most favoured of *ssam* vegetables because it is a refreshing, cooling and energizing food suited to the season. But it is not only wide-leafed vegetables that are used for *ssam*. *Minari* (water dropwort or mugwort) and *sukgat* (crown daisy), which are chive-like narrow leaf vegetables, are commonly used as well. In a seventeenth century scholarly publication, Lee Ik observes that '*ChoSun* people would use any leafy vegetable for *ssam*'.[3] So, basically any vegetable that can be put on one's palm and made into a wrap has been adapted for *ssam* by Koreans.

From the basic, usually lettuce-based, *ssam*, there are many variations for different regions, seasons and holidays. Commonly growing plants like lettuce, sesame leaves and mugwort are chosen for *ssam*, as it is eaten by both working and upper class people. In the past, pumpkins were often grown along fences and in backyards. As a result, pumpkin leaves were an everyday vegetable that could be easily picked, steamed and used as *ssam* greens at home. In modern Korea, steamed pumpkin leaves are sold at many supermarkets. Importantly, not all vegetables are used raw for *ssam*. Fermented foods like *kimchi* (Korea's famous pickled cabbage) is also used for *ssam*, as well as steamed leaves (like pumpkin leaves), thinly-sliced *Mu* (Korean radish) marinated in vinegar and sugar, and blanched vegetables. Even thinly-sliced roots, like beet, which is a non-traditional vegetable for Koreans, are now used for *ssam*, either raw or cooked.

In addition to local plants, the easy accessibility of seafood means various sea vegetables are used for *ssam*, such as *MiYeok* (sea mustard), *DaShiMa* (kelp) and other regional leafy seaweeds. Further inland, some farming areas even use green tea leaves

Koreans' Appetite for Wrapped and Stuffed Foods

as a component of *ssam*. Edible flowers, herbs like coriander, and even small flour or buckwheat crepes can also be used for *ssam*.

Ssam is always accompanied by an appropriate sauce, according to one's taste and the availability of condiments. The base of this sauce is *GoChuJang* (red chilli paste), *DoenJang* (soy bean paste) and/or soy sauce. *Ssam* vegetables can be simple but the sauce can be quite elaborate and use beef, honey, fish, shrimp or other seafood and meats. In Korean palace cuisine, for example, several different sauces were served with *ssam*.[4]

Ssam was a staple of the royal menu when Korea was a monarchy, indicating that it was enjoyed by the aristocracy and upper classes. According to Han Bok Lyeo's *Royal Cuisine and Seoul Food*, different *ssam* sauces made from seafood and meats and a small bowl of sesame seed oil accompanied the king's meal.[5] Basic *ssam* vegetables, such as lettuces, *ssukgat* and young spring onions with meat or fish would be included in the dish, and a few drops of sesame oil would be added to the *ssam* for a fuller flavour. After the meal, they would drink cinnamon bark tea to balance out the cooling energy of lettuces with the warming energy of tea.[6] The common people's *ssam* meal may not have been as elaborate as the king's, but it was also greatly enjoyed. A nineteenth-century song describes a *ssam* meal eaten by labourers sitting beside a field at mid-day after a hard morning's work. The *ssam* meal described in the lyrics involves cooked barley (not rice, then an expensive grain) and soup with plain chilli paste sauce for the wrap. So, *ssam* was appreciated by all levels of Korean society, from the coast to the mountains to the plains.

Ssam has usually been consumed at home, but in south Korea today *ssam* is served everywhere from high-end restaurants to inexpensive eateries. In a recent episode of the TV cooking program *Korean Confidential*, which screens on Arirang (the English-language channel in South Korea), an Australian chef working at Seoul's Intercontinental Hotel cooks and artistically plates his version of *SsamBap* (wrapped rice). He uses kelp, *kimchi* and cabbage with three varieties of seasoned rice to present his dish. In contrast, *SamGyeopSal* (pork belly barbecue) is a popular Korean menu item for dining on a budget. Sliced pork belly is always accompanied with lettuces and sesame leaves, refilled constantly while dining. Some restaurants offer over twenty different vegetables with pork belly barbecue, including non-traditional *ssam* vegetables such as collard, chicory, chard and radicchio. *Ssam* can be eaten at home or out, either at low cost or pricey restaurants, which shows Koreans' fondness for the dish.

This fondness for wrapping also comes from the everyday utensils – chopsticks. The traditional dish *GuJeolPan* has nine different delicacies that are wrapped in small crepes, made with flour and water batter, or thinly sliced Korean radish, just before eating. One needs good chopstick skills, otherwise the whole wrap could fall apart while dipping in sauce and eating it. Chopsticks make wrapping useful, and many ingredients can be used to wrap rice or other fillings. *GwaMeGi*, a regional food of KyungSang (in the south-east) now eaten nationally, is salted herring or saury, hung to cold-dry during winter. *GwaMeGi* is served with sea mustard, *gim*, kelp and/or sesame leaves, spring onion heads, chilli, sliced garlic and a sweet-and-sour red chilli paste sauce. A piece of fish is wrapped with any or all of the above ingredients using chopsticks. *BoSsam* is another unique dish that combines meat and vegetables and requires chopstick wrapping skills. Pork is cooked and served with a wrapping vegetable, such as lettuce or quick sweet-and-sour pickled Chinese cabbage, along with something spicy, like dried radish seasoned with chilli paste or seasoned oysters. Again, the pork piece is wrapped, using chopsticks, inside the vegetable leaf.

Some dishes combine fish and meat in a wrapping. Skate is one of the signature fish caught in the Western Sea of the Korean peninsula, and most skate is fermented to give the fish's flesh a firmer bite and a well-rounded tang. Fermented skate is then eaten as is or cooked. Uncooked, skate is often served with braised pork and *kimchi* in a dish called *SamHap*; diners wrap the skate and pork with *kimchi* at the table.

In addition to fillings, fish can serve as wrappings too. Fish skin may seem an odd ingredient to use, but it is a delicacy occasionally used in elaborate cooking. One of the most widely used fish in Korean cuisine is *MyungTae* (Alaskan pollock). It is often cold-dried during the winter and used all year. Fish is used for soups, stews, frying and in many other ways. Using dried *myungtae* skin for wrapping creates a gourmet dish only served on rare events. The skin of dried fish is carefully peeled off and steamed with a meat and vegetable stuffing. Dried fish skin was once used in palace and upper-class cuisine and is still used in South Korea's high-end restaurants. The fish skin enclosing julienned *Minari*, chestnut, *DaeChu* (jujube) and Korean pear provides a crunchy texture and sweetness to the chewy wrap. It is dipped in mustard sauce to give spiciness, or in soy sauce with vinegar for a milder flavour. In the very popular TV series *DaeJangGuem*, the story of a sixteenth-century palace kitchen court lady, *myungtae* skin wrap is served to the king. Such upscale dishes seem surprising even to Koreans used to everyday *ssam*.

MyungTae is not the only fish whose skin is used for wrapping. *ImYeanSu* (mackerel) is also used, as its skin is thick and flavourful. *SunngEo* (mullet) is another popular fish in Korean cooking. (*Sunngeo*'s eggs are used to make the gourmet delicacy of cured roe, *EoRan*.) Mullet skin is not a notable cooking ingredient, but its skin is used for *ssam* in the western regions of Korea. There is an old saying: 'West sea people go bankrupt eating mullet's skin wrap and Kang Won province fishermen sell their ship to eat mackerel skin wrap'.[7] It is also said that, '*ImYeanSu* (mackerel) skin wrap is so tasty that you don't share it with anyone, not even your mistress'. Such folk wisdom shows that fish skin wrap was a pricy delicacy, but one so tasty that working-class fishermen consumed it even while upper-class men tried to keep it all to themselves.

Some wrappings even enclose themselves. *KangHoe* is blanched spring onion and/or *minari* wrapped into a bite-sized portion; both ingredients are used when they are young and tender. The spring onion is blanched whole and then wrapped small, then dipped into a sauce of sweet-and-sour chilli paste. From this basic wrapping, other ingredients like beef, seafood, or eggs (known as *JiDan*) can be combined and wrapped. If eggs are used, the white and yolk are separated, pan fried and cut into serving portions.

Koreans' Appetite for Wrapped and Stuffed Foods

Ssam usually refers to greens and other foods wrapped at the table by diners, but wrapping is also a cooking method. The lotus flower symbolizes Buddhism, and in Korea Buddhist culture is often a metaphor for what a person should be. Hence, cooking with lotus represents more than food, and Koreans use lotus leaves to wrap and cook rice. A mixture of grains and nuts (rice, sweet rice, black rice, pine nuts, chestnuts, walnuts and red dates) are wrapped in parcel form with fresh lotus leaves and steamed. This cooked wrap is served and unwrapped at the table. Its cultural meaning, nutritional value and flavour make lotus leaf-wrapped rice a signature dish at restaurants specializing in 'temple food', and a popular menu item at traditional restaurants as well as being in world-wide demand in online sales.

Lotus is a plant greatly favoured in Korean Buddhist cuisine because the whole plant can be used in cooking. Lotus root is a uniquely shaped firm vegetable with several holes that is often used in traditional cooking as well. Rice cooked in lotus root is a colourful dish made with sweet rice dyed or mixed with edible, plant-based food colouring. Coloured rice is stuffed into each root hole, and the entire root is steamed. The cooked root is then sliced, showing various shades of rice, and usually served as a side dish for everyone to share rather than in individual portions as plain rice is served. In Korean cuisine, stuffing is an easy method to use and employed in a broad range of foods from savoury to sweet.

Stuffing rice into a vessel-like plant, durable enough to hold its shape for rice cooking, is done with bamboo stalk as well. The stalk is cut into small lengths, and a mixture of different types of rice – brown, sweet and black – are combined with chestnuts, ginkgo seeds, red dates and sometimes ginseng, then stuffed into the stalks, which are covered with cooking paper and steamed. Cooked bamboo stalk rice is served as is, one per person, and uncovered at the table.

Like many other meat-eating cultures, Korea has its own version of sausage, *SunDae*. There are two basic types of *SunDae*: a blood sausage-like *SunDae*, which is still made in southern part of Korea (especially on JeJu Island), and stuffed *SunDae* made using grains and vegetables. The basic method of making *SunDae* is simple: mix preferred ingredients, stuff a natural casing with the mixture and cook. Depending on the region, household, cook and ingredients, *SunDae* tastes different.

SunDae is often handmade with grains such as rice, sweet rice and millet, along with vegetables and traditional herbs like bean sprouts, leek, garlic, sesame leaves, garlic chives, ginger and others combined with minced meat and blood. Cooked *SunDae* is dipped in sauces made with chilli powder, shrimp sauce, soy sauce or bean paste before eating. In some regions, over twenty different ingredients are put into the stuffing, often including regional produce like ginseng, bonnet bellflower roots and even apples. Making premium quality *SunDae* takes skill, time and effort. Although it is labour intensive, there are restaurants around the country that still serve handmade *SunDae* made from secret recipes. Many chefs try to keep the traditional, higher quality products, and plenty of consumers are keen to pay more to taste authentic *SunDae*.

Koreans' Appetite for Wrapped and Stuffed Foods

From this stuffed food, Koreans can enjoy a platter of various *SunDaes* or *SunDae* soup, stir fry or stew.

In modern Korea, modified *SunDae* is commercially available, made with glass noodle stuffing rather than grains and vegetables because it is cheaper and less labour intensive. Another modification is that artificial casings are used, which has made *SunDae* more accessible to a larger proportion of the population. Contemporary *SunDae* does not represent regional variations and has grown into one of the most popular street foods. *SunDae* is so loved that an area in Seoul, SilRimDong, is famous as the hub of *SunDae*. And *SunDae* continues to evolve as chefs experiment with imported ingredients such as cheese.

The casing for traditional *SunDae* varies; it is not limited to pig, cow or other farmed animals' edible intestines. Squid is frequently used. Squid *SunDae* is a gourmet food, mostly handmade at restaurants. The fresh squid body is stuffed with cooked ground meat, diced squid legs, bean curd, onions, garlic and other vegetables, closed up and cooked, usually steamed. Squid has long been the most favoured seafood for making *SunDae* in the KangWon area, while Alaskan pollack is preferred in HamKyung. There, fresh pollack is gutted and cleaned to keep the whole fish shape. Pollack *SunDae* taste better when made with fresh fish but can also be made with frozen ones (frozen pollack needs to be thawed before use). When cooking with whole pollack, the fish is gutted through the gill and stuffed with cooked meat (usually pork), vegetables, bean curd and some pollack intestine, and cooked. In winter, fresh pollack *SunDae* was hung outside to freeze and then cooked whenever needed.

Fish and seafood *SunDae* are fine foods, but there is another *SunDae* delicacy made with a still more unusual casing – fish air bladder. *MinEo* (croaker) has been eaten as a summer fish in Korea for centuries. *MinEo's* air bladder, *BuRae*, has been used as top grade natural glue for traditional handcrafts such as bow-making and mother-of-pearl lacquer work. This fish organ is gelatinous, durable and chewy in texture, which makes it suitable as a *SunDae* casing. The full-grown croaker fish can weigh as much as 20 kg, so its air bladder is big enough to stuff with vegetables like cucumber, bean curd, minced beef, bean sprouts and water dropwort. Each end is tied up before cooking. It is no longer easy to find this delicacy, but Koreans' appetite for stuffed food means that an innovative chef is bound to find new casings.

On Korea's Harvest Day, *ChuSok* (one of the major Korean traditional holidays, also known as *HanGaWii*), the main dish is a rice cake called *SongPyun*. What makes *ChuSok*'s *SongPyun* special is that they are made with newly-harvested rice. Grains of rice are powdered and made into dough to use as the wrapper. The wrapper is then stuffed with a mixture of sesame seeds, red beans, mung beans, honey, cinnamon powder and/or chestnuts. *SongPyun* is either stuffed or not: the absence of filling is symbolic, reminding people to be generous and be open minded; stuffed ones urge people to be lively and grateful. *SongPyun* is shaped like small seashells or flowers, made with a variety of colours (yellow, green, pink, deep purple or brown) created from natural food colourings. Traditionally, *SongPyun* is steamed with pine needles to add more flavour and to prevent them from sticking to each other.

Another traditional food made on special occasions and on traditional holidays is *Tteok* (rice cake). Either savoury or sweet, it is made with powdered grains, mostly rice and glutinous rice flour. *Tteok* can be steamed, boiled, pan-fried or even deep-fried. *Tteok* often contains a sweet stuffing. One sweet *Tteok* is called *Bukkumi*, which is made with a glutinous rice or *susu* (millet) flour dough stuffed with honey, nuts, cinnamon and sweetened red bean. Its cooking method is a cross between wrapping and stuffing. The dough is kneaded, made into flat rounded shapes and pan fried with oil. The stuffing is placed in the middle and the 'skin' is folded into a half-moon shape. Then the *Bukkumi* is coated with syrup or honey for serving. In the past, *Bukkumi*'s stuffing was also savoury, using vegetables and Korean herbs. *Bukkumi* was made into different colours and used as a garnish for *Tteok*, being placed on top of a bigger portion of rice cake. Another *Tteok* made for special purpose garnishing is *juAk*. It is a smaller and colourful version of *SongPyon*, with sweet stuffing like jujube, cinnamon powder, honey and sesame seeds or preserved fruits. It is deep- or pan-fried, dipped into honey while hot and used to garnish other flat rice cakes.

ManDu (Korean dumpling), an easily-made and handy-to-eat wrapped food, is one of the most popular stuffed foods in Korean cuisine. *ManDu*'s skin, which wraps the stuffing, is simple flour dough. Flour is now an everyday ingredient, but in the past flour was a very rare, pricey ingredient that could only be obtained by the wealthy since Koreans did not cultivate wheat. Therefore, a bowl of *ManDu* soup once represented wealth and power. Thinly rolled out *ManDu* skin was stuffed with finely chopped meat like pheasant, beef or pork as well as vegetables such as mushrooms, bean curd and kimchi. Regional location, as well as the season and shape of *ManDu*, also determined stuffing ingredients. There is the common half-moon shaped *ManDu* as well as the parcel-like *ManDu*, which is eaten in summer with cold stock. Sea cucumber-shaped *ManDu* (*GuASan*), with cucumber stuffing, used to be prepared as a summer dish in the court. There was even *ManDu* within *ManDu* to keep the *ManDu* warm and moist, when banquets were held outdoors. As Koreans believed and hoped that fortune could be wrapped, *ManDu* was a special food for feasts, banquets and New Year's Day celebrations.

Today, prepared *ManDu* are cooked in many different ways, which also contributes to its popularity. *ManDu* can be steamed, put into soup with a rice cake, made into stew, pan fried and even deep fried. Now, a variety of *ManDu* can be easily bought at supermarkets, restaurants and even on the street as a snack. In South Korea's cities, you can easily spot casual *ManDu* restaurants, which have skilled chefs demonstrating their *ManDu*-making via big windows facing busy streets to attract customers. Frozen *ManDu* is a 280 billion Korean-won (approximately £152 million) per-year business.[8] This instant food is often accused of being one of the contributors to contemporary obesity and unhealthy lifestyles that cause many illnesses. However, since making

Koreans' Appetite for Wrapped and Stuffed Foods

ManDu at home from scratch takes time and effort, many Koreans continue to consume frozen *ManDu*. *ManDu*'s wrapper can also be made with fish fillets. Fish *ManDu*, *EoManDu*, was once a delicacy made at the court. It took great skill to fillet fish to act as a wrapper and hold the stuffing. *ManDu*'s wrapper can also be made with potatoes and leafy vegetables, like cabbage, that can contain stuffing during the making and cooking process. No matter what is used as a wrapper, it is the stuffing's ingredients which contribute to the taste of *ManDu*. That is why Koreans say to 'stuff' *ManDu*, not 'wrap' *ManDu*.

For food-makers from domestic cooks to professional chefs, wrapping and stuffing is a traditional technique that is still widely practised in South Korea. As in previous centuries, today stuffed and wrapped foods can be savoury or sweet and are enjoyed by all levels of society, whether as cheap street food or as expensive restaurant cuisine. *Bokssam* is a wrapping to celebrate the first full moon, and to wish for good fortune in the coming (lunar) year. Hence, consuming wrapped food (*ssam*) has the symbolic meaning of bringing prosperity and good luck into people's households. The wide variety of wrapped and stuffed foods, from savoury dishes to sweets, from simple to lavish meals, from treats to garnishes, tell us that wrapped and stuffed food and cooking methods still are an important part of Korean culinary heritage and cuisine. While wrapping and stuffing are still a daily practice in Korean cuisine, many Koreans are no longer aware of its cultural and historical significance. Despite being unaware of these long-established traditional eating and cooking customs, their fondness for these delicious dishes remains.

Appendix 1: Glossary of Korean culinary words and terms

Bo or *BoJaGi*: squared wrapping cloth made of cotton or silk, plain or elaborately embroidered. Used for gift wrapping, rituals, weddings, to carry items and to cover food, to name but a few functions.

Bok: luck, good fortune, prosperity.

BukKuMi: a type of *Tteok* (rice cake). Often made with rice and sweet rice-dough with sweet fillings.

BokSsam: wrapping prepared for the celebration of the full moon according to the lunar calendar. It was used to wish for good fortune.

BuRae: air bladder of *MinEo*. Used as casing to make special sausage.

ChuSok: Korean harvest day in Fall. One of the biggest traditional celebrations.

Chwi: wild Aster leaves are used to make side dish and wrapper.

DaeBoreum: celebration of the first full moon of the year.

DaeChu: Korean date, jujube or red date. Eaten raw or dried.

DaShiMa: kelp.

EoManDu: dumpling made with fish fillet as the wrapper.

EoRan: seasoned and dried fish roe in whole, one of the more favoured delicacies.

Gim: dried sea laver sheets

GottGamSsam: dried persimmon stuffed with walnuts.

GuASang: summer dumpling shaped like sea cucumber.

GuJeolPan: platter of nine delicacies with small crepes to wrap the delicacies.

GwaMeGi: cold dried herring or mackerel pike.

HanGaWii: see *ChuSok*.

ImYeanSu: mackerel.

Koreans' Appetite for Wrapped and Stuffed Foods

JiDan: egg whites and yolks are beaten separately and thinly pan-fried.
JuAk: garnishing rice cake, pan fried or deep dried stuffed with nuts and honey.
KangHoe: blanched spring onion or *minari*, wrapped to a bite size.
KimChi: fermented vegetables.
ManDu: Korean dumpling.
MinEo: brown croaker.
MinNaRi: water dropwort or mugwort.
MiYeok: sea mustard.
Mu: Korean radish. It's bigger than usual radish sold in western countries.
MyungSsam: see *BokSsam*.
MyungTae: walleye pollock.
O-KokBap: five different grains and beans with rice.
SamGyopSal: pork belly cut. Often sliced and barbecued. Whole cut can be poached or braised.
Ssam: general name for wrapped food or wrapping.
SsamBap: cooked rice wrapped with vegetables.
SaamHap: combination of braised pork, skate and *kimchi*.
SongPyun: signature rice cake made on *HanGaWi*, Korean harvest.
SukGat: crown daisy.
SuJungGua: sweet beverage made of ginger and cinnamon.
SunDae: Korean sausage.
SunngEo: flathead mullet.
SuSu: millet.
Tteok: rice cake made with powdered rice and sweet rice. Dough stuffed with nuts, beans and sweetener like sugar or honey.

Notes

1. Rice, sweet rice, red beans, millet, barley and any other regional grains are cooked and eaten all day.
2. Kim Yong Suk, *Encyclopaedia of Traditional Medicine at Home* (Pulroyokeunjip, 2009).
3. DongA: http://news.donga.com/3/all/20110420/36579706/1.
4. Han Bok Lyeo, *Royal Cuisine and Seoul Food* (Daewonsa, 2004).
5. Han.
6. Han Bok Jin, *100 Dishes We Need to Know* (Hyunamsa, 2000).
7. National Fisheries Research Development Institute: http://portal.nfrdi.re.kr/bbs?id=lit&flag=pre&boardIdx=403.
8. StyleM News: http://stylem.mt.co.kr/styview.php?no=2011120616194529136&type=1.

The Most Frugal of the Phyllo-wrapped Pies (or How to Feed a Crowd with a Handful of Meat)

Aglaia Kremezi

I consider *pites* – the traditional thin, phyllo-wrapped pies of all kinds – as the eastern Mediterranean equivalent to a sandwich, where both pastry and filling play an equally important role in creating delicious, crunchy and nourishing dishes. Pies as we know them today seem to be closely related to the Roman *placenta* that Cato describes in detail as alternating sheets of dough and crumbled cheese mixed with honey.[1] The top and bottom layers, the casing of the *placenta*, were made with fine flour and brushed with olive oil, while the intermediate sheets of dough were kneaded with a mixture of flour and 'emmer groats'.[2] Ilaria Gozzini Giacosa mixes couscous with flour in her modern interpretation of the Roman dish which she calls '*Torta* with Cheese and Honey'.[3] Interestingly enough in Romania *plăcintă* is the word for a common cheese-filled skillet pie. But there seem to be other variations closer to Cato's ancient dish.[4] A young American-Romanian blogger from Montana gives the recipe for *plăcintă de branza* – she calls it 'Cheese *Burek*' or 'Cheese Filled Phyllo pie'.[5] Like the original *placenta*, it has alternating layers of dough. In her modern interpretation she uses commercial phyllo and a filling of feta and cottage cheese with eggs. Being in America she brushes the phyllo with butter, not olive oil. She writes, 'My dad often remembers eating this type of cheese pie (*placinta de branza*) in Romania, at bakery shops, called "*Placintarii*". He would stop by a bakery shop and buy a piece. However big you wanted...they would cut it, place it on the scale, and weigh it for you'. Similar layered cheese pies (*tyropita*) are common in central and northern Greece, and of course in Turkey (*Börek* or *burek*).

Rolling phyllo

Placenta, the ancient layered bread and cheese/honey dish, was probably very different from the modern Eastern Mediterranean pies and *börek*. In his entry on 'filo' in *The Oxford Companion to Food*, Charles Perry writes that the origin of the thin pastry layers can be traced back to the Tatars and the nomadic Turks of Central Asia who, like ancient Greeks, baked thin breads on the hearth and often folded or stacked them one on top of the other.[6]

Regardless of the specific origins, it is clear that the flatbreads, or the sheets of dough in the *placenta,* underwent a serious transformation in order to become the crunchy, paper-thin phyllo of today. This transformation probably occurred in the vast kitchens of the Ottoman sultans in the Topkapi palace in Istanbul. The hordes of skilled cooks who had to invent and perfect new dishes every day, as their lives depended on it, rolled the traditional crust thinner and thinner, until finally they developed the technique that turns pieces of simple flour dough into silky translucent sheets of phyllo. With minor adjustments and local variations, phyllo is rolled today repeating the same basic movements, and following a very similar method, throughout the Balkans and the Middle East.

I have never fully mastered the skill of rolling paper-thin phyllo pastry. I used to think that there was some kind of secret in the dough, or in the rolling pin, or the work surface. I took many pages of notes as I watched cooks from all over Greece produce, with incredible ease, large sheets of silky phyllo. Some told me to use club soda instead of water, others to add a pinch of dry yeast in the dough, or to increase the amount of olive oil or use lemon juice instead of vinegar and *raki* – the fiery Greek grappa-like moonshine – to make the phyllo crunchy. All of the above were important and interesting points, but they didn't help me much. I came to believe that – much like riding a bicycle, which I also never mastered – you need to start early in life. One also needs to roll phyllo regularly to fully master the technique, which looks so simple when others do the rolling. Indeed, most of the cooks I talked to repeated more or less the same story: when they were twelve (or thirteen or fourteen) years old, one day their mother was ill (or engaged in the fields, or picking olives) so the young daughters had to roll the phyllo to make the family pie. And they did, proving to their mothers that they had 'grown-up' and were almost ready to start their own homes.

My paternal grandmother came from what Greeks used to call 'northern Epirus' – southern Albania today – and like all cooks in the Epirus area, the mountainous northwestern corner of Greece, she rolled perfect phyllo in minutes. Using the typical thin and long rolling pin – about half an inch thick (1.5 cm) and three feet long (92 cm) – she worked fast on a round board which she placed on the kitchen table. When not in use the board was hung from a nail on the wall. This round board is used by most Greek cooks not only because it can be rotated in all directions to facilitate the rolling, but also because there was no large table or working surface in typical village homes. Sometimes instead of a board a special, very low, round table is used, and the women roll sitting on the floor.

I was too young to learn from my grandmother, and neither of my two aunts ever learned to pass the technique to me. Fortunately my new friends, the immigrant women from southern Albania, patiently taught me the gentle movements, and helped me finally realize that the sheet becomes thinner and thinner stretched under trained hands as it is rolled *on* the pin. The heels of the hands must move gently from the centre to the edges, pushing ever so lightly and stretching the dough towards the ends of the rolling pin. I was under the impression that the sheet was made larger and thinner pushed between the pin and the board, but this was a colossal mistake.

Rolling phyllo is very similar to rolling pasta. The pin is different, but you have to keep rolling in order to make the sheet very thin. In fact, in many parts of Greece the same dough used to make phyllo is also used to make *hilopites*, pasta squares, or

How to Feed a Crowd with a Handful of Meat

Figure 1. Rolling single sheets.

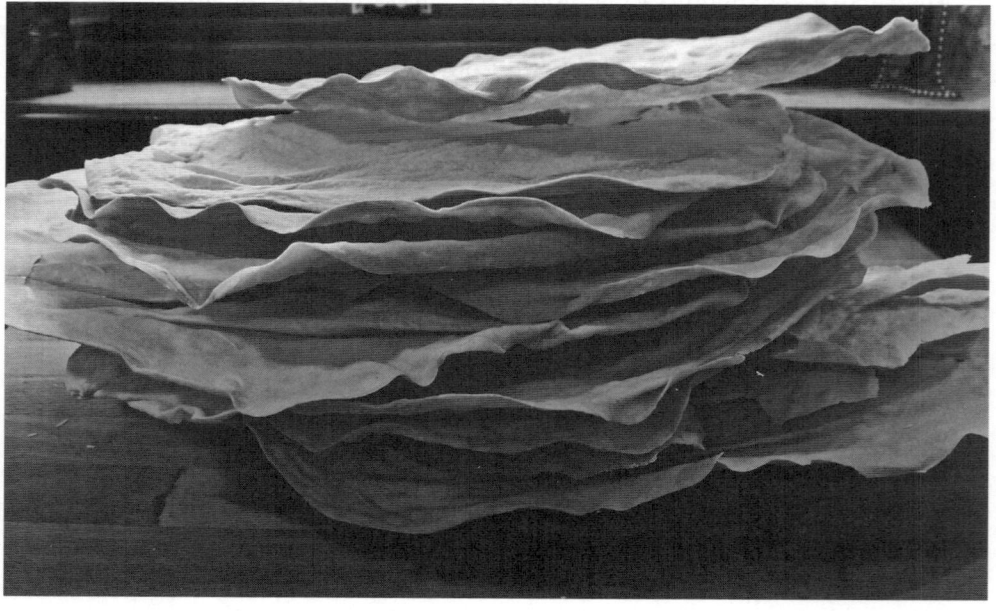

Figure 2. Baked phyllo sheets.

How to Feed a Crowd with a Handful of Meat

Figure 3. Dried goats meat.

Figure 4. Boning meat.

matsata makaronia, the typical fresh *tagliatelle* of Folegandros island. People used to pies made with crunchy and tasty home-made phyllo cannot accept the commercial one. I can now roll acceptable sheets of phyllo thanks to Ela, Stamatia and Polyxeni.[7] They coached me patiently and revealed to me some brilliant shortcuts, like rolling together up to seven sheets – a kind of olive oil puff pastry – that flake and separate as the pie bakes. Polyxeni also taught me to make *mesnik* (or *petanik*), the New Year's festive dish of southern Albania.[8] This unbelievably delicious pie – a kind of meat and herb baklava – is the epitome of frugality; only a handful of dried goat's meat flavours the stuffing of a large, very substantial pie.

The phyllo doubles as stuffing

Early in the winter Albanian families slaughter a couple of sheep or goats; larger and wealthier households may slaughter a calf or even more animals to make the year's supply of *pastërma*, the equivalent of salted pork for the Balkan countries with a Muslim past.[9] They cut meat and bones in small pieces, salt them heavily and hang them from the roof beams and around the hearth. They let the meat dry completely for several weeks, until rock-hard. Then they store the pieces in cloth bags. Every year, before Christmas, my friends receive a bag of *pastërma* from their families in Albania, as no household can be without it. Small pieces of this dried meat are soaked in water overnight to rid them of excess salt. *Pastërma* is added to bean stews or dishes with other pulses, to braised vegetables and greens, to rice and to soups. But most of all, scraps of this sharp-tasting meat flavour all kinds of vegetable pies and are the key ingredient for *mesnik,* the festive New Year's pie.

Like many labour-intensive festive dishes, the preparation of this pie is usually a collective endeavour. *Mesnik* is served at lunch on New Year's day and, as is the case the world over, people wake up late that morning, so the women need to have most of the elements for the pie ready; they just roll the top and bottom phyllo sheets, and assemble and bake the pie the day it is served.

It took us – three experienced cooks – a whole day to make the pie in my semi-professional kitchen. Polyxeni was in charge, as she had prepared *mesnik* a few times before. She and Ela kept rolling phyllo sheets from the dough I had prepared earlier in the KitchenAid with two pounds of bread flour, salt, two-thirds of a cup of olive oil, and enough water to make a smooth elastic dough. I laid each sheet on parchment paper on the oven-rack and baked it for about fifteen minutes, until light brown. 'The sheets need to get some color, otherwise they turn soggy in the pie', Polyxeni explained. Although we used my double convection oven, and the women rolled very fast, it took us about three hours to bake the thirteen sheets needed for *mesnik*. In the villages, they told me, each sheet was baked in the *saçi*, on the hearth (more about this later).[14]

Ela had soaked a few pieces of *pastërma* in several changes of water the previous day, then boiled it in the pressure cooker for about thirty-five minutes until the meat was very tender. We boned the meat, passing the broth through a sieve in a separate bowl.

How to Feed a Crowd with a Handful of Meat

We sautéed in olive oil a bunch of chopped scallions – white plus most of the green part – and two medium onions, until soft and translucent. We added the broth and about four tablespoons of dried mint, and as much thyme from our garden, plus some dried oregano. Polyxeni and Ela explained that while any aromatics were more than welcome, in their homes they only had mint – which they dried for the winter – and wild oregano gathered from the mountains; they used no other spice in their cooking and tasted cumin for the first time in Greece. Polyxeni sprinkled the broth with a good pinch of black pepper, and added some water to bring it to about one and a half quarts. She tasted it and was content; 'not too salty, and very fragrant', she said.

I prepared the old heavy copper pan – my husband's great-grandmother's – which is ideal for pies. I lined it with parchment paper brushed liberally with olive oil, and Ela laid the first five-layered phyllo. Polyxeni rolled another five-layered sheet, and we placed it over the first, after brushing with olive oil. We crumbled a few baked sheets to create a sturdy base for the pie and arranged half the meat pieces over the phyllo. More crumbled sheets covered the meat and we spread the rest of the meat over them. We crumbled the rest of the baked phyllo on top, and Polyxeni started to pour the broth over the pie, taking great care to distribute it all over the pan. Ela rolled the last seven-layered sheet of phyllo to cover the pie. I baked it in a pre-heated 375°F (190°–200°C) oven for one hour and twenty minutes. The advantage of laying the pan with parchment paper is that you can lift it easily to see if the pie is well browned at the bottom. I had to loosely cover the pan with aluminium foil and bake for another 15 minutes to get the proper browning. Then I inverted the pie and let it cool on a rack. I do that with all my pies because I find that if they cool in the pan the bottom becomes soggy.

We feasted on *mesnik* the next day, after we re-heated the pie for about thirty minutes. It was unbelievably delicious; I think that consuming it the next day had made it even better. We were nine around the table: Polyxeni, her husband Joseph and Yannis, their teenaged son, Ela with her husband Stathi, their tween kids, and the two of us. We ate more than one piece each, and we had plenty of leftover pie, which we ate slowly over the next week. It tasted equally delicious, even cold.

Gastra or *saçi*: the portable oven

Having our electric or gas ovens makes us forget that, not so long ago, the difficulty for most cooks was not making the crust for a pie but baking it. A village cook could not bake whenever she chose, for on the nearly treeless Greek islands, for example, wood for the oven was probably the most valuable of the ingredients needed to make a pie. Firing an oven is a lengthy process, and was done once a week. The cook planned to bake a series of dishes, besides the family's bread, in order to use every bit of the precious oven heat.

Pites were usually baked after the bread, as the oven started to cool. Lower temperatures are essential to allow both crust and filling to cook evenly. Unlike the large pies of northern Greece, where the forests provide plenty of wood for the oven, the

Figure 5. Crumbled phyllo first layer.

Figure 6. Crumbled phyllo & meat in layers.

Figure 7. Stuffing doused with broth & herbs.

Figure 8. Putting multiple layers together, ready for rolling.

How to Feed a Crowd with a Handful of Meat

Figure 9. Rolling multiple layers together.

shortage of wood is the reason that many pies on the Greek islands are fried, or shaped into small individual *pitakia* (small pies).

Convenience and scarcity of wood, I believe, led people to invent a bell-shaped clay or metal cover under which one can bake small amounts of food – a pie, pieces of meat with potatoes or vegetables, fish or seafood, cakes and flatbreads – over a few charcoals on the ground or in the fireplace. 'Having previously stoked up the fire [...], place the *placenta* to cook, cover it with the heated crock, and put hot coals around and above it. Be sure to cook it well and slowly. Open to check on it two or three times', writes the Roman Cato, concluding his instructions for the ancient pie.[10] The crock Cato describes brings to mind a *tserepa*, the thick terra-cotta cover made from clay mixed with either hay (in Cephalonia) or goat's hair (in Ithaca) that was still in use on these Ionian islands until twenty years ago. The pan containing the food is placed on a cleaned area in the centre of the hearth and covered with a *tserepa*, which has previously been well heated over the fire. The fading heat from the tiles at the bottom and from the thick bell-shaped cover on top slowly cooks the pie to perfection.

Clay is fragile though, so it was replaced by metal. What we call a *gastra* in Greece – *saçi* in Albania, and *peka* in Croatia – is roughly the same domed cover with a ledge around the outer side to hold the charcoal.[11] Before placing coal on the cover it is important to add a layer of sand or cold ashes, and then heat the underside well over the fire. Only thus can it sustain the even heat needed to cook the food placed under

How to Feed a Crowd with a Handful of Meat

Figure 10. Bottom layer.

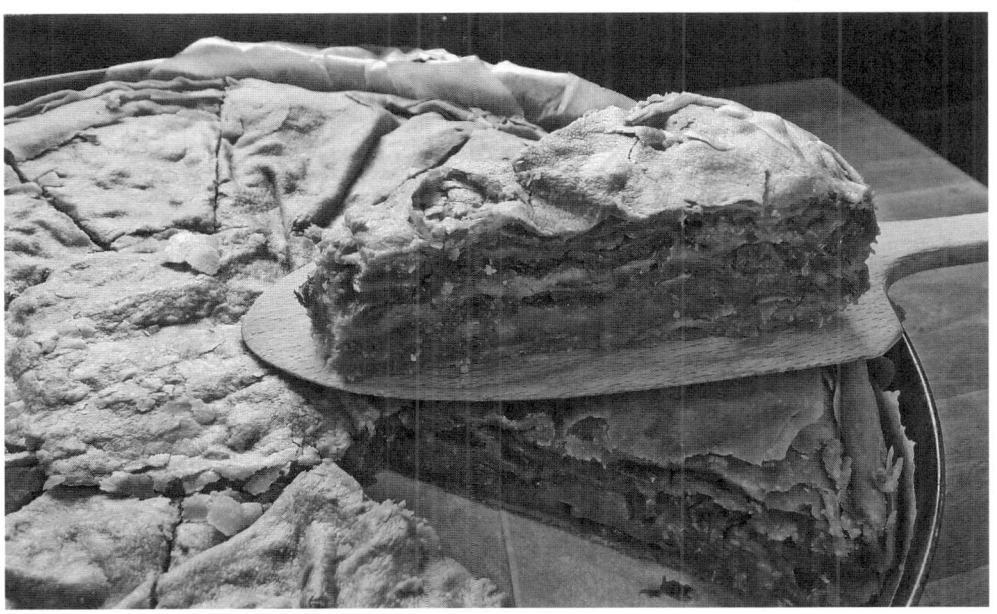

Figure 11. Cutting the pie.

it. Plain live coals burn the outer layer of pita, leaving the inside uncooked, as I learned the first time I used a *gastra*. Patience Gray, speaking about primitive Tuscan kitchens, describes the same portable oven: 'The *forno di campagna* made of tin ... could be set on charcoal or in the ashes in the hearth with live braise on the lid, a kind of rustic oven: cooking between two fires (*fra due fuochi*)'.[12]

My friends' families in southern Albania use the *saçi* regularly, bypassing their new electric ovens – electricity is quite unpredictable in the villages. Pies, breads and even plain vegetables baked with live fire under the dome acquire a unique, addictive, smoky aroma. Like the pies made with home-rolled phyllo, once you taste the difference it is difficult to go back to the convenience of frozen phyllo or sterile electric heat.

Notes

1. Cato *On Farming, De Agricultura*, trans. Andrew Dalby (Totnes, prospect Books, 1998), p. 155.
2. Placenta comes from the Greek word πλακούς (plakous) which is often translated as 'cake' or 'dainty dish'. Plakous is not fully described in the Greek texts but it was probably a rich and enviable delicacy, either containing in the dough, topped, or layered with cheese and honey. Epictetus 3.22.13–14 advises, 'Neither boy, nor girl, nor fame, nor dainties (πλακουντάριον) must have charms for you' (*Dissertationes ab Arriano digestae* Περί Κυνισμού). As Dalby points out, 'The medical use of the word placenta is a modern extension; it had no such implications in classical texts'. Emmer (*Triticum dicoccum*, Latin *far*) was the commonest species of wheat in Cato's Italy, as Dalby notes.
3. Giacosa I. Gozzini, *A Taste of Ancient Rome* (Chicago: University of Chicago Press, 1992), p. 165.
4. http://en.wikipedia.org/wiki/Pl%C4%83cint%C4%83; *Palacsinta* in Hungary is the traditional pancake, while in other Central European countries similar pancakes are called *palatschinken*, and in Croatian and Serbian *palachinke*.
5. http://homecookinginmontana.blogspot.com/2009/12/cheese-burek-or-placinta-de.html.
6. Phyllo, phylo, or filo (from φύλλο) means 'sheet' in Greek.
7. Ela (Manuela) Allamani comes from the village of Katundisht, southern Albania; Satmatia Stylou, from Livinë, belongs to the Greek minority of southern Albania – scolded and persecuted as 'dirty Greeks' during the Hoxha years, when they moved to Greece they continued to be discriminated against as 'dirty Albanians'; and Polyxeni Gjorgji comes from Erseka, a town near Korçë, southern Albania.
8. This is the name my southern Albanian friends used for the pie, but I am almost sure that in different parts of the country the dish may have different names. *Peta* is the Albanian word for phyllo. The term *petanik* is used for various kinds of phyllo-wrapped pies.
9. The Albanian interpretation is a crude version of the common Balkan and Turkish *pastirma*: see http://en.wikipedia.org/wiki/Pastirma for variations of the term, which eventually became the more refined pastrami.
10. The Albanian and Balkan *saçi* or *saç*, although the word sounds much like the Turkish *saj* (see http://en.wikipedia.org/wiki/Saj_(utensil)), is not a flat or convex round griddle.
11. Cato, p. 157.
12. See http://honestcooking.com/2011/04/29/traditionroasted-lamb-under-the-bell/.
13. Patience Gray, *Honey from a Weed: Fasting and Feasting in Tuscany, Catalonia, the Cyclades, and Apulia* (San Francisco: North Point, 1990), p. 25; see the traditional Italian jam tart pasta frolla baked by a young food blogger from Rome *in forno di campagna*: http://www.coquinaria.it/forum/showthread.php?54343-forno-di-campagna-(foto).

Kebabs, Bread, and 'Bread': Perugian History Wrapped up in *Torta al Testo*

Zachary Nowak

'Yes to polenta, no to cous cous'

In 2009 the council of the Tuscan city of Lucca passed an ordinance which declared that in order 'to protect the [local] cooking tradition and the architectural, cultural, structural, historic and décor-related typicalness, no new businesses are allowed whose activity comes from a different ethnic tradition'.[1] Though this particular clause, as well as one that required the use of local ingredients, was later revoked, the requirement that every new restaurant in Lucca's historic centre serve at least one traditional Luccan dish was left in force. The move, clearly aimed at restaurants that offered Chinese fare, or the now-popular kebab, was xenophobia translated into culinary reactionism. The same sentiments had generated 2002 electoral slogans from Italy's separatist Northern League, which read 'Yes to Polenta, No to Cous Cous: Proud of our Traditions'. The fact that Pellegrino Artusi, widely seen as the father of modern Italian cuisine, included a recipe for couscous in his famous cookbook over 120 years ago does not make the dish seem any more Italian. Couscous in this slogan is simply a thinly-veiled metaphor for a Muslim immigrant.

Italy, after decades of sending emigrants abroad, is now one of the primary European 'landing countries' for immigrants, especially illegal immigrants. There are no official Italian government numbers for illegal foreigners, but other estimates are between half a million to a million people.[2] While the number of foreigners legally resident in Italy is just over four million, or about 7 per cent of the population, a recent survey showed that Italians guessed that the percentage of the residents in Italy that were foreigners was 23 per cent.[3] This is likely due to media language about 'invasions' and disproportionate attention to crimes perpetrated by illegal foreigners, and adds to tensions between Italians and foreigners.[4] Populist parties like the Northern League find it easy to refer to these new arrivals with alimentary shorthand and discriminate against them with laws that restrict their cuisine.

What's for dinner has become an important battle for those in Italy who would like to maintain Italian traditions in the face of a perceived foreign invasion. This essay will focus on the rising culinary tension in the city of Perugia, and will examine just how traditional the *torta al testo* indeed is.

University city and farmer region

Perugia, a city of 165,000 residents, is the capital of the central Italian region of Umbria. Like many Italian cities, Perugia's local identity is a complex intersection of its traditions from different epochs, traditions that are both real and invented. While regional tourist information makes much of Umbria as the 'green heart of Italy', a more dispassionate observer points out that the ubiquity of agriculture in Umbria was necessary, not 'natural'. The extension of cultivation into relatively marginal areas (the sides of the Umbrian Apennines) testified not to the region's fertility, but rather to a 'long, slow, tenacious, centuries-old struggle to win land to cultivate from the swamps and forests'.[5]

At the same time as the region of Umbria vaunts its rural traditions, the city of Perugia underlines its history as a university city: Perugia's university, founded in 1307, is Italy's third oldest. Also located in Perugia is the 'University for Foreigners', a state-supported university which has offered Italian courses to foreigners since 1926. These institutions – first the former, then more recently both together – have attracted foreigners to the city, rendering what is ultimately a provincial burg more cosmopolitan than it otherwise would have been. According to the National Statistical Board of Italy, as of 1 January 2009 there were 18,702 foreigners resident in the municipality of Perugia, or about 11.3 per cent of the total population; of these almost 70 per cent are from eastern Europe and South America, with only 20 per cent from northern Africa.[6] The number of foreign residents, while higher than the national average, is still quite low; as indicated above, though, the perception (i.e. of an invasion) is more important than the facts. Perugia has heretofore avoided obvious clashes along racial lines, but in the last several years worry about *extracomunitari* – a term which technically means anyone outside of the EU, but de facto refers to illegal North Africans – and their involvement in crime has frequently been the theme of headlines and local election campaigns.

An integral part of the perception of a 'wave' of foreigners 'invading' the city centre is the dramatic increase in the number of food service outlets offering kebabs in Perugia's historic centre. While the sole Mexican restaurant languishes in a forgotten alley and two Indian restaurants have come and gone, the past ten years has seen an explosion in restaurants offering the eastern Mediterranean kebab. The first kebab stand opened in 2001 and there are currently fourteen in the town's centre; most serve mainly kebabs and perhaps several other side orders (rice and baklava are frequently on sale as well), while others were originally pizza-by-the-slice stands or (in one case) grocery stores that have added kebabs to their offerings. These shops, normally take-out only, are all run by recent immigrants: Kurds, Turks, Palestinians, even Bangladeshis.

One review of the laws like the one in Lucca notes that none of the ordinances referred to by the media as 'anti-kebab' actually refer to kebab stores explicitly; rather they use other means (health laws, promotion of 'traditional food') to restrict the expansion of kebabs and other 'ethnic' restaurants.[7] In Perugia, the assessor of Economic Development and Tourism recently sent a letter to the organizers of all the country festivals (*sagre*) asking them to serve menus 'characterized by the use of typical products of the province, leaving *torta al testo* as the basic dish'.[8] Several weeks later a press release from the same office announced that this suggestion would become law, and that these festivals were moments in which to 'reinforce the connection of the area, also with offering menus that privilege typical products and local drinks'.[9]

Is the recent Umbrian law the first salvo in a culinary war? When asked about why she preferred *torta al testo* to kebabs, one 62-year-old informant replied, 'It's our food, it's our tradition'. Often cited by culinary nativists as an endangered dish, the *torta al testo* is a typical Perugian flatbread that, along with the standard loaf of unsalted bread, has long been the mainstay of the local diet. The *torta al testo* is often served in sit-down restaurants, especially those that make explicit reference to offering 'traditional Perugian fare', but is seemingly being outcompeted by kebabs. Before discussing this competition, the history of the *torta al testo* merits examination.

From Cato to 'exotic cuisines'
Torta al testo literally means 'cake on a tile', though 'cake' in Italian can refer to both sweet and savoury breads. The testo is from Latin *testu*, which translates to plate or (ceramic) lid. Originally the dough was spread out on a terracotta tile or a carefully seasoned fieldstone that had been heated in a fireplace. Hot ashes and coals were spread over the top of the dough and the heat from below (the preheated *testo*) and above (the ashes and coals) cooked the dough into the *torta*, which because of the lack of yeast, remained more or less flat (modern *torta* is about 2cm tall). The ashes were then brushed off, and the flatbread was served. While enthusiasts see the *torta al testo* as a direct lineal descendant of a recipe in Cato the Elder's *De Agricultura*,[10] the procedure is general enough to be common to many cultures. Even within Italy, flatbreads made in the same way (i.e. cooked on a tile) are found all over the peninsula. In Modena the name is *cresciantina*, while in Romagna it is known as the *piadina*; within Umbria the same recipe is called *torta al panaro*, *torta sul testo*, *crescia sul panaro*, and *pizza sotto lu focu*.[11]

While recipes differ, a survey of cookbooks that purport to give traditional recipes suggests something similar to what follows:

Ingredients
500g of [wheat] flour • 2 eggs • 50ml extra virgin olive oil
60g grated pecorino • 1 cube of brewer's yeast • water • salt

Dissolve the yeast in warm water. Mix all other ingredients in a bowl, mixing in the yeast water and more water to get a firm dough. Allow to rise. Roll out in a circular shape, then cook on a cast-iron testo preheated on a gas burner. Toast, flip once, and toast. Split the *torta* into wedges, then cut horizontally and fill.

Torta al testo is a classic stuffed bread: Perugian restaurants divide the *torta* into pizza-like slices and then split the *torta* horizontally. A filling is piled carefully in between the two pieces of *torta*, resulting in a triangular sandwich. While ingredients can include fried bell peppers and onions, melted soft cheese, and prosciutto, the supposedly classic combination is Umbrian sausage and olive oil-soaked *erba*. This last ingredient

– literally 'grass' or 'greens' – is actually a mixture of boiled chicory and kale, classic ingredients of the *cucina povera* ('cuisine of the poor') of Umbria, which has become popular again in recent decades.

That the *torta al testo* is part of the *cucina povera* is something that almost all of the Umbrian cookbooks surveyed make explicit. The pride in this simple-yet-hardy cuisine, born of necessity but enjoyed today because of its uncomplicated good taste, is a common theme in these books. A representative passage from one of the cookbooks' introductions merits a lengthy citation:

> The Umbrian land, rich and generous, produces beautiful and flavourful foods, which its people proudly welcome to their table, foods full of genuine tastes and balanced gastronomic combinations which reflect the cycle of the various agricultural products.
>
> One can assert that Umbria is a farming region, but that does not mean that as a result it offers a limited menu; to the contrary, because of that peculiarity [of being a farming region, a *regione contadina*] its fare is abundant, healthy, and tasty, though not complicated.
>
> In a time like today, in which Italian restaurants and good gastronomic connoisseurs, tired of 'heavily-loaded' and strangely exotic cuisines, turn with correct attention to foods that are healthy, simple, and genuine, Umbrian cuisine, strong with ancient memories as well as rustic nobility, puts up the barricades against every type of béchamel, complicated sauces, and over-elaborate dishes.[12]

This introduction is a declaration of culinary war: the Umbrians, returning to their alimentary heritage, put up the barricades to the invasion of 'strangely exotic' cuisines. But are the adjectives ascribed to Umbrian cuisine – abundant, healthy, and genuine – truly merited in the case of the *torta al testo*?

Bread, 'bread,' and *torta al testo*

While the *torta* is still available everywhere in Umbria, it is a rarity to see the *testo*: indeed, one famous Umbrian restaurant seems to attract customers more for its use of the *testo* (heated in large indoor fireplaces) than for the flavour of its *torta*. While many sources describe the use of a ceramic tile made by resourceful farmers or a *testo* carved from a *pietra morta*, a 'dead stone' dug up from under the ground and thus less likely to crack under thermal pressure, all note that today's *testo* is an industrial product. The restaurant referred to above, Il Faliero, uses prefabricated stone *testi*, but this is a rarity. While some bakeries use pizza stones, nowadays most *torta al testo* is baked like bread in gas-fired ovens or cooked on cast iron *testi*.

References to flatbreads are present in travellers' accounts of Umbria going back to the sixteenth century. In a 1727 call for bids for the contract to make bread in Terni (a city in southern Umbria), the *torta al testo* is conspicuously absent. The announcement is quite detailed about the kinds of bread to be made, their size, and their maximum sale price to the public. Products to be made include a sweet Umbrian doughnut-like cake called *ciambelle*, various kinds of pasta and four types of bread: 'puffed' bread, white bread, brown bread, and soft dough.[13] We can surmise that this absence was due to *torta al testo*'s low position in the classification of breads. City residents and wealthy rural landowners could afford these products, made out of wheat flour; the poor in Italy (i.e. the great mass of people) had to make do with 'bread' made out of the *biade*, or inferior grains.

Food historian Piero Camporesi has shown that wheat flour bread was often a dream for Italian peasants: their 'bread' was a pitiful substitute made from millet, barley, bean flour, chestnuts, acorns, even thistles. The resulting dough, because of its low gluten content, was dark and dense and the taste was never lauded. Camporesi suggests that peasants often intentionally added psychoactive substances to the dough; the consequent drug-induced haze made a miserable life slightly less intolerable.[14] The situation improved slightly after the introduction of maize during the so-called Columbian exchange. New food products from the Americas were incorporated into European diets by being 'translated' into common dishes.[15] Gnocchi, previously made from wheat flour, were now made from potatoes, and corn took the place of grains and other ingredients in peasant 'breads'.

This was the case with Umbrian flatbreads: corn became the main ingredient, as seen in a response from a small city near Perugia to an 1878 inquest into the rural condition, which noted that 'the daily bread of the rural resident [*campangolo*] is a bread that is mainly made of maize, mixed with fava bean flour and flour of other cereals'.[16] The later Jacini Inquest (1884) confirmed that little had changed in the intervening years:

> The ordinary alimentation of the Umbrian sharecropper is largely constituted of maize flour garnished with salt, with which they form a kind of *focaccia* or *torta* which they cook on a ceramic disc. ... The best-off families add in the morning and evening to these pizzas a plate of beans or *fave*, rice garnished with pork, cooked *erba*, or potatoes; on the other hand the rest of the families in the morning add raw onions, cooked potatoes and *erba*, but generally in most cases in the morning one eats simply *torta* made from maize flour.[17]

Important too is the term used for farmers in both inquests: *mezzadro*, not *contadino*. The latter was a general term for someone who worked the land but often referred to a farmer who was also a proprietor, the equivalent of the English yeoman; the former on the other hand explicitly indicated a sharecropper. Umbria was and remained for a long time a region not of farmers (*regione contadina*) but rather of sharecroppers (*regione mezzadrile*);[18] the distinction is not an insignificant one. Landowners, whether noble or ecclesiastical, rented out land to the poor masses, who were required to give a share (often the best share) of all that they produced. The heavy burden of the 'taxes' meant that while they raised pigs and chickens and cultivated wheat, it was the rare sharecropper who had meat more than twice a year, ate fresh eggs, or enjoyed bread made from wheat flour.[19] The resulting poverty and malnutrition caused by a diet that was heavily dependent on maize has been edited out of the fanciful introductions like the cookbook cited above. The land might have been 'rich' and produced 'abundant' products, but these were not enjoyed by those that produced them.

It is clear from these inquests that the only ever-present ingredients for *torta al testo* were water, maize flour, and salt. The better-off farmer might add eggs or cheese, or garnish the *torta* with a sauce, but the only accompaniment for the vast majority of sharecroppers were vegetables: raw onions, cooked potatoes, and boiled greens. The high percentage (likely 100 per cent in most cases) of maize flour relative to wheat flour in the *torta* meant that, like most peasant 'breads,' it was dense. We can further surmise – given the crumbliness of cornbread and the lack of references to fillings – that the *torta* of Umbria's past was not a stuffed bread. If anything, 'garnish' (called *companatico*, literally 'that which goes with bread') was simply placed on top of slices.

Only with the introduction of modern *torta*, made with 100 per cent wheat flour, is there enough elasticity to be able to slice triangles of *torta* to stuff it. In a book written by an engineer-turned amateur historian, we find a description of Perugian foods from the early 1900s. The author characterizes bread in the city of Perugia as 'not bad', while country bread is dark and, at the end of the week, hard, heavy, and bland. When it runs out, it is substituted by *torta al testo*, and 'those who can add a few eggs or a little bit of fat'. The author has the grim determination of a former sharecropper when it comes to describing *torta* made only from maize flour: '*Torta* with maize is on the other hand stomachable. There are those that prefer to eat it hot with cooked *erba*. It remains appetizing only as long as there is a lot of oil as a condiment'.[20] The author explains that *erba* is the basic food of poor people: 'well-cooked and well-dressed they are a pleasure, but without oil or with just a little they are bitter and disgusting, and hard to swallow'.[21] After praising the *torta* as traditional food and giving a recipe with wheat flour, one cookbook notes that 'the difficulty of execution and probably the fact that it is linked to times of poverty have made the maize-flour *torta* almost disappear'.[22]

Theseus' boat and Perugia's *torta*

In Plutarch's *Life of Theseus*, the writer poses a philosophical question about the boat in which Theseus returned from Crete. The boat was supposedly preserved intact in Athens, and with the passage of the years rotten boards were replaced with new ones. If eventually all the boards on the ship were replaced, could the resulting craft still be considered Theseus' boat? The question of the authenticity of the *torta al testo* is perhaps a bit easier to answer. As this essay has shown, nothing remains of the original food but the name: the *testo* is no longer a stone found buried in a field, nor is it a ceramic disc. The only ingredient that has remained constant is water. The 'ingredient drift' was perhaps a gradual process: as conditions improved in the nineteenth century, farmers could afford to mix in more wheat flour, and gradually the percentage of maize flour was reduced from one hundred to zero. Salt, eggs, and cheese were added to the dough.

The *companatico* shifted from being something on top of the bread that was eaten with it to being the filling, an integral part of the dish, as the wheat flour *torta* reduced almost to the secondary role of container. The only echo of the past that we have in the *companatico* is the *erba*, which has been paired with sausage, the latter certainly a novelty.

Certainly the most important shift for the *torta* is semantic, not gastronomic. *Torta al testo* is celebrated today as the classic Umbrian peasant fare: a culinary reminder of a simpler, happier time, a reminder, though, which one can sink one's teeth into, unlike other less concrete reminders. The *torta* of today is thoroughly ahistorical: perhaps as recently as sixty years ago, but definitely one hundred years ago, the majority of Umbrians connected *torta al testo* not with a hearty, healthy cuisine, but rather with pellagra and poverty. *Torta* was not an occasional festive food, but rather a daily – or rather, twice daily – symbol of misery and malnutrition.

How can we understand the fact of the *torta*'s history in the context of today's fiction of the dish? In his essay on the typology of culinary fakelore, Andrew Smith provides a comprehensive list of motivations for the invention of undocumented food myths: journalistic enrichment, local boosterism, 'Big Events Food', founding father dishes, and commercial promotion among them.[23] While slices of the *torta al testo* mythology could fit within a number of these categories, the whole disc does not go into any of them well. *Torta* is not connected to any one festival, there is no story for its origin, nor does it have the journalistic/narrative appeal of the myth that has grown up around the Pizza Margherita.

Food historians have long used the Ranger-Hobsbawm theory of invention of tradition, but a folklore metaphor seems to be more appropriate for the semantic drift in *torta* culture. In a classic paper on the transmission and evolution of folk stories, F.C. Bartlett showed that several principles are at work when subjects tell and retell a story. Each iteration of the original story moves closer to a stable version; while Bartlett describes various mechanisms of change, the most important for our subject is the 'omission of the unpleasant'.[24] As a story is told and retold, unpleasant parts are edited, omitted, and even transformed to make them positive. Thus with repeated recounting and cooking – more likely offhand remarks on 'what we used to eat' than stories – Perugians have slowly transformed *torta al testo* into a healthy, happy food, losing both its negative connotations and gaining much tastier ingredients. This is a common theme in historical linguistics, where a word itself may change very little though what it signifies changes beyond all recognition.[25] As one Umbrian food historian points out, the persistence of 'typical products of ancient tradition' is not due, as is often thought, to their ability to resist change, but rather 'in their flexibility, in their suitability to adaptation, in the capacity to materially change remaining culturally the same'.[26]

In a promotional article for a publication of Perugia's Chamber of Commerce, Giuseppe Agozzino lists the region's typical products: the *torta di Pasqua* (a bread made with cheese and eggs at Easter), the truffles from Norcia, the trout of Clitunno, Cannara onions, broccoli from Lake Trasimeno, the various wines, Umbrian olive oil, and even the *torcolo* (an eel-shaped sweet cake) for Perugia's patron saint, San Costanzo. There is no mention of *torta al testo*; the article was written in 1965.[27] The shift in the meaning of the *torta al testo* happened sometime between then and the present. Recent research on another Perugian food myth relating to the popular unsalted bread (*pane sciapo*) suggests that the folklore related to food myths can develop and spread in a remarkably short time. In the case of *pane sciapo*, most informants insisted they had heard the story long ago, but the first printed source is from 1988.[28] It is possible that the web of meaning ascribed to the *torta al testo* was recent as well. This 'traditionalization' is progressing apace: a master's thesis from 2007 which developed a marketing plan for the *torta al testo* on a national level suggests the name 'Umbrian Focaccia: The Traditional *Torta al Testo*', as well as the outline of Umbria on the package's label.[29]

While one can hypothesize the mechanism of change (repetition and the desire to omit unpleasant details) as well as the timeframe (perhaps relatively recent), the cause is still unknown. This is where the kebab becomes important: I believe that the lionization of the *torta al testo qua* tradition has much to do with the recent popularity of 'foreign' food and the fear of foreigners, especially illegal immigrants. In a book about the Peloponnesian War, anthropologist Marshall McLuhan demonstrates that far from having a long tradition of diametric opposition, Athens and Sparta were until just a half a century before the war very similar. Their opposite cultural stances, seemingly ancient, were in fact an invention born of opposition.[30] While much research has to be done to pinpoint the moment that *torta* begins to be eulogized, as well as the reasons for it, it seems reasonable to hypothesize that the recent acceleration of this process has been in part a reaction to the perceived demographic and culinary invasion. Further interviews with both Perugians and the owners of the kebab stores will elucidate the connection (or lack thereof) between the popularity of the kebab and the sudden importance given to the *torta al testo*.

While the University of Perugia recently announced that they will serve kebab in the student cafeteria, it remains to be seen whether Perugia can draw on its long tradition of openness to foreigners in order to incorporate and Perugianize the new arrival, perhaps making the *torta* the container for the kebab. For now both foods live in uneasy coexistence.

Kebabs, Bread, and 'Bread'

Notes

1. Consiglio communale di Lucca, Delibera del Consiglio communale di Lucca, n.12, 22 January 2009. Lucca has been followed by several other municipalities, among them Reggio Emilia, Bussolengo, and Cittadella. See Magrassi, cited below. Unless otherwise noted, all translations are by the author.
2. M. Antonietta Calabrò, ' "Clandestini, in Italia sono un milione" È la stima della Caritas. Molti hanno già un lavoro, contratto chiesto per settecentomila', *Corriere della Sera*, 22 August 2009: http://www.corriere.it/cronache/09_agosto_10/focus_8c0ab4f0-8572-11de-8be5-00144f02aabc.shtml (Accessed 27 March 2012).
3. 'Immigrati, gli italiani pensano che gli stranieri siano quattrovolte di più', *La Stampa*, 12 December 2009.
4. James Walston, 'Appendix: Immigration Statistics,' *Bulletin of Italian Politics* 2 (2010), 118.
5. Valeria Ventura, 'Agricoltura e condizione contadina in Umbria durante il fascismo' in *Gli Annali della Università per Stranieri* n.16 (Perugia: Università per Stranieri, 1991), p.138. Italy's Fascist regime also made much of the 'green heart of Italy' slogan.
6. ISTAT data as reported in 'Società: gli stranieri residenti a Perugia,' n.d.: http://www.perugia-city.com/2009/10/societa-gli-stranieri-residenti-perugia.html (Accessed 28 April 2012).
7. Mattia Magrassi, 'Le c.d. 'ordinanze anti-kebab', *Le Regioni* 38 (2010), p. 325.
8. Giuseppe Lomurno, Assessor of Economic Development and Tourism of the Municipality of Perugia, 'Somministrazione alimenti e bevande in occasionae di feste sagre,' Letter to Organizers of Festivals and Sagre, in the author's possession, 5 April 2012. *Torta al testo* was the only food explicitly mentioned in the letter.
9. 'Brevi note al Calendario Comunale Sagre anno 2012,' Municipality of Perugia, Office for Government and Development of the Area and of the Economy press release (Perugia, 4 May 2012).
10. Cato gives the following recipe for what he calls *depsticium* in chapter 74: 'Recipe for kneaded bread: Wash your hands and a bowl thoroughly. Pour meal into the bowl, add water gradually, and knead thoroughly. When it is well kneaded, roll out and bake under a crock'. Note that the words 'under a crock' are *sub testu* in Latin. *Marcus Porcius Cato on Agriculture. Marcus Terentius Varro on Agriculture. With an English translation by William Davis Hooper ... Revised by Harrison Boyd Ash* (Cambridge MA: Harvard University Press, 1934), p. 83.
11. The word *panaro* is a synonym for *testo*. The last name translates to 'pizza under the fire' and is interesting because it shows the use of the word 'pizza' outside of Naples, and preserves in the name the original method for cooking (i.e. under the coals and ashes).
12. Annalisa Breschi and Carlo Grassetti, *La cucina umbra: nuovissima guida della cucina umbra, 250 ricette tipiche e di facile sperimentazione* (Perugia: Grassetti, 1991), p. 3.
13. Franco Maroni (ed.), *Appunti per una storia della cucina ternana e…* (Terni: Edizioni Thyrus, 1999), p. 34.
14. See Piero Camporesi, *Bread of Dreams*, trans. by David Gentilcore (Chicago: University of Chicago Press, 1989).
15. Massimo Montanari, *The Culture of Food, The Making of Europe* (Oxford: Blackwell, 1996), pp. 99–101.
16. Anonymous, unpublished responses to the Inchiesta Agraria sulle condizioni igieniche e sanitarie dei coltivatori della terra in Italia [Bertani Inquest], Archives of the Comune di Magione, 1878.
17. AA.VV., *Atti della Giunta per la inchiesta agraria e sulle condizioni della classe agricola*, Vol. XI, t.II (Rome: Forzani e C. Tipografi del Senato, 1885), p. 208.
18. New sharecropping contracts were outlawed in Italy in 1964; the last sharecropping contract expired in 1981.
19. Hasia Diner's chapter on Italian peasants, 'Black Bread, Hard Bread' in her book *Hungering for America. Italian, Irish, and Jewish Foodways in the Age of Migration* (Cambridge, MA: Harvard University Press, 2001) shows how Italian peasants were effectively vegetarians except for a limited number of feast days, as well as underlining the fact that 'bread' for these masses was hardly ever wheat

bread, and then always whole grain.
20. Luigi Catanelli, *Usi e costumi nel Territorio Perugino agli inizi del '900,* ed. Marcello Catanelli (Perugia: l'Arquata, 1987), p. 312. Catanelli uses the word *stomachevole*.
21. Catanelli.
22. Rita Boini, *La cucina umbra: sapori di un tempo,* 3rd edition (Perugia: Calzetti Mariucci, 1998), p. 35.
23. Andrew F. Smith, 'False Memories: The Invention of Culinary Fakelore and Food Fallacies', *Food and the Memory, Proceedings of the Oxford Symposium on Food and Cookery 2000,* ed. Harlan Walker (Totnes: Prospect Books, 2001), pp. 254–60.
24. F.C. Bartlett, 'Some Experiments on the Reproduction of Folk-Stories', *Folklore* 31, 1 (1920), p. 36.
25. This similarity between change in cuisines and languages is brilliantly explored in a series of nine blog posts by Rachel Laudan, 'Cuisine and Language': http://www.rachellaudan.com/2010/11/cuisine-and-language-1-inventories.html (Accessed 4 May 2012).
26. Giancarlo Baronti, 'Dal paese della fame alla città della Cuccagna: Penuria ed abbondanza alimentare nel mondo popolare rurale in Umbria', *Umbria: Saperi e Sapori,* eds. Danilo Fonti, Floriana Cipriani and Giuseppe Merli (Perugia: Regione dell'Umbria, 1999), p. 15.
27. Giuseppe Agozzino, 'Turismo e tradizioni gastronomiche', *Nuova Economia* 9 (Spoleto: Camera di Commercio, Industria, e Agricolture di Perugia, 1965), pp. 31–36.
28. Zachary Nowak and Elisa Ascione, 'Salt War, Folklore: Reflections on the Transmission of a Perugian Urban Legend', unpublished manuscript.
29. Caterina Falconi, 'La pianificazione di marketing per lo sviluppo di un prodotto gastronomico locale nel mercato nazionale: il caso della "Torta al testo" umbra' (master's thesis, Università degli Studi di Perugia, 2008): 8.1.
30. Marshall Sahlins, *Apologies to Thucydides: Understanding History as Culture and Vice Versa* (Chicago: University of Chicago Press, 2004).

Before *Dolma*: A Taxonomy of Medieval Arab Stuffery

Charles Perry

The most characteristic food of the eastern Mediterranean today is stuffed vegetables. Cooks are willing to stuff just about anything – not just eggplants, zucchini and grape leaves, but onions, carrots and even (stretching the category a bit) quinces, though they're as hard as chunks of wood.

But this characteristic taste dates only from the last 500 years – it was the Ottoman Turks who made stuffed vegetables a regular culinary category. In thirteenth-century Arabic cookery books, the only vegetables stuffed were eggplant and snake melon, and before that no vegetables at all. No dish called *dolma* even appears in Şirvani's fifteenth-century Turkish cookery book *Kitâb'üt-Tabîh*, though there is a reference to cabbage *dolmeh* in the sixteenth-century Persian book *Mâddet ol-Hayât*, which observes that it is 'commonly prepared in the land of the Rūm (Turkey) but not well known in Iran'.

Court of Baghdad, tenth century
'Before that' refers to Ibn Sayyar's *Kitāb al-Ṭabīkh*, a tenth-century compilation of recherché Baghdad court dishes of the eighth through early tenth centuries.[1] The stuffed dishes fall into the following categories, most of which would endure for centuries.

Sausage. There are five recipes for *luqāniq* (the Roman *lucanica*) and one for a sausage stuffed in large intestine, *dawwārāt*.[2]

Roasted whole animal. *Jady maḥshū bi-kam'a*[3] is a kid stuffed with truffles and a lot of other ingredients – five stuffings in all, one for the body cavity and one for each of the four limbs, very much the sort of stunt cuisine much admired in medieval courts.

Items wrapped in caul fat. '*Uṣbān lil-Muʿtamid*[4] is livers of a kid and a lamb cut into strips, wrapped in caul fat and tied with small intestine, to make something like an English faggot or a French *crépinette*. *Jady maghmūm bi-dajāja*[5] is more stunt cuisine: a chicken wrapped in caul fat stuffed into a whole kid wrapped in caul fat, the whole thing roasted in a paunch.

Samosa. The recipe for *sanbūsaj*[6] appears in the same chapter as sausages, apparently suggesting that the dough is a substitute for sausage casing.

Sandwich canapé. *Wasaṭ*[7] was a sort of appetizer or *meze* consisting of a split loaf of bread filled with meat, nuts and herbs in sandwich fashion, cut in pieces as canapés.

Flatbread wrap canapé. Rather similar was *bazmāward*,[8] except that the filling was rolled up in flatbread (with a layer of caul fat).

Crepes. *Qaṭā'if*[9] were rolled around sweetened ground nuts.

Deep-fried crepe packets. For *khushkanānaj min qaṭā'if maqlī*,[10] the crepes were fried on one side only, leaving the other slightly tacky, then folded over the nut filling to seal packets that would be deep-fried. The name literally means 'fried *khusākananaj* of crepes', because it was thought to be equivalent to *khushkanānaj* (v. infra), except that it was baked.

Thin pastry wrapper. Lauzīnaj,[11] the most highly regarded medieval pastry, consisted of ground almonds rolled up in a special thin pastry and then cut into pieces in the manner of *bazmāward*.

Rolled cookie or sweet biscuit. Khushkanānaj Abū Isḥāqi muʿarraj[12] were rolled around a nut filling and then twisted into a curved shape for baking. Ordinary *khushkanānaj* was not stuffed.

Molded cookie. Ḥalwā ṭayyiba maḥshuwwa ẓarīfa[13] was formed with the use of a mould which would be lined with one sheet of dough, filled with nuts and sealed with another sheet, the resulting cake being removed and baked.

Cannoli. Ḥalāqīm ('throats')[14] were shaped around a piece of cane, baked like Italian cannoli and stuffed with nuts as a garnish for stews.

Eastern Arab world, thirteenth century

Four major recipe collections were compiled at this time in Syria and Iraq. *Kitāb al-Wuṣla ila al-Ḥabīb*,[15] *Kitāb Wasf al-Aṭʿima al-Muʿtāda* (an expanded version of al-Baghdādī's *Kitāb al-Ṭabīkh*),[16] *Kitāb Zahr al-Ḥadīqa min al-Aṭʿima al-Anīqa*[17] and *Kanz al-Fawāʾid fī Tanwīʿ al-Mawāʾid*.[18]

All the Abbasid savory items continue at this time except the use of caul fat. *Sanbūsaj* is now usually spelled *sanbūsak*.[19] *Bazmāward* and *wasaṭ* (now always in the plural form *ausāṭ*) have exchanged caps – in the later books it's *bazmāward* that is made from a split loaf and *ausāṭ* that is rolled up in flatbread.

All the sweets survive. However, something constructed like *ḥalwā ṭayyiba maḥshuwwa ẓarīfa* is now called *urnīn*,[20] though sometimes stuffed with dates instead of nuts. *Ḥalāqīm* appear under a name still in use (though today referring to a baked pastry made with filo dough), *aṣābiʿ zainab*,[21] but the thirteenth-century pastry is cooked by deep-frying, rather than baking. *Khushkāsnanaj* are now stuffed more often than not.[22] We still find *qaṭāʾif* being rolled around filling after frying.[23] *Khushkanānaj min qaṭāʾif maqlī* is now called *qaṭāʾif maḥshuwwa* (or *maḥshī*).[24]

New items:
Stuffed vegetables. Eggplant appears stuffed with meat,[25] as is in one book snake melon.[26]

Tart nut stuffings. Meats are usually stuffed with nuts (usually walnuts, sometimes with almonds or sesame paste) and a sour ingredient (usually sumac),[27] though once chicken has the sort of sweet nut filling characteristic of pastries.[28] The tart nut filling is particularly common with fish.[29]

Boiled stuffed chicken. In one recipe, it's stuffed with the meat of another chicken, in another with eggs and fried onions.[30]

Stuffing after roasting, strange though it may seem to us. Lamb is stuffed after roasting (and smoking the body cavity) with either breadcrumbs, nuts and herbs, or sesame paste and sumac, or a sort of bread pudding which also serves to stuff one samosa recipe.[31] A chicken is spit-roasted over a pan of breadcrumbs to soak up the running fat and juices and then stuffed with the same crumbs.[32] In one recipe a chicken is partly boiled, then stuffed and wrapped in dough and baked.[33] In another, a fried chicken is stuffed with breadcrumbs, nuts and flavorings; some of this stuffing is reserved, mixed with water and passed as a dipping sauce.[34]

Dates are commonly stuffed with almonds and serve as a garnish.[35] There is also a recipe for dates stuffed with pistachios, then dipped in batter and fried – *ma'mūl* (or *maṣnū') min al-tamr*.[36]

Mukaffan[37] is a thickened confection of nuts and sesame rolled around more nuts, *ausāṭ* fashion.

Kunāfa. The original sense of this word is a thin bread,[38] and *Wuṣla*'s third recipe for *kunāfa mamlūḥa*[39] involves rolling up nuts in it 'like *ausāṭ*'. But for one variety of *lauzīnaj*,[40] a product similar to the vermicelli-like modern pastry, called *kunāfa* in Arabic (though this recipe does not explicitly refer to it by any name), was used the same way.

Katā[41] is a homely Armenian pastry bread of unleavened dough filled with toasted flour which has been rubbed with fat.

Elaborated cookies. Three new forms of stuffed cookie appear, the ring-shaped *ka'k*,[42] *aqrāṣ mukallala*,[43] which was frosted with thick syrup after baking, and *aqrāṣ mukarrara*,[44] which is repeatedly dipped in batter and fried.

Jāmaliyya consists of two pancakes sandwiched around a nut filling and then deep-fried – in effect, *qaṭā'if maḥshuwwa* in circular rather than semicircular form.[45]

Stuffed zulābiyā. Ordinarily *zulābiyā* is a fritter made by dribbling batter into hot fat, but *zulābiyā maḥshuwwa*[46] is a (loosely described) packet of nut-stuffed dough fried in sesame oil.

Western Arab world, thirteenth century

Two books represent the cuisine of North Africa and Moorish Spain, *Faḍālat al-Khiwān*[47] and an anonymous and untitled work generally known as the *Manuscrito Anónimo*.[48] The latter is particularly focused on stuffing – fully 52 of its 395 recipes involve stuffing or wrapping. By the thirteenth century, the eastern and western Arab world had been politically separated for five centuries, and the cuisines had evolved in their own directions. The characteristic savory stuffing in the east is usually meat or nuts, sometimes breadcrumbs, only once eggs. In the west, eggs and cheese are common stuffings.

Sausage was called *mirkās* (merguez). Some have quite unusual stuffings such as cheese[49] or puréed eggplant.[50]

Before *Dolma*: A Taxonomy of Medieval Arab Stuffery

Roasted animals. Anónimo has four recipes for chicken,[51] two for lamb breast,[52] one called lamb roasted 'in its skin' (the wool carefully removed),[53] two for stuffed goose.[54]

Samosa was stuffed with meat as usual[55] but also with sweetened nuts or a mixture of garlic and spices.[56]

Eggplant was usually stuffed with bread crumbs mixed with eggs or meat.[57]

Deep-fried crepe packets[58] were called Abbasid crepes, after the reigning dynasty in Baghdad.

Cookies. *Kaʻk* was called *khushkalān* (for *khushkanānaj*) in Bougie, where it was cut with shears into circles and semicircles. *Kaʻb al-ghazāl* (gazelle's horn) was similar.[59]

Stuffed cakes. *Qurṣa* was a leavened product with a nut stuffing, as was *maqrūḍ* (today the name of a pastry stuffed with dates).[60]

Cannoli. These appear under the name *qanānīṭ*,[61] an Arabic plural of the Spanish *canuto*, 'cane, tube', which happens to be cognate with the Italian word *cannoli*.

Stuffed eggs. In one version the two halves of the egg are held together with a stick,[62] in another they are sealed with raw egg white and fried to seal.[63] These were served as a garnish.

New items:

Meat pies. These were not found in the east, where samosas were the largest in this category.[64]

Cheese pies likewise were not found in the east. There are six recipes in *Anónimo* and eight in *Faḍāla*, some with leavened dough, some with unleavened, and one ('oven cheese pie, which we call Toledan') with puff pastry.[65]

Isfunj was a pastry of leavened dough enriched with eggs made into the shape of a *raghīf* (flat loaf). You would put a nut filling on it, 'then take the *raghīf* with your hand and turn it until it is smooth and round and bite-sized', perhaps an instruction to stuff, and fry.[66]

Baked dough. A very characteristic Moorish dish was *rās maimūn*,[67] 'the monkey's head', which was baked in a pot which would be broken open when removed from the oven. One of the distinctive local developments of the Arabian dish *tharīda* (originally stewed meat mixed with bread) consisted of a mixture of chicken or squab and dough wrapped in more dough and baked with a lot of butter.[68]

Tandoor-roasted meats stuffed with birds. We find a ram stuffed with 'as many plump chickens, pigeons, doves and small birds as you can' (the birds themselves being stuffed)[69] and a calf stuffed with a goose stuffed with a hen stuffed with a pigeon stuffed with a starling,[70] showing that the Moors also knew stunt cuisine.

Animals stuffed with their own meat. Lamb is stuffed with the meat of another lamb,[71] rabbit is stuffed with the meat of another rabbit[72] and there are fully three recipes where a chicken is stuffed with the meat of another chicken.[73] In a special category is a grey mullet gently skinned from the head, leaving the skin hanging from the tail, finally stuffed with its own removed meat as a forcemeat.[74]

Before *Dolma*: A Taxonomy of Medieval Arab Stuffery

Stuffed stuffing. One recipe describes a stuffing which is sent to the oven, pieces of cooked meat having been inserted into it.[75]

Meat as a wrapping. Meat is removed from bones and made into a forcemeat which is formed around the bones, which are cooked in a stew.[76] 'Stuffed asparagus' turns out to be asparagus treated in the same way, coated with meat.[77]

Notes

1. Ibn Sayyar al-Warraq, *Kitāb al-Tabīkh*, ed. Kaj Öhrnberg and Sahban Mroueh (Helsinki: Societas Orientalis Fennica, 1987); English translation by Nawal Nasrallah, *Annals of the Caliphs' Kitchens* (Brill: Leiden and Boston, 2007).
2. al-Warraq, pp. 87–89, Nasrallah, pp. 187–90.
3. al-Warraq, pp. 229–31, Nasrallah, pp. 366–68.
4. al-Warraq, p. 225, Nasrallah, 361.
5. al-Warraq, p. 226, Nasrallah, p. 363.
6. al-Warraq, p. 89, Nasrallah, 190–91.
7. al-Warraq, p. 58, Nasrallah, 149–50.
8. al-Warraq, p. 57, Nasrallah, pp. 149–50.
9. al-Warraq, pp. 274–75, Nasrallah, 422–24.
10. al-Warraq, pp. 271–72, Nasrallah, 420–21.
11. al-Warraq, p. 265–66, Nasrallah, 410–12.
12. al-Warraq, pp. 271–72. Nasrallah, 419–20.
13. al-Warraq, p. 272, Nasrallah, 426.
14. al-Warraq, p. 276, Nasrallah, 425.
15. *Wuṣla* page numbers in this paper refer to MS 1678, Waqfiyya Library, Aleppo.
16. Muhammad b. al-Hasan al-Warraq al-Baghdadi, *Kitab al-Tabikh*, trans. Charles Perry as *A Baghdad Cookery Book* (Totnes: Prospect Books, 2005); *The Description of Familiar Foods*, trans. Charles Perry in *Medieval Arab Cookery* (Totnes Prospect Books, 2001).
17. Shihab al-Dīn Ahmad b. Mubarakshah, *Zahr al-Ḥadīqa fī al-Aṭ'ima al-Anīqa*, MS Orient. A1344, Forschungs- und Landesbibliothek Gotha.
18. *Kanz al-Fawā'id fī Tanwī' al-Mawā'id*, eds. Manuela Marin and David Waines (Wiesbaden: Franz Steiner Verlag, 1993).
19. e.g. *Wuṣla*, p. 12a.
20. *Wasf*, p. 426, Baghdadi, p. 102, *Wuṣla*, p. 24b.
21. *Wasf*, p. 419, *Wuṣla*, p. 21b; Kanz, p. 109.
22. *Wasf*, pp. 425 and 437, Baghdadi, p. 102, *Wuṣla*, p. 27a.
23. *Wasf*, p. 428, Baghdadi, p. 103, *Wuṣla*, p. 27a; Kanz, pp. 108 and. 125.
24. *Wasf*, pp. 428 and pp. 460, Baghdadi, pp. 103–104. *Wuṣla*, p. 23b; Kanz, pp. 108, 123 and 125.
25. *Wuṣla*, p. 62a; Zahr, p. 36a.
26. *Wuṣla*, pp. 63a–b. Snake melon, *Cucumis melo* var. *flexuosus*, is a non-sweet melon which resembles a longish, twisty cucumber with longitudinal grooves. This vegetable (*acur*) is still stuffed in Turkey, often having been dried and then reconstituted out of season. In written Arabic it is also known as *quththā'* and *faqqūs*. In present-day Syria the former name is generally pronounced *mi'ti*, which is actually the classical word *maqtha'a*, 'field of snake melon.' *Quththā'* is cognate with *qishshū'im*, the 'melons of Egypt' for which the children of Israel longed during the Exodus. *Faqqūs* itself is cognate with Hebrew *piqqūs*, which is the word for the process of rubbing off the fuzz on this vegetable. H.S. Paris, 'Semitic

Before *Dolma*: A Taxonomy of Medieval Arab Stuffery

Language Records of Snake Melons (Cucumis melo, Cucurbitaceae) in the Medieval Period and the "piqqus" of the "faqqous"', *Genetic Resource Crop Evolution* 16 February 2011.

27. *Maḥshuwwāt* of chicken, lamb or kid, *Waṣf*, p. 374; chicken stuffing; *Waṣf*, p. 359; Zahr, p. 9a.
28. *Waṣf*., p. 360:
29. *Waṣf*, p. 387 (*samak ṭarī maḥshī*), p. 388 (*samak maqlū maḥshī*) and, p. 394 (*'amal samak fī al-furn*), Zahr, p. 34a (*ṣifat al-maḥshī*) and 18b (*'amal samak mashwī*). The last is followed by 'another recipe for it' which is merely topped with the ingredients of stuffing. Kanz, *'amal al-samak al-mashwī*, p. 90, is preceded by two recipes called stuffed (*maḥshī*) in which the stuffing does not actually enter the fish.
30. *Wuṣla*, p. 48a. Recipe #2 stuffed with meat, #3 stuffed with eggs.
31. *Wuṣla*, p. 60b.
32. *Wuṣla*, p. 45a, *dajāj musamman yuj'al fī sīkh*.
33. *Wuṣla*, p. 45b, *dajāj musamman* #5.
34. *Wuṣla*, p. 45b, *al-muṭayyab*.
35. *Wuṣla*, p.26a, *tamr mulawwaz*; Kanz, p. 129, *ṣifat al-tumūr al-mulawwaza*.
36. *Wuṣla*, p. 14b. This makes it unlike the modern pastry *ma'mūl*, a date-stuffed cookie or cake.
37. Baghdadi, p. 100, *Wuṣla*, p. 22a.
38. Kanz, p. 107, has an odd *kunāfa* which is a fried cake with a filling of toasted semolina.
39. *Wuṣla*, p. 15b, *Waṣf*, p. 419.
40. *Wuṣla*, p. 16a.
41. (*Waṣf*, p. 433; the identical recipe appears in a few MSS of *Wuṣla*, but not including Waqfiyya.)
42. Kanz, p. 12.
43. *Wuṣla* 23b, Baghdadi, p. 103, *Waṣf*, pp. 428 and 430.
44. *Wuṣla* pl. 25a, Baghdadi, p. 104, *Waṣf*, p.429.
45. *Wuṣla*, p. 16b, *Waṣf*, p. 430, Zahr, p. 21a.
46. *Waṣf*, p. 427, *Wuṣla*, p. 67a; recipe ultimately from Ibn Jazla's *Minhāj al-Bayān*.
47. Ibn Razin al-Tujibi, *Faḍālat al-Khiwān*, We 1207 Staatsbibliothek Preussischer Landesbesitz, Berlin.
48. *Kitāb al-Tabīkh fī al-Maghrib wal-Andalus fī 'Asr al-Muwahhidīn li-Mu'allif Majhūl*, ed. Ambrosio Huici Miranda, in *Revista del Instituto Egipcio de Estudios Islamicos en Madrid*, vol. V. 1957. The Spanish translation that appeared under Huici Miranda's name, *Tradducción Española de un Manuscrito Anónimo del Siglo XIII sobre la Cucina Hispano-Magribi*, Madrid, 1966, is not reliable and page references here are to the published Arabic text. An unpolished but generally reliable English translation is available: http://www.daviddfriedman.com/Medieval/Cookbooks/Andalusian/andalusian_contents.htm.
49. Anónimo, p. 10, *mirkās* with fresh cheese/*mirkās bi-jubn raṭb*.
50. Anónimo, p. 154, recipe for eggplant *mirkās*/*ṣifat al-mirkās min bādhinjān*.
51. Anónimo, p. 43, recipe for a hen stuffed without bones/*ṣifat dajāj maḥshū dūn jildihi*; p. 51, a chicken dish/*laun min dajāja* (stuffed with giblets and eggs); p.57, stuffed dish of chicken in the oven/*laun dajāj maḥshī fī al-furn*; p. 39 recipe for hunchbacked (ahdab) chicken/*ṣifat dajāj aḥdab*.
52. Anónimo, p.20 roast lamb breast/*janb mashwī* (stuffed with meat and cheese); another kind of lamb breast/*nau' ākhar min al-janb* (stuffed with breadcrumbs and nuts).
53. Anónimo, p. 18 lamb roast in its skin/*kharūf maḥshī bi-jildihi*.
54. Anónimo, p. 55 recipe for a dish of goose and stuffing/*ṣifat laun min iwazza wa ḥash*; p. 110 stuffed goose/*ṣifat iwazza mahshuwwa*.
55. Anónimo, p. 103 preparation of *sanbūsak*/*'amal al-sanbūsak*.
56. Anónimo, p. 199 *sanbūsak*/*al-sanbūsak*; *sanbūsak* of the common people/*sanbūsak al-'āmma*.
57. Anónimo, p. 37 boiled dish of stuffed eggplants/*maslūq min bādhinjān maḥshī*; p. 112, chicken with stuffed eggplants/*dajāj bi-bādhinjān maḥshī*; p. 154, another type of *mahshi/laun*.
58. Anónimo, p. 200, Abbasid *qata'if*/*ṣifat qaṭā'if 'abbāsiyya*; Faḍāla, p. 16b.
59. Anónimo, p. 56 the preparation of *ka'k*/*ṣun'at al-ka'k*; Faḍāla, p. 13a, *'amal al-ka'k al-maḥshū bil-sukkar wal-lauz*; Faḍāla, p. 14a, *'amal ka'b al-ghazāl*.
60. Anónimo, p. 90, stuffed *qurṣas*/*ṣun'at quraṣ maḥshuwwa*; Faḍāla, p. 15a, *'amal aqrāṣ maḥshuwwa*; p. 19a

Before Dolma: A Taxonomy of Medieval Arab Stuffery

    maqrūḍ.
61. Anónimo, p. 215, stuffed *qanānīt/qanānī maḥshuwwa*.
62. Anónimo, p.79, the making of stuffed eggs/ *'amal baiḍ maḥshī*.
63. Anónimo, p. 121, stuffed eggs/ *baiḍ maḥshī*.
64. Anónimo, p. 47 A pie (*mukhabbaza*) of lamb/*mukhabbaza min laḥm kharūf*; p. 48 a chicken pie/ *mukhabbaza min firākh*; p. 75 a pie of pullets and starlings/*mukhabbaza min firākh wa-zarāzīr*; p. 76, a pie of sea or river fish/*mukhabbaza min ḥūt baḥrī au nahrī*; p. 123, tortoise or mullet pie/*mukhabbaza min salāḥif au būriyyāt*.
65. Anónimo, pp. 185–187; Faḍāla, pp. 20b–22I.
66. Anónimo, p. 37, making stuffed *isfunj/'amal al-isfunj al-maḥshī*.
67. Anónimo, p. 82. the making of *rās maimūn/'amal rās maimūn*; Faḍāla, 38a, *laun ākhar yusammā bi-rās al-maimūn*.
68. Faḍāla, 9a, *tharīda maḥshuwwa bil-dajāj; tharīda maḥshuwwa bil-firākh al-hamam*.
69. Anónimo, p. 17,. stuffed and roast mutton called *al-kamil*, the inclusive/*kabsh maḥshī al-jauf mashwī yusammā al-kāmil*; also in Faḍāla, p 37a, The recipe in Anónimo is followed by a similar recipe for a lamb.
70. Anónimo, p. 18, roast calf made for the Sayyid Abu al-'Ala in Ceuta/ *'ijl mashwī ṣuni'a lil-Sayyid Abī al-'Alā fī Sabta*.
71. Anónimo, p. 17, roast lamb *badī'i/kharūf mashwī badī'ī*.
72. Anónimo, p. 48, stuffed rabbit/*qunaina maḥshī*, p. 50 an extraordinary stuffed rabbit/*qunaina maḥshī 'ajīb*.
73. Anónimo, p. 59, *thurda* of *khabīs* with two chickens; p. 101, preparation of *thurda* of two chickens, one stuffed with the other; p. 126, dish of stuffed chicken.
74. Faḍāla, p. 67a, *laun ākhar*.
75. Anónimo, p. 33, *maḥshi*, a stuffed dish/*ṣan'at al-maḥshī*.
76. Anónimo, p. 50, an extraordinary stuffed rabbit/*qunaina maḥshī 'ajīb* p. 105, stuffed *tafāyā/tafāyā maḥshī*.
77. Anónimo, p. 121, stuffed asparagus/*hilyaun maḥshū*.

Bog Butter: A Gastronomic Perspective

Benedict Reade

People dig for peat. Once dry, this peat burns hot and lets off an evocative smoke that brings to mind the cooking and heating methods of yesteryear. The peat-cutters harvest their quarry from dark brown, water-logged quagmires. Occasionally, these accidental archaeologists discover artifacts left by people long-gone. One such artifact, among the most commonly unearthed items from the watery, misty bogs of Ireland and Scotland, is known as 'bog butter'. Due to the frequency of these findings and its mysterious nature, it has been fairly well studied from an archaeological perspective, perhaps the most thorough investigation being that by Caroline Earwood.[1] In this study I will attempt an exploration of the substance through the eye of a chef and gastronome, combining available literary evidence with our own practical research. We made our own bog butter and subsequent gastronomic analysis with the hope that a new gastronomic perspective on the topic would give us access to a more pragmatic understanding of how and why ancient peoples buried their butter.

Bog butter is butter that has been buried in a peat bog.[2] It has occasionally been confused with animal adipose tissue (most commonly sheep tallow), which has been preserved in the same manner. Over 430 instances of bog butter have been recorded.[3] Of these, 274 have been found in Scotland and Ireland since 1817. These samples are well catalogued by Caroline Earwood. The earliest discoveries are thought to come from the Middle Iron Age (400–350 BC), though this does not exclude the possibility of much more ancient roots. More recently one firsthand account tells of butter being buried for preservation in Co. Donegal 1850–60.[4] In 1892, Rev. James O'Laverty, an advocate of the argument that the butter was buried for gastronomic reasons, dug some butter into a 'bog bank' and left it for eight months. His experiment was carried out in much the same spirit as ours – for analytical purposes and not for a cultural or preserving motive.[5]

This paper aims, by making bog butter using appropriately basic technology, to explore why the *boutyrophagoi*, or 'butter-eaters', across Scotland, Ireland, the Faeroe Islands, Finland and Norway, as well as Kashmir, Assam and Morocco, have buried their butter, with special focus on the Irish, Scottish and Scandinavian traditions.[6] The aim of this paper also extends to a discussion of whether or not butter preserved by this method can have a hedonic value for today's palates, and possibly some use in contemporary cuisine.

Peat bogs are, by their nature, cold, wet places; almost no oxygen circulates in the millennia-old build-up of plant material, which creates highly acidic conditions (our site had a pH of 3.5). Sphagnum moss bogs have remarkable preservation properties, the mechanisms of which are poorly understood.[7] Early food preservation methods have been researched extensively by Daniel C. Fisher, in relation to the preservation of meat. In an attempt to recreate techniques used by Paleoamericans in North America, Fisher sunk various meats into a frozen pond and a peat bog. A key finding from his research is that after one year, bacterial counts on the submerged meats were comparable to control samples which had been left in a freezer for the same amount of time.[8] In fact, suitable foods can probably be aged in many types of soil: salt-rich that will provide dehydration, very cold/freezing that will freeze foods or slow degradation, or, as in our case, anaerobic and acidic conditions to prevent microbial action and oxidation. To our canny ancestors, this preserving characteristic provided an ideal place to bury foods.[9]

Around two-thirds of the bog butter that has been discovered has come in a container or wrapping of some description. These containers are varied; during the spring and summer months when butter was abundant, dairymaids probably used almost anything they could for storage. The most common containers are wooden. These can be described under the broad classifications of kegs, churns, bowls, dishes, boxes, troughs, methers, firkins and piggins.[10] The slowly evolving techniques of the artisan can be seen in these containers and until recently, dates were ascribed to archaeological examples of bog butter in part on account of the workmanship of the container. Willow baskets, staved tubs, or bark wrappings have been used, as have bladders, intestines, and skins or woollen cloth.[11]

Sometimes a combination of materials has been used, such as bark with a bladder, or with a willow basket. One example used a barrel bound in a deerskin to stow the butter into its peaty hiding place.[12] One particularly interesting find, discovered in Rosmoylan (Co. Roscommon, Ireland) dates from the late Iron Age. Within a two-piece barrel, the butter was surrounded with plant fibres from sedge (*Eriophphorum vaginatum*), bent grass (*Agrostis* sp.) and the soft-textured moss, hypnum (*Hypnum cupressiforme*).[13] All three of these plants have a long history of being used by people in mattresses and bedding; the latter takes its name from the Greek 'hypnos' meaning 'sleep'. It is rather poetic that dairymaids had thought of these plants as appropriate for protecting their butter. The butter was wrapped up and made comfortable before being laid down for a long sleep in the bog.

Butter and other dairy products were frequently used as a form of taxation and rent.[14] At Naas Castle in Sweden where we conducted our experiment, butter was a form of tax from the construction of the castle in 1500 until the end of the nineteenth century. One early fifteenth-century manuscript from Scotland, by the Rev. Dr. Archibald Clerk, reports sixteen horse-loads of butter and cheese being found hidden or 'laid-up' near a tenant's house.[15] Butter is valuable: for that reason alone worth hiding, even more so in lawless times. One author testifies that treasures were buried inside fats, so when bog butter was discovered it was pierced from all directions to check for valuables.[16]

Bog Butter: A Gastronomic Perspective

Butter had many uses. It could be used for waterproofing fabric and also a dwelling – one bog house has been discovered where butter and sand have been mixed together to make watertight cement.[17] It might also have been used as a light-source. Angus Grant's 1904 report tells that the found butter was converted into candles but as 'the candles spluttered and crackled, sending sparks of boiling tallow all round…they were voted uncanny, and promptly got rid of'.[18] So while there are many suggestions as to why butter was buried, I propose it was buried not only for its obvious value as a commodity but also for some gastronomic purpose.

While being buried during times of plenty to keep for leaner times, the butter may also have increased its gastronomic value during its time underground. The fact that bog butter never contains salt suggests that it may have been buried to preserve it in times when salt was scarce.[19] During the warmer summers, when rancidity would quickly take hold, burying may have not only been a convenient way of preserving butter, but also of creating a luxury food.[20] As the Danish priest and topographer L.J. Debes said of the Faeroese hoards of buried tallow, 'the longer it is kept being so much the better'.[21] O'Laverty wrote that the Irish buried their butter to 'sweeten it'.[22] He also suggests that it was put into peat to mature it and render it more nutritive.[23] This increased nutrition may be some kind of representation in popular memory of how stored butter could provide for lean times, though it may also refer to a palatable flavour or some biochemical change within the butter itself which renders it more nutritive. Testimonies of bog butter-tasting tend not to describe it as rancid, but many liken the altered fat to cheese. I had to make some to see for myself.

The experiment

From: *The Irish Hiudibras*[24]

But let his faith be good or bad,
In his house great plenty had,
Of burnt oat-bread, and butter found,
With Garlick mixt, in boggy ground,
So strong, a dog, with help of wind,
By scenting out, with ease might find:
And this they call the bravest meat,
That hungry mortals e'er did eat.

So it happened I was introduced to Patrick Johansen, an artisanal butter producer from Sweden. When I heard of his interest in aged butters and experimental butter with wild bacteria, we got to talking. Soon afterward we set to work creating some bog butter of our own. Patrick lives surrounded by great swaths of Swedish forest where elegant birches and enormous oaks grow, interrupted only by the occasional lake and, conveniently, peat bog. His house is a long way from anyone or anything; the water supply is a well in the garden and the only light from paraffin lamps. Patrick learned to make world-class butter from his grandmother, who in turn had learned from the matriarchal line before her. My approach dictated that he decide how everything should be done with the only limitation being that no technology should be used that was not available before the Industrial Revolution.

On the snow-sprinkled morning of 8 April 2012 we embarked on making our twenty-first-century bog butter. We decided that birch bark was to be our material of choice for crafting containers in which to bury the butter. Using an old iron axe we brought down a smooth, tall, straight birch, the bark from which we swiftly peeled. Birch bark unwraps from the trunk with remarkable ease at this time of year; it is soft and pliable yet firm and strong. We peeled the bark and sliced sections out of slightly smaller parts of the tree to make tops and bottoms to our 'barrels'.

We had decided we should make some smaller samples which could be dug up sooner, and then a larger one which will sit underground for some years. *The Irish Hudibras* (1689) asserts that in Ireland, 'butter to eat with their hog, was seven years buried in a bog'.[25] Seven years seems an appropriate length of time for our butter to age.

Although the technology of butter making has changed through the years, the principles remain roughly the same. Butter is made by souring cream, which is then churned until it splits into its fat (butter) and aqueous (butter-milk) phases. The solid butter is removed from the liquid buttermilk, clumped together and washed by kneading it in clean cold water – this removes excess milk solids and buttermilk, thereby increasing the butter's longevity. After washing until the water runs clear, the butter is thrown. This is a process of subjecting the butter to some high impact (literally throwing it against the table), which expels excess water. Now you have butter. The whole process with the latest technology takes about fifteen seconds – for us, it took a little longer.

In earlier times, after milk had been left to stand to allow the cream to rise, it would need to be filtered to remove insects and dirt. Patrick tells me this was often done through grass which, as well as filtering, also supplied the cream with ample lactic acid bacteria. The cow's teat, dairymaid's hands, wooden containers and tools would have also provided plentiful souring bacteria. Filtering could also have been done with a piece of cloth, the advantage being that at the end of the dairy season the cloth could be dried out, preserving spore-forming lactic acid bacteria to be rehydrated and used to inoculate the new batches the following dairy season (non spore-forming bacteria would be lost). For our experiment, in the absence of a cloth from the previous season, we chose to use a 'nest' of grass for filtering. Then the cream was left to sour in a small stone-walled hovel, sunken into the hillside; the kind of dwelling that early pastoralists might have used while in summer pastures.

After souring, the cream must be churned. Traditionally this might have been done by filling a calf's skin with the soured cream and hanging it from a wooden tripod or tree. The skin could then be swung back and forth until the cream split. Many bog butter samples contain large quantities of cow hair, suggesting that perhaps this method of swinging and shaking in a cow skin was often used.[26] To avoid problems of cow hair and in the absence of a calf's skin, we churned our cream by shaking it in a large jar.

The butter was then washed to remove the majority of butter milk. We did this with fresh cold water from the well in the garden – this is quite a simple process of allowing water-soluble parts to be washed out of the butter. Then we removed a large amount of the water by repeatedly picking up the lump of churned and washed butter and throwing it down onto the table. Throwing is an important step in the production of butter to be preserved, so we made sure to do it thoroughly.

We had made four small containers from birch bark and one from pine bark, and we also adapted a large old willow basket to hold a larger sample. In echo of the Rosmoylan bog butter discovery mentioned above we wrapped the butter in hypnum moss, before stuffing these moss-swaddled cylinders into our birch bark barrels – a comfortable bed in which our butter could sleep. Our willow basket held a half-firkin (approx. 12.5 kg) of butter, which was wrapped in a linen apron before being placed in the basket. It was important, as with historical bog butter finds, that the upper surface of the butter be entirely convex, in order that no water collect and stagnate on the top.

Downey et al. note that a large percentage of bog butter discoveries have been made along historic boundary lines.[27] In 1892, James O'Laverty wrote that the butter was dug into 'bog-banks', perhaps another type of territorial confine.[28] Debes's 1673 description of the Faeroe Islands describes how the preserved tallow or 'rue tallow' was buried in a 'dike' which certainly hints at a wall or embankment of some kind.[29] There are many reasons why this should be the case, though it has largely been attributed to ritualistic motivations. I would suggest it may also have been to leave the food in a spot where people were unlikely to dig, and where there was a clear landmark. After looking for an appropriate bog to dig in we found a spot in a sphagnum and birch tree bog. The ground was soft enough to dig easily, and the holes slowly filled up with acidic bog water. We divided our containers between two holes and buried them at around 100cm below the surface. One of these stashes was unearthed and tasted three months after its burial (some notes on these tastings are found below). The second hoard will be allowed to age for a longer time, for seven years in echo of *The Irish Hudibras*, or perhaps left forever as some confusing archaeology for the future: 'It may, therefore, be termed a hidden treasure, which rust doth not consume, nor thieves steel away', as Debes wrote in 1673.[30]

Finally, after counting our steps back to the path, we took a corner off a large rock with the back of our axe. This palm-of-your-hand-sized chunk of rock will now serve as a key. For whoever returns to dig up the butter, the stone key will fit into the rock and the butter will rise up from the bog.

The results
At this point in time, five of our buried containers have been unearthed and tasted, and one remains in its peaty wallow. Tastings of three-month-aged bog butter have

been made at both Nordic Food Lab in Copenhagen, Denmark and at the Oxford Symposium on Food and Cookery 2012 in Oxford, England. Various conclusions can be drawn from these tastings.

In its time underground the butter did not go rancid, as one would expect butter of the same quality to do in a fridge over the same time. The organoleptic qualities of this product were, to many, surprising, causing disgust in some and enjoyment in others. The fat absorbs a considerable amount of flavour from its surroundings, gaining flavour notes which were described primarily as 'animal' or 'gamy', 'moss', 'funky', 'pungent', and 'salami'. These characteristics are certainly far-flung from the creamy acidity of a freshly made cultured butter, but have been found useful in the kitchen especially with strong and pungent dishes, in a similar manner to aged ghee.

As I worked with Patrick to make this bog butter I noticed that all he ate all day was the butter itself. This, he said, is common among butter-makers. A walnut-sized lump will keep one sustained all day. If we consider ancient dairy-based economies, many people may have gone all day eating only butter quite frequently. Occasionally it would be consumed on an oatcake, or with a piece of meat or fish, but often on its own. In times where transhumance brought people to relatively isolated and exposed locations, time spent inside with a fire to keep warm, along with infrequent washing and living-space shared with their animals, may well have meant that stronger foods became more desirable, as they had some character that stood out from the already ripe surroundings.

Taste is, to a large extent culturally defined, and modern tastes have been shaped by myriad modern factors that cannot be removed from the equation. When we tasted this altered butter at this year's Oxford Symposium on Food and Cookery, we had to use some imagination. As O'Laverty wrote of his own bog butter experiment in the late nineteenth century, 'for my own taste I would prefer butter cured in the modern way, but I have no doubt that usage would confer an acquired taste'.[31]

Notes

1. Caroline Earwood, 'Bog Butter: A Two Thousand Year History', *The Journal of Irish Archaeology* 8 (1997), pp. 25–42.
2. Robert Berstan et al., 'Characterization of Bog Butter Using a Combination of Molecular and Isotopic Techniques', *Analyst* 129 (2004), pp. 3–8.
3. L. Downey et al., 'Bog Butter: Dating Profile and Location', *Archaeology Ireland* 75 (2006), pp. 32–34.
4. Earwood.
5. James O'Laverty, 'The True Reason Why the Irish Buried Their Butter in Bog Banks', *Journal of the Royal Society of Antiquities of Ireland* 2 (1892), pp. 356–37.
6. Berstan; David MacRitchie, 'Wooden Dish Found Lately in the Hebrides', *Archaeological Notes, Reliquary* N.S II (1896); E. Estyn Evans, 'Bog Butter: Another Explanation', *Ulster Journal of Archaeology* 3rd. ser, 10 (1947), pp. 59–62; *Proceedings of the Royal Irish Academy* (*PRIA*) vi (1858),

pp. 369–72; personal email exchange with Anders Strinnholm of Stavanger Museum of Archaeology regarding collection item S9457 – three lumps of big butter from the Stavanger area of Norway; James Williams, 'A Sample of Bog Butter from Lachar Moss, Dumfriesshire', *Transactions of the Dumfriesshire and Galloway Natural History and Antiquities Society* 3rd ser., 43 (1966), O'Laverty, 'True Reason'. In Norway a similar practice of burying milk in peat bogs still exists as can be seen here: http://www.nrk.no/nyheter/distrikt/rogaland/jaeren/1.8061809. In Morocco butter is still preserved for long periods of time, sometimes underground, where it is known as *smen*.

7. 'Terence J. Painter', *Carbohydrate Research* 338 (21 November 2003), pp. 2777–78.
8. Sally Pobojewski, 'Underwater Storage Techniques Preserved Meat for Early Hunters', *The University Record*, May 8 1995; retrieved 1/11/2012 from http://www.ur.umich.edu/9495/May08_95/storage.htm.
9. Traditional foods for which burying is a part of the preparation/preservation process, or for which there is evidence that this may have been the case, include: buried eggs (China, eggs); *davuke* (Fiji, bread fruit); *formaggio di Fossa* (Italy, cheese); ghee (India, clarified butter); gravadlax (Scandinavia, salmon); *gubenkraut* (Austria, cabbage); *hákarl* (Greenland, Greenland shark); *igunaq* (Inuit Arctic, walrus); *kiviak* (Greenland, auks in a seal skin): *lutefisk* (Scandinavia, white fish); *muktuk* (Alaska, seal flipper); reindeer's stomach (*Sápmi*, Sweden, stomach with contents); rue tallow (Faeroe Islands & Iceland, sheep's tallow); sealskin poke (Alaska, meat/dried fish with seal fat); *smen* (Morocco, clarified butter); and *surmjølk/myrmjølk* (Norway, milk); Many fermented foods are prepared in fully or partially buried amphoras, including wine in Armenia and soya sauce in Korea.
10. Earwood; F. J. Hunter, 'Iron Age Hoarding in Scotland and Northern England', *Reconstructing Iron Age Societies*, eds. A. Gwilt and C. Hasselgrove, Oxbow Monographs in Archaeology, (Oxford: Oxbow, 1997), p. 71.
11. James O'Laverty, 'Bog-butter', *Ulster Journal of Archaeology* 1st ser., 7 (1859), pp. 288–94.
12. Williams; Earwood.
13. Earwood.
14. O'Laverty, 'Bog-butter'; personal communications between Professor E.C Synnott, Process Engineering Department, University College Cork, Ireland and Dr Alison Sheridon FSA Scot FSA AIFA, Head of Early Prehistory, National Museums Scotland.
15. Rev. Dr. Archibald Clerk, 'Notes on Everything', accessed via Dr. Alison Sheridon FSA Scot FSA AIFA, National Museum of Scotland.
16. Angus Grant, *PSAS* 39 (1904–5), pp. 246–47.
17. Niall Ó Dubhthaigh, 'Summer Pasture in Donegal', *Folk Life* 22 (1984), pp. 42–54.
18. Grant.
19. Earwood; Hunter; O'Laverty, 'True Reason'.
20. Ó Dubhthaigh.
21. James Ritchie, 'A Keg of Bog-butter from Skye', *Proceedings of the Society of Antiquaries of Scotland* 75 (1941), pp. 5–22.
22. O'Laverty, 'Bog-butter'.
23. O'Laverty, 'Bog-butter'; O'Laverty, 'True Reason'
24. Some doubts exist over the author(s) of *The Irish Hudibras*. O'Laverty attributes it to William Moffet in 1855 ('True Reason'). James Farewell (1689) is written in the copy held by the British Library. www.amazon.co.uk attributes the text to 'Multiple Contributors'.
25. O'Laverty, 'True Reason'.
26. O'Laverty, 'Bog-butter'; Ritchie.
27. Downey.
28. O'Laverty, 'True Reason'.
29. *PRIA* vi (1858), pp. 369–72.
30. *PRIA* vi (1858), pp. 369–72.
31. O'Laverty, 'True Reason'.

The Case for Casings

Allyson E. Sgro

Sausages are named by their inner contents; we don't buy 'collagen stuffed with beef' or 'cured hog middle stuffed with garlic and pork', but 'kosher hot dogs' and 'roasted garlic and pork sausage'. For most consumers and home cooks, the casing is an afterthought: an edible wrapping that should not interfere with the stuffing beyond a satisfying snap as we sink our knife or teeth into the meat. Their function appears to be only containing the contents and displaying – thanks to their translucent nature – the stuffing to the consumer. However, relegating sausage casings to this marginal role ignores the other jobs they accomplish. A casing gives a definite and contained shape to what would otherwise be an unwieldy lump of ground meat, and in this sense it is merely a container. However, casings also provide a medium through which we can manipulate stuffings in ways that would not otherwise be possible. Despite being relegated in the modern consumer's mind to the role of a mere edible wrapper, casings are as key to sausages as the meat that is stuffed into them.

To explore what a casing adds to the experience of sausage consumption, we need to break down its contributions. Its first and most obvious role is that of a passive wrapper: our experience of a food begins with our eyes, and the outward appearance of a sausage is both figuratively and literally shaped by its casing. However, the casing doesn't just dictate the form of the sausage: it also contributes to other physical attributes such as colour and perceived texture. Meat colour in particular is often used as an approximation of freshness, and, while a casing can extend the storage time of the meat within, it can also negatively affect our perception of the meat's quality beyond its age. Physical defects or surface aberrations in the casing can change our perception of the contents and risk being an unpleasant reminder of a casing's origins. Appearance is strongly related to preference for a particular kind of sausage and is frequently considered by the food industry when evaluating new casing and stuffing components or processing conditions.[1] While manufacturing convenience is a driving concern in the industry's interest in sausage casings, the reproducibility of a uniform end product also motivates casing research. The food industry understands that the casing's role extends beyond mere wrapper: a highly controlled and homogenous casing substrate helps ensure that each package of sausage promises an identical consumer experience.

In my own attempt to make sausage, this lack of uniform appearance was the primary tipoff that my first experience might not produce the end product I desired. As a friend screwed down the plunger to fill the casing and I guided the casing off the nozzle, I noticed small bulges begin to appear and striations begin to stretch out. A handful of hernias formed and I strategically decided to create new links in the sausage chain to hide them. The casing itself was a little thicker and mottled than the supposedly natural pork casings I'd encountered on my store-bought sausages. It wasn't different enough from my expectations to be unappetizing, but it was a hint that the texture might not be what I expected.

Even more than appearance, casings dictate the tactile sensations a sausage imparts. A crisp, tender casing can give a textural contrast to an emulsified filling, and a rubbery casing that resists both incisor and knife can mar an otherwise perfectly cooked sausage. By moving toward thinner and more processed casings, either artificial or highly modified natural ones, the tactile contributions of a casing can be minimized and thus reduce the potential for a casing to negatively affect the experience of sausage consumption, since the casing's texture and taste are such critical components of the sensory experience. A thin, uniform casing is much easier to sear or roast consistently. A thicker or uneven casing can cook unevenly; sometimes you have to strike a balance between singeing one end and hoping the other will crisp up a bit so you don't have to peel it off before eating. To avoid such issues in controlled studies, the sausage is sometimes cut into small slices or chunks.[2] This technique permits the casing's taste and texture to be ignored in favour of that of the stuffing, but does not change the casing's ability to affect the taste of the stuffing, and thus uncouples the taste of a casing from its effects on the stuffing.

Taste is the primary attribute of the sausage affected by the casing. The casing itself can have a taste, often enhanced by caramelizing the casing in the cooking process, but what makes it transcend the status of edible wrapper is its ability to mediate chemical changes that affect the stuffing's taste. Natural casings are generally composed of the submucosal membrane, just one layer removed from the mucosal membrane that forms the inner surface of the intestine, and this layer's biological role of absorption and secretion makes it well suited to the task of mediating chemical reactions. These membranes are permeable to water vapour and gases that can affect the stuffing and also have the added benefit of interacting with gases during smoking so that their flavour can be affected as well.[3] This role is minimized in most fresh sausages, but it is instrumental in crafting a cured sausage. During curing, the permeable membrane that facilitates the formation of a hospitable environment inside the casing for the bacteria that consume the sugars in the stuffing and generate lactic acid as a waste product.[4] This lactic acid produces the crucial tangy flavour so characteristic of dry fermented sausages.

Biological membranes vary in thickness and diameter, but their generally similar gas permeability and mechanical characteristics make them almost interchangeable as an ingredient. However, artificial casings offer an opportunity to tune the properties of casings that mediate chemical interactions between the contents and the outside world. Materials such as collagen and gelatine provide protection from oxygen while others offer different benefits: gelatine/sodium alginate blends aid in long-term water retention, and pectin-based casings offer protection against lipid oxidation.[5] Collagen casings are particularly popular due to their ease of use in stuffing machinery; from a

The Case for Casings

taste perspective, they rapidly take on the colour and aroma of smoke which allows for shorter smoking cycles to produce the same flavourful result.[6] Casings made entirely from vegetable components have even been developed that don't break or peel during cooking and allow for the development of new vegetarian-friendly sausages.[7] Developing new casings and casing modifications is an active area in food science, but this research primarily seeks the industrial goal of uniformity and increased shelf-life rather than the enhancement of the product as a whole.

Yet casings can be just as important as the stuffing itself. When I bit into both my roasted and sautéed sausages, I was woefully disappointed, and so were my dining companions. Experienced cooks, all of us, and yet here we were stuck with a rubbery membrane around otherwise deliciously seasoned ground meat. What had we done wrong? Here was a standard hog casing like the ones that purported to surround all the sausages we'd expertly cooked in the past, and yet it produced a totally foreign end result. Had our soaking been insufficient thus leaving some salt in the membrane that affected how it cooked? Had we not extruded enough meat into each section of the casing so that it wasn't quite taut? Was the casing itself faulty? Too old? Gone off somehow? We had thought of casings as just a wrapper for so long we had no idea where to begin troubleshooting our failure.

In my first sausage-making attempt, I assumed the casing was infallible and if I treated it as I had countless other casings of the same type it would produce a sausage exterior with the satisfying snap I was craving. Given the range of modifications to the end products that casings facilitate, it is clear that casings serve a function beyond that of a wrapper and are truly an ingredient of the sausage. However, the responsibility of selecting the appropriate casing has mostly shifted to a producer far removed from the consumer; this separation causes the consumer to overlook the casing's key role. I did not appreciate how the casing was just as finicky as any other ingredient and while it could serve its role as a wrapper, it could fail in enhancing the sausage.

My experience illustrates how our perception of sausage has changed in the modern era. Our experience of sausage has not changed because of casing materials, because the classic casings are still the ones most widely in use today despite the new developments in artificial casings. Similarly, the stuffing recipes we commonly use have changed little for hundreds of years.[8] What has changed is our level of contact and experience with casings and thus our appreciation for their role. Sausage has become sanitized and lost its connection to its origins as a food with innards as a wrapper and other mysterious odds and ends of an animal as stuffing. The modern era has mostly relieved consumers of not only their immediate connection to a casing's (unsavoury to some) biological origins but also any need to concern themselves with its role in the sausage. That loss has manifested itself in the consumer's ignorance of the importance of casing selection beyond its utility as a wrapper. We are now provided with a sanitized experience of sausage casings as sausages have evolved from a home-made to a butcher or factory-made food; we do not engage with them in the same way as consumers as we would have during the stuffing process. Rarely are there large variations in the end product to attract our attention to what differences in casings might enhance or detract from the experience beyond the most superficial question of whether or not something is the expected product. When you go through the process of making a food item or cooking a recipe, you develop an appreciation for how each ingredient contributes to the end dish and how variations in the ingredients affect the cooking process. Working with an identical product every time may ensure you have the experience you have come to expect from a particular brand or type of sausage, but it also deprives you of the opportunity to develop an appreciation for how various aspects of a product affect that experience. Casings contribute to every aspect of a sausage from its shape to its taste, and these effects that a casing has on the sensory experience of consuming sausage make it transcend its role as a mere wrapper to become an ingredient.

Notes

1. J. G. Bloukas, E. D. Paneras, and G. C. Fournitzis, 'Effect of Replacing Pork Backfat with Olive Oil on Processing and Quality Characteristics of Fermented Sausages', *Meat Science* 45 (1997), pp. 133–44; J. Flores, J. R. Marcus, P. Nieto, J. L. Navarro, and P. Lorenzo, 'Effect of Processing Conditions on Proteolysis and Taste of Dry-Cured Sausages', *Zeitschrift für Lebensmitteluntersuchung und -Forschung A* 204 (1997), pp. 168–72; S. N. Papadima, I. Arvanitoyannis, J. G. Bloukas, and G. C. Fournitzis, 'Chemometric Model for Describing Greek Traditional Sausages', *Meat Science*, 51 (1999), pp. 271–77.; Y. Sanz, R. Vila, F. Toldrá, and J. Flores, 'Effect of Nitrate and Nitrite Curing Salts on Microbial Changes and Sensory Quality of Non-Fermented Sausages', *International Journal of Food Microbiology* 42 (1998), 213–17; Ragnhild Solheim, 'Consumer Liking for Sausages Affected by Sensory Quality and Information on Fat Content', *Appetite* 19 (1992), pp. 285–92.
2. Cheorun Jo, Ju-Woon Lee, Kyung-Hwan Cho, Hong-Sun Yook, and Myung-Woo Byun, 'Quality Properties of Sausage Made with Gamma Irradiated Natural Casing from Intestine of Pork or Lamb', *Radiation Physics and Chemistry* 63 (2002), pp. 365–67, p. 365; A. Conte, R. Marino, A. Della Malva, A. Sevi, and M. A. Del Nobile, 'Influence of Different Casings on Salami Produced with Meat from Buffalo and Podolian Cattle', *Journal of Food Quality* 35 (2012), pp. 127–36, p. 129; Solheim, p. 286.
3. Gunter Heinz and Peter Hautzinger, *Meat Processing Technology for Small-to Medium-Scale Producers* (Bangkok: FAO Regional Office for Asia and the Pacific, 2007), p. 249; Michael Ruhlman and Brian Polcyn, *Charcuterie: The Craft of Salting, Smoking, and Curing* (New York: Norton, 2005), pp. 104–105.
4. Juan A. Ordóñez, Eva M. Hierro, Jose M. Bruna, and Lorenzo de la Hoz, 'Changes in the Components of Dry-Fermented Sausages During Ripening', *Critical Reviews in Food Science and Nutrition* 39 (1999), pp. 329–67, p. 331; Ruhlman and Polcyn, p. 172.
5. L. Liu, J. F. Kerry, and J. P. Kerry, 'Application and Assessment of Extruded Edible Casings Manufactured from Pectin and Gelatin/Sodium Alginate Blends for Use with Breakfast Pork Sausage', *Meat Science* 75 (2007), pp. 196–202, pp. 198, 200; K. S. Miller and J. M. Krochta, 'Oxygen and Aroma Barrier Properties of Edible Films: A Review', *Trends in Food Science & Technology* 8 (1997), pp. 228–37, p. 235.
6. Milda E. Embuscado, *Edible Films and Coatings for Food Applications* (New York: Springer, 2009), p. 248; Joshua Lipsky, 'Casings: A Sausage's Best Friend', *National Provisioner* 219 (2005), pp. 88, 90, 92, p. 88.
7. Lipsky, p. 92.
8. Hannah Glasse, *The Art of Cookery Made Plain and Easy* (Bedford, MA: Applewood Books, 1998), p. 152; Janet Hinson (translator), 'Le Menagier De Paris' (1393): <http://www.daviddfriedman.com/Medieval/Cookbooks/Menagier/Menagier.html> [accessed 31 May 2012]; Ruhlman and Polcyn, p. 116; D. L. Salsbury, 'All About Sausage Casings', *Countryside and Small Stock Journal* (1999), 80–82, p. 80.

A Case for Culinary Mongrelism

May Rosenthal Sloan

During a discussion with a group of Jewish-British women from Leeds, filmed for the 2011 television programme *Jamie's Great Britain*, Jamie Oliver stated, 'We think that fish and chips is ours, but it's not ours, it's theirs … but we consider it ours, which is a compliment to them'. This rhetoric of 'us and them' – at play in a UK media production which otherwise seemingly embraced the concept of multi-ethnic influences on the food of a particular region – is outdated. It exemplifies the confused and often divisive manner in which identities based on fixed notions of religion, ethnicity or nationhood remain central to our culinary consciousness. From Glaswegian deep-fried pizza to Trinidadian doubles, both eaten on a sunny Brooklyn street, wrapped and stuffed foods make an interesting starting point for delving into the world of what I would tentatively term, culinary mongrelism. This idea is influenced by the work of historian Panikos Panayi who, pointing to the long history of multi-ethnic influences on British food, asserts that 'to suggest that we have moved from an "English" cuisine in 1900 to an international one a hundred years later distorts the truth.'[1]

I would further this assertion by suggesting that all dishes, 'cuisines' and indeed forms of culinary expression are more ethnically diverse than they might initially seem and that, in assigning them 'pure' national or ethnic identities, we are falsely constructing culinary restrictions. In this paper, I attempt to reclaim the idea of the mongrel food as a positive concept by encouraging breaking down these restrictions and embracing ethnic complexities. As such, I suggest that we are all culinary mongrels.

Recent examples I have consumed include the deep-fried pizza, or crispy slice, an Italian baked flatbread, transported to Scotland, probably via the United States, and influenced by Jewish fish-cooking techniques, whereby a protective layer of batter is wrapped around the food to be fried. Doubles, fried flatbreads, called *bara*, stuffed with a spiced chickpea mixture, are sold by Asian Trinidadians, the descendants of indentured immigrants, to black Caribbean-Americans in New York. Then there is French baguette stuffed to bursting with sizzling catfish, hot with bird's eye chillies, sour and salty with a dressing made of fish sauce and lime, sweetened with a little sugar. Topped with long batons of carrot, shredded lettuce and fragrant coriander, *Bánh Mì* has become deservedly popular in New York, London and Sydney. As well as having been transported from Vietnam to the English-speaking West, *Bánh Mì*, like a good deal of southern Vietnamese food, is an example of the influence of the colonizing French upon Vietnam.[2] All of these foods have geographical and ethnic influences which are varied. In this paper, I will discuss in more detail three wrapped or stuffed dishes whose component parts demonstrate the theory that I am forming as part of my doctoral research. These are foods which I have encountered either whilst carrying out fieldwork in London and New York, where my research is based, or on other travels where food has invariably played a central role to my sense of environmental understanding.

My doctoral work evolved from a project that looked at the history of a market in east London, close to where I grew up. One of the first stuffed foods to capture my attention for its hybrid nature was the jerk-chicken bagel, which came out of this market, or more specifically a bakery in it. When I was a child in the area, the bakery in question sold bagels, *challah*, chopped herring and cream cheese. It was run by Jews and aimed at Jewish customers, although many others used it. Good smoked salmon was available elsewhere in the market that had for years had a large Jewish presence both in terms of custom and trading. As a number of Caribbean migrants settled in the area from the 1960s onwards, their presence began to be felt in the market, and the numbers of Jewish traders decreased. By the mid-1980s, a guide to London markets stated that 'the loud-coloured shirts and dresses of the West Indians, equally loud reggae music and stalls heaped with yams, cassavas and green bananas evoke a calypso atmosphere more like Jamaica than Dalston'.[3] Ridley Road did not appear by this point to be an obviously Jewish market.

However, there did not need to be a large, local Jewish population for foods of that group to be sold and enjoyed. Having largely moved on, the Jews of Dalston had left their legacy. By the mid-1990s, the Ridley Road Bagel Bakery had changed hands, and its selection of bagels was becoming more varied. In 1996, the *Independent* deemed the bakery one of the top ten places in London to eat the boiled and baked breads, citing in particular its 'blueberry, granary and garlic varieties'.[4] The choice of bagel would soon become even more unusual when, at the end of the decade, the bakery was taken over by Pakistani owners who recognized the market for Jewish baked goods with a Caribbean flavour. Now fillings included jerk or brownstew chicken, and ackee and saltfish. Patties and other Caribbean foods were available alongside, whilst the legacy of the area's Jewish past remained.

I interviewed the young manager, Aydan, who was born in southern Turkey but moved to London when he was a child. It was evident throughout his interview that his interest in the food he sold was entirely business-related. With little ethnic or culinary investment in either the bread or its filling, Aydan stated that customers spent '*crazy money … On the bagels itself, so it's like, I'll give you example, the jerk chicken bagel, bagel with a bit of chicken, three pounds thirty which is, they really make a profit*'.[5] The jerk chicken bagel represents, in many ways, the changes that have occurred in the area over the last century or more. The bread serves as a lingering legacy of Dalston's Jewish settlers who came to the area from the late-nineteenth century onwards. Its highly spiced, juicy chicken filling, rich with allspice and chilli, reminds us of the immigration of people from Jamaica and other Caribbean islands from the mid-twentieth century. But this stuffed bread also tells of the groups who have taken opportunities to sell foods which may seem ethnically charged, but have little to do with them, other than in an economic sense. In this case, Pakistani and Turkish entrepreneurs have little investment in the meaning or even taste of the food but know that it makes a profit. This in turn offers a comparison with white British traders on the market, many of whose families have had stalls there for generations, and who have responded to the influx of Caribbean and African custom by picking up the trade in yams, cassava and other such produce.

Travelling over 6000 miles, but remaining in a highly spiced, plastic-chaired and linoleum-floored site of sale much like that of the previous snack, Singapore is perhaps one of the most interesting places to look at the ethnic complexity of many wrapped and stuffed foods, affected as it is by a complex history of migration and colonialism. In 1967, two years after Singapore had become a nation state, Dr Goh Keng Swee, then the Minister of the Interior and Defence, stated that 'We are a complex, multi-racial community with little sense of common history, with a group purpose which is yet to be properly articulated. We are in the process of rapid transition towards a destiny which we do not yet know'.[6] A country with as many as four official languages is likely to be defined by a similarly diverse hybrid of food cultures. A recent guidebook to the country asserted that 'No subject arouses as much Singaporean passion, or is likelier to provoke an argument than food ... It would be easier to win a consensus on climate change at the UN than it would be to find two Singaporeans who agree on the best place to eat something'.[7] This is a country where a discussion of the ethnic make-up of food is particularly appropriate.

Furthermore, being as full as it is of street food, Singapore is rich in the realm of the wrapped and stuffed. The snack food *Roti John* is an interesting case through which aspects of Singaporean ethnic history are visible. Using the word *roti* to refer simply to bread, *Roti John* consists of a soft bread roll, filled with highly spiced mutton, sardines or anchovies. It is usually dipped into an egg-based batter and fried. Once cooked, it is often served crisscrossed with stripes of tomato ketchup and mayonnaise. Two articles in the Singaporean newspaper *The Straits Times* in 1986 and 1988 assigned ownership of the snack to a Malay hawker who had made the first version for 'an English "John", explaining that the name John is often used in Malay speech to refer to an unknown English man'.[8] Thus the real John for whom this dish was named remains a mysterious and unknown figure, symbolizing more than anything else a cultural distance between Singaporean ethnic groups.

In a discussion of nation-building and ethnicity, Michael D. Barr and Zlatko Skrbiš paint a picture of a colonial history in which the 'The Malays were viewed by both the Chinese and the colonial administration as being "endowed with the traits of complacency, indolence, apathy, infused with a love of leisure and an absence of motivation and discipline".'[9] This complex and difficult inter-ethnic relationship adds to the idea of 'John' as a culturally distant character.

Roti John combines a filling of the spiced meat or fish of much Malay food, with 'French' bread (in fact far softer in most cases than a baguette) of the *roti* itself, a marker perhaps of culinary exchange between Europe and Asia. It also provides a link to the United States, with legend suggesting that the 'John' for whom it was first made was in fact requesting a hamburger from the Malay hawker.[10] This in turn points to the Americanization of British food culture during the latter half of the twentieth century, when, according to Panayi, 'multinationals, above all McDonalds, ... also introduced foreign foods, symbolized by the hamburger, into Britain'.[11] By the mid-1960s, when *Roti John* entered into the world via a Malay Singaporean, a hamburger had become a perfectly normal thing for a British tourist or expatriate (for who knows where 'John' lived?) to order from a restaurant or street vendor.

To further push the idea of *Roti John* as a symbolically mongrel food, one might examine this very familiar item of now-international fast food. For, of course, the hamburger which is so symbolic of the United States of America, was in fact transported to the New World from Europe. In his account of New York food and drink between 1624 and 1898, Andrew Smith describes a Manhattan establishment run by an immigrant, August Ermisch, which 'featured a number of traditional German dishes, including a "Hamburger steak",' and tells how within a decade the dish had become familiar throughout the country. Stuffed into bread rolls by street vendors, it made a convenient working lunch the type of which 'John' would have been requesting'.[12]

Finally, the garish condimental zigzags atop a *Roti John* add to the story. The addition of mayonnaise, like the link of the bread and the lingering thought of hamburgers, returns us to Europe and to France. More interesting is the ketchup, which in this case is almost certainly the Heinz tomato variety, with the odd salty and sour note but predominantly sweet and, well, red-tasting. Ketchup gives the dish a further link to the United States and Pittsburgh in particular, where the son of German immigrants founded a company that would boast 57 varieties. However the history of the sauce adds a pleasingly cyclical element to the story of *Roti John*, for its origin was not in the west at all. *The Oxford Companion to Food* states that 'the word "ketchup" comes from the Chinese (Amoy dialect) *kêtsiup*, meaning a fermented fish sauce, probably via a Malay word *kechap*, now spelled *kecap*, which means soy sauce'.[13]

From Singapore and Malaysia via Britain, the United States and Germany, this egg-and-bread dish stuffed with spiced fish or mutton is truly an excellent symbol of mongrel foods, even without starting on the complexities of the spice trade, which could not be done justice in a piece of this length.

To finish with a more personal story, which is just a little bit surreal, we travel back to east London, to an interview-respondent called Renford. His description of a unique dish he had created, consisting of jellied rice wrapped in a layer of choux pastry tiles, seemed to encompass many issues of cultural exchange, both immediate to his experience and more widely indicative of my approach to mongrelizing foods.

To properly understand these issues, a little background on the creator of the dish is required. Born in 1937, Renford moved from Montego Bay, Jamaica, to London in the

1960s and started work as a kosher caterer for, amongst other people, the Ford Motor Company. By the time I met him, Renford had for some years run his own company, a bakery, in an east London market. Throughout his interview, he regularly expressed appreciation for the Jewish culture with which he had been surrounded as a newcomer to the country. This desire to associate with the more established minority, who had settled before most Jamaican immigrants, can be seen as symbolic of his desire to be viewed as an established settler. This would also be reinforced by his distancing himself from those migrants from Asian and African countries subsequently arriving in this part of London.

When discussing the various ethnic groups visible in the diverse market, Renford offered the following philosophical explanation: 'To me, race is like vegetable. You got turnip, you got carrot, you got cabbage, you got beetroot. If you don't like beetroot, eat carrot. If you don't like that [*chuckling*], eat turnip. But *all* is vegetable. See what I'm saying? … and I like *all* vegetable'.[14] However, questioned about the changes that he has witnessed in the market in the forty-odd years he has been working there, his views of those from other cultures became less abstract and more complex:

> It changed because, yeah in the sixties, market in, in *here*, we have more Jewish people in here. You got more, more variety of stuff. Yeah? … All these butcher over here used to be English butcher. Now if you look now they all Asian. Quality has gone down … and um, the African people they … they have got to bring back the stock, that Caribbean people don't *eat*. Lot of the African stock, Caribbean people don't *buy* from them so they don't eat that stuff. You have snails in the shells, some *black fish* they, we never eat them. … [*In a low voice*] I don't know what it is and we have *never* eaten those kind of things. So Caribbean people do not buy those kind of things. … You understand, so that's where the market, gradually change and more and more African come in and more and more *Asian*.[15]

Asked whether he felt more connected with the Jewish element of the market, he responded with conviction, 'Yes, yes, it is, it is. That's true, yes.'[16] He then went on to describe the trust between himself and the Jewish traders who had existed on the market, in comparison with the Asian traders who, he asserted, sometimes fiddled with the scales. Renford's adamant stance that 'Caribbean' and 'African' food were wholly dissimilar was set against his opinion that 'Caribbean' and 'Jewish' foods shared many characteristics. Both of these responses to the foods around him appeared to reflect the position he felt he occupied in the densely layered ethnic landscape of the area.

When describing the banquets that he used to cater for Ford, Renford talked of the centrepieces he painstakingly made from a curious assortment of ingredients to resemble pineapples. These drew on the classic French cookery techniques he had been taught in Jamaica. They also replicated the produce of Renford's native country as well as referencing English Victorian table decoration. They were then recreated in

A Case for Culinary Mongrelism

London for a kosher, Jewish audience. Renford explained patiently how one of these centrepieces was constructed:

> I have something from Ford's, we used to make artificial stuff. Like um, I … used to make pineapple, but is not pineapple, look *just* like a pineapple. … I used to, wi' gelatine, and put it into a rice, bowl a rice, and you get the shape of the rice like a pineapple, yeah? Then you make choux paste … and you drop the choux paste like the pineapple pit that you see in the pineapple, and then try put it in the oven, come to that colour. … So the rice become firm … Yeah? So you done

A Case for Culinary Mongrelism

all these fancy bit like, wi' the choux paste, you bake that up and you stick them on the rice, like, like a pineapple, look *just* like a pineapple ...and you never noticed that when you finished; you just had a pineapple.[17]

Of course, this description immediately served as a challenge to me. Step by step, I cooked the rice, set it in gelatine in bowls and placed these together, skewering them until set. I then made a choux pastry, piped and baked it in small squares. I wrapped the rice jelly in a blanket of these choux tiles, and topped the whole with slivers of green 'lunchbox bars' which according to Renford's instructions, should have been angelica. And five or six hours later, I had to agree that this complex and involved method produced a centrepiece which did not look wholly unlike a pineapple.

From Montego Bay to London, taking in a little of France and aiming at a Jewish table, this dish, which I call a Montego Bay Kosher Choux Pineapple is a curious one which tells a little of one man's journey through his life and the world. When I asked Renford how the dish tasted, he looked surprised, blinked and said, 'We don't *eat* it!'.[18] Having tasted a little of my recreation, I can see why. However, even if devoid of culinary charm, this nonetheless edible dish, like the jerk chicken bagel, *Roti John* and other wrapped and stuffed foods are particularly satisfying dishes to separate into their various elements in order to explore the diverse ethnic and geographical histories existing within them, and begin to argue the case for culinary mongrelism.

A Case for Culinary Mongrelism

Notes

1. 'Immigration and Food in 20th-Century Britain, Exchange and Ethnicity', *Journal for the Study of British Cultures* 13.1 (2006).
2. Alan Davidson, ed., *The Oxford Companion to Food* (Oxford: Oxford UP, 1999), pp. 829–30.
3. Alec Foreshaw and Theo Bergström, *Markets of London, a Complete Guide with Maps and Photographs* (Middlesex: Penguin, 1983), p. 86.
4. Collette Harris, 'Ten Places to Buy Bagels', *The Independent*, 3 March 1996.
5. Interview with Aydan, conducted by the author, July 2010.
6. Qtd. in Ernest C.T. Chew and Edwin Lee, *A History of Singapore* (Oxford: Oxford University Press, 1991), p. 363.
7. Joshua Samuel Brown, *Singapore Encounter* (Victoria: Lonely Planet, 2010), p. 158.
8. 'A Sandwich Once Made for "John"', *The Straits Times*, 2 November 1986; 'Local Spreads', *The Straits Times*, 17 September 1988.
9. *Constructing Singapore, Elitism, Ethnicity and the Nation-Building Project* (Copenhagen: Nordic Institute of Asian Studies, 2008), p. 88.
10. 'Local Spreads'.
11. *Spicing Up Britain, The Multicultural History of British Food* (London: Reaktion Books, 2008), p. 9.
12. Andrew F. Smith, 'The Food and Drink of New York from 1624 to 1898', *Gastropolis: Food & New York City*, eds. Annie Hauck-Lawson and Jonathan Deutsch (New York: Columbia University Press, 2009), p. 45.
13. Davidson, p. 433.
14. Interview with Renford, conducted by the author, July 2010.
15. Ibid.
16. Ibid.
17. Ibid.
18. Ibid.

'Four and Twenty Blackbirds Baked in a Pie': A History of Surprise Stuffings

David C. Sutton

Sing a song of sixpence
A pocket full of rye
Four and twenty blackbirds
Baked in a pie
When the pie was opened
The birds began to sing
O wasn't that a dainty dish
To set before the king?

This is one of the best known of English nursery rhymes, still sung by young children, and still found in children's books, often with pictures of happy blackbirds flying up from an improbably small pie. One tradition associates the song with a real incident which is said to have occurred during Anne Boleyn's seductive invitation of King Henry VIII to Hever Castle, and a few accounts wickedly suggest that the blackbirds were not only dead but rank (with 'sing' meaning stink to high heaven).

Blackbirds, thrushes and smaller birds were indeed baked in English pies from medieval times until much more recently. In the 1860s Mrs Isabella Beeton famously included a recipe for blackbird pie in her guide to household management. It seems fairly clear, however, that this particular nursery rhyme is referring to a stranger tradition: the medieval practice of surprise stuffings, a form of 'subtlety'. Whether or not the song dates from the 1520s and concerns Anne Boleyn, the blackbirds are likely to have been alive.

The use of live animals in pies (blackbirds, thrushes, pigeons, even frogs) or on the floor of the banqueting hall (peacocks, rabbits, swans, even foxes) derives originally from decadent periods of the Roman Empire, but re-emerged as a typical feature of the *entremets* of the grandest medieval banquets.

Entremets

Entremets literally means 'between dishes', and in the classic French cuisine of the nineteenth and twentieth centuries had come to mean a small dish served between the cheese and the dessert (this is still the primary definition in the *Dictionnaire Larousse*). In the medieval banquet, however, and particularly from the fourteenth century to the seventeenth centuries, the *entremets* became an elaborate entertainment course featuring illusion foods (live chickens plucked and disguised as roasted dead birds), extravagant fancies (pike's heads breathing fire), musical interludes (musicians emerging from stage-props, and even occasionally from huge pies), architectural constructions such as miniature castles and ostentatious displays of wealth in gold and silver trappings.[1]

The extravagances of the *entremets* led to severe criticism by the Church, but the great medieval princes (and some prelates) found the competition in producing ever more spectacular dishes and entertainments too alluring. Cooked peacocks were painstakingly re-dressed in their feathers; huge hedgehogs were built out of almonds; according to the *Magia naturalis* a goose was roasted and carved while still alive and walking around; for Lenten banquets, fish would be cooked and then disguised as pheasants; cooked swans and herons were decorated with leaves of real gold; Pope Clement VI was served from a beautiful fountain which dispensed five different wines (Vernaccia, Greco, Bielna, Saint-Pourçain and Rhenish); a *pâté de Lorraine* was cut open and a flight of live birds escaped.

To the modern reader there is a strong element of the ridiculous about these *entremets* exuberances. We are prompted to remember that the French word for stuffing is *farce*. A highly critical assessment of these old-fashioned excesses began during the fastidious reign of King Louis XIV. From around 1660 new attitudes of gastronomic taste-matching, serious appreciation and respect for the flavour of each individual food were becoming the norm in France. The self-indulgence of the *entremets* was seen as archaic, disrespectful and ridiculous. A key destructive text was *Le repas ridicule* (1666) by Boileau (Nicolas Boileau-Despréaux). Within a decade of its publication, the medieval *entremets* had disappeared.

Subtleties

The medieval banquet and its *entremets* were certainly not subtle, in the most usual modern sense of the word. They might be described as dazzling, astonishing, bizarre, extravagant, grotesque – anything but subtle. And yet the dishes served at the *entremets* stage of the feast, especially the elaborate sugary confections, were known in England as subtleties (often spelt 'sotelties'), using the word subtlety in the sense of ingenuity.

The Oxford Companion to Food has a dismissive entry on Entremets, but a helpful account under the heading Subtleties:

> While medieval diners ate, at formal meals, they observed the spectacle that was performed between courses. The course was called a met; the activities between courses were therefore the entremets. The contemporary English term was 'soteltie'. …
>
> The line between entremets made to be eaten and for allegorical purposes was not strictly observed. At Charles the Bold's festivities a course at one meal consisted of some thirty pies, each enclosed in a silk pavilion and each bearing

the name of a walled town under Charles's rule. The visual effect was that of a military encampment; the message was clearly a statement of Charles's military strength. A more pastoral, poetic conception appeared at the last of these wedding feasts. Thirty platters were made up to look like gardens, each with a golden hedge surrounding a different kind of fruit tree; each tree bore the name of a ducal abbey. Around the trees were figures of peasants harvesting the fruit while others held baskets with candied spices and fruit for the guests to eat. Other entremets at these festivities were more fantastic: a court dwarf rode in on the back of a lion and was given to the bride, Margaret of York, to whom he sang a song and presented a daisy (in French *marguerite*).[2]

These fifteenth-century Burgundian subtleties represent the apogee of the practice. It was difficult to imagine how any future banquet could surpass their superabundance. In England subtleties were usually more subdued and more sugary. One early example (from the *Collection of Ordinances of the Royal Household*, around 1425, quoted in the *Oxford English Dictionary*) was a sugar model of Saint George on horseback slaying the dragon. Bishop Latimer in 1552 gives an even more placid account (by Burgundian standards): 'At the end of the dinner they have certain subtleties, custards, sweet and delicate things'. In Portugal, several accounts state that in 1513 King Manuel offered the Pope a life-size effigy of himself surrounded by twelve cardinals and three hundred candles, all made of sugar.[3]

Other countries of Europe tended to think of France (and not only fifteenth-century Burgundy) as the country where *entremets* and subtleties were most extraordinary. Chaucer visited France on a number of occasions, and in 'The Frankeleyns Tale' (written in the 1380s) his franklin describes a French banquet where an imitation river was created in the banqueting hall, with a barge sailing on it, watched by jugglers and a live lion.

Subtleties were intended at least to surprise and impress, sometimes to astonish, and occasionally to amaze. The surprise stuffings – and especially the stuffings with live animals – clearly came at the amazing end of this spectrum.

Frog pie

The accounts of live birds emerging from pies, epitomized by our twenty-four blackbirds, are fairly frequent from the fourteenth to the seventeenth centuries – although the number of incidents is perhaps not many more than the number of accounts. Internet searches on *oiseaux vivants* and *uccelli vivi* lead to numerous French, Burgundian and Italian examples.

The flying birds were by far the most common surprise stuffing, and they were brought into other aspects of the medieval banquet as well. In 1513, for example, the city of Rome offered a special banquet to the Medici family which began with a beautiful cloth napkin at each place-setting. Inside each napkin was a small bird, and the birds, of course, all flew up into the air as the napkins were shaken out.[4]

A History of Surprise Stuffings

Although small birds were favoured, any lively living creature could be used for a surprise stuffing. Clearly, it was important that they should be not only alive but vigorous when the pie came to be opened. The pie therefore needed to have not only a supply of fresh air, but ideally some food for sustenance (such as 'a pocket-full of rye'). Here is a classic recipe for a pie to contain living creatures, published in *Epulario* in 1516, with the English translation appearing in 1598:

> Make the coffin of *a great pie* or *pasty*, in the bottome thereof make a hole as big as your fist, or bigger if you will, let the sides of the coffin bee somewhat higher than ordinary pies, which done put it full of *flower* and bake it, and being baked, open the hole in the bottom, and take out the flower. Then having *a pie of the bigness of the hole in the bottom of the coffin aforesaid*, you shal put it into the coffin, withall put into the said coffin round about the aforesaid pie *as many small live birds as the empty coffin will hold*, besides the pie aforesaid. And this is to be done at such time as you send the pie to the table, and set before the guests; where uncovering or cutting up the lid of the great pie, all the birds will flie out, which is to delight and pleasure shew to the company.[5]

It would be anachronistic to think of such 'surprise pies' as a waste of good pastry, since pie-pastry would not have been considered as part of the food at the tables of the rich even if it contained the most delicious fillings. Pastry and pies were regarded as containers, to be discarded once their contents had been enjoyed (or, alternatively, to be eaten by the servants).

An extreme example of a surprise stuffing is found in a fairly late source, Robert May's *The Accomplisht Cook*, first published in 1660.[6] Having studied French food habits and learned about frogs as a food, May included several frog recipes in his book, including marinated frogs and baked frogs. He also included this astonishing proposal for an *entremets* event structured around a surprise stuffing:

> Make the likeness of a Ship in Paste-board, with Flags and Streamers, the Guns belonging to it of Kickses, bind them about with packthread, and cover them with close paste proportionable to the fashion of a Cannon with Carriages, lay them in places convenient as you see them in Ships of war, with such holes and trains of powder that they may all take Fire; Place your Ship firm in the great Charger; then make a salt round about it, and stick therein egg-shells full of sweet water, you may by a great Pin take all the meat out of the egg by blowing, and then fill it up with the rose-water, then in another Charger have the proportion of a Stag made of course paste, with a broad Arrow in the side of him, and his body filled up with claret-wine; in another Charger at the end of the Stag have the proportion of a Castle with Battlements, Portcullices, Gates and Draw-Bridges made of Past-board, the Guns and Kickses, and covered with course paste as the former; place it at a distance from the ship to

fire at each other. The Stag being placed betwixt them with egg shells full of sweet water (as before) placed in salt. At each side of the Charger wherein is the Stag, place a Pye made of course paste, in one of which let there be some live Frogs, in each other some live Birds; make these Pyes of course Paste filled with bran, and yellowed over with saffron or the yolks of eggs, guild them over in spots, as also the Stag, the Ship, and Castle; bake them, and place them with guilt bay-leaves on turrets and tunnels of the Castle and Pyes; being baked, make a hole in the bottom of your pyes, take out the bran, put in your Frogs, and Birds, and close up the holes with the same course paste, then cut the Lids neatly up; To be taken off the Tunnels; being all placed in order upon the Table, before you fire the trains of powder, order it so that some of the Ladies may be perswaded to pluck the Arrow out of the Stag, then will the Claret-wine follow, as blood that runneth out of a wound. This being done with admiration to the beholders, after some short pause, fire the train of the Castle, that the pieces all of one side may go off, then fire the Trains, of one side of the Ship as in a battel; next turn the Chargers; and by degrees fire the trains of each other side as before. This done to sweeten the stink of powder, let the Ladies take the egg-shells full of sweet waters and throw them at each other. All dangers being seemingly over, by this time you may suppose they will desire to see what is in the pyes; where lifting first the lid off one pye, out skip some Frogs, which make the Ladies to skip and shreek; next after the other pye, whence come out the Birds, who by a natural instinct flying in the light, will put out the Candles; so that what with the flying Birds and skipping Frogs, the one above, the other beneath, will cause much delight and pleasure to the whole company: at length the Candles are lighted, and a banquet brought in, the Musick sounds, and every one with much delight and content rehearses their actions in the former passages.[7]

This late account appears to be in earnest, although some commentators have assumed it to be a parody, and almost beyond parody.

Roman surprise stuffings

These entertainments of the medieval banqueting halls had their origins in certain periods of the Roman Empire, the previous golden age of European decadence. Above all they call to mind the *Cena* section of the *Satyricon* of Petronius (often known as 'Trimalchio's feast'), where first a huge boar is brought into the banqueting hall, apparently cooked and decorated with baskets of dates. When the boar's side is cut open, out into the room flies a flock of thrushes. Trimalchio has a group of fowlers ready with limed twigs, and the thrushes are caught, cooked and presented, one for each diner. This is followed later by an elaborate hoax with a pig. The pig is chosen and sent away to be cooked; it comes back bulging, and the chef is stripped for punishment for having apparently forgotten

A History of Surprise Stuffings

to remove the intestines; at the last minute, however, the pig is cut open and out pours a selection of sausages and blood-puddings, ready to eat.

The *Satyricon* is usually assumed to be a moral satire of the age of Nero, and of Nero's own court in particular. As Nero has long been a byword for tastelessness, savagery and immorality, it is curious that our medieval banqueters were not more reticent about imitating him. The imitation featured shared elements such as the baked thrushes, but it was the surprise stuffings above all which linked the medieval banquets to the time of Nero.

As well as Neronian excess, the *Satyricon* is usually seen as exemplifying Saturnalian licence. The characteristics of this festival, as summarized by Kronos in Lucian's *Saturnalia*, were the forbidding of any serious behaviour, any athletic training or any financial transactions; the encouragement of drinking, noise, games, dice, singing naked; licensed drunkenness; and the overturn of social positions, with slaves allowed to mock and revile their owners.

There is a clear imitation of Trimalchio's feast in a banquet described by the Byzantine writer Theodoros Prodromos. This is Gobryas' feast, in the course of which Artaxanes is served with a whole lamb, tears at the side of it, and sees a flight of baby sparrows emerging into the dining room.[8]

Three great banquets

Descriptions of several great medieval banquets have survived in considerable, though sometimes confused, detail. The main characteristics of these banquets are often similar, and surprise stuffings always play an important role.

The grandest banquet of all is usually said to be that of the vow of the pheasant (*le festin du voeu du faisan*). This spectacular feast was arranged by Philippe le Bon, Duke of Burgundy, in Lille in 1454 as a response to the Turkish capture of Constantinople. The ostensible purpose of the banquet was to invite princes from all over Christendom to agree a latter-day crusade against the Ottomans, and to swear a crusading oath on a live pheasant. Above all, however, the banquet was a celebration of the grandeur and wealth of the Burgundians.

In fact, a succession of banquets was held in January and February 1454, all on the same theme. The first banquet featured a huge silver swan on the main table, apparently pulling a boat. But it was the third banquet which became the talk of the courts of Europe. Held on 17 February 1454, it featured several architectural *entremets de paintrerie*, huge constructions of wood, metal and cloth, mounted on the tables, with fountains spouting, and within a huge model church an organ which could be heard playing. An immense whale was towed into the hall, from which emerged a troupe of dancers; there was a live lion in the hall at one stage, and two live falcons pursued an unfortunate heron. Many courses of food, in large quantities, were wheeled in and out of the hall on trolleys. Depictions of Burgundian glory were everywhere, alongside *tableaux* reminding the guests of Saracen conquests and Christian defeats. There was

A History of Surprise Stuffings

even a giant Saracen leading a live elephant, and music specially written by Gilles Binchois and performed by a group of musicians – variously numbered at twenty-four and twenty-eight – sitting inside an enormous pie.

Finally a live pheasant was presented, supposedly from the Black Sea state of Colchis, and all the knights and grandees present swore an oath on the pheasant, committing themselves to a new crusade. The crusade never took place, and the banquet was condemned not only for its decadence but also for its blasphemous representations of religious motifs.

Some accounts specifically link the twenty-four musicians in the Burgundian pie with our nursery rhyme about twenty-four singing blackbirds, giving us a choice of distinctive origins for that particular surprise stuffing.

A less well-known banquet for which full descriptions survive was that given by Gaston IV de Foix-Béarn for the ambassadors of the King of Hungary at Montil-les-Tours on Christmas Day 1458.[9] The banquet consisted of six services, and several *entremets*. The third service (the *ragoûts de gibiers*) is especially striking, comprising partridges, rabbits, peacocks, herons, swans, woodcocks, wild geese and, most surprisingly, *vautours et outardes* (vultures and bustards). Herons and peacocks provided the most prized meats at many of these banquets. The richest and largest of the *entremets* was pulled into the hall by twenty-four servants (twenty-four once more), in the form of a mountain raised on a dais. From one side of the mountain emerged two fountains, one flowing with water flavoured with fragrant nutmeg (*muscade*), the other with rose water. With the hall thus wonderfully perfumed, the mountain opened again and released a crowd of live rabbits and little birds which scampered and flew around the hall – *pour la plus grande joie de l'assistance*. A beautifully bejewelled horseman then rode into the room and presented all the ladies with bouquets of flowers. One cannot help imagining the twenty-four servants then struggling to retrieve the frightened rabbits and little birds before the delicacies of the next course (which highlighted fried oranges) could be served.

Our third banquet was organized by Giovanni II Bentivoglio to celebrate the marriage of his son Hannibal. It was held in Bologna in 1487 and was chronicled by Cherubino Ghirardacci. The banquet lasted for seven hours, from eight in the evening until 3 a.m. It opened modestly enough with tiny *hors d'oeuvres* and a selection of sweet wines. There followed roasted pigeons and pigs' livers *en papillotte*; plates of baked thrushes; and partridges stuffed with *confits* of olives and grapes. A huge sugar castle was then served as an *entremet*; once opened it was found to be full of live birds, which emerged and flew around the room, to general admiration. When the birds had been retrieved, great plates were presented bearing roasts of a whole deer and a whole ostrich, surrounded by calves' heads, capons, sausages and sauces. These were followed by a magnificent course of roasted peacocks, one peacock per male guest, each peacock decorated with a fan of its own tail-feathers. Hares and roe-deer were roasted and returned to their skins, and served in a fine display of taxidermy. Cakes of sugar, almonds and ricotta came next, and then another castle was drawn into the hall. This one turned out to be full of live rabbits, which duly scampered across the drawbridge and all around the room. This spectacle was accompanied by a service of rabbit *pâté*. Before the end of the meal there were more courses of roasts and cakes and bonbons and *dragées desserts*, and a third and still larger castle. Unfortunately, the denizen of the third castle was a large and unhappy pig, who set up a great grunting and squealing, but declined to leave the castle and join the company on the floor of the banqueting hall. Our chronicler notes again and again that these dishes were presented or exposed, rather than served. The whole meal was an enormous and extravagant performance.

Conclusion: subtlety explanations

It appears that the banqueting practices between about 1250 and 1500 reverted, consciously or unconsciously, to the previous period of great private wealth and luxury in Europe, between about AD 50 and 350. As we have seen, there were even echoes of the appalling reign of the Emperor Nero.

It is difficult for modern readers to understand the great attraction of these subtleties and *entremets*, which often appear grotesque or crazy. This conclusion looks at a range of attempts to explain these medieval phenomena, whose extinction marks the beginning of modern attitudes to dining (around the year 1660).

Some scholars regard banqueting subtleties as a mysterious aberration, foolish and inexplicable. As great a medievalist as Johan Huizinga seems to shrug his shoulders in exasperation at these practices. If Huizinga struggles to get inside this particular medieval mind-set, regarding *entremets* as insipid and ugly, as lamentable exhibitions of 'almost incredible bad taste', then the modern reader's bafflement at what the diners were thinking may perhaps be excused.

To take one extreme example, when the papal court at Avignon was presented with a plate of meticulously culled cockerels' testicles disguised as chickpeas (peasant food), what were the diners expected to think? And how did their host, in this case the Avignon pope, expect them to respond?

Clearly these extravaganzas of mealtime entertainment were intended as displays of power and wealth. There were, however, other factors involved. There seems to be a strong element of fun and mischief in these illusion foods, perhaps a sense of transgression, of pushing beyond normal boundaries, of rule-breaking, even of Saturnalian licence. On occasion the *entremets* would come close to mockery of religion. There was a pleasure in ostentation: a delight in the display of kitchen skill, artistry, sheer cleverness. We note also a love of theatre and colour. The desire to demonstrate power and glory could become a triumph of quantity, scale and hugeness. It was important to astonish and to dazzle, but also (especially in the case of the Burgundians) to go one step further and to over-awe. Perhaps the host wanted above all to leave his diners feeling overwhelmed and full of deference in the face of his mastery and ability to reshape nature.

There is a rather different view presented by Barbara Wheaton in the *Oxford Companion to Food*. Her approach relates medieval subtleties to manuscript illustrations and the manuscript page, with its 'fantastic ornaments and drolleries'. For Wheaton the medieval banquet was a setting for the events that went on around it in the same way that manuscript lettering provided the setting for wonderful illuminations and embellishments.[10]

This seems to me to be a delightful and enlightening analogy rather than an explanation. Certainly it moves us beyond Huizinga's view of the banquets as 'a barbarous manifestation', but for full explanations we need to consider the social history of the period, the lifestyles, the concerns and the attitudes of the banqueters.

Medieval social history provides us with two keys to these strange practices: the rise of personal wealth and the growth of social instability.

The two periods of extravagant, and apparently decadent, banqueting – during the Roman Empire and the late-medieval era – coincided with times when personal wealth among members of the upper classes reached exceptional levels, but also when social mobility and social upheaval led to uncertainty and insecurity amongst those same wealthy individuals.

In very general terms, European life for about 600 years after the fall of the Roman Empire (roughly between the years 450 and 1050) was not characterized by accumulation of disposable personal wealth. Although hoarding of treasure continued, the banking industry almost disappeared during these centuries and there were very few individuals who could be described as the leisured rich. Banqueting and feasting became functions or adjuncts of other activities (alliance, conquest, coronation) rather than structured pleasures in themselves.

The revival of the banking industry in Europe was partly linked to the need to fund the Crusades, but the growing importance of money and credit also led to a wider group of moneyed individuals who sought a life-style commensurate with their wealth. The ostentation of banquets was a by-product of this rise of personal wealth which perhaps reached a peak in the period 1250–1300.

The new wealth is a major factor in the return of grand banqueting in the Roman style. It does not in itself, however, provide much of a reason for the return of the banqueting follies of the wealthy – subtleties, conceits, *entremets* and surprise stuffings.

A strong theory is that, especially in the period from the fourteenth to the sixteenth centuries, the upper classes, albeit newly wealthy, were threatened by waves of protests, riots and revolts. Peasants marched on the cities; labour shortages encouraged militancy; guilds defended workers' rights; city-states (even those as grand as Venice and Genoa) provided unstable political structures; the advances of Islam menaced the Christian West. There appeared to be political analogies with the last days of the Roman Empire.

Embattled, threatened and uncertain, the upper classes, according to this theory, shut themselves away in their own introverted world. They emphasized their separation from the people and popular culture; they created a self-referential world of their own, with its own rules and its own comforting absurdities. The very absurdities, together with all the exotic importations, underlined the class-separation. The period from 1300 to 1600 marked the greatest possible distinction and separation of the life-styles and aspirations of the social classes, the rich and the poor, and the extravagances of the banqueting hall can be seen as a highly visible and defiant, expression of this distinction and separation.[11] From about 1660 the reign of Louis XIV, the Sun King, witnessed a new era of stability, certainty, elegance and gastronomic style.

Whichever explanation is favoured, the age of the *entremets* and the surprise stuffing appears to us now as a sealed-off piece of food history. It is easier for a modern historian to empathize with the food habits of the ancient Egyptians or Chinese than with our own late-medieval predecessors. The four-and-twenty blackbirds provide a curious link to a strange disappeared world which seems barely connected to our own.

Notes

1. These accounts draw upon Jean-Marc Albert, *Aux tables du pouvoir* (Paris: Armand Colin, 2009); Massimo Montanari, *La fame e l'abbondanza: storia dell'alimentazione in Europa* (Roma: Editori Laterza, 1994); Jean Verdon, *Le plaisir au Moyen Âge* (Paris: Perrin, 1996): especially pp. 117–151; Pierre Tucoo-Chala, 'L'art de la table à la fin du Moyen Âge', *Généalogie des Pyrénées-Atlantiques* 38 (juin 1994), pp. 2–10; and, above all, Bruno Laurioux: *Manger au Moyen Âge: pratiques et discours alimentaires en Europe au XIVe et XVe siècles* (Paris : Hachette Littéraires, 2002) and Agathe Lafortune-Martel, *Fête noble en Bourgogne au XVe siècle : le banquet du Faisan (1454): aspects politiques, sociaux et culturels* (Montréal: Bellarmin; Paris: Vrin, 1984). See also Johan Huizinga, *The Waning of the Middle Ages* (London: Arnold, 1924) and *Splendeurs de la cour de Bourgogne : récits et chroniques*, dir. Danielle Régnier-Bohler (Paris: Laffont, 1995).
2. Barbara Wheaton, 'Subtleties', *The Oxford Companion to Food*, ed. Alan Davidson (Oxford : Oxford University Press, 1999), p. 760.
3. e.g. Kenneth Pomeranz and Steven Topik, *The World that Trade Created* (Armonk: M. E. Sharpe, 1999), p. 88; Colin Spencer, *British Food: An Extraordinary Thousand Years of History*, new ed. (London: Grub Street, 2011), p. 365.
4. See Béatrix de L'Aulnoit and Philippe Alexandre, *Des fourchettes dans les étoiles: brève histoire de la gastronomie française* (Paris: Fayard, 2010), p. 34.
5. Qtd. Esther B. Aresty, *The Delectable Past: The Joys of the Table from Rome to the Renaissance, from Queen Elizabeth I to Mrs. Beeton*, new ed. (London: Allen and Unwin, 1965), p. 33.
6. On Robert May, see Esther B. Aresty: op. cit., p. 86; and Kenneth James: *Escoffier: The King of Chefs* (London: Hambledon, 2002), p. 80.
7. Robert May, *The Accomplist Cook*, text from the 5th edition, 1685, original spelling retained.
8. See Tim Whitmarsh: *The Cambridge Companion to the Greek and Roman Novel* (Cambridge: Cambridge UP, 2008), p. 275.
9. Pierre Tucoo-Chala, op. cit., for the 1458 banquet, and Massimo Montanari, op. cit., for the 1487 banquet.
10. Wheaton, pp. 760–761.
11. Dr Deborah Jenkins had suggested an analogy with behaviour in City of London champagne bars during the recessionary crisis of 2008–09, and this provoked interesting discussion during the 2012 Oxford Symposium. In the same discussion, Carolin C. Young (writer on food, art, culture and Paris) helpfully reminded the audience that the impulse to ostentation through banquet–displays continued and even expanded after 1660 (though without live animals).

Food for Feasting or Food for Fasting? Rabbinical *Krepelach*

Susan Weingarten

Rabbinical literature throughout the ages is a rich but barely tapped source for what foods Jews (and sometimes their non-Jewish neighbours) ate. The rabbis were always very concerned to define what was permissable under the laws of *kashrut* (kosher food), and most research on their writings in the past has concentrated on these religious and regulatory aspects. However, in the course of these discussions, the texts often provide valuable details of how foods were made, an aspect which was only of secondary interest to earlier researchers. This paper will concentrate on a number of rabbinical texts mostly from medieval and early modern northern Europe (Ashkenaz), written in Hebrew, to see what they can tell us about the food called *krepelach*.

The term *krepelach*, singular *krepel*, diminutive *krepelin*, appears to be derived from the French or German for a fried dough (cf. modern *crèpe*, *krapfen*), with the Yiddish plural ending *–ich* or *–ach*. All these forms refer to dough pockets, stuffed either with meat or cheese, or less often with fruits and nuts.

Krepelach or *krepelin(s)* do not appear as such in the late antique talmudic literature, but medieval and later rabbis sometimes identify them with an obscure talmudic term '*pat ha-ba'a be-kisnin*,' literally 'bread that comes with *kisnin*.' It is unclear what the original meaning of the term *kisnin* was, but one of the early medieval rabbinical interpretations related this term to the word '*kis*', a pocket, and hence to *krepelach*, which appear to have been made with bread dough until comparatively recently. By the beginning of the thirteenth century, Rabbi Isaac ben Moses of Vienna, in his book *Or Zaru'a* (The Light is Sown), identifies what he calls *krepelins* with '*aravoli*'. This clearly refers to *ravioli*, and in fact it appears to be the earliest mention of this food, long before it features in Italian or other European literature.[1]

Rabbinical questions: *krepelach* dough and bread dough

The rabbinical discussions of *krepelach* fall into a number of categories. The first of these is about the definitions of bread. This was important to the rabbis for two reasons. First of all, if a woman made a large quantity of dough for bread, she was obliged by rabbinic law to take off a small part of it ($1/24$) for the priests' portion, *hallah*.[2] When there was a Temple in Jerusalem, this bit of dough seems to have been actually given to the priests, but today it is simply removed with a blessing and burnt. However, there were other things a woman could do with her dough than just bake it for bread – she could boil it for *itriot*, pasta, for example, and the rabbis argued over whether dough intended for non-bread foods needed to have the priests' portion taken from it. On the face of it, this was unnecessary, but what if the woman changed her mind half way through? When it came to *krepelach*, some rabbis said they had the status of bread, and the priests' portion must be taken from the dough. The filling might be thought to cancel this status, but since, like *kneidelach*, dumplings, but unlike *gremzils* (*vermicelli*), *krepelach* 'have the shape of bread,' they could come within the category of bread. Given these discussions, *krepelach* dough in the Middle Ages would seem to have been bread dough. Today *krepelach* are made with noodle dough, i.e. eggs and flour. It is not clear when this change happened.

Another type of rabbinical discussion was related to this question: if only baked dough could be considered bread, what exactly was baking? Did any case where 'the fire went under the dough' produce bread? If so, what about frying? And even if only baking made bread, what if the dough was fried then baked, or baked then fried? In the thirteenth century, the *Or Zarua* says '*kreplins* which we call *aravoli*' must have the priests' portion taken and have the blessing for bread made over them since they are made of kneaded dough, and even if they are fried, since 'the fire goes under them' they are still included in the category of bread.[3] So *krepelach* in the thirteenth century could be baked or fried.

Meat and cheese filled *krepelach*

There is a further category of rabbinical discussions about *krepelach*, this time concerning not the dough covering, but the filling. Three times the Hebrew Bible tells us that Jews are forbidden to 'boil a kid in its mother's milk.'[4] This ban has been developed over the ages by the rabbis into strict separation of foods containing meat from foods containing milk, to the extent that present day religious Jews now have separate, colour-coded sets of crockery and cutlery for meat and dairy foods, and some even have separate sinks for washing them, and separate ovens for cooking.[5] Medieval *krepelach* were made with either meat or cheese fillings, but what if these got mixed up? There are a number of cases where this sort of accident was discussed by the rabbis, which also give us some insight into how this food was made.

The first case is to be found in the thirteenth-century writings of Rabbi Isaac ben Moses, the *Or Zaru'a*, whom we met above. Rabbi Isaac writes that he was visiting Rabbi Simhah in the town of Speyer, in the Rhineland, on the eve of the Sabbath, when Samuel ben Abraham haLevi came in to ask what he should do.[6] A non-Jewish maidservant had poured buttermilk into a pot of meat-filled *krepelach* in some sort of liquid. Rabbi Isaac's solution here was to add lots of water to the pot, since there is a rabbinic principle that if a forbidden liquid is accidentally added to a permitted liquid, it need not be thrown away if the proportion of forbidden to permitted is less than one in sixty. Nowadays this solution would not be acceptable *post factum*: it is allowed only if there had been sixty parts of water in the pot before the single part of buttermilk was added. However, there is a further rabbinic principle which enjoins taking a lenient view in the case of considerable loss: presumably in medieval Speyer the loss of a whole pot full of meat *krepelach* would have been sorely felt by the family concerned. The imminence of the Sabbath, when it is forbidden to cook, was probably also a factor here. We can perhaps learn incidentally that cheese-filled *krepelach* were served in a buttermilk sauce, rather than the richer sour cream more common today.[7]

Further evidence of how *krepelach* were made comes from fourteenth-century Mainz, from Rabbi Jacob ben Moses haLevi Moelin, known as the Maharil, who writes:

> Unless fat ... was prepared especially for Passover, it is not customarily eaten on Passover because of the way in which it is used for *hametz* [leavened foods], such as porridge of flour or cooked wheat or barley or *frimsels* [*vermicelli*] or *krepelach*: people are not [always] careful not to put in a *hametz* spoon to take out fat with it for their food. And also when they heat up goose skin in a frying pan they are not careful about *hametz*.[8]

The Maharil here is concerned that people should not use fat on Passover that might have been accidentally contaminated with *hametz*, leavened food, which is forbidden on Passover. He includes *krepelach* in his list, although it is not clear whether the fat was used for the filling, for greasing the pan or for frying the *krepelach*. Although he carries on to discuss rendering goose fat, he does not actually say this was used for the *krepelach*, but we see from other sources that this was often the case. Claudia Roden and Ariel Toaff have both discussed the extensive involvement of medieval Rhineland Jews in raising and eating geese.[9] *Schmalz krepelach*, i.e. *krepelach* fried in *schmalz* (animal fat), are mentioned in the *Sefer Mitzvot haNashim* (The Book of Women's Commandments) by Rabbi Benjamin Slonik, published in Cracow in the sixteenth century, which deals with taking *hallah*, among other things.[10]

More clearly, the *Noda beYehudah*, a collection of reponsa written in eighteenth-century Prague by Rabbi Ezekiel ben Judah haLevi Segal Landau, reports the case of a woman who borrowed two iron bowls (or perhaps baking trays) to bake *krepelach* in. Not knowing that her neighbour used them for meat, she greased them with butter and baked *krepelach* in them. She did not tell this to her neighbour when she gave them back, and within a hour the original owner greased them with meat fat and used them to bake meat *krepelach*, together with seven other bowls- or trays-full. The question, again, is whether these *krepelach* can be eaten. A number of rabbis have discussed the questions raised in this case, and they disagree.[11] Some say the *krepelach* in the two bowls must be discarded. Others find ways of being more lenient: some say since this is a considerable loss it is permitted to use them; others say since these are a minority in a majority it is permitted (this is a loop-hole normally applied to liquids only). But others say that since it was goosefat which was used, and geese are not mammals like cows or goats which have mother's milk, so the prohibition against using them with butter is only an extra rabbinical addition, not part of the original biblical prohibition.

Zvi Pesah Frank, a nineteenth- and early twentieth-century rabbi born in Lithuania who became chief rabbi of Jerusalem, was known for his lenient views and attempts to help the poor. He suggests that if there is a problem of mixing meat and milk, even if the *krepelach* are cooked in a sauce, which gives its taste to the *krepelach*, as long as the filling is covered on all sides with dough, the sauce will only give its taste to the outer dough casing of the *krepelach*, so it is possible to strip this off and just eat the meat inside.[12]

Shaping *krepelach*

Aside from these issues of religious regulations, the *Noda be Yehudah* records a method of baking *krepelach* in iron bowls or trays. The Maharil in the fourteenth century, whom we saw above, writes of baking *krepelach*, or at least keeping them warm or heating them up, on top of a tiled stove. There are also a few mentions in the rabbinic literature of the 'iron things with which people make/form *krepelach*', mentioned together with other metal objects used in cooking. What were these iron things? The *Hokhmat Adam*, written by Rabbi Abraham Danziger from late eighteenth-century Vilna, talks about the 'iron troughs' in which they form *krepelach* and *kichelach*, little cakes or biscuits. Were these baking trays? Pastry shape-cutters? Trays with indentations? And what shape *krepelach* did they produce? In an encyclopaedia article written by Bertha Fishberg, wife of a Jewish anthropologist in early twentieth-century New York, there is evidence for the shape of *krepelach*:

> *Kreplech* or *krepchen* is another dish peculiar to eastern European Jews. It is prepared in the following manner: Flour and eggs are mixed into a dough. This is rolled into sheets and cut into three-inch squares. On each square of dough is placed fine-chopped meat, to which salt, pepper, and onions are added. The edges of the rolled dough are then brought together and well pasted. This is then placed in a soup previously prepared for the purpose. This kreplech is eaten at least three times a year by every pious Jew – on Purim, on the day preceding the Day of Atonement, and on Hosha'na Rabbah. On occasions when meat is not eaten, chopped cheese is placed inside the kreplech.[13]

So Bertha Fishberg's *krepelach* would have been triangular. Other descriptions specify round shapes for *krepelach* dough, which produce semi-circular *krepelach*.[14] Today most *krepelach* dough is either cut as a square or a circle, which is then folded in half to give a triangular or semi-circular *krepel*. Sometimes the corners are then stuck together before cooking, giving a shape like a little hat, like *tortellini* or *cappelletti*. Neither squares nor circles would have needed dedicated shape-cutters, but it is interesting to note that a colleague of mine, Mimi Kresh, has published a shape-cutter for making dozens of hexagonal *krepelach* at the same time.[15]

Were these the 'iron things for making *krepelach*'? At the 2012 Oxford Symposium, Sharon Hudgins showed an identical utensil called a *pelmenitsa*, which comes from present-day Siberia and is used for making *pel'meni*, filled dough pockets very similar to

krepelach.[16]

Krepelach and their Jewish cousins

We saw earlier that the *Or Zarua* identifies *kreplins* with *aravoli*, which we interpreted as *ravioli*. Elsewhere he puts *aravoli* together with *calzoni* when categorizing them as 'bread'. *Calzoli* or *calcioli*, and *arvili* are also mentioned together as bread foods in the *Sefer haAgur*, published in Naples, whose author, Rabbi Jacob ben Judah haAshkenazi (from Ashkenaz), moved from Germany to Italy in the fifteenth century.[17] These are presumably related to present-day Italian *calzoni*, which are also stuffed pasta pockets. These pasta pockets have a long history. They seem to appear first in rabbinic literature in *Sefer Ra'avyah*, written by Eliezer ben Joel haLevi, a rabbi from twelfth-century Bonn. Here they are called *calesins* or *calosenos*, listed together with *verimzelis* (*vermicelli*). They still exist under a very similar name in the Sephardi Jewish kitchen. Claudia Roden, in her book on modern Jewish foods, describes *calsones* as 'large ravioli' which were served on Friday nights with *reshteh* (*tagliatelle*) in modern Aleppo, where she suggests they may have arrived from Italy with Jewish emigrants from the sixteenth century onwards.[18] Roden notes that *calsones* can be rectangular or half-moon-shaped. Edda Servi Machlin, in her book on Italian Jewish foods, identifies *calzonicchi*, pasta pockets filled with calf brain, as a legacy of ancient Roman Jews.[19] She makes them by placing spoonfuls of filling two inches apart all over a sheet of egg dough, covering this with another sheet of dough, and cutting out the *calzonicchi* with a glass into what she calls half-moon shapes, although she presumably means full-moons.[20] In case we had any doubts about identifying *calsones/calzoni/calzonicchi* with *krepelach*, we find them thus identified in the fourteenth century by Rabbi Moses Parnas of Rothenberg in Germany in his *Sefer haParnas*, where he writes of '*calsinos* which are called *kreplins*'.

There is a further food which is identified with *krepelach* in Poland in the seventeenth century, *hoisen blasen*. Rabbi David haLevi Segal, from Ostrow in seventeenth-century Poland, author of the *Turei Zahav* (Columns of Gold) and known as the Taz, writes about *krepelach* and *hoisen blasen*, which can either be made of dough kneaded with honey, or ordinary dough fried in honey. In the first case they are not considered 'bread', but in the second case they are. This discussion is continued by Rabbi Abraham Abeli haLevi Gombiner from Gombin, Poland, author of the *Magen Avraham* (Shield of Abraham), later in the seventeenth century. He says the definition as 'bread' is dependent on whether the honey and spices in the filling of the *krepelach* or *hosen blasen* are larger in quantity than the flour, or not. He adds that some people knead the dough for *hosen blasen* with fat and vinegar.

Thus *hoisen blasen* are clearly also a stuffed dough food, apparently usually stuffed with a sweet filling, unlike *krepelach* which can be either savoury or sweet. They were noted but not identified by Samuel Krauss in his paper 'Aus der jüdischen Volksküche'.[21] A search of Yiddish dictionaries and help from Karin Vanecker finally led me to translate this term as 'puffy pants' or 'clown's trousers'.[22] Karin said this made her laugh, and her laughter solved the problem of identification, for Claudia Roden also writes that she and her family giggled about the name of *calsones*, which means 'underpants' in Ladino.[23] Alan Davidson writes that Italian non-Jewish *calzoni*, originally dough-covered sausages, are named after trouser legs.[24] Thus we might translate both these versions of *krepelach*, *calsones* and *hoisen blasen*, as bloomers, a covering for flesh!

Food for feasting or food for fasting?

Feasting

As Bertha Fishberg noted, nowadays traditional Jews eat *krepelach* particularly on three special occasions: *krepelach* are eaten with a meat stuffing on both the eve of the fast of the Day of Atonement and on Hoshanah Rabbah (the day of final judgement on the festival of Tabernacles); they can be eaten with either a meat or a cheese stuffing on the joyous festival of Purim. Sometimes, because of the cheese they are also eaten on Shavuot, the festival of the Giving of the Law when it is customary to eat only dairy foods, although nowadays it is more common to eat cheese-stuffed *blintzes*. In sixteenth-century Poland there was a special form of Purim *krepelach*, according to the *Emeq haBerakhah* (The Valley of Blessing), which deals with the blessings to be made over different foods. The author, Rabbi Abraham b Shabetai Sheftel Horowitz, tells us that the dough for these Purim *krepelach* was kneaded with honey and different spices, and the whole was filled with fruit or conserve. This filling resembles that which we saw earlier for *krepelach* and *hoisen blasen,* but it is also reminiscent of one of the early medieval writers on the *pat ha-ba'a be-kisnin*, which was seen by some rabbis as the forerunner of *krepelach*. In the *Arukh*, an eleventh-century dictionary written in Rome, the entry for *kisnin*, after quoting the Babylonian Talmud (BT Berakhot 41b etc.), goes on to cite the eleventh-century Rabbenu Hannanel of Kairouan in present-day Tunisia, who interprets *kisnin* as pockets filled with sugar, fruit and nuts.²⁵ The nineteenth-century Hungarian editor of the *Arukh*, Alexander Kohut, thought that they could be cannabis seeds. This would certainly have given a very happy Purim.

The festival of Purim commemorates the deliverance of the Jews of Persia from the plots of the wicked Haman, who wanted to kill them all. They were saved through Esther, who became queen. The celebration of the festival includes 'sending presents of portions [of food], each man to his neighbour', as well as gifts for the poor and the ceremonial public reading of the story in the biblical *Book of Esther*. Since the deliverance took place through a woman, women are obliged to listen to the reading of *Esther*, but in the seventeenth and eighteenth century, the *Shevut Ya'aqov* (The Remnant of Jacob), written by Rabbi Jacob b Joseph Reischer from Prague and the Rhineland, questions whether women are also obliged to send portions of food.²⁶ Since the biblical text says each *man* is liable, does *man* include women? He concludes that women may give portions to other women only, and records that it is traditional for women to give *krepelach*. In other places there is a discussion of how much food to give, and it is concluded that since 'portions' is in the plural, there should be at least two different sorts of foods. We have already seen that the covering of the *krepelach* was seen as totally distinct from the meat or cheese filling. Later we shall see that a single *krepel* was seen as two different foods.

Before we leave the festival of Purim, however, we should note that it was, and indeed still is, a very joyous festival. The reading of *Esther* is done in a carnival atmosphere with the community in fancy dress, and noisy instruments are beaten every time the wicked Haman's name is read out. More wine is drunk than on any other occasion in the Jewish calendar, and much food is eaten. Because the festival celebrates a reversal in the fortunes of the Jews there is a tradition of celebrating in a topsy-turvy way: it is forbidden, as noted above, to eat a kid cooked in its mother's milk, or indeed any meat cooked with milk; on Purim it became traditional in some Polish Jewish communities to eat chicken cooked in almond milk.²⁷ Similarly, although Jews in countries where non-Jews drank alcohol were generally abstemious, drinking only a few sips from the prescribed cups of sacramental wine, on Purim it was said to be a commandment to drink until one could no longer tell the difference between 'damn Haman' (the enemy) and 'bless Mordechai' (Esther's uncle and the other Jewish hero of the book). In keeping with this permissive carnival atmosphere, Purim *krepelach* can be filled with anything: cheese, meat, nuts or fruit – presumably the custom varied from place to place.

Leaving the festivities of Purim, we find that *krepelach* filled with meat are served in chicken soup on the eve of Yom Kippur, the Day of Atonement, a twenty-five hour fast when food and drink are equally forbidden. It is usual to serve bland food before the fast, without too much salt or spice so as not to increase thirst. So meat covered in bland dough fits the bill nicely. On the Day of Atonement, it is believed that God seals man's fate for the next year: having judged him ten days earlier on the New Year, he now sentences him to live or die. (This time *man* certainly includes woman). The day is spent in breast-beating confessions of past misdeeds and promises to turn over a new leaf. But neither the divine nor the human decision is necessarily final, it is believed. Ten days later still, God looks again to see whether people are carrying out their New Year's resolutions. This is the half-festival of Hoshanah Rabbah, when Jews call to God to save them (hoshanah=hoseannah), beating willow twigs till the leaves fall off. This last day of the week of Tabernacles is a serious moment before the rejoicing of the law. Here too it is traditional to eat meat-filled *krepelach*.

A number of reasons have been given for the eating of *krepelach* on these festivals: one eats them, it is is said, whenever one beats (*krachen*): on Purim we beat things at the name of Haman, on Hoshanah Rabbah we beat willow twigs, and on the Day of Atonement we beat our breasts in confession – so we eat *krepelach* which are made of chopped and beaten meat or cheese.[28] I have also read another explanation. On the Day of Atonement and Hoshanah Rabbah, we think of our sins and hope for God's mercy (which was granted to us on Purim). The meat, the animal product that is got by killing, represents God's justice, i.e. what we deserve; it is covered by a vegetable covering of wheat dough which represents God's mercy, which we hope will cover our just deserts.[29] Personally, I doubt whether these were the real original reasons for eating *krepelach* on these occasions: but given that there was such a custom, rabbis through the ages have a tendency to rationalize and explain both food and behaviour.

Fasting

Purim is preceded by a day-long fast: Esther's original three-day fast has been cut to more manageable proportions. The Eve of the Day of Atonement meal precedes a fast, while Hoshanah Rabbah looks back to a fast. On all these occasions we eat *krepelach*, which were therefore strongly associated in the Jewish mind with food for fasting. The rabbis thus ask why we should not eat *krepelach* before other fasts in the Jewish calendar, in particular the fast of Tish'a beAv, the ninth day of the month of Av, which commemorates some of the great catastrophes of the Jewish calendar: the destruction of the First and Second Temples and the expulsion from Spain. The fast of Tish'a beAv is preceded three weeks earlier by a shorter fast on the seventeenth of the month of Tammuz, when the walls of Jerusalem were breached by the besieging Roman army that eventually destroyed the Temple three weeks later on the ninth of Av. The three weeks of the battle for Jerusalem in the first century of our era are now commemorated by bodily restrictions: bans on haircuts, new clothes, marriages, ending with a ban on eating meat or drinking wine for the first nine days of the month of Av. Clearly, meat filled *krepelach* were not allowed, but we have seen that *krepelach* can be filled with cheese. But on the eve of the ninth Av the rabbis decreed that eating before the fast, which was necessary to sustain you through the twenty-four-hour deprivation of food and drink in the heat of the Middle Eastern summer, should not be too enjoyable. In the week before the fast, meat and wine had been banned: now they insisted on banning eating more than one foodstuff at the *se'udah mafseqet*, the meal where you stopped eating before the fast.³⁰ In antiquity, when the diet of many was bread, bread and more bread, having many varieties of food was a sign of plenty and enjoyment; at the Passover meal, which symbolized deliverance, Jews were enjoined to have more than one food: at least two, the rabbis said. So on the sad eve of the ninth Av some rabbis forbade more than one sort of cooked food:³¹ not even two different sorts of pasta – and *krepelach*, they said, as we saw on Purim, were really two foods, the filling and the dough, and hence were specifically forbidden, in spite of the associations with other fast days.³² The other fasts, it should be stressed, were joyful occasions, paradoxical as this may seem to members of a Symposium dedicated to food, for whom fasting may seem anathema. The joyful feasting of Purim, preceded by a fast, celebrates a fast which worked, and led to deliverance. On the Day of Atonement we also confidently expect deliverance: indeed by the end of the fast we are purified and become like angels (who are supposed not to eat). And of course it is assumed that we must have kept our New Year resolutions. But the final deliverance is not yet here; the Temple has not yet been rebuilt, so the seventh Tammuz and the ninth Av are still sad fasts. As such, they are not preceded by eating *krepelach*.

Notes
1. Susan Weingarten 'Medieval Hanukkah Traditions: Jewish Festive Foods in Their European Contexts', *Food and History* 8.1 (2010), pp. 41–62.
2. Not to be confused with present-day *halleh*, which is the name given to the Sabbath bread.
3. Rabbinical convention often refers to authors by the name of their book, as here, the *Or Zarua*, or by an acronym made up of the initial letters of their name, e.g. below, the *Maharil*.
4. Exodus 23.19; 34.26; Deuteronomy 14.21.
5. David Kraemer, *Jewish Eating and Identity through the Ages* (New York: Routledge, 2007).
6. On Jews in Speyer, see Robert Chazan, *Reassessing Jewish Life in Medieval Europe* (Cambridge: Cambridge University Press, 2010), pp. 101ff.
7. See Gil Marks *Encyclopedia of Jewish Food* (Hoboken, NJ: Riley, 2010): sv kreplach/krepl.
8. Sefer Maharil (minhagim) *Hilkhot maakhalot assurot beFesah* 7.
9. Claudia Roden, *The Book of Jewish Food: An Odyssey from Samarkand and Vilna to the Present Day* (London: Penguin, 1997), p. 111; A.Toaff in a lecture 'Is there a Jewish gastronomy?' at the conference on Jewish Food, Bar Ilan University, Israel, 21 June 2004, has said that whatever food medieval non-Jews made from pigs, Jews made from geese. Cf. Gilian Riley, *The Oxford Companion to Italian Food* (Oxford: Oxford University Press, 2007): sv Jewish gastronomy. My late father-in-law, Abraham Weingarten, whose family moved from White Russia to Moscow to Leipzig at the end of the nineteenth century, spoke with nostalgia of eating goose fat spread on his Passover *matzah* in his childhood. When I presented rabbinical *krepelach* in Safed, Israel in 2012, a member of the audience told me that she would render goose fat to make *griben*, cracklings, which she crushed and added to the *krepelach* filling.
10. Non vidi. Cited by Mordechai Kosover, *Yidishe makholim* (New York: 1954), p. 74.
11. Including Rabbi Abraham Danziger *Hokhmat Adam* (18th century Vilna); Rabbi Abraham Zvi Hirsch

Eisenstadt Pithei Teshuva, a collection of responsa on the Code of Jewish Law written in Bialystock in Lithuania at the beginning of the nineteenth century.
12. Rabbi Zvi Pesah Frank Har Zvi: *Yoreh Deah* 87.
13. *Jewish Encyclopedia* (New York: 1925): sv cookery: Eastern Europe. Creplech also appear in the first edition of the *Settlement Cook Book* (1901): http://digital.lib.msu.edu/projects/cookbooks/coldfusion/display.cfm?ID=sett&PageNum=122, accessed 15 October 2012.
14. Cf 'Makin' kreplach': http://www.youtube.com/watch?v=-VuI9FiE_L4 accessed 17.05.2012.
15. wordpress.com/2008/10/08/mimi-makes-kreplach/ I am grateful to Mimi for permission to use her picture.
16. Hudgins refers to a film showing how to use the *pelmenitsa*: http://www.youtube.com/watch?v=8eq-jmFGp40.
17. Sefer haAgur Hilkhot Seudah 215.
18. Roden, p. 405.
19. Edda Servi Machlin, *The Classic Cuisine of the Italian Jews* (New York: Giro, 1993), pp. 123–24. She also notes *ravioli* di Purim, spinach-stuffed *ravioli* made by Italian Jews on the festival of Purim (p. 126).
20. Joan Rundo, *La cucina ebraica in Italia* (Casale Monferrato, 2003), p. 30 makes them triangular.
21. Samuel Krauss, 'Aus der jüdischen Volksküche', *Mitteilungen zur Jüdischen Volkskunde* 18 (1915) 31: Hosenblasen (?).
22. Krauss, as a learned German scholar of the late nineteenth century, is scornful of Yiddish, calling it demeaningly 'jargon' (op. cit. previous note).
23. Roden, p. 111.
24. Alan Davidson *Oxford Companion to Food* (Oxford: Oxford University Press, 2006): sv *calsones*. Davidson is presumably relying on Carol Field, *The Italian Baker* (New York: Harper & Row, 1985), p. 270, who writes that *calzoni* look very much like the baggy pants Neapolitan men wore in the eighteenth and nineteenth centuries. I am grateful to Gillian Riley for finding this reference for me, and her caveat (in a personal communication) that we should be 'a bit wary of the fixed certainties that would locate them in a particular region at such and such a time'.
25. Alexander Kohut, ed., *Aruch Completum* (NY, 1878–85, repr. 1955).
26. Appropriately for this paper, Rabbi Jacob was also known as Rabbi Jacob Backofen!
27. Rabbi Shabetai b Meir Cohen (Sha"kh), (Poland, 17th century), commentary on Yoreh De'ah 87, 6. He concludes that this is permissible as long as there are a few whole almonds around to demonstrate the origin of the 'milk'.
28. Krauss, n. 20.
29. A.I. Sperling, *Sefer Ta'amei haMinhagim* (Lvov, 1896) section 736.
30. Mishnah Taanit iv, 7.
31. It was customary to sit on the ground and eat mourning food, such as an egg, but some rabbis enjoined bread and water only.
32. Rabbi Abraham Danziger, *Hayei Adam* (Vilna, 1809), pt 2–3 Hilkhot Shabbat veMoadim: 134, 1) forbids *farfel* and *lokshen*, and defines *krepelach* filled with cheese as two foods.